3-46

THE AMERICAN LEGACY OF LEARNING

Readings in the History of Education

THE LIPPINCOTT FOUNDATIONS OF EDUCATION SERIES

Under the Editorship of

John Hardin Best and James E. Wheeler

Rutgers University

THE AMERICAN LEGACY OF LEARNING

Readings in the History of Education

Edited by
John Hardin Best, *Rutgers University*
and
Robert T. Sidwell, *State University of New York at Oswego*

J. B. Lippincott Company
Philadelphia and New York

If your plan is for one year, plant rice;
For ten years, plant trees;
For a hundred years, educate men.
                    Confucian saying

Preface

From a glance at the pages of this book it is apparent that a great many people, from Vergerius to James Bryant Conant, contributed to its making. Their names appear in the contents and throughout the volume. Not so apparent are the names of those who contributed otherwise to the book; these contributions we acknowledge with grateful appreciation: J. J. Chambliss and James E. Wheeler, our colleagues at Rutgers who discussed many of these ideas at length; Charles O. Burgess of University of Washington and Joe Park of Northwestern University who read and criticized the manuscript; graduate students Dennis Gillan, Gray Lewis, Nadine Schwartz, and Charles Thompson for graduate student doings; Maria Leccese for secretarial and clerical help on the manuscript; the Rutgers University Library for assistance in securing documents and in photo-duplicating services; and finally Charlotte Taylor Best.

October, 1966

ROBERT T. SIDWELL
JOHN HARDIN BEST

Contents

PART 2

The National Period 1789-1877   99

PART 3

An Era of Expansion and Reform 1877-1960   241

Prologue

I T has become almost obligatory to preface works of readings or anthologies with something of a caveat to the reader. With the universe of choices open to the editor, he must, perforce, exercise judgment, preference, even prejudice, to select those items that he will include within the limitations imposed by the space available to him. Inherent in this culling process is the knowledge that in so doing, he will inevitably alienate a certain percentage of his readers who will disagree with both his inclusions and his omissions. This work will be no exception. Some readers will wonder, no doubt, at the obtuseness —nay, even the downright perverseness—of the editors in including this and excluding that. As there is no escaping this contretemps, one might just as well face up to it, here at the beginning, and move along to more pleasant thoughts.

This book, like Caesar's Gaul, is divided into three parts. Unlike Gaul, however, the division is not entirely arbitrary. It does attempt to delineate three generally equal parts of American educational history. The first spans the "Colonial Era" from the landing of the first European colonists at Jamestown in 1607 to the establishment of the Republic under the Constitution in 1789. The second part is the "National Era" from the early years of the new nation to the reunification at the end of Reconstruction in 1877. Third is the "Era of Expansion and Reform," the transition of America from late nine-

1

teenth century to contemporary times. Each of these parts is preceded by a rather lengthy essay, in which the editors attempt to set forth an interpretive "line" for the period under consideration. This "line" has, to a large degree, governed choice of the selections of readings included in that part. The parts have been sectioned in order to focus upon one or another aspect of education during the period. The essays provide an introduction and brief overview for each part or historic period, outlining the particular intellectual, social, economic, political or other forces that interacted with the educational endeavors of that period. It is the view of the editors that the process of education is an integral and interrelated part of the total matrix of any period in time; to treat education in isolation, divorced from the other processes and forces that mold an era, is, of course, misleading.

Some of the interpretive "lines" may seem a bit on the radical side. This has been done often intentionally, hopefully to stimulate, to open new intellectual vistas, to generate critical discussion. Part Two, for example, was to a large degree derived from the work of F.S.C. Northrop in legal philosophy. The extrapolation from Professor Northrop's provocative theses to the field of educational history helps to make the national era more comprehensible in terms of its educational aims and efforts.

As one source of annoyance with books of readings generally has been their tendency to present one reading after another with little or no explanation to indicate any connection between them other than pure caprice on the part of the editor, commentaries have been provided for all selections, to link them into a continuing narrative.

The editors have, in short, endeavored to avoid the "cut and paste" sort of a collection that so frequently leaves the reader with a sense of having received a confusing exposure to disjointed and unrelated bits and parts of the whole fabric. This decision has, unfortunately, necessitated the omission of some of the interesting aspects of educational history in America. The colonial era, for instance, could well have contained some evidence of efforts to educate non-white residents of America. But this was a complex undertaking; so much so that it was felt that rather than give it the scanty exposure that space would permit, it would be better to omit it entirely. Reluctantly, therefore, the work of John Eliot and the Mayhews and of Wheelock and Bray was not included. The same problem arose regarding an account of the struggles to establish church-related systems of parochial schools in late nineteenth and twentieth century America. Again the decision was made to omit any systematic study of the area.

The fruits of these labors are presented with full cognizance of imperfections and omissions, in the hope that through its pages the students of the history of American education will be able to experience something of that invaluable past that is their truly remarkable "legacy of learning."

GENERAL REFERENCES

Bailyn, Bernard. *Education in the Forming of American Society.* Chapel Hill: University of North Carolina Press, 1960.

Boyd, William (ed.). *The Emile of Jean Jacques Rousseau.* New York: Teachers College, Columbia University, 1956.

Brubacher, John S. *A History of the Problems of Education.* New York: Macmillan Co., 1947.

Brubacher, John S., and Rudy, Willis. *Higher Education in Transition.* New York: Harper, 1958.

Butts, R. Freeman. *The American Tradition in Religion and Education.* Boston: Beacon Press, 1950.

Butts B. Freeman, and Cremin Lawrence A. *A History of Education in American Culture.* New York: Henry Holt & Co., 1953.

Cremin, Lawrence A. *The Wonderful World of Ellwood Patterson Cubberley.* New York: Teachers College, Columbia University, 1965.

Cubberley, Ellwood P. *Public Education in the United States.* Boston: Houghton Mifflin, 1919.

Cubberley, Ellwood P. *Readings in Public Education in the United States.* Boston: Houghton Mifflin, 1934.

Cubberley, Ellwood P. *Readings in the History of Education.* Boston: Houghton Mifflin, 1920.

Curti, Merle. *Social Ideas of American Educators.* New York: Scribner's, 1935.

Curti, Merle. *The Growth of American Thought.* New York: Harper, 1943.

Gabriel, Ralph H. *The Course of American Democratic Thought*. New York: The Ronald Press, 1956.

Good, H. G. *A History of American Education*. New York: Macmillan Co., 1956.

Hofstadter, R., and Smith, Wilson. *American Higher Education*. Chicago: University of Chicago Press, 1962.

Knight, Edgar W. *A Documentary History of Education in the South Before 1860*. 5 vols. Chapel Hill: University of North Carolina Press, 1949-1953.

Knight, Edgar W., and Hall, Clifton L. *Readings in American Educational History*. New York: Appleton-Century-Crofts, 1951.

McCluskey, Neil G. *Public Schools and Moral Education*. New York: Columbia University Press, 1958.

Monroe, Paul (ed.). *A Cyclopedia of Education*. 5 vols. New York: Macmillan Co., 1911-1913.

Monroe, Will S. *Bibliography of Education*. New York: D. Appleton & Co., 1897.

Park, Joe. *The Rise of American Education: An Annotated Bibliography*. Evanston Illinois: Northwestern University Press, 1965.

Parrington, Vernon L. *Main Currents in American Thought*. New York: Harcourt, Brace, 1927-1930.

Randall, John H., Jr. *Making of the Modern Mind*. Boston: Houghton Mifflin, 1940.

Robinson, James H. *The Mind in the Making*. New York: Harper, 1950.

Rudolph, Frederick. *The American College and University*. New York Alfred A. Knopf, 1962.

Ulich, Robert. *History of Educational Thought*. New York: American Book Co., 1945.

Welter, Rush. *Popular Education and Democratic Thought in America*. New York: Columbia University Press, 1962.

Wiggin, Gladys A. *Education and Nationalism*. New York: McGraw-Hill, 1962.

PART 1

Colonial American Education
1607-1789

I SEVENTEENTH-CENTURY ORIGINS

THE early settlers of America crossed the expanse of the Atlantic equipped with a far more valuable cargo than mere material possessions. They came as the living and articulate representatives of a way of life and thought that had its roots deep in the old world. Among their intellectual effects, these early settlers carried certain ideas and plans of institutions and practices to be transplanted in the virgin soil of the new world.

It is by no means necessary to pledge allegiance to a "geographical determinism" to admit that the very geographic conditions of the new world were bound to influence and transform the educational ideas of a classic European vintage that the colonists carried to its shores. The rude encounter of highly civilized and cultured Europeans with the overwhelming immensity of a barbaric continent was highly significant for the development of American education. To call this an encounter with a "frontier" is perhaps to introduce a term which is somewhat misleading. "Frontier" here must be understood as representing a geographic condition as well as a sociological force, both of which operate and interact with one another. A frontier condition contains, of course, the immediate geographic physical factor of free and abundant land. In addition it contains other factors, as Frederick Jackson Turner pointed out, of a sociological nature such as a temporary lowering of civilized standards and a weakening of the power of tradi-

5

tional institutions as church and school.[1] It is with these latter, socio-logical, factors of their frontier that the early American settlers were greatly concerned. Indeed, their efforts to combat the threat of these aspects of the frontier condition may well have provided the matrix within which the foundation and development of colonial American education took place. The chief characteristic of American history, suggests Avery O. Craven, is that it presents a series of recurring social evolutions as people advanced to colonize the continent. The major peculiarity of institutions in such a process, says Craven, is constant readjustment.[2] The institution of education in America, as shall be seen, presents the historian with indisputable evidence of this process of readjustment under the influence of the American frontier acting upon the transported European social and intellectual ideals.

The immediate sources of these ideals may be found in the ethical and religious thinking of the Reformation and, to a lesser degree, in the humanist tradition of the Renaissance. The colonists, especially the New England Puritans, brought their ideals to the new world with the avowed intention of transplanting them directly in soil uncorrupted by the evils of English society. The result was to be a "New Zion" in a new world, or so the colonists thought, replete with all of the wis-dom of the old but with none of the perversion and impurity that char-acterized European conditions. It is worth noting that the ideals of the old world were quite acceptable to the colonists and that no radical revision of social ideals was contemplated. Rather, there would be a purification of old ideals through a new start in a clean and uncor-rupted environment. The result would serve as a model for a decadent Europe to imitate and envy.

The educational system of England that the colonists left behind had been undergoing reform and upheaval for nearly a century. It had become more secularized and attractive to a Protestant, urban, middle-class culture that saw in the process of education the means to both a godly life and a worldly success. This education was traditional

---

[1] David M. Potter, *People of Plenty* (Chicago: University of Chicago Press, 1954), p. 144.

[2] Avery O. Craven, "Frederick Jackson Turner," in W. T. Hutchinson, ed., *Marcus W. Jernegan Essays in American Historiography* (Chicago: University of Chicago Press, 1937), p. 254.

(classically oriented) but by no means unrealistic or obsolete. It was, as a matter of fact, highly utilitarian. Knowledge of classical languages was of considerable practical value to one seeking a clerical or governmental career, as well as being a requirement for other professions. The immediate confrontation in the new world with a wilderness that began as soon as one left the ship on which he had arrived, however, effectively precluded the transplanting, *in toto,* of education on the English model. It was immediately and frighteningly apparent that the taming and civilizing of the wilderness of America was going to take some time and considerable effort. The leisurely development of education was simply not feasible under these conditions; the children of the colonists would be grown and have children of their own long before the frontier could be properly civilized to the extent of permitting the support of an educational system of the nicety of England's. And yet, education could not be neglected either; for to do so was to create a dangerous condition that would effectively negate the whole body of ideals and purposes of coming to a new world. In a word, the children exposed to frontier conditions, without education, might very well lose any interest in matters educational or cultural. They might, it was feared, end up simply as barbarians in a barbarous land if something was not done immediately. The level of civilization that the Puritan founders held so necessary for a "New Zion" could, in one generation, sink to a point so low as to be beyond regeneration.

The ideals that produced and supported these fears on the part of the early settlers were derived from two traditions: the Renaissance ideal of an education based primarily upon classical languages and letters and the Reformation requirement of an educated ministry with a literate congregation. This combination is well expressed by the Puritan writer and divine, Richard Mather, in his description of the founding of Harvard College in 1636. In this description from Mather's often quoted *New England's First Fruits* (1643), one can clearly feel his pride in the fact that the Puritans, although in a veritable wilderness, were not allowing that fact to result in any intellectual degeneration and were preserving the intellectual heritage of antiquity and the Renaissance (see Selection 3).

The maintenance of a learned and educated clergy to spread the religious ethic, a literate citizenry to receive it, and the responsibility of maintaining a high level of civilization in the face of the threat of frontier conditions were the motivating forces that spurred the rapid advance of education in the New England colonies. These dual demands of Reformation and Renaissance seem perhaps to us today as rather far removed from reality. To the early settlers, however, particularly the New England settlers, these were very real and living doctrines. The education necessitated by the demands for a learned clergy and a literate populace was derived from the classical tradition of Renaissance humanism. Although traditional in content, this education was viewed as a means, and not as an end in itself. It was, therefore, education for a very practical purpose—a utilitarian curriculum. Although the preparation of a learned clergy is not, perhaps, what many of us would call a utilitarian endeavor today, that is only because we are, for the most part, committed to other ends (such as the preparation of scientists, for example, to contribute to cold war armaments) which require different means. The historical *faux pas* of judging the past by the standard of values of the present is hard to avoid, but it must be realized that what is today a matter of academic interest might well have been a matter of utmost practicality to the people of the past (and vice versa). The useful of today's world can quickly become the ornamental of tomorrow's, as a glance at the curriculum of the medieval university will easily demonstrate. It was this tradition of New England colonial education, its basic utilitarian grounding, that permitted its transformation and flexibility in the light of the changing socio-economic conditions and demands of the eighteenth century.

The direction and motivation of education by what was essentially institutionalized religion is one of the striking aspects of education, particularly in New England, in the seventeenth century. This is hardly surprising in the light of the forgoing discussion and not at all surprising when it is recalled that it was Calvin who was the guiding religious spirit of the majority of the colonists. Calvin had stated his position clearly regarding the relationship of education and the church. Unlike Luther, who saw the church as subservient to the state in the matter of control of education, Calvin visualized no problems with a church-state dichotomy of power. He clearly subsumed both state and education under the rule of the church. Hence, American colonial Calvinists, when they gave educational control to the church, were simply manifesting good Calvinistic doctrine.

The rapid establishment of education (rather startlingly rapid when it is recalled that the Massachusetts Bay Colony only began in 1630 and had the nucleus of a college by 1636) can thus be largely explained in terms of the interaction of the frontier of the American continent, with the blended influences of the Renaissance and Reformation ideals that the colonists carried with them to the "New Zion." An educated leadership was an absolute necessity, and the means for the perpetuation of this sort of leadership had to be literally hewn from the wilderness of the promised land. The fact that educational institutions were rapidly created and (albeit tenuously) maintained by a group that was struggling for its bare existence in an unfamiliar and uncivilized land is a striking indication of the strength of their belief in the power and necessity of education.

Paralleling the founding of grammar schools and colleges, institutions which were designed for the gentlemanly upper class and preparation for the learned professions, there was equally strong interest (for similar motives) in insuring at least literacy for the common folk. Essential in the Puritan religious scheme was the literate congregation, the necessity for creating every man his own priest. The responsibility traditionally lay with the family to see that every child should grow up with an understanding of the values, ethical and otherwise, of the culture. The child should have some knowledge of the Holy Writ, along with a considerable respect for the learning of the clergy. He should come to know his place in the patriarchal Puritan society and to accept the rule of his earthly superiors under an Almighty God. In the wilderness of America, however, the old order of "acculturation," the informal education of the young through family and apprenticeship, did not seem to work.

By the time the first generation of American born were growing into adulthood, it was clear that emergency measures were necessary to insure continuity of the culture and its values.[3] The General Court

[3] For a discussion of the sociological factors in the beginnings of the common schools in New England, see Bernard Bailyn, *Education in the Forming of American Society* (Chapel Hill: University of North Carolina Press, 1960), pp. 15-49.

of the Massachusetts Bay Colony in 1642 acted to require parents, guardians, and masters of apprentices to ensure that their charges were instructed in basic literacy, as well as taught a trade, in order that the young should grow into responsible, self-sustaining members of society. Specifically, the parents and masters were enjoined to teach their children or apprentices to read and to understand "the principles of religion and the capital laws of the country." The strictly emergency nature of the 1642 Act was manifest in its minimal educational requirements—writing, languages, and the like were not specified therein. A weak and virtually unenforcable law, the Act of 1642 reflected the sense of desperation that undoubtedly inspired its passage.

Five years later, a much more drastic and inclusive piece of educational legislation was put on the books of the Bay Colony. Whereas the 1642 Act had said nothing about schools, per se, the 1647 law provided specifically for the initiation and maintenance of schools. This law required each town of fifty householders to provide a school for instruction in reading and writing; towns of one hundred or more householders had to provide and support a teacher able to instruct in Latin and Greek.

The involvement of the state with educational matters was justified in the Act's famous preamble: "It being one chief project of the old deluder, Satan, to keep men from the knowledge of the scriptures. . . ."[4] Schools are necessary, it stated, not on the grounds that education is a positive good in and of itself, but, rather, because they are required to accomplish a particular desirable end. Possibly that end was presented as a religious one to make the act palatable to the public; it seems doubtful that it was entirely non-secular in intent. The end advanced in the 1647 Act was simply that learning was necessary to thwart the schemes of the devil. Satan in the form of ignorance would subvert the basic values of the society, values which were fundamentally religious but which included the secular as well.

Although the primacy of the Congregational-Puritan tradition of local control and support was maintained for the first time in the new world, the state entered the educational scene by providing general

---

[4] Ellwood P. Cubberley, *Readings in the History of Education* (Boston: Houghton Mifflin, 1920), p. 299.

regulatory requirements. The method of school support was to be determined by the individual towns, of which there were probably about thirty in 1647. This educational tradition of local control and support of schools under general state requirements, of course, has permeated the American structure of education.

The secular motives for the 1647 Act establishing common schools can be seen as an attack on indigence, a sort of seventeenth-century war on poverty. It was thought, no doubt rightly, that the failure of common education could create a whole segment of society which not only lacked a sense of the religious and ethical values but which also lacked the means for self-support, for earning a living at an honest trade. Such a failure of education, of course, could eventually lead to widespread pauperism and burdens to the taxpayer far heavier than the support of common schools. Thus the preservation of the social and ethical foundations of colonial society demanded that the common folk be properly educated, if not informally, then of necessity formally through the institutional means of the school.

It is clear that these early educational efforts were dictated and hastened by the situation in which the colonists found themselves. In a sense, these efforts constituted a "crash" legislative program in an attempt to circumvent frontier conditions (in their sociological aspect) that were perceived as potentially debilitating and even decivilizing. This was no academic theory detached from environmental realities but, rather, the first steps towards that "readjustment" of educational institutions that typified reaction to the American frontier. These were very real emergency efforts to solve problems arising from a very real and threatening intellectual environment.

Puritan New England provides the major focus for early American educational history in illustrating the problems in education and the colonial's response to them. The vigor of the Puritans in raising the questions, defining the problems, and initiating the struggles in education accounts for this focus of attention. There was, of course, considerable diversity from New England to the Carolinas in educational developments due to such variables as geography and climate and the cultural and religious differences in European origin. By the end of the seventeenth century, though these differences continued to exist, the colonies—North, Middle-Atlantic, and South—were engaged in educational struggles generally along the New England lines. With the start of the new century, however, the direction and development of education throughout the American colonies began to undergo profound and significant change.

II   EIGHTEENTH-CENTURY TRANSITIONS

Since its inception, education in America has been characterized by an evolutionary nature. As the socio-economic conditions of the growing and developing country changed, education also changed to meet the demands. The flexible and utilitarian spirit of its earliest educational structures has been a persistent principle in the nation's educational history; though there have always been those who have insisted that educational patterns once established should be maintained, per se, in the face of change in other social institutions (which change they generally also decry). A utilitarian curriculum of the past runs a certain risk in that it may gain the stature of immutability, on the basis of its antiquity and long lineage, in a present that has completely different needs. Our evolving educational structure contains in its social fabric both progressive and reactionary elements—utilitarian as well as antiquarian dimensions. This ambiguous pattern is seen educationally in the eighteenth century, a century of rapid growth and change, both economically and socially, in America. American education endeavored to meet the challenge in its own ambivalent way; it was willing to remain utilitarian in spirit but reluctant to admit that that which was needed in terms of utility was any different from that which had been needed in the past.

Expansion of commerce and the development of a degree of economic diversification in the seaboard cities of America in the eighteenth century were the major economic changes. Opportunity in the form of cheap western land and a chronically short supply of labor in a rapidly expanding economy gave impetus to a changing social pattern. In New England the theological oligarchy was uprooted by internal doctrinal struggles and by secularizing tendencies in its own body. It became involved in a life and death struggle with new social patterns, a battle that was to end in the demise of the Puritan oligarchy. Although Calvinism in the eighteenth century found a polished spokesman in Jonathan Edwards, its course as the dominant force of New England largely was run. Economic interests were asserting their demands over idealistic interests. The Puritan was becoming a Yankee, and he was enjoying thoroughly the profitable transformation.

The transforming of the Puritan of New England into an economic creature, par excellence, in the eighteenth century is a fascinating phenomenon. Actually, the step from saint to businessman was not such a strange leap as one unfamiliar with the intricacies of Puritan theology might think. As John Cotton had observed:

> There is another combination of virtues strangely mixed in every lively, holy Christian: and that is, diligence in a worldly business, and yet deadness to the world. Such a mystery as none can read but they that know it.[5]

This mystery has been partially read by Max Weber and R. H. Tawney, the economic and social theorists, who coined for it the name, "The Protestant Ethic." The Puritan theology saw man in the world as a working animal, demanded of each man that he find his "calling" and work steadfastly at it. No activity was beyond the scope of the holy purpose, but the work was for the glory of God, not for the worker.

This basic ethic was transformed in the eighteenth century into a secular ethic of success through economic endeavor. Striving and yet remaining disinterested in the rewards seemed more and more impossible to many and ridiculous to others. While the ethic of hard and diligent work continued to carry with it its Puritan connotation of "goodness" and a route to both worldly and spiritual fulfillment, the latter was becoming redundant for many. The ethic, in the eighteenth century, remained Puritan but became a secularized Puritanism.

The rising middle class merchants and tradesmen who followed the ethic to its logical secular conclusion were quick to observe that the educational offerings of the times were woefully inadequate to meet

[5] See Perry Miller, *The American Puritans* (Garden City, New York: Doubleday & Co., 1956), p. 171 ff.

their needs. Education was still geared to the preservation of an elite class that was elite no longer and to the maintenance of a level of civilization on a frontier that had long since been pushed westward. It was clearly out of step with the needs of a dynamic and mobile class that sought the more mundane ends of personal advancement and worldly success. The gentlemanly Latin grammar schools and classically oriented colleges obviously did not provide the means for a man on the move to bigger and better things. The Yankee was a trader, not a theologian. His educational ends had changed, but the means available (educationally) had not. Languages, he saw, would be a splendid acquisition for a man who traded on all of the seven seas of the world. But Latin? Greek? Hardly. French or Spanish certainly would help in a venture to foreign ports, but the number of people with whom he was likely to trade who might communicate in classical Greek was obviously limited. The struggling merchant or his ambitious young clerk could see that mathematics would be a real help in doing accounts, but classical Euclidean geometry never balanced any merchant's books.

Apprenticeship, the traditional agency of education in mundane or commercial subjects, was a long process, and the quality, by and large, of instruction was shallow in content.

Private schoolmasters, like the Sophists of Athens, tried to fill the gap between the narrow classical curriculum of the schools and the radically altered educative requirements of a secularized society by offering instruction to the new class in a variety of "practical" (and cultural) subjects. In Charleston, for example, in 1733, a private master, John Miller, taught "these sciences: Arithmetic, Algebra, Geometry, Trigonometry, Surveying, Dialling, Navigation, Astronomy, Gauging, Fortification. The Stenographic and Orthographic Projection of the Sphere. The use of the Globe and the Italian Method of Book-keeping."[6] Two night schools provided instruction in a similar array of subjects for Charlestonians whose work precluded their attendance during the day. In Philadelphia, in New York, Boston, or Richmond, the practical vernacular education of the private-venture schools with

6 Carl Bridenbaugh, *Cities in the Wilderness* (New York: The Ronald Press, 1938), p. 450.

their increased emphasis on business and vocational training was in considerable demand by the early decades of the eighteenth century.

But instruction with a private schoolmaster carried with it certain risks for an eager and sincere student. There might always be a suspicion that one was being short-changed—not getting the genuine article. The aspiring merchant's clerk might essay a course in Portuguese; but until he actually encountered someone who spoke that language and put his instruction to the pragmatic test of effective communication, he had no guarantee that what he had laboriously (and expensively) learned was not Latin spoken with a Boston accent in three-quarter time. Foreign languages, after all, have but one commonality to the untrained ear; they all sound foreign. To find he had spent his hard-earned money in the pursuit of pig-latin under the guise of Portuguese could be disillusioning. In short, there was a potentially dangerous lack of any control or regulation of educational offerings. It should in fairness be noted, however, that the majority of private masters were honest and capable educators.

The upshot of the socio-economic changes in the America of the eighteenth century was a demand on the part of the rising and ambitious middle class for an education that would provide the effective means of personal advancement, an education that had a real conversion value into tangible economic and social profits. What was wanted was an education that would prepare for the new and changed world of expanding opportunity. Perhaps no single person saw so clearly what was needed in education for this class than a man who had himself arisen from their midst to a position of great trust and leadership in the country—Ben Franklin.

Freed from the static societal and political fetters of the seventeenth century, the new American looked forward into a future that he could, in some measure, control. His personal advancement in this world, he saw, depended upon the amount of this control that he could exert; and he looked to education to provide him with the means to this end. Education and learning were seen as the instruments of progress in a world that seemed to beg to be conquered, both for the individual and for the nation. After the American Revolution, the school was further intrusted with the responsibility of being the teacher of democracy—the solidifier and the preserver of the national and political ideals of the new nation.

Within the intellectual environment of eighteenth-century America, there existed in theory the seeds that would eventually transform education to meet the demands of a democracy. Although it remained for the nineteenth-century to accomplish the reality (and then only after a bitter and prolonged struggle) of a democratically oriented educational process, the theoretical supports could be found in the Enlightenment of the eighteenth-century. John Locke's psychological theory, with its clear message of the potential force of education acting upon the *tabula rasa* of the mind (*all* minds were equally blank slates at birth), presents not only an educational method but an ideal as well. Combined with the democratic ideal that every man should have the opportunity of having his *tabula rasa* adequately and fully filled by the process of education, the Lockean message provided a powerful theoretical rationale for a new education appropriate for a democratic nation. Taken as a whole, the fusion of democratic ideals with Lockean psychology provided theoretical support of liberty (each individual could be free to advance himself through education), equality (every man is equipped mentally alike at birth), and fraternity (a democratic national brotherhood could be formed through a system of mass education, schools open to all). By the end of the century, the educational theory existed which seemed to make attainable the democratic social and political ideals of liberty and equality in the American nation.

This brief and cursory overview of American colonial education has stressed the changing role of education in a changing world. From the original confrontation and modification of the ideals of education brought to America with the continent of America itself, the history of American education has revolved around change and transformation, ultimately resulting in an educational system that is unique in all the world—uniquely American. In the colonial period, education was seen originally as the means of the propagation of a religious ethic, and this was modified by the very continental wilderness to include provision for the maintenance of a level of civilization, a provision obviously unthought of and unnecessary in Europe. With chang-

ing conditions in the eighteenth century, we have seen that education
was transformed still further and viewed as both the means of individual
success in a secularized world and, after the Revolution, as the means
for the teaching of democracy and the making of a new nation.

SECTION 1

Origins of Seventeenth-Century Educational Ideas

The intellectual beginnings of education in America in the seventeenth century reflect the combining of the Renaissance humanist
with the Protestant Reformationist thinking in education. The selections included illustrate the dual European influences along with
an example of a very early American product of the blending.

The essay entitled *De Ingenuis Moribus* was written by the Italian
humanist, Petrus Paulus Vergerius, for a young nobleman named
Ubertinus of Carrara in 1404. The writing represents humanist educational thought at a highly sophisticated level, reflecting a deep respect for the classical literary tradition with a real enthusiasm for
its possibilities in educating the complete man. From the complete
essay of some twenty-five pages in length, selections are included
here.

1. A Treatise on the Humanist Education

Petrus Paulus Vergerius

§ 1.   Your grandfather, Francesco I., a man distinguished for his
capacity in affairs and for his sound judgment, was in the habit of saying

Reprinted from William Harrison Woodward, translator and editor, *Vittorino da
Feltre and Other Humanist Educators* (Cambridge: Cambridge University Press,
1897), pp. 96-97, 102, 105.

that a parent owes three duties to his children. The first of these is to bestow upon them names of which they need not feel ashamed. For not seldom, out of caprice, or even indifference, or perhaps from a wish to perpetuate a family name, a father in naming his child inflicts upon him a misfortune which clings to him for life. The second obligation is this: to provide that his child be brought up in a city of distinction, for this not only concerns his future self-respect, but is closely connected with the third and most important care which is due from father to son. This is the duty of seeing that he be trained in sound learning. For no wealth, no possible security against the future, can be compared with the gift of an education in grave and liberal studies. By them a man may win distinction for the most modest name, and bring honour to the city of his birth however obscure it may be. But we must remember that whilst a man may escape from the burden of an unlucky name, or from the contempt attaching to a city of no repute, by changing the one or quitting the other, he can never remedy the neglect of early education. The foundation, therefore, of this last must be laid in the first years of life, the disposition moulded whilst it is susceptible and the mind trained whilst it is retentive.

This duty, common indeed to all parents, is specially incumbent upon such as hold high station. For the lives of men of position are passed, as it were, in public view; and are fairly expected to serve as witness to personal merit and capacity on part of those who occupy such exceptional place amongst their fellow men. You therefore, Ubertinus, the bearer of an illustrious name, the representative of a house for many generations sovereign in our ancient and most learned city of Padua, are peculiarly concerned in attaining this excellence in learning of which we speak. Our name, our birthplace, are not of our own choice. Progress in learning, on the other hand, as in character, depends largely on ourselves, and brings with it its own abiding reward. But I know that I am urging one who needs no spur. Can I say more than this?—continue as you have begun; let the promise of the future be consistent with your performance in the past.

To you, therefore, I have addressed this tractate upon the principles of Learning and of Conduct: by which I intend the subjects and the manner of study in which youth may be best exercised, and the actions which it behoves them to pursue, or to avoid, in the course of their daily life. Although addressed to you, it is intended for all who, blessed by nature with quickened minds and lofty aims, desire to shew by their lives their gratitude for such gifts. For no liberal mind will readily sink into mere sloth or become absorbed in the meaner side of existence.

· § 3.   We call those studies *liberal* which are worthy of a free man; those studies by which we attain and practise virtue and wisdom; that edu-

cation which calls forth, trains and develops those highest gifts of body
and of mind which ennoble men, and which are rightly judged to rank
next in dignity to virtue only. For to a vulgar temper gain and pleasure
are the one aim of existence, to a lofty nature, moral worth and fame.
It is, then, of the highest importance that even from infancy this aim,
this effort, should constantly be kept alive in growing minds. For I may
affirm with fullest conviction that we shall not have attained wisdom in our
later years unless in our earliest we have sincerely entered on its search. Nor
may we for a moment admit, with the unthinking crowd, that those who give
early promise fail in subsequent fulfilment. This may, partly from physical
causes, happen in exceptional cases. But there is no doubt that nature has
endowed some children with so keen, so ready an intelligence, that without
serious effort they attain to a notable power of reasoning and conversing
upon grave and lofty subjects, and by aid of right guidance and sound learning reach in manhood the highest distinction.

Indeed the power which good books have of diverting our thoughts from
unworthy or distressing themes is another support to my argument for the
study of letters. Add to this their helpfulness on those occasions when we
find ourselves alone, without companions and without preoccupations—
what can we do better than gather our books around us? In them we see
unfolded before us vast stores of knowledge, for our delight, it may be,
or for our inspiration. In them are contained the records of the great achievements of men; the wonders of Nature; the works of Providence in the past,
the key to her secrets of the future. And, most important of all, this Knowledge is not liable to decay. With a picture, an inscription, a coin, books share
a kind of immortality. In all these memory is, as it were, made permanent;
although, in its freedom from accidental risks, Literature surpasses every
other form of record.

Literature indeed exhibits not facts alone, but thoughts, and their expression. Provided such thoughts be worthy, and worthily expressed, we
feel assured that they will not die: although I do not think that thoughts
without style will be likely to attract much notice or secure a sure survival.
What greater charm can life offer than this power of making the past, the
present, and even the future, our own by means of literature?

An international council of Calvinist churches, the Synod of Dort,
meeting in 1618-1619 in Holland, had significant influence on the
direction of the Reformed Churches both in Europe and America.
The deep concern of the Synod with the promotion of education

and the necessity for unifying efforts of all institutions in the society to this end is expressed with urgency and conviction in these Resolutions. Reformed Protestant educational thinking was to be translated into organization and action.

2. Calvinist Resolutions on the Promotion of Instruction

The Synod of Dort

In order that the Christian youth may be diligently instructed in the principles of religion, and be trained in piety, three modes of catechising should be employed. I. *In the house, by parents.* II. *In the schools, by schoolmasters.* III. *In the churches, by ministers, elders and catechists especially appointed for the purpose.* That these may diligently employ their trust, the Christian magistrates shall be requested to promote, by their authority, so sacred and necessary a work; and all who have the oversight of churches and schools shall be required to pay special attention to this matter.

I. The office of parents is diligently to instruct their children and their whole household in the principles of the Christian religion, in a manner adapted to their respective capacities; earnestly and carefully to admonish them to the cultivation of true piety; to engage their punctual attendance on family worship, and take them with them to the hearing of the Word of God. . . . Parents who profess religion, and are negligent in this work, shall be faithfully admonished by the ministers; and, if the case requires it, they shall be censured by the Consistory, that they may be brought to the discharge of their duty.

II. Schools, in which the young shall be properly instructed in the principles of Christian doctrine, shall be instituted not only in cities, but also in towns and country places where heretofore none have existed. The Christian magistracy shall be requested that well-qualified persons may be employed and enabled to devote themselves to the service; and especially that the children of the poor may be gratuitously instructed, and not be excluded from the benefit of the schools. In this office none shall be employed but such as are members of the Reformed Church, having certificates of an upright faith and pious life, and of being well versed in the truths of the Catechism. They are to sign a document, professing their belief in the Confession of Faith and the Heidelberg Catechism, and promising that they will give catechetical instruction to the youth in the principles of Christian truth according to the same. . . .

Reprinted from Henry W. Dunshee, *History of the School of the Collegiate Reformed Dutch Church* (New York: Aldine Press, 1883), pp. 3-4.

III. In order that due knowledge may be obtained of the diligence of the schoolmasters, and the improvement of the youth, it shall be the duty of the ministers, with an elder, and, if necessary, with a magistrate, to visit all the schools, private as well as public, frequently, in order to excite the teachers to earnest diligence, to encourage and counsel them in the duty of catechising, and to furnish an example by questioning them, addressing them in a friendly and affectionate manner, and exciting them to early piety and diligence. If any of the schoolmasters should be found neglectful or perverse, they shall be earnestly admonished by the ministers, and, if necessary, by the Consistory, in relation to their office.

With considerable pride Richard Mather pointed out the preservation in America of the great traditions of learning of the Renaissance and the Reformation. *New England's First Fruits* was printed in London in 1643, the year after the first class, with its nine members, was graduated from Harvard College.

3. New England's First Fruits

Richard Mather

After God had carried us safe to New England, and we had builded our houses, provided necessaries for our livelihood, reared convenient places for God's worship, and settled the civil government, one of the next things we longed for and looked after was to advance learning and perpetuate it to posterity, dreading to leave an illiterate ministry to the churches when our present ministers shall lie in the dust. And as were thinking and consulting how to effect this great work, it pleased God to stir up the heart of one Mr. Harvard (a godly gentleman and a lover of learning, there living amongst us) to give the one half of his estate (it being in all about £1700) towards the erecting of a college, and all his library. After him, another gave £300, others after them cast in more, and the public hand of the state added the rest. The college was, by common consent, appointed to be at Cambridge (a place very pleasant and accommodate) and is called (according to the name of the first founder) Harvard College.

The edifice is very fair and comely within and without, having in it a

Reprinted from Perry Miller, ed., *The American Puritans: Their Prose and Poetry* (Garden City, New York: Doubleday Anchor Books, 1956), pp. 323-327.

spacious hall (where they daily meet at common lectures, exercises), and a large library with some books to it, the gifts of divers of our friends, their chambers and studies also fitted for and possessed by the students, and all other rooms of office necessary and convenient, with all needful offices thereto belonging. And by the side of the College, a fair grammar school, for the training up of young scholars and fitting of them for academical learning, that still as they are judged ripe they may be received into the College. Of this school, Master Corlet is the master, who hath very well approved himself for his abilities, dexterity and painfulness, in teaching and education of the youth under him.

Over the College is Master Dunster placed as president, a learned, conscionable and industrious man, who hath so trained up his pupils in the tongues and arts, and so seasoned them with the principles of divinity and Christianity, that we have to our great comfort (and in truth, beyond our hopes) beheld their progress in learning and godliness also. The former of these hath appeared in their public declamations in Latin and Greek, and disputations logical and philosophical, which they have been wont (besides their ordinary exercises in the College hall), in the audience of the magistrates, ministers and other scholars, for the probation of their growth in learning, upon set days, constantly once every month, to make and uphold. The latter hath been manifested in sundry of them by the savory breathings of their spirits in godly conversation, insomuch that we are confident, if these early blossoms may be cherished and warmed with the influence of the friends of learning and lovers of this pious work, they will, by the help of God, come to happy maturity in a short time.

Over the College are twelve overseers chosen by the General Court: six of them are of the magistrates, the other six of the ministers, who are to promote the best good of it, and (having a power of influence into all persons in it) are to see that every one be diligent and proficient in his proper place.

Rules and precepts that are observed in the College:

1. When any scholar is able to understand Tullius [Cicero] or such like classical Latin author *extempore,* and make and speak true Latin in verse and prose, *suo ut aiunt marte* ["to stand, as they say, on his own feet"], and decline perfectly the paradigms of nouns and verbs in the Greek tongue, let him then, and not before, be capable of admission into the College.

2. Let every student be plainly instructed and earnestly pressed to consider well: the main end of his life and studies is "to know God and Jesus

Christ, which is eternal life" (John 17. 3), and therefore to lay Christ in the bottom, as the only foundation of all sound knowledge and learning.

And seeing the Lord only giveth wisdom, let everyone seriously set himself by prayer in secret to seek it of Him (Prov. 2. 3).

3. Everyone shall so exercise himself in reading the scriptures twice a day that he shall be ready to give such an account of his proficiency therein, both in theoretical observations of the language and logic, and in practical and spiritual truths, as his tutor shall require, according to his ability: seeing "the entrance of the word giveth light; it giveth understanding unto the simple (Psal. 119. 130).

4. That they, eschewing all profanation of God's name, attributes, word, ordinances and times of worship, do study with good conscience carefully to retain God and the love of His truth in their minds. Else, let them know that (notwithstanding their learned) God may give them up "to strong delusions" (II Thess. 2. 11, 12), and in the end "to a reprobate mind" (Rom. 1. 28).

5. That they studiously redeem the time, observe the general hours appointed for all the students, and the special hours for their own classes; and then diligently attend to lectures, without any disturbance by word or gesture. And if in anything they doubt, they shall inquire as of their fellows, so (in case of "non-satisfaction") modestly of their tutors.

6. None shall, under any pretense whatsoever, frequent the company and society of such men as lead an unfit and dissolute life.

Nor shall any, without his tutor's leave or (in his absence) the call of parents or guardians, go abroad to other towns.

7. Every scholar shall be present in· his tutor's chamber at the seventh hour in the morning, immediately after the sound of the bell, at his opening the scripture and prayer; so also at the fifth hour at night, and then give account of his own private reading (as aforesaid in particular the third), and constantly attend lectures in the hall at the hours appointed. But if any (without necessary impediment) shall absent himself from prayer or lectures, he shall be liable to admonition, if he offend above once a week.

8. If any scholar shall be found to transgress any of the laws of God or the school, after twice admonition, he shall be liable, if not *adultus,* to correction; if *adultus,* his name shall be given up to the overseers of the College, that he may be admonished at the public monthly act.

. . . . .

Every scholar that on proof is found able to read the originals of the Old and New Testament into the Latin tongue, and to resolve them logically, withal being of godly life and conversation, and at any public act hath the approbation of the overseers and master of the College, is fit to be dignified with his first degree.

Every scholar that giveth up in writing a system or synopsis, or summa, of logic, natural and moral philosophy, arithmetic, geometry and astronomy, and is ready to defend his theses or propositions, withal skilled in the originals as abovesaid, and of godly life and conversation, and so approved by the overseers and master of the College at any public act, is fit to be dignified with his second degree.

SECTION 2

Instruction, Curriculum, Textbooks, and Materials

Instruction in the common schools of seventeenth-century America was based almost entirely on the Bible, psalm books and testaments, and on hornbooks and primers composed of religious materials adapted for the use of children. The hornbook was usually a single horn-covered sheet filled with letters and numbers, and it served to introduce the young scholar to learning. The primer was a more sophisticated text which included the basics of rhymed alphabet, syllables and spelling words, as well as religious verses and catechism. The *New England Primer* was the first primer to be printed in the colonies and the one most widely used in numerous editions and revisions. Its sixty or more pages, of which selections are included, summarize much of the spirit of seventeenth-century common-school instruction.

Reprinted from Paul Leicester Ford, *The New England Primer* (New York: Dodd, Mead & Company, 1899). This is a facsimile reprinting of a 1727 edition of the *Primer;* also reissued in Classics in Education series (New York: Bureau of Publications, Teachers College, Columbia University, 1962).

4. The New England Primer

In Adam's Fall
We sinned all.

Thy Life to mend,
God's Book attend.

The Cat doth play,
And after flay.

A Dog will bite
A Thief at Night.

The Eagle's Flight
Is out of Sight.

The idle Fool
Is whipt at School

As runs the Glass,
Man's life doth pass.

My Book and Heart
Shall never part.

Job feels the Rod,
Yet blesses God.

Proud Korah's troop
Was swallow'd up.

The Lion bold
The Lamb doth
hold.

The Moon gives light
In Time of Night.

Nightingales sing
In Time of Spring.

The royal Oak, it
was the Tree
That sav'd his roy-
al Majesty.

Peter denies
His Lord, and cries.

Queen Esther comes
in royal State,
To save the Jews
from dismal Fate.

Rachael doth mourn
For her first born.

Samuel anoints
Whom God ap-
points.

Time cuts down all,
Both great and small.

Uriah's beauteous
Wife
Made David seek
his life.

Whales in the Sea
God's Voice obey.

Xerxes the Great
did die,
And so must you
and I.

Youth forward slips,
Death soonest nips.

Zaccheus, he
Did climb the Tree,
His Lord to see.

Now the Child being entred in his Letters and Spelling, let him learn these and such like Sentences by Heart, whereby he will be both instructed in his Duty, and encouraged in his Learning.

The Dutiful Child's Promises,

I Will fear GOD, and honour the KING.
 I will honour my Father & Mother.
I will Obey my Superiours.
I will Submit to my Elders,
I will Love my Friends.
I will hate no Man.
I will forgive my Enemies, and pray to
   God for them.
I will as much as in me lies keen all God's
  Holy Commandments.

I will learn my Catechism.
I will keep the Lord's Day Holy.
I will Reverence God's Sanctuary,
 For our GOD is a consuming Fire.

DUTY OF CHILDREN TOWARDS
THEIR PARENTS.

God hath commanded faying, Honour thy Father and Mother, and whofo curfeth Father or Mother, let him die the Death.   Mat. 15. 4.

Children obey your Parents in the Lord, for this is right.

2. Honour thy Father and Mother, (which is the first Commandment with Promise).

3. That it may be well with thee, and that thou mayst live long on the Earth.

Children, obey your Parents in all

Things, for that is well pleasing unto the Lord.   Col. 3, 20.

The Eye that mocketh his Father, and despiseth the Instruction of his Mother, let the Ravens of the Valley pluck it out, and the young Eagles eat it.

Father, I have sinned against Heaven, and before thee.   Luke 15, 10.

19. I am no more worthy to be called thy Son.

No man ever hated his own flesh, but nourisheth and cherisheth it. Ephes. 5, 19.

I pray thee let my Father and Mother come and abide with you, till I know what God will do for me. I Sam. 22, 3.

My Son, help thy Father in his Age, and grieve him not as long as he liveth.

12. And if his Understanding fail, have patience with him, and despise him not when thou art in thy full Strength.

Whoso curseth his Father or his Mother, his Lamp shall be put out in obscure Darkness.   Prov. 20, 20.

· VERSES.

I in the Burying Place may see.
   Graves shorter there than I;
From Death's Arrest no Age is free,
   Young Children too may die;
My God, may such an awful Sight,
   Awakening be to me!
Oh! that by early Grace I might
   For Death prepared be.

AGAIN

First in the Morning when thou dost
   awake,

To God for his Grace thy Petition
make,
Some Heavenly Petition use daily to
say,
That the God of Heaven may bless
thee alway.

Good Children muſt,
Fear God all Day,   Love Chriſt alway,
Parents obey,   In Secret Pray,
No falſe thing ſay, Mind little Play,
By no Sin ſtray,   Make no delay,
        In doing Good.

Awake, ariſe, behold thou haſt
Thy Life a Leaf, thy Breath a Blaſt;
At Night lye down prepar'd to have
Thy ſleep, thy death, thy bed, thy grave.

Learn theſe four Lines by Heart.

Have Communion with few.
Be Intimate with ONE.
Deal juſtly with all.
Speak Evil of none.

MR. John Rogers, Miniſter of
the Goſpel in London, was
the firſt Martyr in Q. Mary's Reign,
and was burnt at Smithfield, February the fourteenth, 1554. His Wife,
with nine ſmall Children, and one
at her Breaſt, following him to the
Stake, with which ſorrowful ſight
he was not in the leaſt daunted,
but with wonderful Patience died
couragiouſly for the Goſpel of
Jeſus Chriſt.

Some few Days before his Death,
he writ the following Exhortation
to his Children.
    . . .
GIve ear my Children to my words,
    whom God hath dearly bought,
Lay up his Laws within your heart,
    and print them in your thought.
I leave you here a little Book,
    for you to look upon:
That you may ſee your Fathers face,
    when he is dead and gone.
Who for the hope of heavenly things,
    while he did here remain,
Gave over all his golden Years
    to Priſon and to Pain.
Where I among my Iron Bands,
    incloſed in the dark,
C

Then pray the Lord my Soul in Heav'n
   may be with Glory crown'd.
Come welcome Death, the end of fears,
   I am prepar'd to die ;
Those earthly Flames will send my Soul,
   up to the Lord on high.
Farewel my Children to the World,
   where you must yet remain,
The Lord of Host be your defence
   till we do meet again.
Farewel my true and loving Wife,
   my Children and my Friends,
I hope in Heaven to see you all,
   when all things have their ends
If you go on to serve the Lord,
   as you have now begun,
You shall walk safely all your days,
   until your life be done.
GOD grant you so to end your days,
   as he shall think it best,
That I may meet you in the Heav'ns,
   where I do hope to rest.

The

In wide use by the late eighteenth century was the speller, a text similar to the primer but somewhat expanded in length and more secular in orientation than the primer. The most commonly used of the spellers in America was Thomas Dilworth's *A New Guide to the English Tongue*. It was first published in England in 1740 but, like the primer, had many editions and revisions in the colonies. Dilworth's speller actually comprised the entire text material for what was generally taught in the common schools of the eighteenth century. The title page, reprinted here, contains thus a concise outline of the curriculum of the common learning.

5. Dilworth's Speller

Thomas Dilworth

(The title page of *A New Guide to the English Tongue* and the outline of the curriculum appear on pages 30 and 31.)

The above title page of a 1797 edition published in Lancaster, Pennsylvania, is reproduced by courtesy of The Rutgers University Library.

A NEW GUIDE

TO THE

English Tongue.

IN FIVE PARTS.

CONTAINING,

I. Words, both common and proper, from one to six syllables: the several sorts of monofyllables in the common words being distinguished by tables into words of two, three, and four letters, &c. with six short leffons at the end of each table, not exceeding the order of syllables in the foregoing tables. The several forts of pollyfyllables alfo, being ranged in proper tables, have their fyllables divided, and directions placed at the head of each table for the accent, to prevent false pronunciation; together with the like number of leffons on the foregoing tables, placed at the end of each table, as far as to words of four fyllables, for the eafier and more speedy way of teaching children to read.

II. A large and useful table of words, that are the fame in found, but different in fignification; very neceffary to prevent the writing one word for another of the fame found.

III. A fhort, but comprehenfive, grammar of the Englifh Tongue, delivered in the moft familiar and inftructive method; neceffary for all fuch perfons as have the advantage only of an Englifh education.

IV. An ufeful collection of fentences in profe and verfe, divine, moral, and hiftorical; together with a felect number of fables adorned with proper fculptures, for the better improvement of the young beginners. And,

V. Forms of prayer for children, on feveral occafions.

The whole being recommended by feveral Clergymen and eminent Schoolmafters, as the moft ufeful Performance for the inftruction of youth.

LANCASTER,
PRINTED BY HENRY AND BENJAMIN GRIMLER.

Studies in the Latin grammar schools and colleges, though based on the ancient languages and the classic literature, were nonetheless thoroughly religious in spirit. These institutions were, of course, generally for the upper classes, designed to prepare the gentlemanly student for entry into one of the learned professions, especially for the church. Instruction in the Latin grammar school was essentially just that, Latin grammar, with perhaps some exposure to Greek. Classes were taught in Latin, and the emphasis was placed on preparing the young scholar for college work using the ancient languages. Yet the reading of Caesar, Cicero, and Virgil represented an exposure at least to history, geography, and a variety of areas of the humanities and social sciences.

The college curriculum was a continuation on a more sophisticated level of the classical studies that had been started in the Latin school. New areas of study introduced in the college included the languages of the Holy Writ, rhetoric, and declamation—essentially the professional clerical uses of learning. The college curriculum and the level of study are illustrated here first in the schedule for a Harvard class for each day (see chart on page 34) and second in a compilation of the holdings of the Harvard library early in the eighteenth century.

6. Latin-Grammar and Collegiate Studies

Samuel Eliot Morison

The Harvard College Library was the largest single collection in New England at the end of the [seventeenth] century. Begun in 1638 by John Harvard's bequest of about four hundred volumes, of which a catalogue is fortunately preserved, it gradually increased by donation and bequests from scholars in both Englands. In 1698, through the proceeds of selling over a hundred duplicates, the college was able to order for the library two important German annuals of science and general literature, the *Acta Eruditorum* and the *Miscellanea Curiosa, sive Ephemerides Medico-Physicarum Germanicarum.* By 1723 when the first catalogue of the College Library was printed, it composed about three thousand five hundred volumes, which I have analyzed as follows:

Reprinted by permission from Samuel Eliot Morison, *The Intellectual Life of Colonial New England* (New York: New York University Press, 1956), pp. 146-147.

*Number
of Volumes*

Theology, Bibles, Patristic Works, and Scholastic Philosophy	2,183
Ancient Philosophy, Logic, Ethics, Metaphysics	137
History, Politics, Geography, Description, and Travel	367
Physics, Natural History, General Science	131
Mathematics, Astronomy, Architecture, Navigation, Warfare	124
Hebrew and Other Oriental Languages	99
Greek Grammar and Literature	58
Latin Grammar and Literature	63
Dictionaries, Encyclopaedias, Lexicons	105
Modern Literature (French, English, Italian, Renaissance Latin).	45
Law and Statutes	65
Medicine	58
Manuals of Rhetoric, *flores*, etc.	35
Miscellaneous and Unidentified	47
Total (of which 1,340 were in folio)	3,517

Although President Dunster had attempted to obtain money for law and medical books for the College Library, it was still weak, in 1723, in all subjects but theology; and for the very good reason that it was intended largely for what we should call graduate students in that subject. Undergraduates were expected to buy or borrow their textbooks, and were not encouraged to use the Library or permitted to borrow books from it without express permission. Nevertheless Samuel Lee, who knew books, called it a 'handsome library' in 1690.

7. Harvard Regulations

the Lawes Liberties & orders of Harvard Colledge confirmed by the Overseers & president of yᵉ Colledge in the Yeares 1642, 1643, 1644, 1645, & 1646. and published to ye Scholars for ye perpetuall preservation of their welfare & governement

Regulations governing Harvard students in the seventeenth century offer an interesting insight into the life of the college. In the official view at least, pursuit of the higher learning was a rigorous and soberly religious undertaking.

THE TIMES AND ORDER OF THEIR STUDIES

FIRST YEAR

	8–9 a.m.	9–10	10–11	2–3 p.m.	3–4	4–5
M. & T.	Logic i–iii; PHYSICS iv	study	study	Disputations	study	study
Wed.	GREEK GRAMMAR[1]	study	study	*Grammatical practice*	study	study
Thurs.	HEBREW GRAMMAR	study	study	*Hebrew Bible readings*	study	study
Fri.	RHETORIC	Declamations	study Rhetoric rest of day			
Sat.	DIVINITY CATECHETICAL	study		History ii, iii; NATURE OF PLANTS, i, iv		

SECOND YEAR

	8–9 a.m.	9–10	10–11	2–3 p.m.	3–4	4–5
M. & T.	ETHICS & POLITICS	study	study	study	Disputations	study
Wed.	GREEK GRAMMAR[2]	study	study	study	*Greek Poetry*[3]	study
Thurs.	ARAMAIC	study	study	study	*Aramaic readings*[4]	study
Fri.	RHETORIC	Declamations	study Rhetoric rest of day			
Sat.	DIVINITY CATECHETICAL	study				

THIRD YEAR

	8–9 a.m.	9–10	10–11	2–3 p.m.	3–4	4–5
M. & T.	study		ARITH. & GEOM. i–iii; ASTRONOMY iv	study	study	Disputations
Wed.	"Perfect their [Greek] Theory before noone"			*Greek Composition*[5]	study	
Thurs.	study		SYRIAC	study	study	*Readings in Syriac N. T.*
Fri.	RHETORIC	Declamations	study Rhetoric rest of day			
Sat.	DIVINITY CATECHETICAL	Commonplaces	study			

[1] "Etymologie and Syntax."   [2] "Prosodia and Dialects."   [3] "Practice in Poësy, Nonnus, Duport, or the like."
[4] "Ezra and Daniel."   [5] "Exercise Style, Composition, Imitation, Epitome both in Prose and Verse."

Chart reprinted by permission of the publishers from Samuel Eliot Morison, *Harvard College in the Seventeenth Century* 2 volumes (Cambridge, Mass.: Harvard University Press, 1936), I, p. 140.

See yᵉ same B. 3. p. 19 &c

1. When any Schollar is able to Read Tully or such like classicall Latine Authour ex tempore, & make and speake true Latin in verse and prose suo (ut aiunt) Marte, and decline perfectly the paradigmes of Nounes and verbes in yᵉ Greeke toungue, then may hee bee admitted into yᵉ Colledge, nor shall any claime admission before such qualifications.

2. Every one shall consider the mayne End of his life & studyes, to know God & Jesus Christ which is Eternall life Joh. 17. 3.

3. Seeing yᵉ Lord giveth wisdome, exery one shall seriously by prayer in secret, seeke wisdome of him. prov. 2 2, 3 &c.

4. Every one shall so exercise himselfe in reading yᵉ Scriptures twice a day that they bee ready to give an account of their proficiency theerein, both in theoreticall observations of Language & Logicke, and in practicall & spirituall truthes as their tutour shall require according to their severall abilities respectively, seeing the Entrance of ye word giveth light &c psal. 119. 130.

5. In the publike Church assembly they shall carefully shunne all gestures that shew any contẽpt or neglect of Gods ordinances and bee ready to give an account to their tutours of their profiting and to use ye helpes of Storing themselves with knowledge, as their tutours shall direct them. & all Sophisters & Bachellors (until themselves make common place shall publiquely repeate Sermons in yᵉ Hall whenever they are called forth.

6. they shall eschew all prophanation of Gods holy name, attributes, word, ordinances, and times of worship, and study with Reverence & love carefully to reteine God & his truth in their minds.

7. they shall honour as their parents, Magistrates, Elders, tutours & aged persons, by beeing silent in their presence (except they bee called on to answer) not gainesaying, shewing all those laudable expressions of honour & Reverence in their presence, that are in use as bowing before them standing uncovered or ye like.

8. they shall bee slow to speake, & eschew not onely oathes, Lies, & uncertaine Rumours, but likewise all Idle, foolish, bitter scoffing, frothy wanton words & offensive gestures.

9. None shall pragmatically intrude or intermeddle in other mens affaires.

10. During their Residence, they shall studiously redeeme their time, observe ye generall houres appointed for all ye Scholars, & yᵉ speciall hour for their owne Lecture, & then diligently attend ye Lectures without any disturbance by word or gesture: And if of any thing they doubt they

Reprinted by permission from "Harvard College Records," *Publications of Colonial Society of Massachusetts,* Vol. XV. (1925), p. 24-29.

shall inquire as of their fellowes so in case of non-resolution modestly of their tutours.

11. None shall under any pretence whatsoever frequent the company & society of such men as lead an ungirt & dissolute life.

Neither shall any without licence of ye overseers of yᵉ Colledge bee of the Artillery or traine-Band.

Nor shall any without yᵉ Licence of yᵉ Overseers of yᵉ Colledge, his tutours leave, or in his absence yᵉ call of parents or Guardians goe out to another towne.

12. No Scholar shall buy sell or exchange any thing to ye value of sixe-pence without ye allowance of his parents, guardians, or tutours. And whosoever is found to have sold or bought any such thing without acquainting their tutour or parents, shall forfeit ye value of ye Commodity, or ye Restoring of it, according to ye discretion of yᵉ president.

13. the Scholars shall never use their Mother-toungue except that[t] in publike Exercises of oratory or such like, they bee called to make them in English.

14. If any Scholar beeing in health shall bee absent from prayer or Lectures, except in case of urgent necessity or by yᵉ Leave of his tutour, hee shall bee liable to admonition (or such punishment as the president shall thinke meet) if hee offend above once a weeke.

15. Every Scholar shall be called by his Sirname onely till hee bee invested with his first degree; except hee bee fellow-commoner or a Knights Eldest Sonne or of superiour Nobility.

16. No Scholars shall under any pretence of recreation or other cause what-ever (unlesse foreshewed & allowed by ye president or his tutour) bee absent from his studyes or appointed exercises above an houre at Morning-Bever, halfe an houre at afternoone-Bever; an houre and an halfe at Dinner & so long at Supper.

17. If any Scholar shall transgresse any of ye Lawes of God or the House out of perversnesse or apparent negligence, after twice admonition hee shall bee liable if not adultus to correction, if Adultus his name shall bee given up to ye Overseers of ye Colledg[e] that he may be publikely dealth with after ye desert of his [fau]lt but in [gros]ser offenses such graduall proceeding shall not bee ex[pected].

18. Every Scholar that on proofe is found able to read ye originall of ye old & New testament into ye Latin toungue, and to Resolve them Logically withall beeing of honest life & conversation and at any publike act hath ye approbation of ye overseers, & Master of ye Colledge may bee invested with his first degree.

19. Every Scholar that giveth up in writing a Synopsis or summa of Logicke, Naturall & morall Philosophy, Arithmeticke, Geometry; &

Astronomy, & is ready to defend his theses or positions, withall Skilled in ye originals as aforesaid & still continues honest and studious, at any publicke act after triall hee shall bee capable of ye 2^d degree of Master of Arts.

Orders agreed upon by ye Overseers at a meeting in
Harvard Colledge, May: 6th: 1650.

No Schollar whatever w^thout ye fore acquaintance & leave of ye President & his Tutor, or in ye absence of either of them two of ye ffellowes shal bee present at or in any of ye Publike Civil meetings or Concourse of people as Courts of justice, elections, fayres, or at military exercise in ye time or howers of ye Colledge exercise Publike or private neither shal any schollar exercise himself in any Military band, unlesse of knowne gravity & of approoved, sober & vertuous conversation & y^t wth leave of ye President & his Tutor.

No scholar shall take Tobacco unlesse permitted by ye President wth ye Consent of their parents or guardians, & on good reason first given by a Physitian & then in a sober & private manner.

To ye Intent y^t no scholar may mispend his time, to ye dishonour of God & society or ye greif & disappointment of his friends, but y^t that ye yearly progresse & sufficiency of Scollars may bee manifest: Its therefore order'd: that hence forth there shall bee three weeks of visitation yearly foresignifyed publikely by ye Præsident of ye Colledge between ye tenth of June & the Commencement wherein from 9 of ye Clock to 11 in ye fore-noone & from one to 3 in the afternoon of ye second & third day of ye week all scholars [t]wo years standing & upward shall sit in ye Hall to bee examined by all Commers in ye Latine, Greek & Hebrew tongues & in Rhetoricke, Logike & Physicks. & they that expect to proceed Batchelours that year to bee examined of their sufficiency according to ye Lawes of ye Colledge. & such that expect to proceed masters of Art to exhibit their Synopses of Arts required by ye Lawes of ye Colledge. & in Case of any of ye Sophisters Questionists or Inceptors faill in ye premises required at their hands according to their standings respectively or bee found insuffi-cient for y^eir time & standing in ye Judgment of any three of the visitors being overseers of ye Colledge they shall bee deferred to ye following Year but they that are approved sufficient for their degrees shall pro-ceed; & ye Sophisters publickly approved shall have their names publickely set in up in ye Hall

Whereas by experience wee have found it prejudicial to the pmoting of Learning & good manners in the Colledge to admit such yong Schollars who have been negligent in their studyes & disobedient to their masters in the Schools & so by an evill custome or habit become utterly unfit to improove for their owne pfit according to their freinds expectation the liberty of students in th^e Colledge: It is therefore ordered by the President & ffellows of Harvard Colledge that no Schollar whatsoever where these bee published shall thenceforth bee admitted from any such Schools unlesse having the Testimony of the Master of the said School of his obedience & submission to all Godly School-discipline & of his studiousnes & diligence at leastwise for one quarter of a year last before his comeing thence, or in case of discontinuance from School then it is expected hee shall bring the testimony of his sober & studious conversation under the hand of a Magistrate, or Elder or two or three competent pious witnesses.

SECTION 3

Teaching, Teachers, and Learners

". . . the preservation of the means of knowledge among the lowest ranks is of more importance to the public than all the property of all the rich men in the country."

John Adams, A Dissertation on
the Canon and Feudal Law (1765)

This section presents some representative readings relevant to the "preservation of the means of knowledge" in colonial America. Among the "lowest ranks," this generally took the form of provision in indentures of apprenticeship whereby the master agreed to provide (in a variety of ways) for the education of the apprentice. The first part of this section, therefore, illustrates these educational provisions in some selected indenture contracts.

The three essential ingredients of institutional education are, of course, the teacher, the pupil, and the curriculum. Examples of educational conditions with reference to teachers and students are included in this section, as well as some comments by both on the curriculum.

Finally, this section contains a sampling of the advertisements printed by the private-school masters of the eighteenth century (in the northern and southern colonies) which illustrate the metamorphosis that the curriculum was going through in the eighteenth century—a metamorphosis that was, at least initially, confined to the flexible nature of private educational ventures. As the subsequent section will demonstrate, there were attempts to carry this new "useful" educational orientation into the more formal educational offerings of newly conceived "academies," but these attempts were largely unsuccessful during the colonial period.

The concluding portion of this section presents some selections from the diaries kept by two interesting personalities who taught in the colonial South—Philip Vickers Fithian and John Harrower. These selections illustrate the colonial education process through the eyes of resident tutors in the homes of the wealthy southern gentry.

APPRENTICESHIP EDUCATION

The apprentice system of colonial America was modeled after the English system of apprenticeship as stated in the English Statute of Artificers and the Poor Law of 1601. Although initially inaugurated in order to produce a supply of skilled labor, it developed into an important elementary educational agent. The apprenticing to a master to learn a trade was accepted colonial-American practice as early as 1631 on Boston, and the English apprentice system was adopted in New York after 1675. In Philadelphia before 1690 provincial authorities handled all indentures of apprenticeship. By the close of the seventeenth century, apprenticeship was a part of the labor picture in all of the towns of colonial America.*

The famous 1642 Massachusetts education law required parents and masters to provide for, among other things, the education of their charges—particularly with regard to basic literacy. A subsequent

* Carl Bridenbaugh, *Cities in the Wilderness* (New York: The Ronald Press, 1938), pp. 46-48.

law made the inclusion of compulsory book-learning provisions manditory in all Massachusetts indentures of apprenticeship.

Other colonial towns generally followed suit in adopting the English system, frequently requiring provisions for education in the indenture contracts, usually with reference to reading, writing, and ciphering.

In the eighteenth century, this manditory instruction was largely relegated to the evening school, and the indenture contracts of this century increasingly contained a clause that specifically provided for school attendance during a specified part of the year. One investigator found 108 indentures in New York province alone containing such provisions.* This schooling was usually a matter of one-quarter of a year in attendance at an evening school for each year of indenture. Carl Bridenbaugh, an authority on colonial American social history, concludes that far more children received their elementary education by this system than by any other.†

Affixing his mark to the indenture in Selection 8, John Maisters (Masters) of York county (Maine) contracted not only to learn the secrets of carpentry (and keep them to himself), but to conduct his personal affairs in exemplary fashion. His master, William Partridg, for his part bound himself to attempt to convey to young Maisters the elements of carpentry, to provide him with board and lodging, and to bestow upon his apprentice the magnificent stipend of "seaven pounds" for each of his four years of servitude. Note that Partridg also bound himself to teach his apprentice to "write and siffer" (cipher). This last, of course, only if young Maisters demonstrated that "hee bee capable."

8. A Seventeenth-Century New England Indenture of Apprenticeship

This Indenture witnesseth that I John Maisters of Wells, In the County of Yorke, with the Consent of my father Nathall Masters doe bind my selfe an

Reprinted by permission from Richard B. Morris, *Government and Labor in Early America* (Copyright 1946 by Richard B. Morris; Torchbook edition, Harper & Row, 1966), p. 366.

* Robert F. Seybolt, as cited in Bernard Bailyn, *Education in the Forming of American Society* Chapel Hill: University of North Carolina Press, 1960), p. 33.
† Bridenbaugh, *op. cit.*, p. 289.

apprentice to William Partridg of Wells Carpenter, in the same County, to continew with, abide and faithfully serve him my master as a faithfull apprentice out to doe, the full and Just tearme of four years, to bee fully ended from the date thereof; The sayd apprentice his sd Maister faithfully to serue, his lawfull secrets keepe, hee shall not play at unlawfull games, nor vnseasonably absent him selfe from his sayd Maisters busines, hee shall not frequent Tavernes, nor lend, nor spend the goods or victualls of his sd Maister, without his leaue, hee shall not Contract Matrimony, or Committ fornication, but truely and trustily obserue his sd Maisters lawful Comands as a faithfull servant out to due. The sd Maister his sd apprentice shall teach, and Instruct in the Trade of a Carpenter, to the best of his skill, according to what his sayd apprentice is Capable of, and alsoe doe promiss to teach him to write and siffer, If hee bee Capable, and to giue him a set of Tools at the end of his tyme, and to prouide him dureing the sd apprentishipe, Convenjent Meate drinke, lodging and washing, and seaven pounds per Ann: for to bind him aparell, and provided his Maister shall goe out of the County, hee shall not haue him his sayd servant to goe along with him, without his sd apprentice Consent. In witness wr of [whereof] Wee haue here unto set our hands and seales interChangeably this sixteenth day of Septembr, one thousand six hundred seaventy foure:

John Maisters his marke	[his seale]
William Partridg	[his seale]

The following illustrations are typical of the apprenticeship contracts of the eighteenth century. In the first contract, Jonathan Stoughton of Connecticut is to be taught not only the trade of a blacksmith but the "art of arithmatick" as well. This "arithmatick" is clearly of a practical nature, designed to assist young Stoughton to balance his accounts. Note that this contract further contains a "medicare" provision—at least to the extent of providing "phisick in sickness and health."

9. A New England Eighteenth-Century Indenture of Apprenticeship

This Indenture witnesseth that Jonathan Stoughton, son of Thomas Stoughton of Windsor in the county of hartford and Coloney of Con-

Reprinted from H. R. Stiles, *The History of Ancient Windsor Connecticutt* (New York: C. B. Norton 1859), I, p. 442.

necticut in new england, with his father's consent hath put him selfe an apprentice to Nathan day of the aboue sd windsor county and coloney: blacksmith and white smith to Learn his art, trade or mystery after the manner of an Apprentice to serue him until the sd Jonathan Stoughton attaines the age of twenty-one years, during all which time the sd apprentice his master faithfully shall serue, his secrets keep, his Lawfull commands gladly obaye he shall not do any damage to his sd master nor see it don by others without giveing notice thereof to his sd master. he shall not waste his sd master's goods or Lend them unLawfully to aney, he shall not commit fornication nor contract matrimony within the sd terme, at cards, dice or any other unlawfull game he shall not play whereby his sd master may suffer damage. he shall not absent himself day nor night from his master's service without his leave. nor haunt ale houses, Taverns or playhouses butt in all things behave himselfe as a faithfull apprentice ought to do during ye sd terme, and the sd master shall do his utmost to teach and Instruct ye sd apprentice In the boue mentioned blacksmith and white smiths trade and mistery and to teach or caus the sd apprentice to be Taught the art of Arithmatick to such a degree that he may be able to keep a book well, and provide for him meat, drink, apparel, washing and lodging and phisick in sickness and health suitable for such an apprentice during the sd terme, and att the end of sd terme the sd master shall furnish the sd apprentice with two good new suits of apparel boath wooling and lining for all parts of his body suitable for such an apprentice besids that apparel he carrieth with him and for the performance of all and every the sd convenants and agreement either of the sd parties bind themselves unto the other by these presents in witness whereof they have interchangeably put their hands and seals this first day of September in the year of our Lord god, 1727.

In the following contract, William Mathews agrees to serve a full seven year apprenticeship with Thomas Windover of New York City in order to learn the trade of a "Cordwiner" [cordwainer, a shoemaker]. In addition to the standard restrictions and benefits, Windover would also provide tuition for his apprentice to attend night school for "one quarters schooling" every winter. There were numerous private venture masters who would, for a fee, be happy to instruct this young apprentice in any one of a bewildering variety of subjects. (See below for illustrations of some of the advertised offerings of these private school masters.)

10. A New York Eighteenth-Century Indenture of Apprenticeship

This Indenture Wittnesseth that I, William Mathews, son of Marrat of the City of New York, Widdow, hath put himself and by these Presents doth voluntarily and of his own free Will and Accord and by the Consent of his said Mother put himself Apprentice to Thomas Windover of the City aforesaid Corwiner with him to live and (after the Manner of an Apprentice) to serve from the fifteenth day of August last Anno Dom one thousand and seven hundred and Eighteen untill the full Term of seven years be Compleat and Ended. During all which Term the said Apprentice his said Master Thomas Windover faithfullly shall serve his secrets keep, his lawfull Commands gladly every where Obey, he shall do no damage to his said Master nor see to be done by Others without letting or giving Notice to his said Master, he shall not waste his said Masters Goods, nor lend him unlawfully to any, he shall not Committ fornication nor Contract Matrimony within the said Term. At Cards, Dice or any Other unlawfull Game he shall not play whereby his said Master may have Damage with his Own Goods or the Goods of those during the said Term without Lycense from his said Master he shall neither buy nor sell. He shall not absent himself day or night from his Masters service without his leave, nor haunt Alehouses, Taverns or Playhouses, but in all things as a faithfull apprentice he shall behave himself towards his said Master and all his during the said Term. And the said Master during the said Term shall, by his best means or Method that he can Teach or Cause the said Apprentice to be taught the Art or Mystery of a Cordwiner, and shall find and provide unto the said Apprentice sufficient Meat, Drink, Apparel, Lodging and washing fitting for an Apprentice, and shall during the said Term every winter at Nights give him one Quarters schooling, and at the Expiration of the said Term to provide for the said Apprentice a sufficient New Suit of Apparell four shirts and two Necletts, for the true Performance of all and every the said Covenants and agreements Either of the said parties bind themselves unto the Other by these Presents.

In Witness whereof they have hereunto Interchangeably put their hands

Reprinted by permission from Richard B. Morris, *Government and Labor in Early America* (Copyright 1946 by Richard B. Morris; Torchbook edition, Harper & Row, 1966), pp. 366-367.

and seals this twenty fifth day of September in the fifth year of his Majesties Reign, Annoque Domini One thousand seven hundred and Eighteen. The Marke of William Mathews (seal) sealed and delivered in the Presence of John Rushton, H. D. Meyer, New York Sept. 26th Ao 1718 then appeared before me Jacobus Kip one of his Majties Justis of the Peace for the City and County of New York the within Named Apprentice and acknowledge the signing and sealing of this Indenture to be his Voluntary Act and Deed.

Jacobus Kip, Justice of the Peace

The final illustration reveals an early teacher-training situation. John Campbell desired to earn his living as a schoolmaster; hence he contracted with George Brownell to complete an apprenticeship of ten years and three months. Note that master Brownell is rather uncertain as to whether his work is properly defined as an "art trade or calling," a confusion that seems quite typical with schoolmasters past and present. John Campbell chose an excellent mentor to learn the "art trade or calling of a Schoolmaster." Brownell was a well-traveled, private-school master who taught in Boston and Philadelphia as well as in New York. He is, however, probably best remembered due to the later success of one of his Boston pupils, a young chap named Ben Franklin. Franklin remembered Brownell in the *Autobiography* as ". . . a skillful master, and who succeeded very well in his profession by employing gentle means only, and such as were calculated to encourage his scholars."

11. Indenture for Teacher Training

This Indenture Wittnesseth that John Campbell son of Robert Campbell of the City of New York with the consent of his father and mother hath put himself and by these presents doth Voluntarily put and bind himself Apprentice to George Brownell of the Same City Schoolmaster to learn the Art Trade or Mystery and with the Said George Brownell to Serve from the twenty ninth day of May one thousand seven hundred and twenty one for and during the Term of ten years and three Months to be Compleat and Ended During all which term the said Apprentice his said Master and

City of N. York Indentures, February 19, 1694 to January 29, 1707, pp. 145-47 (Ms. folio, City Hall, New York). Reprinted in Robert F. Seybolt, *Source Studies in American Colonial Education* (Urbana: University of Illinois Press, 1925), pp. 85-86.

Mistress faithfully Shall Serve their Secrets keep and Lawfull Commands gladly everywhere obey he Shall do no damage to his said Master or Mistress nor suffer it to be done by others without Letting or Giving Notice thereof to his said Master or Mistress he shall not Waste his said Master or Mistress Goods or Lend them Unlawfully to any he shall not Commit fornication nor Contract Matrimony within the Said Term at Cards Dice or any other unlawfull Game he shall not Play: he Shall not absent himself by Day or by Night from his Said Master or Mistress Service without their Leave; nor haunt Alehouses Taverns or Playhouses but in all things behave himself as a faithfull Apprentice ought to Do towards his said Master or Mistress during the Said Term. And the said George Brownell Doth hereby Covenant and Promse to teach and Instruct or Cause the said Apprentice to be taught and instructed in the Art Trade or Calling of a Schoolmaster by the best way or means he or his wife may or can if the Said Apprentice be Capable to Learn and to find and Provide unto the Said Apprentice sufficient meat Drink Apparel Lodging and washing fitting for an Apprentice during the Said Term: and at the Expiration thereof to give unto the Said Apprentice one Suit of Cloth new Consisting of a coatvest coat and Breeches also one New hatt Six New Shirts Three pair of Stockings one pair of New Shoes Suitable for his said Apprentice. In testimony Whereof the Parties to these Presents have hereunto Interchangeably Sett their hands and Seals the third day of August in the Eighth year of the Reign of our Sovereign Lord George King of Great Britain &c. Anno Domini One thousand seven hundred and Twenty One. John Campbel. Signed Sealed and Delivered in the presence of Mary Smith Cornelius Kiersted Memorandum Appeared before me John Cruger Esq. Alderman and One of his Majesties Justices of the Peace for this City and County. John Campbell and Acknowledged the within Indenture to be his Voluntary Act and Deed New York the 9th Aprill 1722.

THE TEACHERS

Good teachers are always a chronic shortage in any era, no less so in Colonial America. In addition to recruiting schoolmasters by means of apprenticeship to a qualified teacher, the colonies imported teachers from abroad.

The following letter, written in 1685 by William Penn to friends T. Loyd, Thomas Holmes, William Hampton, and Secretary Markham in Philadelphia, illustrates one manner in which new teachers were introduced into the colonies. John Saxby apparently is well-qualified to teach in the classical tradition of the sevententh century and comes highly recommended for employment in the Quaker city.

12. Letter to His Friends

William Penn

DEAR FRIENDS,

My dear & unfeined love salutes you & y^{rs} desireing all ye wellfaire, here & hereafter the Bearer is one John Saxby a bred Scholler, capable of teaching the latin, Greek writing & Arethmatick very well, so y^t either by himselfe if room or as instructer & M^{rs} of learning under Christopher whos own business will rather be Superintendency of manners & hous Goverm^t I desire you to encourage & employ him, he has an accurate short way of teaching the latin wch is very valuable he has a good name, & is an honest man, & t'will be wisdom as well as kindness & charity to indulge & encourage him; hous room gratis, ye first winter will do something, there way because for that & if he be soon in employ he will do well enough, he also has a son an excellent Scribe to learn writeing assuredly ye Man has useful abilitys & a simplicity no more, but ye Lord be wth you wth his fear & blessings

Your true frd

KENSINGTON   WM. PENN.
7th 6mo 85

The teacher's life was almost as carefully regimented as that of his student. He was frequently provided with detailed instructions with regard to his many duties and obligations. The manifold duties of the colonial-American school master are reflected by the following

Reprinted from "Letter of William Penn," *Pennsylvania Magazine of History and Biography*, XXXIII (1909), p. 303.

extract from a New England "Town Book" dealing with required
activities of a master in 1661:

13. Duties of a School Master

1) Act as court-messenger
2) Serve summonses
3) Conduct certain cermonial church services
4) Lead Sunday choir
5) Ring bell for public worship
6) Dig graves
7) Take charge of school
8) Perform other occasional duties

In addition to being fully occupied, teachers were often required to
be licensed to teach. This could either be a formal license, per se,
or the approval of the town government for an individual to open
and conduct a school. The following document is a formal license
to teach in Albany, New York, in 1665. Notice that in this particular
instance, a monopoly is granted in this Dutch community to English
teacher, John Shutte. The licensing was usually done by the clergy,
and the contract was drawn by civil authorities. A 1701 Massachusetts
law required, for example, that every grammar-school master "be
approved by the minister of the town and the minister of the two
next adjacent towns, or any two of them by certificate. . . ."

14. License to Teach

Whereas, the teaching of the English tongue is necessary in this government; I have, therefore, thought fitt to give license to John Shutte to be
the English Schoolmaster at Albany; And, upon condition that the said

"Duties of a School Master" is reprinted from E. D. Grizzell, *Origin and Development of the High School in New England Before 1865* (New York: Macmillan
Co., 1923), p. 24.
"License to Teach" is reprinted from *Records of ye Towne Meetings of Lyn
1691-1701/2,* Part One (Lynn, Massachusetts: Lynn Historical Society, 1949), p. 39.

John Shutte shall not demand any more wages from each Schollar than is given by the Dutch to their Dutch Schoolmasters, I have further granted to the said John Shutte that hee shall bee the onely English Schoolmaster at Albany.

Given under my hand, at Fort James in New York, the 12th day of October, 1665.

RICH'RD NICOLLS

A less formal contract with a teacher is seen in the following extract from the records of the town meeting of Lynn, Massachusetts, at the close of the seventeenth century. At a "Meeting of the select Men of Lyn January: 13: 1695/5" we learn that:

> The select men did agree with Mr. Normenton to bee scoole mastor for ye town for ye year Ensewing and the town to give him five pounds for his labour and ye town is to pay twenty-five shillings towards the hire of Nathaniell Newhalls house for one year to keep scoole in and ye sd Mr. Normenton to hire ye sd house. . . .

In 1701, the town meeting of Lynn was somewhat more specific with regard to the duties of the "scoole master," as the following extract indicates.

15. Duties of the Scoole Master

. . . at a town meeting held in Lyn Nouemye: 5th 1701 Voated to have a grammar schoole master to keep schoole in the town.

at ye same meeting

Voated thirty pounds money for the maintenance of a grammar schoole master for one year beginning when such schools master shall be settled in the town to teach such as shall be sent to him Latten or to Write cipher and Read

at ye same meeting

Voated that Theophilus Burrill shall take care to procure a schools master fourth with or as soone as may be. . . .

[The following year (1702), this town meeting further]

Reprinted from: *Records of ye Towne Meetings of Lyn 1701-1717,* Part Two (Lynn Massachusetts: Lynn Historical Society, 1956), p. 10.

Voated ten pounds money for part of ye maintenance of a grammar schoolemaster quallyfied according to Law for one year beginning when such schoolemaster shall be settled in the schoole to teach such as shall be sent to him to Reed write cipher and to lern Latten and such school master to have over and above the said ten pounds: 2d: pence p week for such as are sent to Reed: 3: Cipher: and 6: pence p weak for them that are sent to lern Latten to be paid by parants and masters that sends their children or servants to learn as afore sd

[at the same meeting]

Voated that the selectmen shall take care to procure a schoole master fourth with or as soone as maybe. . . .

[Finally, a glance at the record of the meeting held "in Lyn January: 12 1702/3" confirms what has been long suspected by members of the teaching fraternity but rarely so clearly enunciated. After voting an additional ten pounds for part of the maintenance of a "grammar schoole master," the meeting further specified]

. . . the selectmen should obtain a school master for this present year *as cheap as they can* [emphasis added]

THE LEARNERS

The educational process is, of course, a dialogue and not a monologue. The student also had his view of education (and of teachers). These perceptions are valuable in any understanding of the total picture of education in colonial times in America.

The author of the following piece, Alexander Graydon (1752–1818), was a lawyer, author, and sometime captain in the Continental Army. His experience here related of his entrance into the Academy of Philadelphia (known since 1755, as Graydon points out, as the "College, Academy and Charitable School of Philadelphia") provides an interesting picture of pre-revolutionary education.

The two teachers that he mentions (Kinnersley and Beveridge) were both notable educators. Ebenezer Kinnersley was the master of the English school at the time of Graydon's experience, having suceeded the able David James Dove in 1753. Dove, incidently, had lost his academy position due to his insistence on maintaining a private school for girls. John Beveridge, the "native of Scotland who retained the smack of his vernacular tongue in its primitive purity," was a poet.

Graydon spent some four years in the Latin School of the Academy and became a "drop-out" at the age of fourteen.

16. A Colonial School-Boy

Alexander Graydon

Being now, probably, about eight years of age, it was deemed expedient to enter me at the academy, then, as it now continues to be, under the name of a university, the principal seminary in Pennsylvania; and I was accordingly introduced by my father, to Mr. Kinnersley, the teacher of English and professor of oratory. . . . The task, of the younger boys, at least, consisted in learning to read and to write their mother tongue grammatically; and one day in the week (I think Friday) was set apart for the recitation of select passages in poetry and prose. For this purpose, each scholar, in his turn, ascended the stage, and said his speech, as the phrase was. This speech was carefully taught him by his master, both with respect to its pronunciation, and the action deemed suitable to its several parts. . . . More profit attended my reading. After Æsop's fables, and an abridgment of the Roman history, Telemachus was put into our hands; and if it be admitted that the human heart may be bettered by instruction, mine, I may aver, was benefited by this work of the virtuous Fenelon. . . .

. . . A few days after I had been put under the care of Mr. Kinnersley, I was told by my class mates, that it was necessary for me to fight a battle with some one, in order to establish my claim to the honor of being an academy boy. . . . I found that the lists were appointed, and that a certain John Appowen, a lad who, though not quite so tall, [was] yet better set and older than myself, was pitted against me. . . . A combat immediately ensued between Appowen and myself, which for some time, was maintained on each side, with equal vigor and determination, when unluckily, I re-

Reprinted from Alexander Graydon, *Memoirs of a Life Chiefly Passed in Pennsylvania within the Last Sixty Years* (Harrisburg: John Wyeth, 1811), pp. 16-18, 24-25, 31.

ceived his fist directly in my gullet. The blow for a time depriving me of breath and the power of resistance, victory declared for my adversary, though not without the acknowledgment of the party, that I had at last behaved well, and shown myself not unworthy of the name of an academy boy. . . .

I have said that I was about to enter the Latin school. The person whose pupil I was consequently to become, was Mr. John Beveridge, a native of Scotland, who retained the smack of his vernacular tongue in its primitive purity. His acquaintance with the language he taught, was I believe, justly deemed to be very accurate and profound. But as to his other acquirements, after excepting the game of backgammon, in which he was said to excel, truth will not warrant me in saying a great deal. He was, however, diligent and laborious in his attention to his school; and had he possessed the faculty of making himself beloved by the scholars, and of exciting their emulation and exertion, nothing would have been wanting in him to an entire qualification for his office. But unfortunately, he had no dignity of character, and was no less destitute of the art of making himself respected than beloved. Though not perhaps to be complained of as intolerably severe, he yet made a pretty free use of the ratan and the ferule, but to very little purpose. . . .

. . . as my evil star would have it, I was thoroughly tired of books and confinement, and her [his mother's] advice and even entreaties were overruled by my extreme repugnance to a longer continuance in the college, which, to my lasting regret, I bid adieu to when a little turned of fourteen, at the very season when the minds of the studious begin to profit by instruction. We were at this time reading Horace and Cicero, having passed through Ovid, Virgil, Cæsar and Sallust. . . .

Graydon's subsequent critique of the education that he received at the academy is noteworthy in that it reflects the inadequacies of the academy instruction in terms of the realities of eighteenth-century Philadelphia. In short, the result of Graydon's educational venture was exactly the result that Franklin had feared—it failed to provide for a business or calling. Graydon expressed this as follows:

17. Critique of His Education

Alexander Graydon

From a pretty close application, we were well grounded in grammar, and had passed through the elementary books, [but after the first two years] became possessed of the demons of liberty and idleness. . . . One boy thought he had Latin enough, as he was not designed for a learned profession; his father thought so too, and was about taking him from school. Another was of the opinion that he might be much better employed in a counting house, and was about ridding himself of his scholastic shackles. As this was a consummation devoutly wished by us all, we cheerfully renounced the learned professions for the sake of the supposed liberty that would be the consequence. We were all, therefore, to be merchants, as to be mechanics was too humiliating."

The following letter, written by young John Ten Broeck from his boarding school in Stamford to his proud parents in Albany, is illustrative of the amazingly consistent behavioral patterns of schoolboys—patterns that transcend time and place. Put into modern terminology and spelling, this letter could well be sent out today without, one suspects, arousing any more surprise on the part of the recipient than it probably did on the part of Myneer Ten Broeck in 1752.

In addition to providing testimony to the effect that the colonial schoolboy's appetite was as insatiable as his modern counterpart's, Master John, has, alas, forgotten to pack his extra pair of "schuse." Note also that our young scholar makes the most of this oversight to request, not any old pair of shoes, but "a pare of indin's schuse." Naturally, a plea for additional funds is also included—a plea that the Ten Broeck family will undoubtedly find a familiar refrain in subsequent letters in the months to come.

Reprinted from Alexander Graydon, *Memoirs of a Life Chiefly Passed in Pennsylvania within the Last Sixty Years* (Harrisburg: John Wyeth, 1811), p. 31.

18. Schoolboy's Letter Home

John Ten Broeck

"TO MR. CORNELIUS TEN BROECK
                    att Albany.
"Stamford, the 13th Day of October, 1752.
    "HONORED FETHAR,
    "These fiew Lines comes to let you know that I am in a good State of Health and I hope this may find you also. I have found all the things in my trunk but I must have a pare of Schuse. And mama please to send me some Ches Nutts and some Wall Nutts; you please to send me a Slate, and som pensals, and please to send me some smok befe, and for bringing my trunk 3/9, and for a pare of Schuse 9 shillings. You please to send me a pare of indin's Schuse. You please to send me som dride corn. My Duty to Father and Mother and Sister and to all frinds.
                    "I am your Dutyfull Son,
                            "JOHN TEN BROECK.
    "Father forgot to send me my Schuse."

Another student's-eye view of educational activities during the eighteenth century is expressed in the following document. It also reveals some of the expense involved in attending school for one quarter. Interestingly enough, the school bill (which was made out in blank by student, Charles Mifflin, and filled in by schoolmaster, P. Webster) provided an accounting of what Mifflin's time would have been worth had he not been attending school. This sum was added to the cost of the quarter's attendance. The item labeled "schooling" referred to tuition cost, as opposed to cost of living expenses. The master's certificate indicated (perhaps) to Mifflin's guardian, that the money had been well spent. Note the high proportion of lecture time devoted to Latin grammar as compared with English grammar. History and geography were also studied at this school.

Reprinted by permission from A. M. Earle, *Child-life in Colonial Days* (New York: Macmillian Co., 1915), pp. 80-81.

19. School Bill

UNION SCHOOL

Quarter Bill for Preceding Quarter.

Dr. Cha[s] Mifflin to Board & Lodging @ £30 per ann.	7	. 10	. 0
Cloathing at £12. per Ann	3	. 0	. 0
Books 9/ paper, Quills, ink, &c 3/4		12	. 4
Pocket Money at 6d per week		6	. 6
Time wou[d] have been worth		10	. 0
	£11	. 18	. 10
Schooling		17	. 6
Whole Cost	£12	. 16	. 4

Cr. Began to Keep a Diary, June 26 in which Time I said 64 morning Lessons; Read Eng. History, 59 times, Read Poetry 26 times, Read Roman History 24 times, Attended Lecture on Latin Gram. 62, Attended Lecture on Eng. Gram. 48 times, Said 82 Lessons in Corn. Nepos, Made 48 Latin Ex[r] Had Tryals for Places at the Table 12 times, Place in 1st Class Head 3 times, Foot none, Absent none, Read 113 Chapters in the Holy Bible, Attended Divine worship at the Friends meeting 12 times, Had 8 Lectures on Geog. Maps. Wrote 8 Copies.

Masters Certificate that Charles Mifflin has performed his Ex[r] well, Studies diligently makes a Very Desirable progress in Learning.

P. WEBSTER.

To MR THOMAS WHARTON (his Guardian).
Sep. 24, 1764.

The Germans were one of the groups in colonial America who were quite concerned with pedagogical theory and practice, and one of the keenest observers and recorders amongst this group was the Mennonite teacher, Christopher Dock. During his long tenure as a Pennsylvania teacher, Dock observed and thought a great deal about education. This resulted ultimately in his writing one of the first treatises in British America on the subject of education—the famous

Reprinted from: "Notes and Queries," *Pennsylvania Magazine of History and Biography,* XXXIII (1909), pp. 365-366.

Schul-Ordnung (1770). In the following selection (written in 1750),
Dock explained how children should be received and treated in school.

20. Reception and Treatment of School Children

Christopher Dock

The children arrive as they do because some have a great distance to
school, others a short distance, so that the children cannot assemble as
punctually as they can in a city. Therefore, when a few children are present,
those who can read their Testament sit together on one bench; but the boys
and girls occupy separate benches. They are given a chapter which they
read at sight consecutively. Meanwhile I write copies for them. Those who
have read their passage of Scripture without error take their places at the
table and write. Those who fail have to sit at the end of the bench, and
each new arrival the same; as each one is thus released in order he takes up
his slate. This process continues until they have all assembled. The last one
left on the bench is a "lazy pupil."

When all are together, and examined, whether they are washed and
combed, they sing a psalm or a morning hymn, and I sing and pray with
them. As much as they can understand of the Lord's Prayer and the ten
commandments (according to the gift God has given them), I exhort and
admonish them accordingly. This much concerning the assembling of
pupils. But regarding prayer I will add this additional explanation. Children say the prayers taught them at home half articulately, and too fast,
especially the "Our Father" which the Lord Himself taught His disciples
and which contains all that we need. I therefore make a practice of saying
it for them kneeling, and they kneeling repeat it after me. After these
devotional exercises those who can write resume their work. Those who
cannot read the Testament have had time during the assemblage to study
their lesson. These are heard recite immediately after prayer. Those who
know their lesson receive an O on the hand, traced with crayon. This is
a mark of excellence. Those who fail more than three times are sent back
to study their lesson again. When all the little ones have recited, these are
asked again, and any one having failed in more than three trials a second
time, is called "Lazy" by the entire class and his name is written down.
Whether such a child fear the rod or not, I know from experience that this
denunciation of the children hurts more than if I were constantly to wield
and flourish the rod. If then such a child has friends in school who are able

Reprinted from Martin B. Brumbaugh, *The Life and Works of Christopher Dock*
(Philadelphia: J. B. Lippincott Co., 1908), pp. 105-108.

to instruct him and desire to do so, he will visit more frequently than before. For this reason: if the pupil's name has not been erased before dismissal the pupils are at liberty to write down the names of those who have been lazy, and take them along home. But if the child learns his lesson well in the future, his name is again presented to the other pupils, and they are told that he knew his lesson well and failed in no respect. Then all the pupils call "Diligent" to him. When this has taken place his name is erased from the slate of lazy pupils, and the former transgression is forgiven.

The children who are in the spelling class are daily examined in pronunciation. In spelling, when a word has more than one syllable, they must repeat the whole word, but some, while they can say the letters, cannot pronounce the word, and so cannot be put to reading. For improvement a child must repeat the lesson, and in this way: The child gives me the book, I spell the word and he pronounces it. If he is slow, another pupil pronounces it for him, and in this way he hears how it should be done, and knows that he must follow the letters and not his own fancy.

Concerning A B C pupils, it would be best, having but one child, to let it learn one row of letters at a time, to say forward and backward. But with many, I let them learn the alphabet first, and then ask a child to point out a letter that I name. If a child is backward or ignorant, I ask another, or the whole class, and the first one that points to the right letter, I grasp his finger and hold it until I have put a mark opposite his name. I then ask for another letter, &c. Whichever child has during the day received the greatest number of marks, has pointed out the greatest number of letters. To him I owe something—a flower drawn on paper or a bird. But if several have the same number, we draw lots; this causes less annoyance. In this way not only are the very timid cured of their shyness (which is a great hindrance in learning), but a fondness for school is increased. Thus much in answer to his question, how I take the children into school, how school proceeds before and after prayers, and how the inattentive and careless are made attentive and careful, and how the timid are assisted.

Quakers too, were very conscious of educational problems in colonial America. The following document is by the Quaker leader, Thomas Budd, written in the seventeenth century. In this selection, taken from his *Good Order Established in Pennsylvania and New Jersey in America* (1685), Budd proposed a school law and suggested some particulars with regard to the business of education. Note that his was a very "practical" orientation, the "most useful arts and sciences" should be taught to both girls and boys.

21. Proposal of School Law

Thomas Budd

1. Now, it might be well if a law were made by the governours and general assemblies of Pennsilvania and New Jersey, that all persons inhabiting the said Provinces to put their children seven years to the publick school, or longer, if the parents please.

2. That schools be provided in all towns and cities, and persons of known honesty, skill, and understanding be yearly chosen by the governour and general assembly, to teach and instruct boys and girls in all the most useful arts and sciences, that they in their useful capacities may be capable to read and to write true English and Latine and other useful speeches and languages, and fair writing, arithmetick, and book-keeping; and the boys to be taught and instructed in some mystery or trade the making of mathematical instruments, joynery, turnery, the making of clocks and watches, weaving, shoe making, or any other useful trade or mystery that school is capable of teaching; and the girls to be taught and instructed in spinning of flax and wool, and knitting of gloves and stockings, sewing, and making of sorts of needle-work, and the making of straw-work, as hats, baskets, etc., or any other useful art or mystery that the school is capable of teaching.

3. That the scholars to be kept in the morning two hours at reading, writing, book keeping, etc., and other two hours at the work in that art, mystery, or trade that he or she most delighteth in, and let them have two hours to dine and for recreation and in the afternoon two hours at work at their several employments.

4. The seventh day of the week the scholars may come to the school only in the forenoon, and at a certain hour in the afternoon let a meeting be kept by the school masters and their scholars, where, after good instruction and admonition is given by the masters to their scholars, and thanks returned to the Lord for his mercies and blessings that are daily received from him, then let a strict examination by the masters of the conversation of the scholars in the past week, and let reproof, admonition, and correction

Reprinted from U. S. Bureau of Education Circular of Information No. 1, 1899. Contributions to American Educational History #23. *History of Education in New Jersey* by David Murray (Washington, D. C., U. S. Printing Office, 1899), pp. 17-18.

be given to the offenders according to the quantity and quality of their faults.

5. Let the like meetings be kept by the school-mistresses and the girls apart from the boys. By strictly observing this good order, our children will be hindered from running into that excess of riot and wickedness that youth is incident to, and that will be a comfort to their tender parents.

6. Let one thousand acres of land be given and laid out in a good place to every publick school that shall be set up, and the rent or income of it to go towards defraying the charge of the school.

7. And to the end that the children of the poor people and the children of the Indians may have the like good learning with the children of the rich people, let them be maintained free of charge to their parents, out of the profits of the school arising by the work of the scholars, by which the poor and the Indians, as well as the rich, will have their children taught; and the remainder of the profits, if any be, to be disposed of in building of school-houses and improvements to the thousand acres of land which belongs to the school.

THE PRIVATE MASTERS

The efforts to fill the educational void that existed between the realistic needs of a rising commercial middle class and the classical offerings of the existing schools were largely made by the private schoolmasters. They advertised at great length, setting their educational wares before a public that was demanding an education somehow coordinated with the actual conditions of the times. From bookkeeping to shorthand, modern languages to navigation, the private masters provided instructions in any and all varieties of learning. As will be noted, many also gave instruction in the classical subjects and in those subjects such as music, dancing, fencing, and needlework that would add to one's polish, savior faire, and general façade of gentility. Night or day to males and females, these masters were at work. Evening schools, oriented towards education for the urban apprentice, were generally providing the more vocational subjects, but they also offered classical subjects. As a matter of fact, so many of these evening schools opened in commercial Philadelphia that, "to prevent trouble," eleven of the principal evening schoolmasters jointly advertised in 1767 that they would start evening classes on October 12th, and fees would be standardized at twelve-shillings-six-pence per quarter for writing and reading. (This price included supplies such as pens, ink, and the necessary fire).*

Some interesting pedagogical techniques were evolved by these private masters. In Philadelphia, for example, Paul Fooks instituted an early "area study program" for those who were interested in West-Indian trade. In addition to French and Spanish, Fooks included lectures of a practical nature on trade and business in the West Indies based on his own experiences. Anthony Lamb (father of Revolutionary War General, John Lamb) used the "case method" to teach such subjects as navigation, utilizing actual journals of voyages as texts for this subject.

The following advertisements are typical of the announced offerings of the eighteenth-century private masters. The first group is representative of southern masters, the second of the northern colonies.

22. Southern Private Masters

This is to give Notice, to all young Gentlemen and Ladies inclinable to be taught the Art of DRAWING, That an Evening School for that Purpose will be open'd on the first of November next, at my House in Friend street, where every Branch of that Art will be taught with the greatest Exactness by

Jeremiah Theus
—*The South-Carolina Gazette*, Nov. 5, 1744.

JOHN BRUCE, M. A.

WILL give very good Encouragement to a Person of irreproachable Morals, capable of assisting him to teach the GREEK, LATIN, and ENGLISH LANGUAGES. Such a Person's being acquainted with the different Branches of the MATHEMATICKS, and excelling in WRITING, will be an additional Recommendation. Application may be made to him-

Reprinted by permission from E. W. Knight, ed., *A Documentary History of Education in the South Before 1860* (Chapel Hill: Univ. of North Carolina Press, 1949), I., pp. 660-661.

* Carl Bridenbaugh, *Cities in Revolt* (New York: Capricorn Books, 1964), p. 377.

self, at his own Room, over against the Church, Head of *Cumberland* Street, *Norfolk.—The Virginia Gazette* ([Williamsburg], Alex. Purdie and John Dixon), December 31, 1772, p. [3].

The Subscriber begs leave to inform his friends That he intends opening a school, on Monday the 20th of this instant April, at the house of Mr. Christian Camphire, adjoining the Collector William Spencer, Esq., where he. . . . designs teaching Latin, Reading, Writing, and Arithmetic.

James Whitefield

N.B. A few Masters and Misses will be also lodged and boarded.—*The Georgia Gazette,* (Savannah), April 8; April 15, 1766.

A single man of good character who Teacheth the Principles of the Latin, the French as accented in Paris, the right Spanish Castellans, and children to Read and Write English, would be glad of employment in a Latin School as an assistant, or in a private family in town or country. Any gentlemen or ladies desirous to employ him in such capacity may hear of him by applying to the printer.—*Georgia Gazette* (Savannah), Sept. 23; Oct. 7, 1767.

As Mr. Beaufort has attended to the house mentioned in his former advertisement, and has not met with such encouragement as he deserves in teaching the French, he intends to continue by one month if no better encouragement; he hopes that such gentlemen and ladies that intend to be taught that useful and genteel language, will not neglect this opportunity, as he is wanted where he may have encouragement suitable to his merit.—*North Carolina Gazette* (James Davis), March 13, 1778.

The Rev. Benj. Lindsay and Robert Walker, lately from the U. of Edinburgh, whose testimonials will bear the minutest inspection, intend to open an Academy, on the 1st of September next in the house formerly occupied by the Rev. Mr. Bowen . . . . The terms are as follows, viz. On admission, One Guinea. For Greek, Latin, French, and Mathematics, Two Pounds Sterling per Quarter. For English, Writing and Arithmetic, Thirty Shillings Sterling per Quarter. . . . N.B. The patronage of the inhabitants of Savannah and its vicinity is solicited, as long as the proficiency of the pupils committed to their charge shall merit it. The strictest attention to morals, as well as other improvements, may be depended on.—*The Georgia Gazette,* (Savannah), Aug. 28, 1788. (Repeated Sept. 11, 18, 25)

Theophilus Field

—*The Virginia Gazette* (Williamsburg, William Hunter),
March 27, 1752, p. [3]; April 3, 1752, p. [3], April 10,
1752, p. [4].

Williamsburg, June 12, 1752.

MR. SINGLETON takes this Opportunity of informing Gentlemen and Others, That he proposes to Teach the VIOLIN in this City, and Places adjacent, at a Pistole each *per* Month, and a Pistole Entrance, provided a sufficient Number of Scholars can be engaged, (not less than Six in any one Place:) He will give Attendance at *York, Hampton,* and *Norfolk,* on the aforesaid Terms.—*The Virginia Gazette* (Williamsburg, William Hunter), June 12, 1752, p. [2]

23. Northern Private Masters

1709

Opposite to the Mitre Tavern in Fish-street near to Scarlets-Wharff, Boston, are Taught Writing, Arithmetick in all its parts; And also Geometry, Trigonometry, Plain and Sphaerical, Surveying, Dialling, Gauging, Navigation, Astronomy; The Projection of the Sphaere, and the use of Mathematical Instruments: By Owen Harris.

Who Teaches at as easie Rates, and as speedy as may be.

1718

Mr. Browne Tymms Living at Mr. Edward Oakes Shopkeeper in Newbury Street, at the South End of Boston, keeps Merchants & Shopkeepers Books, also writes Bills, Bonds, Leases, Licences, Charter-parties, &c. for any Person that may have Occasion, at reasonable Rates. And likewise teacheth Young Men Arithmatick and Merchants Accounts.

1720

At the house formerly Sir Charles Hobby's are taught Grammar, Writing after a free and easy manner, in all the hands usually practiced, Arithmetick Vulgar and Decimal in a concise and practical Method, Merchants Accompts, Geometry, Algebra, Mensuration, Geography, Trigonometry, Astronomy, Navigation and other parts of the Mathematicks, with the use of the Globes and other Mathematical Instruments, by Samuel Grainger.

They whose Business won't permit 'em to attend the usual School Hours, shall be carefully attended and instructed in the Evenings.

Reprinted by permission of the publishers from Robert Seybolt, *The Private Schools of Colonial Boston* (Cambridge, Mass.: Harvard University Press, 1935), pp. 11, 14, 15, 19, 36.

1728

Caleb Philipps Teacher of the New Method of Short Hand, is remov'd opposite to the north door of the Town House in King-street. As this way of Joyning 3, 4, 5 &c. words in one in every Sentence by the Moods, Tenses, Persons, and Verb, do's not in the least spoil the Long Hand, so it is not anything like the Marks for Sentences in the Printed Character Books being all wrote according to the Letter, and a few Plain and Easy Rules.

N.B. Any Persons in the Country desirous to Learn this Art, may by having the several Lessons sent Weekly to them, be as perfectly instructed as those that live in Boston.*

1753

For the benefit of Persons confin'd in Business in the Day-Time, Notice is hereby given, that they may be taught Writing, Arithmetick, Algebra, Navigation, Gauging, Book-keeping, &c. &c. in the best Manner during the Winter Season, from Candlelight till Half an Hour past Eight o'Clock in the Evening,

Due to the conditions (economic and geographical) of the southern colonies, a large number of families who could afford education for their children resided at a distance from urban centers (such as Charleston) where there were schools. Under such a situation, one could either send over children to board at an urban schoolmaster's establishment or bring a schoolmaster out to reside at one's residence. Both alternatives were employed; hence a number of resident tutors plied their intellectual trade throughout the southern colonies.

Two such tutors kept diaries of their experiences; selections from these documents constitute the readings of this section. These men were of entirely different backgrounds and were acting under entirely different circumstances. Philip Fithian was a Princeton graduate and erstwhile clergyman who acted as a tutor during the interim between college graduation and the assumption of ministerial duties and ordination. John Harrower, on the other hand, was an indigent Scotsman who was forced by circumstances to sign as an indentured servant, leaving wife and child in Europe. Neither tutor was partic-

---

* This is surely one of the earliest evidences of a "correspondence course" to appear in this country.

ularly eager to assume the teaching position; for both men their tutorial experience was viewed as a temporary expedient.

The diaries are rich and fascinating, providing a rare day-by-day account of educational experiences as well as social life in the colonial South. Excerpts from these diaries are selected here for reading.

24. A Tutor's Diary

Philip Fithian

[ANDREW HUNTER, JR., TO PHILIP VICKERS FITHIAN]

Nassau-Hall June 26th 1773.

SIR.

I expected notwithstanding your small offence you would have let me know before this time whether you had made any determination different from what you designed when I left you. If you design teaching before you get into business, there are now several considerable offers made to young men who are willing to go to Virginia by some of the first gentlemen in the colony; one particularly who will give as good as 60 £, the best accomodations, a room to study in and the advantage of a library, a horse kept and a servant to wait upon you.

Dr Witherspoon is very fond of getting a person to send him. I make no kind of doubt but if you were to write to the doctor but he would engage it to you, the terms are exactly as I write you as I have informed myself that I might let you know—

There are a number of our friends and class-mates getting into business as fast as possible, whether they are called or not I cannot pretend to judge, this much I would say that I think it is not any ones duty to run too fast. No less than four Debow, Reese, McCorkle, Allen, under trials by a presbytery, and Bryan trying to get license to plead law in some of the best courts on the continent, if infamy were law or lies were Gospel he might get license either to plead or preach.

We have had the pleasure of Laura's company here for some weeks past, I hope you will not envy us considering that continual pleasure is too much for such mortals as we to bear.

Reprinted from Hunter Dickinson Farish, ed., *The Journal and Letters of Philip Vickers Fithian 1773-1774: A Plantation Tutor of the Old Dominion* (Williamsburg, Virginia: Colonial Williamsburg, Incorporated, 1957), pp. 3-4.

I beg that you may no longer refrain from writing, as I should be very glad to hear many things from you and other of my friends in Cohansie which you can relate with little trouble. If you have been trying with me who could keep from writing longest, I own fairly beat. The number of our students are considerably increased, and our school consists of thirty-nine—I have heard there are some disagreeable stories going through your country I wish you would let me know something about them. Doctr Ward spent part of yesterday with me in his return.

My love to Mr and Mrs Green.

I am, Sir,

Your very friend,

ANDW HUNTER.

[J O U R N A L]

July 1. [1773]
Rose at five. Read in the greek Testament, the third Chapter of the Acts. Breakfasted at seven. Busy the greater part of this Day in coppying off some loose miscellanous Pieces. P. M. Read the Spectator in my Course. Received in the Evening, by the Stage, a Letter from Mr and: Hunter jur In which he invites me to remove, & accept a School, of very considerable Consequence, in Virginia. He also informs me that four of our Class-Mates, are on Trial, under a Presbytery, for Preachers; & one has applied for Licence to plead Law in Maryland; Poor Boys! hard they push to be in the midst of Tumult, & Labour.

[PHILIP V. FITHIAN TO ANDREW HUNTER, JR.]
Deerfield July 3. 1773.

SIR
I am sorry you impute neglect of writing in me to so wrong a cause, as an old trivial offense, I confess that I am to blame, and am willing to stand reproved by you, for having been so long silent. If I should offer any thing in excuse it would be great hurry arising from the duty of my station, on which account I have wrote only two or three letters since you left us. The school in town, which I had in view, as I make no doubt you know, is now occupied by Mr *Lynn.* And the terms of the school at *Blandensburg* are I think too low, to divert me from the course of my business. I would not however forego a good offer in a school abroad, for some short time. What you write concerning the offer of a Gentleman in Virginia, is, I think of considerable consequence, provided the conditions of teaching are not over burdensome; I should speedily agree to go and apply for the place, were I made satisfied as to this.

I shall however, beg the assistance of your friendship, to enquire in what county the school is; what number and degrees of scholars there are; and if you think the place suitable, and if the Docter shall think proper to appoint me to it, I am not unwilling to remove and accept it. Please to mention this to the Docter; and if he has not engaged a teacher, and is pleased to accept me, I hope you will acquaint me as speedily as may be, with what you can learn as to the time of beginning, the custom of the school, &c. You mentioned four in your last, who have applied to Presbytery, and are on tryal, I can tell you another, Mr Heith; he applied to the Philadelphia Presbytery; but came to town, I understood so late, that before he made application the Presbytery was dissolved, some of the Members however, being still in town, at his request, gave him sundry pieces of exercise, which it is expected the Presbytery will acknowledge, so that he is the fifth out of our class who is designing soon to appear in public!

I am Sir yours, &c.

PHILIP V. FITHIAN

Monday Novemr 1st

We began School—The School consists of eight—Two of Mr Carters Sons—One Nephew—And five Daughters—The endest Son is reading Salust; Gramatical Exercises, and latin Grammer—The second Son is reading english Grammar Reading English: Writing, and Cyphering in Subtraction—The Nephew is Reading and Writing as above; and Cyphering in Reduction—The eldest daughter is Reading the Spectator; Writing; & beginning to Cypher—The second is reading next out of the Spelling-Book, and beginning to write—The next is reading in the Spelling-Book—The fourth is Spelling in the beginning of the Spelling Book—And the last is beginning her letters—

Teusday 2.

Busy in School—begun to read Pictete[40]—

[LETTER OF PHILIP V. FITHIAN TO THE REVEREND ENOCH GREEN].

Westmoreland, Novr 2d 1773.

REVD SIR.

According as I appointed I take this early oppertunity of acquainting you that I am arrived safe; and I am to assure you that I find the place fully equal to my highest expectations—I am situated in the *Northern-Neck,* in a most delightful Country; in a civil, polite neighbourhood; and in a family remarkable for regularity, and oeconomy, tho' confessedly of the highest quality and greatest worth of any in *Virginia*. I teach only Mr Carters children, and only one of them is to learn Languages, and he is reading

Salust and the Greek grammer, is seventeen years old, and seems to be a Boy of Genius—the other two learn writing and Arithmetic—But he has four Daughters, young Misses that are at times to be taught writing and English—I have the terms as I expected, and find the place wholly agreeable—and am strongly solicited to stay many years—But money nor conveniency shall detain me long from my most important connections at home—You may expect me in may at the *Synod*. Please to have my compliments to Mrs Green, to Miss Betsy if at Deerfield, and to my acquaintances that shall enquire and accept to yourself the

Respect of your humble Servt

PHILIP V. FITHIAN

[JOURNAL]

Wednesday 3.
Busy in School—
Thursday 4.
Busy in School—To day the two eldest Daughters, and second Son attended the Dancing School.
Fryday 5.
Busy in School—

[LETTER OF PHILIP V. FITHIAN TO THE REVEREND ENOCH GREEN]

Decemr 1st 1773.

REVD SIR.

As you desired I may not omit to inform you, so far as I can by a letter, of the business in which I am now engaged, it would indeed be vastly agreeable to me if it was in my power to give you particular intelligence concerning the state and plan of my employment here.

I set out from home the 20th of Octr and arrived at the Hon: Robert Carters, of Nominy, in Westmorland County, the 28th I began to teach his children the first of November. He has two sons, and one Nephew; the oldest Son is turned of seventeen, and is reading Salust and the greek grammer; the others are about fourteen, and in english grammer, and Arithmetic. He has besides five daughters which I am to teach english, the eldest is turned of fifteen, and is reading the spectator; she is employed two days in every week in learning to play the Forte-Piana, and Harpsicord —The others are smaller, and learning to read and spell. Mr Carter is one of the Councellors in the general court at Williamsburg, and possest of as great, perhaps the clearest fortune according to the estimation of people here, of any man in Virginia: He seems to be a good scholar, even in classical learning, and is remarkable one in english grammar; and notwithstanding his rank, which in general seems to countenance indulgence to children, both himself and Mrs Carter have a manner of instructing and dealing with children far superior, I may say it with confidence, to any I have ever seen, in any place, or in any family. They keep them in perfect subjection to themselves, and never pass over an occasion of reproof; and I blush for many of my acquaintances when I say that the children are more kind and complaisant to the servants who constantly attend them than we are to our superiors in age and condition. Mr Carter has an over-grown library of Books of which he allows me the free use. It consists of a general collection of law books, all the Latin and Greek Classicks, vast number of Books on Divinity chiefly by writers who are of the established Religion; he has the works of almost all the late famous writers, as Locke, Addison, Young, Pope, Swift, Dryden, &c. in Short, Sir, to speak moderately, he has more than eight times your number— His eldest Son, who seems to be a Boy of Genius and application is to be sent to Cambridge University, but I believe will go through a course either in Philadelphia or Princeton College first. As to what is commonly said concerning Virginia that it is difficult to avoid being corrupted with the manners of the people, I believe it is founded wholly in a mistaken notion that persons must, when here frequent all promiscuous assemblies; but this is so far from truth that any one who does practise it, tho' he is accused of no crime, loses at once his character; so that either the manners have been lately changed, or the report is false, for he seems now to be best esteemed and most applauded who attends to his business, whatever it be, with the greatest diligence. I believe the virginians have of late altered their manner very much, for they begin to find that their estates by even small extravagance, decline, and grow involved with debt, this seems to be the spring which induces the People of fortune who are the pattern of all behaviour here, to be frugal, and moderate. You may expect me at home by the permission of Providence the latter end of april next, or the beginning of May; and as I proposed I shall present my exercises for the examination of the Presbytery; and if they think proper I shall gladly accept of a licence in the fall: I must beg your favour to mention me to such of my acquaintances in Deerfield as you think proper, but especially to Mrs Green, Miss *Betsy,* your family, and Mrs Pecks—I must also beg you to transmit so much of this intelligence to Mr Hunter as that my relations in Greenwich may know that I am through the mercy of heaven in good health. I beg, Sir, you will not fail to write, and let it be known to Mr Hunter, that a letter will come as secure by the Post as from Cohansie to Philadelphia; the Letters are to be directed to me thus, To Mr Philip V. Fithian at Mr *Carters* of Nominy, to be left at Hobes Hole

I am, Sir, yours

PHILIP V. FITHIAN

25. Journal

John Harrower

Wednesday, 26th.   This day I being reduced to the last shilling I hade was obliged to engage to go to Virginia for four years as a schoolmaster for Bedd, Board, washing and five pound during the whole time. I have also wrote my wife this day a particular Acco^t. of every thing that has happened to me since I left her until this date; At 3 pm this day I went on board the Snow Planter Capt. Bowers Com^r. for Virginia now lying at Ratliff Cross, and imediatly as I came Onb^d. I rec^d. my Hammock and Bedding. at 4 pm came Alex^r. Steuart onb^d. the same Ship. he was Simbisters Servt. and had only left Zetland about three weeks before me. we were a good deall surprised to meet w^t. on another in this place.

[interim is description of the voyage]

About 4 pm I was brought to Colonel Daingerfield, when we imediatly agreed and my Indenture for four years was then delivered him and he was to send for me the next day. at same time ordred to get all my dirty Cloaths of every kind washed at his expense in Toun; at night he sent me five shillings onb^d. by Capt. Bowers to keep my pocket.

Friday, 27th. This morning about 8 AM the Colonel delivered his three sons to my Charge to teach them to read write and figure. his oldest son Edwin 10 years of age, intred into two syllables in the spelling book, Bathourest [Bathurst] his second son six years of age in the Alphabete and William his third son 4 years of age does not know the letters. he has likeways a Daughter whose name is Hanna Basset   Years of age. Soon after we were all sent for to breackfast to which we hade tea, Bread, Butter and cold meat and there was at table the Colonel, his Lady, his Children, the housekeeper and myself. At 11 AM the Colonel and his Lady went some where to pay a visite, he upon horseback and she in her Charriot. At 2 pm I dined with the Housekeeper the Children and a stranger Lady. at 6 pm I left school, and then I eat plenty of fine strawberries, but they

Reprinted from *The Journal of John Harrower (American Historical Review)*, VI (1900-1901), pp. 72, 78, 79, 82-85, 106-107.

neither drink Tea in the afternoon nor eat any supper here for the most part. My school Houres is from 6 to 8 in the morning, in the forenoon from 9 to 12 and from 3 to 6 in the afternoon.

Sunday, 29th. There is no church nearer Belvidera than Fredericksburgh, and for want of a sadle I was oblidged to stay at home all day and when I was alone in the school I thought on the following verses.

Thursday, 23d. This day entred to school John Edge son to the above named M^r. Sam: Edge. he is a lad about 14 years of age and is both deaf and dum.

To Mrs John Harrower
Lerwick, Zetland

BELVIDERA 14th. June 1774.

My Dearest Life

I wrote you from London on Wednesday 26th. Jany. last which Im hopefull came safe to hand, and found you and my dear Infants in perfect health, and am hopefull this will find both you and them in the same state, As I am at present and have been I bless God since I left you. You will remember when I wrote you last, I informed you that I was to go for Baltimore in Maryland, But I altred my design in that and came here it being a more healthy pleace. I sailed from London on Freiday the 4th. Feby. last, and arrived in Hampton roads in Virginia on the 27 April, having been a Month of the time at Spithead in England. As to particulars of our Voyage &^{ca} it would take up too much room here to insert it. But I have a Journal of every days transactions and remarcable Occurances since the morning I left you which will be amusing to you when please God we are spared to meet, for I design to see and prepare a way for you all in this Country how soon I am able.—I shall now aquaint you w^t my situation in this Country. I am now settled with an Colonel W^m. Dangerfield Esqr. of Belvidera, on the Banks of the River Rappahannock about 160 miles from the Capes or sea mouth, and seven Miles below the Toun of Fredericksburgh. My business is to teach his Children to read write and figure, Edwin his oldest son about 8 years of [age] Bathurest his second 6 years of age and William his youngest son 4 years of age. he has also a Daughter whose name in Hanna Basset. I came to this place on Thursday 26th. May and next morning I received his three sons into my charge to teach, the two youngest boys I got in A:B:C. and the oldest Just begun to syllab and I have now the two youngest spelling and the oldest reading. I am obliged to teach in the English method which was a little aquard to me at first but now quite easy. I am also obliged to talk english the best I can, for Lady Dangerfield speacks nothing but high english, and the Colonel hade his Education in England and is a verry smart Man. As to my agreement it is as follows Viz^t. I am obliged to continue with Col. Dangerfield for four years if he insists on it, and for teaching his own children I have Bed, Board, washing and all kind of Cloaths during the above time, and for what schoolars I can get more than his Children I have five shillings currency per Quarter for each of them, which is equall to four shillings sterling, and I expect ten or twelve to school next week, for after I hade been here eight days and my abilities and my behavior sufficiently tried, the Colonel rode through the neighbouring Gentlemen and Planters in order to procure scollars for me, so that I hope in a short time to make something of it. And as I have no Occasion to spend a farthing on myself every shill^g. I make shall be carefully remitted you, for your support and my Dear Infants. But I must be some time here before any thing can be done, for you know every thing must have a beginning.

. . .

Munday, 27th. At 9 AM I went to M^r. McAlleys and staid teaching his Son and sister untill dark and then rode home bringing with me 1½ Yd. Linen for summer breeches.

Thursday, June 6th. In the afternoon I went to M^r. Becks, when he told me that M^{rs}. Battle wanted to see me and to talk to me about teaching her two daughters to write, upon which I imediatly waited upon her and engaged to return upon Saturd next by 1 pm and begin them to write but made no bargain as yet.

Saturday, 8th. At noon I went to M^{rs}. Bataile's and entred two of her Daughters to writting, Viz. Miss Sallie and Miss Betty and continoued teaching them until night, when I agreed to attend them every Saturday afternoon and every other Sunday from this date until 8th. June 1777 (If it please God to spare me) for four pound Virginia currancy.

Sunday, 9th. After breackfast I rode to M^r. McAlleys and teach'd his son to write untill 4 pm and then came home in the evening.

Wednesday, 10th. At 6 pm went to M^{rs}. Battaile's and teach'd untill sunset and then return'd home and soon after hea[r]d a great many guns fired towards Toun. about 12 pm the Col^o. Despatched Anth^y. Frazer there to see what was the cause of [it] who returned, and informed him that there was great rejoicings in Toun on Acco^t. of the Congress having declared the 13 United Colonys of North America Independent of the Crown of great Britain.

SECTION 4

Theory of the Realist School

A new direction in American education in the eighteenth century had its intellectual beginnings in the theory of the "realist" school. This theory placed learning squarely on the basis of the sensory and the environmental, which in this view was the essential reality. Learning thereby must necessarily begin with the child's immediate surroundings, sensorily perceived, and proceed always from the concrete to the abstract, from the simple to the increasingly difficult in efficiently graded steps. This new approach had been first outlined in the preceding century by Johann Amos Comenius, a Moravian bishop and teacher whose ideas were spread mainly through his series of graded, illustrated Latin textbooks called *Orbis Pictus*. The study of Latin in the Comenian style offered the child the language as a tool, a useful instrument, for further learning; and it largely ignored in the process whatever aesthetic values might inhere in the literature. This precursor of "Dick and Jane" was in sharp contrast to the reverent, almost mystical, humanist approach to the ancient tongue, however painful that approach to its learning might be. The school that seemed to arise from these sensory theories in language instruction was a school consciously based on the economic, social, as well as intellectual demands of the young, a school fitted to the environment of the learner.

The Comenian ideas were discussed and debated throughout Europe in the mid-seventeenth century. On a visit to London in 1641, Comenius outlined his educational ideas in an address to the Royal Society, and he was received with highest respect and honor by Samuel

Hartlib and other of the Commonwealth educators, the leading English educational theorists of the day. It was Hartlib who asked John Milton to comment on the realist school ideas, which he did at length in his *Tractate on Education*. John Locke, a young man at the time of the Comenius visit to England, was clearly impressed by the current of Comenian sensory theories of the time. Almost a century later, Benjamin Franklin designed a plan for a realist school in America which reflected the theoretical background, from Milton, Locke and others, of the sense-realist approach in education.

John Milton's *Tractate on Education,* written in 1644, is an essay of some twenty-five pages of which is included here the introductory section. In the essay Milton expresses his firm Protestant Calvinism as well as his classical humanist thinking as the proper basis for educational planning. In the humanist aspect he is reminiscent of the earlier Italian humanism of Vergerius. Yet in his criticisms of the schools of his times, in particular his remarks on language and its teaching, he expresses a receptivity to the new ideas of the realist approach in education.

26. Humanistic Realism

John Milton

The end then of Learning is to repair the ruines of our first Parents by regaining to know God aright, and out of that knowledge to love him, to imitate him, to be like him, as we may the neerest by possessing our souls of true vertue, which being united to the heavenly grace of faith makes up the highest perfection. But because our understanding cannot in this body found it self but on sensible things, nor arrive so clearly to the knowledge of God and things invisible, as by orderly conning over the visible and inferior creature, the same method is necessarily to be follow'd in all discreet teaching. And seeing every Nation affords not experience and tradition enough for all kind of Learning, therefore we are cheifly taught the Languages of those people who have at any time been most industrious after Wisdom; so that Language is but the Instrument conveying to us things usefull to be known. And though a Linguist should pride himself to have all the Tongues that *Babel* cleft the world into, yet, if he have not studied the solid things in them as well as the

Reprinted from John Milton, *Areopagitica and Of Education,* George H. Sabine, ed., (New York: Appleton-Century-Crofts, Inc., 1951), pp. 59-62.

Words and Lexicons, he were nothing so much to be esteem'd a learned man, as any Yeoman or Tradesman competently wise in his Mother Dialect only. Hence appear the many mistakes which have made Learning generally so unpleasing and so unsuccessful; first we do amiss to spend seven or eight years meerly in scraping together so much miserable Latine and Greek, as might be learnt otherwise easily and delightfully in one year. And that which casts our proficiency therein so much behind, is our time lost partly in too oft idle vacancies given both to Schools and Universities partly in a preposterous exaction, forcing the empty wits of Children to compose Theams, Verses and Orations, which are the acts of ripest judgment and the final work of a head fill'd by long reading and observing, with elegant maxims, and copious invention. These are not matters to be wrung from poor striplings, like blood out of the Nose, or the plucking of untimely fruit: besides the ill habit which they get of wretched barbarizing against the Latin and Greek *idiom,* with their untutor'd *Anglicisms,* odious to be read, yet not to be avoided without a well continu'd and judicious conversing among pure Authors digested, which they scarce taste, whereas, if after some preparatory grounds of speech by their certain forms got into memory, they were led to the praxis thereof in some chosen short book lesson'd throughly to them, they might then forthwith proceed to learn the substance of good things, and Arts in due order, which would bring the whole language quickly into their power. This I take to be the most rational and most profitable way of learning Languages, and whereby we may best hope to give account to God of our youth spent herein: And for the usual method of teaching Arts, I deem it to be an old errour of Universities not yet well recover'd from the Scholastick grossness of barbarous ages, that in stead of beginning with Arts most easie, and those be such as are most obvious to the sence, they present their young unmatriculated Novices at first comming with the most intellective abstractions of Logick and Metaphysicks: So that they having but newly left those Grammatick flats and shallows where they stuck unreasonably to learn a few words with lamentable construction, and now on the sudden transported under another climate to be tost and turmoil'd with their unballasted wits in fadomless and unquiet deeps of controversie, do for the most part grow into hatred and contempt of Learning, mockt and deluded all this while with ragged Notions and Babblements, while they expected worthy and delightful knowledge; till poverty or youthful years call them importunately their several wayes, and hasten them with the sway of friends either to an ambitious and mercenary, or ignorantly zealous Divinity; Some allur'd to the trade of Law, grounding their purposes not on the prudent and heavenly contemplation of justice and equity which was never taught them, but on the promising and pleasing thoughts of litigious terms, fat contentions, and flowing fees; others betake them to State affairs, with souls so unprincipl'd in vertue, and true generous breeding, that flattery, and Court shifts and tyrannous Aphorisms appear to them the highest points of wisdom; instilling their barren hearts with a conscientious slavery, if, as I rather think, it be not fain'd. Others lastly of a more delicious and airie spirit, retire themselves knowing no better, to the enjoyments of ease and luxury, living out their daies in feast and jollity; which indeed is the wisest and safest course of all these, unless they were with more integrity undertaken. And these are the fruits of mispending our prime youth at the Schools and Universities as we do, either in learning meer words or such things chiefly, as were better unlearnt.

I shall detain you no longer in the demonstration of what we should not do, but strait conduct ye to a hill side, where I will point ye out the right path of a vertuous and noble Education; laborious indeed at the first ascent, but else so smooth, so green, so full of goodly prospect, and melodious sounds on every side, that the Harp of *Orpheus* was not more charming. I doubt not but ye shall have more adoe to drive our dullest and laziest youth, our stocks and stubbs from the infinite desire of such a happy nurture, then we have now to hale and drag our choisest and hopefullest Wits to that asinine feast of sow-thistles and brambles which is commonly set before them, as all the food and entertainment of their tenderest and most docible age. I call therefore a compleat and generous Education that which fits a man to perform justly, skilfully and magnanimously all the offices both private and publick of Peace and War. And how all this may be done between twelve, and one and twenty, less time then is now bestow'd in pure trifling at Grammar and *Sophistry,* is to be thus order'd.

A new sensory psychological theory of learning, implied in the sense-realist thinking of the seventeenth century, was given formal statement in John Locke's *Essay Concerning Human Understanding* published in 1690. The *tabula rasa* theory, the blank mind of the child at birth, passive, open, ready to receive through the senses the impressions of experience, was a theory revolutionary in its implications, socially, politically, and educationally. It seemed to imply that environmental influence, education or the lack of it, was the prime force in bringing about the distinction of prince from pauper. Actually Locke did not posit such complete environmentalism. He was careful to point out that the mind did indeed play some active function, however small, through the "reflective" faculties in receiving the sensory impressions. Yet it seemed to many interpreters of Locke's *Essay,* particularly to some of the enlightened French, that if only education could be redesigned, reformed along realist lines, to answer the needs of all men, education could become indeed the key to the advancement of man as well as the means for achieving social and political equality among men.

27. Concerning Human Understanding

John Locke

1. *Idea is the object of thinking.*—Every man being conscious to himself that he thinks, and that which his mind is applied about whilst thinking being the ideas that are there, it is past doubt that men have in their minds several ideas, such as are those expressed by the words whiteness, hardness, sweetness, thinking, motion, man, elephant, army, drunkenness, and others: it is in the first place then to be inquired. How he comes by them? I know it is a received doctrine, that men have native ideas and original characters stamped upon their minds in their very first being. This opinion I have at large examined already; and, I suppose, what I have said in the foregoing book will be much more easily admitted, when I have shown whence the understanding may get all the ideas it has, and by what ways and degrees they may come into the mind; for which I shall appeal to everyone's own observation and experience.

2. *All ideas come from sensation or reflection.*—Let us then suppose the mind to be, as we say, white paper, void of all characters, without any ideas; how comes it to be furnished? Whence comes it by that vast store, which the busy and boundless fancy of man has painted on it with an almost endless variety? Whence has it all the materials of reason and knowledge? To this I answer, in one word, from experience. In that all our knowledge is founded, and from that it ultimately derives itself. Our observation, employed either about external sensible objects, or about the internal operations of our minds, perceived and reflected on by ourselves, is that which supplies our understandings with all the materials of thinking. These two are the fountains of knowledge, from whence all the ideas we have, or can naturally have, do spring.

3. *The object of sensation one source of ideas.*—First, our senses, con-

Reprinted from John Locke, *Essay Concerning Human Understanding,* Book II: "Of Ideas," Chapter I. (Chicago, Ill.: Gateway Editions, Inc., 1956), pp. 19-23.

versant about particular sensible objects, do convey into the mind several distinct perceptions of things, according to those various ways wherein those objects do affect them; and thus we come by those ideas we have of yellow, white, heat, cold, soft, hard, bitter, sweet, and all those which we call sensible qualities; which when I say the senses convey into the mind, I mean, they from external objects convey into the mind what produces there those perceptions. This great source of most of the ideas we have, depending wholly upon our senses, and derived by them to the understanding, I call *sensation*.

4. *The operations of our minds the other source of them.*—Secondly, the other fountain, from which experience furnisheth the understanding with ideas, is the perception of the operations of our own mind within us, as it is employed about the ideas it has got; which operations when the soul comes to reflect on and consider, do furnish the understanding with another set of ideas which could not be had from things without; and such are perception, thinking, doubting, believing, reasoning, knowing, willing, and all the different actings of our own minds; which we, being conscious of, and observing in ourselves, do from these receive into our understandings as distinct ideas, as we do from bodies affecting our senses. This source of ideas every man has wholly in himself; and though it be not sense as having nothing to do with external objects, yet it is very like it, and might properly enough be called *internal sense.* But as I call the other sensation, so I call this *reflection,* the ideas its affords being such only as the mind gets by reflecting on its own operations within itself. By reflection, then in the following part of this discourse, I would be understood to mean that notice which the mind takes of its own operations, and the manner of them, by reason whereof there come to be ideas of these operations in the understanding. These two, I say, viz., external material things as the object of sensation, and the operations of our own minds within as the objects of reflection, are, to me, the only originals from whence all our ideas take their beginnings. The term *operations* here, I use in a large sense, as comprehending not barely the actions of the mind about its ideas, but some sort of passions arising sometimes from them, such as is the satisfaction or uneasiness arising from any thought.

5. *All our ideas are of the one or the other of these.*—The understanding seems to me not to have the least glimmering of any ideas which it doth not receive from one of these two. *External objects* furnish the mind with the ideas of sensible qualities, which are all those different perceptions they produce in us; and *the mind* furnishes the understanding with ideas of its own operations.

These, when we have taken a full survey of them, and their several modes, [combinations, and relations,] we shall find to contain all our whole stock of ideas; and that we have nothing in our minds which did not come in one of these two ways. Let anyone examine his own thoughts, and thoroughly search into his understanding, and then let him tell me, whether all the original ideas he has there, are any other than of the objects of his senses, or of the operations of his mind considered as objects of his reflection; and how great a mass of knowledge soever he imagines to be lodged there, he will, upon taking a strict view, see that he has not any idea in his mind but what one of these two have imprinted, though perhaps with infinite variety compounded and enlarged by the understanding, as we shall see hereafter.

6. *Observable in children.*—He that attentively considers the state of a child at his first coming into the world, will have little reason to think him stored with plenty of ideas that are to be the matter of his future knowledge. It is by degrees he comes to be furnished with them; and though the ideas of obvious and familiar qualities imprint themselves before the memory begins to keep a register of time or order, yet it is often so late before some unusual qualities come in the way, that there are few men that cannot recollect the beginning of their acquaintance with them: and, if it were worth while, no doubt a child might be so ordered as to have but a very few even of the ordinary ideas till he were grown up to a man. But all that are born into the world being surrounded with bodies that perpetually and diversely affect them, variety of ideas, whether care be taken about it or not, are imprinted on the minds of children. Light and colors are busy at hand everywhere when the eye is but open; sounds and some tangible qualities fail not to solicit their proper senses; and force an entrance to the mind; but yet I think it will be granted easily, that if a child were kept in a place where he never saw any other but black and white till he were a man, he would have no more ideas of scarlet or green than he that from his childhood never tasted an oyster or a pineapple has of those particular relishes.

7. *Men are differently furnished with these according to the different objects they converse with.*—Men then come to be furnished with fewer or more simple ideas from without, according as the objects they converse with afford greater or less variety; and from the operations of their minds within, according as they more or less reflect on them. For, though he that contemplates the operations of his mind cannot but have plain and clear ideas of them; yet, unless he turns his thoughts that way, and considers them attentively, he will no more have clear and distinct ideas of all the operations of his mind, and all that may be observed therein, than he will have all the particular ideas of any landscape, or of the parts and motions of a clock, who will not turn his eyes to it, and with attention heed all the parts of it. The

picture or clock may be so placed, that they may come in his way every day; but yet he will have but a confused idea of all the parts they are made of, till he applies himself with attention to consider them each in particular.

28. Thoughts Concerning Education

John Locke

§ 1.   A sound mind in a sound body, is a short but full description of a happy state in this world: he that has these two, has little more to wish for; and he that wants either of them, will be but little the better for any thing else. Men's happiness or misery is most part of their own making. He whose mind directs not wisely, will never take the right way; and he whose body is crazy and feeble, will never be able to advance in it. I confess, there are some men's constitutions of body and mind so vigorous, and well framed by nature, that they need not much assistance from others; but, by the strength of their natural genius, they are, from their cradles, carried towards what is excellent; and, by the privilege of their happy constitutions, are able to do wonders. But examples of this kind are but few; and I think I may say, that, of all the men we meet with, nine parts of ten are what they are, good or evil, useful or not, by their education. It is that which makes the great difference in mankind. The title, or almost insensible, impressions on our tender infancies, have very important and lasting consequences: and there it is, as in the fountains of some rivers, where a gentle application of the hand turns the flexible waters into channels, that make them take quite contrary courses; and by this little direction, given them at first, in the source, they receive different tendencies, and arrive at last at very remote and distant places.

§ 2.   I imagine the minds of children as easily turned this or that way, as water itself; and though this be the principal part, and our main care should be about the inside, yet the clay cottage is not to be neglected.

Reprinted from John Locke, *Some Thoughts Concerning Education*, Peter Gay, ed., (New York: Bureau of Publications, Teachers College, Columbia University, 1964), pp. 19-20.

Benjamin Franklin in his proposals for an academy in Philadelphia outlined a detailed plan of a realist school, a school which would offer not only the proper learnings of the Latin Grammar Schools but also the "practical and useful" studies that were available only irregularly and uncertainly in the private-venture schools of colonial America. Here was an "opportunity" school designed to fit the needs of a rising class of farmers and tradesmen who would not be constrained by bounds of birth and privilege but who needed an educational institution to help develop their capabilities. Though Franklin's own life and experience was probably the main basis of the academy idea, Franklin indicates in the elaborate foot-noting the theoretical origins of his *Proposals Relating to the Education of Youth in Pennsylvania,* from Milton, Locke, and others. The plan called for the establishment of an English School in a position of equal status with the Classical School within the new Academy. Though the curriculum of the two branches would be essentially the same in stressing the traditional studies of grammar, rhetoric, and logic, the important innovation of the English School, and it was a striking one, was that instruction itself would be not in Latin but entirely in English. The time saved with the use of the vernacular could be enormously important; the oft-quoted statement from the *Proposals* speak to this point: "As to their STUDIES, it would be well if they could be taught every Thing that is useful, and every Thing that is ornamental: But Art is long, and their Time is short. It is therefore propos'd that they learn those Things that are likely to be most useful and most ornamental. Regard being had to the several Professions for which they are intended."

Franklin's *Idea of the English School* which follows here, though it preceded the formulation of the *Proposals,* was not published until 1751, two years after the establishment of the Academy in Philadelphia. The English School marks the beginning of the nineteenth-century American academy movement and in many ways looks forward to the struggle to achieve universal popular education in America.

29. Idea of the English School, Sketch'd Out for the Consideration of the Trustees of the Philadelphia Academy

Benjamin Franklin

[1751]

It is expected that every Scholar to be admited into this School, be at least able to pronounce and divide the Syllables in Reading, and to write a legible Hand. None to be receiv'd that are under [   ]* Years of Age.

FIRST OR LOWEST CLASS

Let the first Class learn the *English Grammar* Rules, and at the same time let particular Care be taken to improve them in *Orthography*. Perhaps the latter is best done by *Pairing* the Scholars, two of those nearest equal in their Spelling to be put together; let these strive for Victory, each propounding Ten Words every Day to the other to be spelt. He that spells truly most of the other's Words, is Victor for that Day; he that is Victor most Days in a Month, to obtain a Prize, a pretty neat Book of some Kind useful in their future Studies. This Method fixes the Attention of Children extreamly to the Orthography of Words, and makes them good Spellers very early. 'Tis a Shame for a Man to be so ignorant of this little Art, in own Language, as to be perpetually confounding Words of like Sound and different Significations; the Consciousness of which Defect, makes some Men, otherwise of good Learning and Understanding, averse to Writing even a common Letter.

Let the Pieces read by the Scholars in this Class be short, such as Croxall's Fables, and little Stories. In giving the Lesson, let it be read to them; let the Meaning of the difficult Words in it be explained to them, and let them con it over by themselves before they are called to read to the Master, or Usher; who is to take particular Care that they do not read too fast, and that they duly observe the Stops and Pauses. A Vocabulary of the most usual difficult Words might be formed for their Use, with Explanations; and they might daily get a few of those Words and Explanations by Heart, which would a little exercise their Memories; or at least they might write a Number of them in a small Book for the Purpose, which would help to fix the Meaning of those Words in their Minds, and at the same Time furnish every one with a little Dictionary for his future Use.

Reprinted from John Hardin Best, ed., *Benjamin Franklin on Education* (New York: Teachers College, Columbia University, 1962), pp. 165-171.

* Left blank in the original; Franklin later suggested that the boys should be from eight to sixteen years of age.

The Second Class to be taught

Reading with Attention, and with proper Modulations of the Voice according to the Sentiments and Subject.

Some short Pieces, not exceeding the Length of a *Spectator,* to be given this Class as Lessons (and some of the easier *Spectators* would be very suitable for the Purpose.) These Lessons might be given over Night as Tasks, the Scholars to study them against the Morning. Let it then be required of them to give an Account, first of the Parts of Speech, and Construction of one or two Sentences; this will oblige them to recur frequently to their Grammar, and fix its principal Rules in their Memory. Next of the *Intention* of the Writer, or the *Scope* of the Piece; the Meaning of each Sentence, and of every uncommon Word. This would early acquaint them with the Meaning and Force of Words, and give them that most necessary Habit, of Reading with Attention.

The Master then to read the Piece with the proper Modulations of Voice, due Emphasis, and suitable Action, where Action is required; and put the Youth on imitating his Manner.

Where the Author has us'd an Expression not the best, let it be pointed out; and let his Beauties be particularly remarked to the Youth.

Let the Lessons for Reading be varied, that the Youth may be made acquainted with good Stiles of all Kinds in Prose and Verse, and the proper Manner of reading each Kind. Sometimes a well-told Story, a Piece of a Sermon, a General's Speech to his soldiers, a Speech in a Tragedy, some Part of a Comedy, an Ode, a Satyr, a Letter, Blank Verse, Hudibrastick, Heroic, &c. But let such Lessons for Reading be chosen, as contain some useful Instruction, whereby the Understandings or Morals of the Youth, may at the same Time be improv'd.

It is requir'd that they should first study and understand the Lessons, before they are put upon reading them properly, to which End each Boy should have an English Dictionary to help him over Difficulties. When our Boys read English to us, we are apt to imagine *they* understand what *they* read because *we* do, and because 'tis their Mother Tongue. But they often read as Parrots speak, knowing little or nothing of the Meaning. And it is impossible a Reader should give the due Modulation to His Voice, and pronounce properly, unless his Understanding goes before his Tongue, and makes him Master of the Sentiment. Accustoming Boys to read aloud what they do not first understand, is the Cause of those even set Tones so common among Readers, which when they have once got a Habit of using, they find so difficult to correct: By which Means, among Fifty Readers we scarcely find a good One. For want of good Reading, Pieces publish'd with a View to influence the Minds of Men for their own or the publick Benefit, lose Half their Force. Were there but one good Reader in a Neighbourhood, a publick Orator might be heard throughout a Nation with the same Advantages, and have the same Effect on his Audience, as if they stood within the Reach of his Voice.

THE THIRD CLASS TO BE TAUGHT

Speaking properly and gracefully, which is near of Kin to good Reading, and naturally follows it in the Studies of Youth. Let the Scholars of this Class begin with learning the Elements of Rhetoric from some short System, so as to be able to give an Account of the most usual Tropes and Figures. Let all their bad Habits of Speaking, all Offences against good Grammar, all corrupt or foreign Accents, and all improper Phrases, be pointed out to them. Short Speechs from the Roman or other History, or from our *Parliamentary Debates,* might be got by heart, and deliver'd with the proper Action, &c. Speeches and Scenes in our best Tragedies and Comedies (avoiding every Thing that could injure the Morals of Youth) might likewise be got by Rote, and the Boys exercis'd in delivering or acting them; great Care being taken to form their Manner after the truest Models.

For their farther Improvement, and a little to vary their Studies, let them now begin to read *History,* after having got by Heart a short Table of the principal Epochas in Chronology. They may begin with Rollin's *Antient and Roman Histories,* and proceed at proper Hours as they go thro' the subsequent Classes, with the best Histories of our own Nation and Colonies. Let Emulation be excited among the Boys by giving, Weekly, little Prizes, or other small Encouragements to those who are able to give the best Account of what they have read, as to Times, Places, Names of Persons, &c. This will make them read with Attention, and imprint the History well in their Memories. In remarking on the History, the Master will have fine Opportunities of instilling Instruction of various Kinds, and improving the Morals as well as the Understandings of Youth.

The Natural and Mechanic History contain'd in *Spectacle de la Nature,* might also be begun in this Class, and continued thro' the subsequent Classes by other Books of the same Kind: For next to the Knowledge of *Duty,* this Kind of Knowledge is certainly the most useful, as well as the most entertaining. The Merchant may thereby be enabled better to understand many Commodities in Trade; the Handicraftsman to improve his Business by new Instruments, Mixtures and Materials; and frequently Hints are given of new Manufactures, or new Methods of improving Land, that may be set on foot greatly to the Advantage of a Country.

THE FOURTH CLASS TO BE TAUGHT

Composition. Writing one's own Language well, is the next necessary Accomplishment after good Speaking. Tis the Writing-Master's Business to take Care that the Boys make fair Characters, and place them straight and even in the Lines: But to *form their Stile,* and even to take Care that the Stops and Capitals are properly disposed, is the Part of the English Master. The Boys should be put on Writing Letters to each other on any common Occurrences, and on various Subjects, imaginary Business, &c. containing little Stories, Accounts of their late Reading, what Parts of Authors please them, and why. Letters of Congratulation, of Compliment, of Request, of Thanks, of Recommendation, of Admonition, of Consolation, of Expostulation, Excuse, &c. In these they should be taught to express themselves clearly, concisely, and naturally, without affected Words, or high-flown Phrases. All their Letters to pass through the Master's Hand, who is to point out the Faults, advise the Corrections, and commend what he finds right. Some of the best Letters published in our own Language, as Sir William Temple's, those of Pope, and his Friends, and some others, might be set before the Youth as Models, their Beauties pointed out and explained by the Master, the Letters themselves transcrib'd by the Scholar.

Dr. Johnson's *Ethices Elementa,* or first Principles of Morality, may now be read by the Scholars, and explain'd by the Master, to lay a solid Foundation of Virtue and Piety in their Minds. And as this Class continues the Reading of History, let them now at proper Hours receive some farther Instructions in Chronology, and in that Part of Geography (from the Mathematical Master) which is necessary to understand the Maps and Globes. They should also be acquainted with the modern Names of the Places they find mention'd in antient Writers. The Exercises of good Reading and proper Speaking still continued at suitable Times.

FIFTH CLASS.

To improve the Youth in *Composition,* they may now, besides continuing to write Letters, begin to write little Essays in Prose; and sometimes in Verse, not to make them Poets, but for this Reason, that nothing acquaints a Lad so speedily with Variety of Expression, as the Necessity of finding such Words and Phrases as will suit with the Measure, Sound and Rhime of Verse, and at the same Time well express the Sentiment. These Essays should all pass under the Master's Eye, who will point out their Faults, and put the Writer on correcting them. Where the Judgment is not ripe enough for forming new Essays, let the Sentiments of a *Spectator* be given, and requir'd to be cloath'd in a Scholar's own Words; or the Circumstances of some good Story, the Scholar to find Expression. Let them be put sometimes on abridging a Paragraph of a diffuse Author, sometimes on dilating or amplifying what is wrote more closely. And now let Dr. Johnson's *Noetica,* or first Principles of human Knowledge, containing a Logic, or Art of Reasoning, &c. be read by the Youth, and the Difficulties that may occur to them be explained by the Master. The Reading of History, and the Exercises of good Reading and just Speaking still continued.

SIXTH CLASS.

In this Class, besides continuing the Studies of the preceding, in History, Rhetoric, Logic, Moral and Natural Philosophy, the best English Authors may be read and explain'd; as Tillotson, Milton, Locke, Addison, Pope, Swift, the higher Papers in the *Spectator* and *Guardian,* the best Translations of Homer, Virgil and Horace, of *Telemachus, Travels of Cyrus,* &c.

Once a Year, let there be publick Exercises in the Hall, the Trustees and Citizens present. Then let fine gilt Books be given as Prizes to such Boys as distinguish themselves, and excel the others in any Branch of Learning; making three Degrees of Comparison; giving the best Prize to him that performs best; a less valuable One to him that comes up next to the best; and another to the third. Commendations, Encouragement and Advice to the rest; keeping up their Hopes that by Industry they may excel another Time. The Names of those that obtain the Prizes, to be yearly printed in a List.

The Hours of each Day are to be divided and dispos'd in such a Manner, as that some Classes may be with the Writing-Master, improving their Hands, others with the Mathematical Master, learning Arithmetick, Accompts, Geography, Use of the Globes, Drawing, Mechanicks, &c. while the rest are in the English School, under the English Master's Care.

Thus instructed, Youth will come out of this School fitted for learning any Business, Calling or Profession, except such wherein Languages are required; and tho' unacquainted with any antient or foreign Tongue, they will be Masters of their own, which is of more immediate and general Use; and withal will have attain'd many other valuable Accomplishments; the Time usually spent in acquiring those Languages, often without Success, being here employ'd in laying such a Foundation of Knowledge and Ability, as, properly improv'd, may qualify them to pass thro' and execute the several Offices of civil Life, with Advantage and Reputation to themselves and Country.   B. F.

SECTION 5

Enlightenment and Colonial Education

"Preach my dear Sir, a crusade against ignorance; establish and improve the law for educating the common people."
                                        Thomas Jefferson, Letter to
                                        George Wythe, August 13, 1786.

The mainstream of colonial American thought was fed by the admixture of two dominant European intellectual tributaries or strains. The first of these tributaries, that of Puritanism, was transported to these shores in the seventeenth century. The second, that of the Enlightenment, was largely an eighteenth-century import. Each of these strains influenced the subsequent development of American education. As has been seen, the American-Puritan educational movement was itself a product of the synthesis of Reformation and Renaissance ideals; the Enlightenment was similarly a result of the fusion of several facets of European thought—of Lockean psychology, Newtonian physics, Rousseau's romantic agrarianism, and others. It is important to realize that what is here described as "Puritanism" and "Enlightenment" were not formulated systematic philosophies, but rather sets of basic assumptions and primitive postulates. Puritanism was not a single philosophy but, rather, a flexible framework erected deductively upon the foundation of a set of postulates regarding the nature of man and his relationship with God and society. Thus, there was room for variation in the framework; it could (and did) take alternate forms, sharing, however, a basic allegiance to a particular set of basic postulates and assumptions.

These assumptions and basic postulates have in part been indicated by the studies of Max Weber, who concluded that Christianity was, above all a bourgeois religion. Although this sweeping judgment does some violence to the class-transcending appeal of Christianity, there remains a large kernel of truth in Weber's generalization, particularly with regard to the Protestant faction of Christianity. In the psychology of the middle class, therefore, one may find several constant features which are reflected in its religious doctrines. Primary among these factors (basic postulates) was a high development of individual self-

conciousness. This, coupled with the rise of the bourgeosie as a revolutionary element directed against feudal restrictions, gave impetus
to a social doctrine permeated by a concern with individual liberty
and natural rights, a highly personalized ethic of individual salvation
and individual moral righteousness. It is important to note, however,
as H. Richard Niebuhr has observed, that this ethic may produce a
real heroism of self-discipline and personal responsibility but does
not lead to a hopeful passion for social justice. Its martyrs, notes
Niebuhr, die for liberty, not for equality and fraternity.* Its heroes
are patrons of individual enterprise, not the great benefactor of the
brotherhood of mankind.

These postulates (which, as shall be seen, are quite different from
those of the Enlightenment) may, in education, lead to a
demand for better and more widespread educational opportunity;
but such demands will not be predicated upon fraternal or equalitarian
ideals. Such an attitude may be seen (in education) in the statements
of the Puritan, John Adams:

> . . . no practicable or possible advancement of learning can ever
> equalize knowledge among men to such a degree that some will not
> have more influence in society than others; and, consequently, that
> some will always be aristocrats and others democrats . . .†

Such sentiments, however, did not restrict the Puritan from being
an advocate of the extension of educational opportunity—far from
it. As Adams expressed it:

> Laws for the liberal education of youth, especially of the lower class
> of people, are so extremely wise and useful that to a humane and
> generous mind no expense for their purpose would be thought
> extravagant.‡

Although holding to the view that knowledge on the whole, promoted virtue and happiness (hence, education should be supported),
Adams, the Puritan, was forced to observe that there was no necessary and automatic connection between knowledge and virtue. Simple
intelligence had no association with morality. The diffusion of knowl-

---

* H. Richard Niebuhr, *The Social Sources of Denominationalism* (New York:
Henry Holt & Co., 1929), p. 87.
† John Adams, "Letter to John Taylor," quoted in *The Political Writings of John
Adams* (New York: Liberal Arts Press, 1954), p. 209.
‡ John Adams, "Thoughts on Government," quoted *ibid.*, p. 91.

edge, per se, was a necessary and virtuous activity; but in itself and without "information of abuses, redification of errors and the dissipation of pernacious prejudices," it could lead merely to the destruction of "all decorum, discipline, and subordination, anarchy and insecurity of property . . . so that nations will soon wish their books in ashes, seek darkness and ignorance . . . and follow that standard of the first mad despot . . . who will endeavor to obtain them."*

In short, education was no social panacea because people were not born with equal powers and faculties, to equal influence in society, or to equal property and advantages. The idea that all men were perfectible was, therefore, "mischievous nonsense." This fact of human existence, Adams never ceased to stress, should never lessen "our utmost exertions to amend and improve others and in every way ameliorate the lot of humanity."†

(That Adams practiced what he preached may be clearly seen in his inclusion in the state constitution of Massachusetts [Chapter VI, Section II] of a provision that recognized the necessity of a state to encourage and cherish the interests of learning, science, and literature.)

The movement we know as the Enlightenment is a similar structure, based upon a different set of postulates and conceptions. As this section will deal with the Enlightenment in colonial American education, it would be well to attempt to delineate some of these postulates. Upon these postulates, as upon those of the Puritans, a number of frameworks may be erected—hence the Enlightenment too took different forms in different parts of the Western world. The assimilation of the body of postulates that constituted the Englightenment into the corpus of colonial American conditions produced something quite different here than, for example, in England or France.

One of the basic postulates of the Enlightenment had to do with the perfectability of Man and the inevitability of progress. Believing, therefore, that humanity could be made over and brought upward, en masse, to a higher level of perfection, the men of the Enlightenment found a potent instrument for their perfection in education. Newtonian physics had effectively relegated supernatural intervention in the affairs of men and nature to a barely minimal rôle and had

* John Adams, "Discourses on Davila," quoted *ibid.*, p. 189.
† John Adams, "Letter to Vander Kemp," quoted in Page Smith, *John Adams* (New York: Doubleday & Co., 1962), 2 Vols. II, p. 1078.

demonstrated the power of man's rational faculty to comprehend the universe itself (which was found to operate according to logical mathematical laws). This being the case, it is hardly surprising to note the optimistic faith in reason and the intellectual process that formed another of the basic postulations of the Enlightenment. If the universe itself could be fully comprehended by rational means, then surely it was reasonable to conclude that a better society could be achieved through the same agency. This was certainly an exciting thought. Reason would reign supreme; supernatural superstitions would be replaced by the cool judgment of reason; and man's progress would be totally a resultant of the sustained application of his rational faculty.

This reason, as Locke had shown, was no mysterious entity. It was, as a matter of fact, one of the faculties of the mind which could be developed through exercise, just as a muscle of the body. People were not born complete with a varying amount of reason, rather with minds that were simply wax tablets. All men, therefore, had the potentiality of developing reason—they were, to that extent, equal. The process by which reason was developed was, of course, education. Although this faith in the process of education to instrumentally assist the advance and progress of mankind was a shared, common postulate of the men of the Enlightenment, the specifics of just what sort of education would be most advantageous was a matter of some dispute. As will be seen in the following selections, the type of curriculum deemed suitable was open to a wide range of speculation. None of the Enlightenment thinkers, however, had any doubts that education and reason would ultimately lead mankind onward and upward to perfection through continual progress. The ultimate triumph of reason in the world of man and nature was a basic and unquestioned assumption, and this exercise of reason would culminate in new and undreamed levels of perfection. This assumption generated all of the attributes of a secular religion, all of the assurance of a prophetic and inevitable evolutionary process. It produced a secular faith not at all dissimilar in quality to the faith of a proportion of the modern world in the ultimate and inevitable final synthesis of Marxist dialectic.

The selections following reveal this faith, as articulated in the area of education. The basic postulates of man's perfectibility through education, of the ultimate supremacy of reason, and of a humanitarian concern with the perfection and progress of all men are all eloquently demonstrated.

With respect to the relationship of the Enlightenment strain and the Christian Puritan strain, it becomes clear that at the heart of the movements there were primitive postulates and assumptions which were at variance. In essence, it was the assumption of the nature of man that was the real dividing line. Adams, representing the Puritan view, could not neglect what he took to be the evidence of history and Puritan dogma that man, while he had a capacity for good, had a tendency to evil. Reason and knowledge, therefore, could be utilized for either good or evil purposes; alone neither was any assurance of virtue. The more philosophic Enlightenment position followed the assumption that man was inherently good, not evil, and all that was necessary to insure continual progress and perfection was to remove those factors *external* to man which hindered his natural goodness and perfection, i.e., ignorance, poverty, corruption of society, etc. His natural goodness would then shine through, and progress would be assured. The application of reason to these externally contaminating factors would free the inherent goodness in all men.

These basic assumptions on the nature of man and the rôle of reason in his affairs were the source of the disagreements which marked the greater part of the relationship between Jefferson, the man of the Enlightenment, and Adams, the Puritan. Adams, though he could readily subscribe to the notion that reason *ought* to govern the affairs of men, could not find evidence for an assertion that in reality it ever had. Taking human nature as he found it in reality, as revealed in history and supported by Christian beliefs, he was forced to conclude that it was highly unlikely that reason ever *would* govern the affairs of men. To proceed on any other assumption, he felt, was a denial of history and of the realities of human nature.

The evolution of a synthesis between this Puritan Christian thesis (in terms of basic postulates) and the Enlightenment antithesis can be seen as the story of the development of the basic postulates that govern American thinking. The educational structure of this synthesis is the content of the subsequent chapters.

Thomas Jefferson was, and is, to many the epitome of the Age of Enlightenment. His intellectual virtuosity and far-ranging interests are a part of American tradition. His eloquent statement of Lockean democratic principles in the Declaration of Independence has never been surpassed either for clarity or for emotional conviction.

The ultimate repository of the essence of a democratic society lay, not in a theory, but in its citizens. If, said Jefferson, ". . . we think them not enlightened enough to exercise their control with a wholesome discretion, the remedy is not to take it [control] from them, but to inform their discretion by education." Ignorance and freedom in a state are antithetical; true representative government has as its ultimate foundation the enlightenment of the people. Jefferson's entire orientation and plea for educational opportunity rested squarely upon this conviction; his educational views are truly and wholly an extension of his enlightenment political views. Clearly, as has been already noted, underlying all of their specific manifestation was the basic postulate of the Enlightenment with regard to the essential goodness of the nature of man and a passionate faith in the power of reason to elicit this goodness by freeing man from the chains of ignorance.

Jefferson's plea for the extension of educational opportunity is based on both humanitarianism and instrumental grounds. The cultivation of free men for a free society was an ethic that took into account both the humanistic belief in the inalienable right of man to liberty and the pursuit of happiness, and the instrumental use of education to provide for the intelligent and responsible leadership that was necessary to ensure such a free society.

Jeffersonian education was, therefore, to be constituted of the liberal arts, not in the stultified modern sense of the term but rather in the sense of the ancient *artes liberales,* the liberating arts. Man was to be liberated from ignorance and irrationality, freed to fully participate as a free man with other free men in society. In his enlightened participation in such a society, the free man was the only guarantee for the perpetuation of a free society.

30. To Diffuse Knowledge More Generally

Thomas Jefferson

Another object of the revisal is, to diffuse knowledge more generally through the mass of the people. This bill proposes to lay off

Reprinted from Paul Leicester Ford (ed.), *The Works of Thomas Jefferson,* (N.Y.: G. P. Putnam, 1904), IV, pp. 60-65.

every county into small districts of five of six miles square, called hundreds and in each of them to establish a school for teaching, reading, writing, and arithmetic. The tutor to be supported by the hundred, and every person in it entitled to send their children three years gratis, and as much longer as they please, paying for it. These schools to be under a visitor who is annually to chuse the boy of best genius in the school, of those whose parents are too poor to give them further education, and to send him forward to one of the grammar schools, of which twenty are proposed to be erected in different parts of the country, for teaching Greek, Latin, geography, and the higher branches of numerical arithmetic. Of the boys thus sent in any one year, trial is to be made at the grammar schools one or two years, and the best genius of the whole selected, and continued six years, and the residue dismissed. By this means twenty of the best geniuses will be raked from the rubbish annually, and be instructed, at the public expense, so far as the grammar schools go. At the end of six years instruction, one half are to be discontinued (from among whom the grammar schools will probably be supplied with future masters); and the other half, who are to be chosen for the superiority of their parts and disposition, are to be sent and continued three years in the study of such sciences as they shall chuse, at William and Mary college, the plan of which is proposed to be enlarged, as will be hereafter explained, and extended to all the useful sciences. The ultimate result of the whole scheme of education would be the teaching all the children of the State reading, writing, and common arithmetic; turning out ten annually, of superior genius, well taught in Greek, Latin, geography, and the higher branches of arithmetic; turning out ten others annually, of genius who, to those branches of learning, shall have added such of the sciences as their genius shall have led them to; the furnishing to the wealthier part of the people convenient schools at which their children may be educated at their own expense.—The general objects of this law are to provide an education adapted to the years, to the capacity, and the condition of every one, and directed to their freedom and happiness. Specific details were not proper for the law. These must be the business of the visitors entrusted with its execution. The first stage of this education being the schools of the hundreds, wherein the great mass of people will receive instruction, the principal foundations of future order will be laid here. Instead, therefore, of putting the Bible and Testament into the hands of the children at an age when their judgments are not sufficiently matured for religious inquiries, their memories may here be stored with the most useful facts from Grecian, Roman, European, and American history. The first elements of morality too may be instilled into their minds; such as, when further developed as their judgments advance in strength, may teach them how to work out their own greatest happiness, by shewing them that it does not depend on the condition of life in which chance has placed them, but is always the result of a good conscience, good health, occupation, and freedom in all just pursuits.—

Those whom either the wealth of their parents or the adoption of the state shall destine to higher degrees of learning, will go on to the grammar schools, which constitute the next stage, there to be instruction in the languages. The learning Greek and Latin, I am told, is going into disuse in Europe. I know not what their manners and occupations may call for: but it would be very ill-judged in us to follow their example in this instance. There is a certain period of life, say from eight to fifteen or sixteen years of age, when the mind like the body is not yet firm enough for laborious and close operations. If applied to such, it falls an early victim of premature exertion; exhibiting, indeed, at first, in these young and tender subjects, the flattering appearance of their being men while they are yet children, but ending in reducing them to be children when they should be men. The memory is then most susceptible and tenacious of impressions; and the learning of languages being chiefly a work of memory, it seems precisely fitted to the powers of this period, which is long enough too for acquiring the most useful languages, ancient and modern. I do not pretend that language is science. It is only an instrument for the attainment of science. But that time is not lost which is employed in providing tools for future operations; more especially as in this case the books put into the hands of youth for this purpose may be such as will at the same time impress their minds with useful facts and good principles. If this period be suffered to pass in idleness, the mind becomes lethargic and impotent, as would the body it inhabits if unexercised during the same time. The sympathy between body and mind during their rise, progress and decline, is too strict and obvious to endanger our being misled while we reason from the one to the other.—As soon as they are of sufficient age, it is supposed they will be sent on from the grammar schools to the university, which constitutes our third and last stage, there to study those sciences which may be adapted to their views.—By that part of our plan which prescribes the selection of the youths of genius from among the classes of the poor, we hope to avail the state of those talents which nature has sown as liberally among the poor as the rich, but which perish without use, if not sought for and cultivated.—But of all the views of this law none is more important, none more legitimate, than that of rendering the people the safe, as they are the ultimate guardians of their own liberty. For this purpose the reading in the first stage, where *they* will receive their whole education, is proposed, as has been said, to be chiefly historical. History, by apprising them of the past, will enable them to judge of the future; it will avail them of the experience of other times and other nations; it will enable them to know ambition under every disguise it may assume; and knowing it, to defeat its views. In every government on earth is some trace of human weakness, some germ of corruption and degeneracy, which cunning will discover, and wickedness insensibly open, cultivate, and improve. Every government degenerates when trusted to the rulers of the people alone. The people themselves therefore are its only safe depositories. And to render even them safe, their minds must be improved to a certain degree. This indeed is not all that is necessary, though it be essentially necessary. An amendment of our constitution must here come in aid of the public education. The influence over government must be shared among all the people. If every individual which composes their mass participates of the ultimate authority, the government will be safe; because the corrupting of the whole mass will exceed any private resources of wealth and public ones cannot be provided but by levies on the people. In this case every man would have to pay his own price. The government of Great Britain has been corrupted, because but one man in ten has a right to vote for members of parliament. The sellers of the government, therefore, get nine-tenths of their price clear. It has been thought that corruption is restrained by confining the right of suffrage to a few of the wealthier of the people; but it would be more effectually restrained by an extension of that right to such numbers as would bid defiance to the means of corruption. . . .

Dr. Benjamin Rush of Philadelphia, who wrote the following selections, deserves to be better known to Americans. Like Jefferson, Rush was a true man of the Englightenment, versatile, volatile, and highly verbal. His wide-ranging interests and penetrating intellect led him to the roles of pioneer psychiatrist, abolitionist, penal reformer, humanitarian, and political radical. He also found time to affix his signature to the Declaration of Independence.

Rush represented the more radical wing of the Enlightenment. His political radicalism was fully expressed by Thomas Paine, to whom he was friend and confidant. It was Rush, as a matter of fact, who suggested to Paine the title *Common Sense* for one of his fire-eating political treatises.

No one was more convinced than Benjamin Rush of the necessity of enlisting education in the service of democracy. With Helvetius, he believed universal education to be the cure for most of the ills of mankind, particularly with regard to matters of government. His conviction was gently but firmly negated by his friend John Adams, who expressed the more cynical belief that such education would more likely produce ". . . a greater number of able and ambitious men who would understand the better how to worry one another with greater art and dexterity . . ." (Adams at the time was still recovering from the trials and tribulations of the Presidency.)

Rush, however, was undeterred in his view by such suggestions; education was the handmaiden of Democracy. A product of the "middling class," Rush was far more sensitive on the matter of class structures than the aristocratic Jefferson. As our political structure had changed radically with the Revolution, so too should education undergo revolutionary change to reflect the new independent and democratic status. The classics, for example, he maintained had no place in a democratic educational structure. A classical education suggested to Rush a class education and violently contradicted his egalitarian principles as the unwelcome vestige of an unenlightened past. (To this thought, John Adams replied that he would as soon think of closing his shutters to see more clearly as banish the classics to improve republican ideas.) As others of his Englightened colleagues, such as Samuel H. Smith and Samuel Knox, Rush set down his ideas for a broad system of public instruction ranging from literacy to the higher learning.

An interesting proposal for a federal university was one of the operational suggestions by Rush to revolutionize education and to insure the inculcation of proper democratic principles. Although the idea of a federal university died a lingering death through several federal administrations, Rush's clearly articulated belief in a universal education based firmly on democratic ideals and his rejection of a class (elite) curriculum in favor of a more practical "common" curriculum, remained an educational manifesto that would be even more forcibly ennunciated in the years to come.

31. Education Agreeable to a Republican Form of Government (1786)

Benjamin Rush

Before I proceed to the subject of this essay, I shall point out, in a few words, the influence and advantages of learning upon mankind.

I. It is friendly to religion, inasmuch as it assists in removing prejudice, superstition and enthusiasm, in promoting just notions of the Deity, and in enlarging our knowledge of his works.

II. It is favourable to liberty. Freedom can exist only in the society of knowledge. Without learning, men are incapable of knowing their rights, and where learning is confined to a few people, liberty can be neither equal nor universal.

III. It promotes just ideas of laws and government. "When the clouds of ignorance are dispelled (says the Marquis of Beccaria) by the radiance of knowledge, power trembles, but the authority of laws remains immovable."

IV. It is friendly to manners. Learning in all countries, promotes civilization, and the pleasures of society and conversation.

V. It promotes agriculture, the great basis of national wealth and happiness. Agriculture is as much a science as hydraulics, or optics, and has been equally indebted to the experiments and researches of learned men. The highly cultivated state, and the immense profits of the farms in England, are derived wholly from the patronage which agriculture has received in that country, from learned men and learned societies.

Reprinted from Benjamin Rush, *Essays, Literary, Moral and Philosophical* (Philadelphia: Bradford, 1798), pp. 1-6.

VI. Manufactures of all kinds owe their perfection chiefly to learning—hence the nations of Europe advance in manufactures, knowledge, and commerce, only in proportion as they cultivate the arts and sciences.

For the purpose of diffusing knowledge through every part of the state, I beg leave to propose the following simple plan.

I. Let there be one university in the state, and let this be established in the capital. Let law, physic, divinity, the law of nature and nations, economy, &c. be taught in it by public lectures in the winter season, after the manner of the European universities, and let the professors receive such salaries from the state as will enable them to deliver their lectures at a moderate price.

II. Let there be four colleges. One in Philadelphia, one at Carlisle, a third, for the benefit of our German fellow citizens, at Lancaster, and a fourth, some years hence at Pittsburgh. In these colleges, let young men be instructed in mathematics and in the higher branches of science, in the same manner that they are now taught in our American colleges. After they have received a testimonial from one of these colleges, let them, if they can afford it, complete their studies by spending a season or two in attending the lectures in the university. I prefer four colleges in the state to one or two, for there is a certain size of colleges as there is of towns and armies, that is most favourable to morals and good government. Oxford and Cambridge in England are the seats of dissipation, while the more numerous, and less crowded universities and colleges in Scotland, are remarkable for the order, diligence, and decent behaviour of their students.

II. Let there be free schools established in every township, or in districts consisting of one hundred families. In these schools let children be taught to read and write the English and German languages, and the use of figures. Such of them as have parents that can afford to send them from home, and are disposed to extend their educations, may remove their children from the free school to one of the colleges.

By this plan the whole state will be tied together by one system of education. The university will in time furnish masters for the colleges, and the colleges will furnish masters for the free schools, while the free schools, in their turns, will supply the colleges and the university with scholars, students and pupils. The same systems of grammar, oratory and philosophy, will be taught in every part of the state, and the literary features of Pennsylvania will thus designate one great, and equally enlightened family.

But, how shall we bear the expense of these literary institutions?—I answer—These institutions will *lessen* our taxes. They will enlighten us in the great business of finance—they will teach us to increase the ability of the state to support government, by increasing the profits of agriculture, and by promoting manufactures. They will teach us all the modern improvements and advantages of inland navigation. They will defend us from hasty and expensive experiments in government, by unfolding to us the experience and folly of past ages, and thus, instead of adding to our taxes and debts, they will furnish us with the true secret of lessening and discharging both of them.

But, shall the estates of orphans, bachelors and persons who have no children, be taxed to pay for the support of schools from which they can derive no benefit? I answer in the affirmative, to the first part of the objection, and I deny the truth of the latter part of it. Every member of the community is interested in the propagation of virtue and knowledge in the state. But I will go further, and add, it will be true economy in individuals to support public schools. The bachelor will in time save his tax for this purpose, by being able to sleep with fewer bolts and locks to his doors—the estates of orphans will in time be benefited, by being protected from the ravages of unprincipled and idle boys, and the children of wealthy parents will be less tempted, by bad company, to extravagance. Fewer pillories and whipping posts, and smaller gaols, with their usual expenses and taxes, will be necessary when our youth are properly educated, than at present; I believe it could be proved, that the expenses of confining, trying and executing criminals, amount every year, in most of the countries, to more money than would be sufficient to maintain all the schools that would be necessary in each county. The confessions of these criminals generally show us, that their vices and punishments are the fatal consequences of the want of a proper education in early life.

I submit these detached hints to the consideration of the legislature and of the citizens of Pennsylvania. The plan for the free schools is taken chiefly from the plans which have long been used with success in Scotland, and in the eastern states* of America, where the influence of learning, in promoting religion, morals, manners and good government, has never been exceeded in any country.

The manner in which these schools should be supported and governed —the modes of determining the characters and qualifications of schoolmasters, and the arrangement of families in each district, so that children of the same religious sect and nation, may be educated as much as possible together, will form a proper part of a law for the establishment of schools, and therefore does not come within the limits of this plan.

* There are 600 of these schools in the small state of Connecticut, which at this time have in them 25,000 scholars.

REFERENCES

Bailyn, Bernard. *Education in the Forming of American Society*. Chapel Hill: University of North Carolina Press, 1960.

Best, John Hardin (ed.). *Benjamin Franklin on Education*. New York: Teachers College, Columbia University, 1962.

De La Fontainerie Francois. *French Liberalism and Education in the Eighteenth Century*. New York: McGraw-Hill, 1932.

Hansen, O. A. *Liberalism and American Education in the Eighteenth Century*. New York: Macmillan Co., 1926.

Kiefer, Monica. *American Children Through Their Books, 1700-1835*. Philadelphia: University of Pennsylvania Press, 1948.

Knight, Edgar W. *A Documentary History of Education in the South Before 1860*. vols. 5 Chapel Hill: University of North Carolina Press, 1949-1953.

Lee, Gordon C. (ed.). *Crusade Against Ignorance: Thomas Jefferson on Education*. New York: Teachers College, Columbia University, 1961.

Meriweather, Colyer. *Our Colonial Curriculum, 1607-1776*. Washington, D.C.: Central Publishing Co., 1907.

Seybolt, Robert F. *Apprenticeship and Apprenticeship Education in Colonial New England and New York*. New York: Teachers College, Columbia University, 1917.

Seybolt, Robert F. *The Private Schools of Colonial Boston*. Cambridge, Mass.: Harvard University Press, 1935.

Seybolt, Robert F. *The Public Schools of Colonial Boston, 1635-1775*. Cambridge, Mass.: Harvard University Press, 1935.

PART 2

The National Period
1789-1877

I A CONCEPT OF "NATION"

THE underlying concept that explains and connects the particular events of the era from 1789 to 1877 is, as the title indicates, the concept of a nation. Properly understood, this concept may provide a key with which to understand the educational ideas and practices of the period in all of their manifest diversity. Hence, consideration of education in the national period may begin by turning attention initially to the underlying concept of a nation.

SOME BASIC ASSUMPTIONS OF THE UNITED STATES

That a contiguous geographic area can adequately define a nation is a tempting but obviously fallacious notion. One has but to look at geographically bifurcated Pakistan, or even at geographically detached Hawaii and Alaska, to quickly invalidate this definition. Similarly, one can as easily dispense with other immediately experienced variables— such as language, appearance, dress, cephalic indices, or what have you. These simply will not do; there are too many exceptions that effectively negate all of these as adequate definitions of a nation. *To understand a nation, one must first understand the basic premises and elementary concepts shared by the majority of individuals in that nation—for these are what link these individuals together as a nation.*

With this definition of the symbol "nation," attention may now more profitably be turned to the period under examination and to ask with de Crèvecoeur—just what is this new man, this American? De Crèvecoeur has been partially answered by the above suggestion that the American is an individual who shares certain basic elementary concepts and premises with other individuals, who are therefore also designated Americans. These concepts define a national philosophy, which in turn provides the basis of national behavioral responses. As a contemporary professor of philosophy has expressed this thought: "The State is not merely a formal organization of political, economical, and military activities, but, what is more important, a community in which the moral ideas may be realized by way of these organized activities."[1] The use of the term "community" is a happy choice, for, as John Dewey pointed out, the similarity between "community" and "communicate" is by no means accidental. One can truly communicate only from a common base of beliefs and meanings. Even when such communicants disagree, they in a sense agree to disagree, and by virtue of this agreement there is a basis of eventual reconciliation.

Although the basic beliefs and assumptions which form the nucleus of a national philosophy are for the most part held unconsciously, there was at least one time in this nation's history when they were brought into conscious focus. This time was at the nation's founding, and the philosophy was made conscious and articulated by a few leaders— generally referred to as the "founding fathers." The talented and facile pen of Thomas Jefferson articulated what is probably the key concept in our national philosophy when, in the Declaration of Independence, Jefferson stated in memorable prose, "We hold these truths to be self-evident, that all men are created equal. . . ." This phrase is familiar, perhaps too familiar, to most Americans, but how many have stopped to analyze its meaning? Such an analysis, however, like that of "nation," is vital for understanding.

To begin with, consider the source of this belief in the equality of all men. Jefferson states that it is not derived from any particular doctrine or philosophy but is "self-evident." As such, this belief must transcend individual doctrines, philosophies, etc., for it must be self-

---

[1] Thomé H. Fang, *The Chinese View of Life* (Hong Kong: The Union Press, 1957), p. 242.

evident to all. This point may be further clarified when it is seen that Jefferson was not stating a moral relationship between men but, rather, a legal relationship. Being self-evident, this legal relationship is prior to, and transcendent of, courts and legislature.

Jefferson offers no proofs, however, and rests his case on the self-evidency of "natural law." He later claimed no originality for his Declaration philosophy, stating that he had only written down what was common knowledge and belief. In other words, to use the convenient terminology of the legal sociologist Eugen Ehrlich, Jefferson was putting the "living law" in positive form.[2]

All this has a great deal to do with the history of American education.

II EDUCATION IN THE NATIONAL PERIOD

If all men were created equal before God and the law, obviously this equality must be expressed economically, politically, and educationally in the new democracy. Jefferson never pretended to the naive belief that all men were biologically or intellectually equal. Quite obviously they were not. Legally, however, they were equal; hence their status (to borrow the word of Sir Henry Maine) could not be allowed to determine their legal position.[3] Educationally, this meant that inferior status (poverty, for example) could not be the determining factor in educational availability. If the child could benefit from education, his low status could not be allowed to interfere with his equality with other children of equal brightness but higher status. Jeferson's educational proposals rest on this concept of equality, spelled out in such proposals as his *Bill for the More General Diffusion of Knowledge*. Equality before the law, as both Jefferson and Benjamin Rush saw, could not be operationally exercised without education. Rush particularly stressed the necessity of educating the populace in order to make democracy work. The people could hardly participate in or perpetuate a democratic form of government based on legal

[2] See Eugen Ehrlich, *Fundamental Principles of The Sociology of Law*. Translated by W. L. Mall, Harvard Studies in Jurisprudence, Vol. V (Cambridge, Mass.: University Press, 1936), pp. 121-136.

[3] On the "law of status" concept, see Sir Henry Maine, *The Ancient Law* (London: John Murray, 1908).

equality if they were unaware of the bases of democracy and equality. Political power would soon pass back into the eager hands of an educated status group.

Ignorance was the deadly enemy of democratic government; education was its bulwark. It was to insure that all federal officers were properly grounded in democratic theory that Rush proposed his federal university. Graduation from this "University of Democracy" would be a prerequisite for governmental office and would assure the electorate that the incumbant official understood the national philosophy.

Charles Pinckney suggested the creation of a national university and tried, though unsuccessfully, to extend congressional control over education in general. Joel Barlow planned a National Institute to educate scientists, civil servants, and artists. Similar plans were evolved by Noah Webster, Samuel Knox, Nathaniel Chipman, James Sullivan, Robert Coram, Samuel Smith, and others.[4]

The concept of legal equality was extended by some leaders of the era to embrace the idea of equality of opportunity—economic, political, and social. This idea would provide a rationale for universal education. But popular suspicion of a powerful central government precluded wide support for any federalized education. While many would agree with the requirement for a educated citizenry, educational endeavors retained their traditional moral and religious connection in the minds of the majority of the populace. State-controlled and supported education had to wait for the future; education was still entwined with church and religion in the view of most of the people—an association that organized religion showed no inclination to dissolve.

The academy movement, noted in the previous section, was precisely to provide operationally for equality of economic opportunity. Educational preparation, rather than status of birth or position, would insure this economic equality. Indeed, the academy so well represented a means of putting into practice the national philosophy of

---

[4] R. B. Nye, *The Cultural Life of the New Nation* (New York: Harper Bros., 1960), pp. 155-156. On the history of some of these plans, see G. B. Goode, "The Origin of the National Scientific and Educational Institutions of the United States," *Papers of the A. H. A.*, IV (April, 1890).

equality that it quickly became the dominant institution of secondary education in every region of the agrarian America of this period. The academy was actually an institution with a dual purpose, as illustrated by Franklin's proposal for an English and classical faculty in his academy. It was to prepare for college entrance on the one hand with a four-year classical course or for business and certain semi-professional activities on the other, with an English course of three years duration. Some academies included teacher-training (for the lower schools) as well as provision for female instruction. The diversity of learning and levels of instruction offered in the various academies, was indeed almost all-inclusive.

One could even learn to act as the social equal of anyone—through academy offerings in dancing, manners, and the like. Typically, the academy was a boarding school—well suited to an America that was largely rural, a society of farms and small towns. It was a "private" school in that it was governed by a private board and supported in the main from tuition payments or, in a few instances, from endowments. Many academies received occasional grants of public monies from the communities they served, but they were denied full or systematic tax support. It was a "public" institution (in the British sense of the term) in that it was open to all comers and indeed served the public. Seldom if ever, it was pointed out, was the poor but deserving scholar turned away from any academy. The popularity of this public-private institution provides ample evidence for the astuteness of Jefferson's perception of the "living law" of the times. Eventually, the academy was superseded by the publicly controlled and supported high school (the first established in Boston in 1821), and the equalitarian and utilitarian mission of the original academies was taken up by this new urban-centered institution. Academies remained on the scene, of course, as they still do, but except for the name they are far removed from their prototypes, retaining only the college preparatory function. By the 1870's, the public high school had assumed the dominant role in secondary education in an America becoming increasingly urban and industrial.

There were, naturally, other forces at work in the National period which influenced education. Politically, the doctrine of equality received added operational emphasis with the election of Andrew Jackson. This ushered in the so-called "age of the common man." Actually, what happened was that the common man gained the power (through Jackson) to demand his equality. As a part of the national philosophy, it must be remembered, this was nothing really new in theory or belief. What *was* different was that the theory acquired a spokesman with the power to affect change. Not surprisingly, the result was a sort of a reverse snobbery. Not only was the "common man" endowed with equality, the more "common" one could appear, the more "equal" one could be. Status returned with a vengeance, but in reversed order. Some saw in this movement of the veneration and virtual deification of the "common man" the dangers of a Rousseauian democratic revolution in the French manner, a "tyranny of the majority" rule. The basic underlying national philosophy, however, was based on Locke and not Rousseau, hence the reaction to any radical Jacksonian "leveling" that extended equality beyond Lockean limitations.

There was, clearly, a marked difference between a radical Jacksonian equalitarianism and the Jeffersonian expression of equalitarianism. With respect to education, it will be recalled that Jefferson asked for an extension of educational opportunity, and he emphasized that that this education should be in the classical liberal arts tradition. Jeffersonian equalitarianism argued that this classical education should be available to all who could benefit from it, not merely to a socioeconomic élite. The availability of classical liberal education, which Jefferson saw as the only suitable education to provide leadership for society, must be extended in a democracy to all children, whatever their socio-economic status level, who possessed the requisite talent or potential. The classical educational curriculum would serve as a filter, screening out the intellectually unfit, so that eventually the cream (intellectually) of the lower classes would rise to the top to take their places of leadership in the country, as well educated in the classical learning as any aristocrat. Some have named this notion "qualitarianism," as opposed to "equalitarianism."

The Jacksonian version of equalitarianism (a frame of mind, actually, not limited to Jackson personally) differed from the Jeffersonian views by its rejection of any hierarchy of educational values. As such, it ran counter to the Jeffersonian conviction that one specific type of education (the classical liberal arts curriculum) should constitute the educational standard or serve as a filter through which all potential leaders in a democracy must pass. Although Jefferson sought to limit political power to a specifically prepared educational and intellectual group (demanding that admission to this group be determined by ability and not socio-economic status), he was not concerned with those who could not mold or articulate their aspirations into the frame of reference of the classical liberal arts. Jacksonianism, holding to an equalitarian doctrine of all knowledge and ability, viewed the attainments of a farmer or a merchant on the same level as the accomplishments of a classically educated scholar. One was on no "higher" level than the other, and all were equally fitted for social or political power.

This difference of opinion, it might be noted, has resulted in endless educational dispute to the present time.

Some, like the astute Horace Mann, saw in Jacksonian political power the means to actualize a new educational concept—the common school—not a school for the common man, but a school common to all men. To remove the dangers of perpetuating vested (status-oriented) interests, this school would be a thoroughly public, tax-supported institution. Among the major vested interests were the religious denominations, who supported many of the existing academies and perpetuated their denominational creeds thereby. To insure complete "commonality" and freedom from vested influences, Mann proposed at first to eliminate religion from the common schools. As might be expected, the denominations protested vigorously. This, they claimed, would undermine the moral fibre of the youth; for morality and ethics, it seemed, were clearly based upon religion. Mann had to fall back and regroup his thoughts, stating that of course he was not advocating moral anarchy or a debilitating atheism. He proposed finally that religion should also be equalized by taking from each the common factors shared by all. Thus, religion would be preserved, and at the same time no denomination could come to dominate the others in the school.

There were, of course, other obstacles to be met and overcome. Taxation was (theoretically, at least) bearable if one could see some benefits from it to oneself. What benefit from a school tax to the unmarried or childless? Merely, said Mann, in terms of an overall improvement in society. What, claimed the wealthy, do we get out of this tax? We send our children to academies and pay tuition there. Why should we also be called upon to pay for the education of other people's children? To answer this, Mann had to construct a particularly ingenious parry. The parry was turned into a sharp reposte when Mann attacked the weakest link in the armor of the wealthy, their basic fear of a radically leveling social revolution. He could play upon the fears of a status-determined class who saw themselves threatened by a great assemblage of "common men" who for the first time had a spokesman (Jackson) with real political power. It could be indirectly pointed out to be wealthy that investment in a common school might have class-survival value, for in such a school any thoughts of revolutionary action and radical social leveling could and would be educated out of the young in favor of change through the democrative processes. The school would also insure a supply of educated workers who could eventually be trained to fill lower and middle management positions.

There was yet another problem to be faced by the determined Horace Mann, that of persuading the "common man" himself that the common school was an appropriate institution for his children. On a practical level, the "common man" quite clearly felt that the income he received by virtue of his offspring's going to work rather than to school was a formidable argument against the common school idea. This Mann countered by pointing out that with schooling; the potential income would be magnified and in the long run would far outweigh the limited financial contribution that the uneducated child could make. Such an argument was pursuasive indeed to the public of the Jacksonian era, composed of an expanding, commercially oriented society, far less intellectually than economically inclined. The majority will, which was essentially non-intellectual, did tend to demean the goals of intellectual pursuit. Yet, on the other hand, this same entrepreneurial spirit led to an expansion of the educational role to include responsibility for individual self-development and economic security, for civic and moral virtue, and for social betterment.

All in all, it was a tremendous task for Mann and his followers. That they succeeded is a real testimony to their astuteness and determination. The success of the movement, however, was ultimately assured by the fact that its basic principle of equality was in accord with the unconsciously held basic philosophy of the nation.

The religious movements during this period are also of great interest to the historian of education—again illustrative of a behavioral manifestation of the national philosophy. Curiously enough, while the hithertofore rigidly orthodox Northeast was changing to the more liberal Unitarian-Universalist theology, the previously religiously liberal South was becoming more rigidly orthodox. By 1850, southern Protestantism was closer in temper and ideals to seventeenth-century New England than to Jefferson's Virginia of 1750.[5] Slavery was undoubtedly one cause of this southern movement to a religious neo-orthodoxy. A free-thinking liberal atmosphere could not be tolerated in a society forced more and more to justify the "peculiar institution." In the East, however, the rise of non-trinitarian Unitarianism, stressing the unity, not the trinity of God, represented another behavioral correlate of the national philosophy. Based on the *jus naturae* or natural law apprehended by the use of reason, this denomination rejected the supernaturalism of trinitarian religion and built its religious edifice upon the belief in natural man and natural reason.[6] The secular intellectual movement associated with this religious belief is called Transcendentalism. What was "transcended" was essentially the man-made *jus civile* (civil law) in favor of the transcendent *jus naturae*. Nature, therefore, was exalted and usually romanticized in the process; the famous "over-soul" of Emerson was nothing more than a somewhat romantic expression of the *jus naturae*. Emerson spent much time, however, in trying to transmit the concept of the over-soul through the medium of a language remarkably unequipped for the task. Painting,

[5] R. B. Nye, *op. cit.,* p. 233.
[6] As William Ellery Channing stated it: "I am surer of rational nature from God than that any book [Bible] is."

as the orientals found, was a much more appropriate medium, as it could be directly experienced.[7]

In any event, the result of the transcendental notion was a genuine concern with the circumstances of others. Under the *jus naturae* (or *jên* or *Tao*), man is clearly his brother's keeper. Indeed, that which separates man from man is a false and illusory dichotomy (to be transcended). Hence, humanitarian reform was the behavioral response of this movement. Educationally, the common school movement drew on this humanitarianism, as did the educational movement called the Lyceum. This last was a nationally organized lecture bureau designed to expose all men to the benefits of education—to improve their lot—and enrich their lives. Originally these lectures were aimed at very direct, economic improvement (in farming methods, bee-keeping, and the like), but they became in time more and more attuned to the improvement of the general level of culture.

Differences in southern thinking in these matters of humanitarian reform can be well illustrated in the denominational schisms between northern and southern branches of the Protestant churches that occurred before and continued after the Civil War.[8] Ostensibly the denominational groups disagreed along political and economic lines, specifically with regard to slavery, but the real split was on a much deeper level.

It will be recalled that the unconscious postulates and assumptions underlying a national philosophy are held by a majority, but not all, of the inhabitants. The South had very early in its history accepted a different set of postulates from those of Locke and Jefferson.[9] It is

[7] Curiously enough, the oriental flavor one finds in Emerson and Thoreau (frequently directly referred to) is perfectly in accord with the idea of a *jus naturae*. Oriental thought expresses the concept as Tao or *jên* or "suchness," but it is the same concept. The important difference is in the form of knowing. The oriental finds that Tao solely by a radically empirical method—accentuated by such practices as meditation. The Stoic Roman found the *jus naturae* through an intellectual use of the imageless postulates of mathematical physics. For a full development of the point, see F. S. C. Northrup, *The Complexity of Legal & Ethical Experience* (Boston: Little, Brown, and Company, 1959), p. 143 ff.

[8] See H. Richard Niebuhr, *The Social Sources of Denominationalism,* (New York: Henry Holt and Company, 1929).

[9] See Peter Laslett "Sir Robert Filmer," *William and Mary Quarterly,* Vol. V No. 4, 3rd sec., pp. 523-546.

perhaps ironic in this case that Lockean philosophy was set forth by the southerner, Jefferson. As a recent study indicates, it was the status-based legal forms set forth by Sir Robert Filmer (the same Filmer against whom Locke wrote in his *Second Treatise on Government*) that were introduced into colonial Virginia (via the Virginia Company). Thus, a portion of the inhabitants of the United States derived their living law not from the equalitarian *jus naturae* tradition, but from the aristocratic, patriachal law of status concepts of Filmer and Richard Hooker. The living law of the old South was, therefore, not equalitarian but thoroughly patriarchal and status oriented, concerned with differentiations of birth, family, color, and the like.

This patriarchal living law does not, of course, preclude humanitarian reforms or educational provisions. It does, however, preclude a philosophy of equality. The southern stress on family and background, which holds sway to this day, is neither egotism nor eccentricity. It is merely the response of a patriarchal living law.

EDUCATIONAL ACCOMPLISHMENTS OF THE NATIONAL PERIOD

We have touched thus far on a few of the positive educational accomplishments of this period (and the readings will illustrate many others). To establish a normative judgment of these accomplishments is a difficult task. To speak from the benefits of the historian's 20/20 hindsight is one matter; to attempt to see the period in terms of its own needs and limitations is quite another. It has been said (correctly) that the period was rather non-intellectual in its education. Even in higher education—and the remarkable spirit in the founding of colleges during the period was indeed one of its educational high points—the stress seemed to be more towards educating for character rather than in rigorous pursuit of ideas. It must be understood, however, that the underlying force of this period was to create a character—a national character. This was a time of nation building and of the building of a national character. From Webster's attempts in his many textbooks to create a distinctly American language[10] to Rush's proposal for

[10] In his efforts to create a uniquely "American" language structure, Webster was proceeding from sound philosophical linguistic principles. A language, in its "Meta" function, contains an expression of the basic concepts and assumptions of a people.

a national university, this element is clearly recognizable. Education was to establish the priority of collective values, to establish what Gustave R. Radbruck has called a "transindividualistic" value orientation.

The apparent threat of a rising secular emphasis in society and education was in part responsible for the generally non-intellectual state of affairs in educational institutions. Secularization and the ideas of individual equality were clearly seen as threats by the church-dominated colleges, for example. Although the initial purpose of producing a learned clergy had long since waned (Harvard, for example, sent 70 per cent of its graduates into the ministry in 1650; one hundred years later it sent only about 45 percent), the idea of producing a Christian had not disappeared.

After the Revolutionary War, the nationalistic need for useful and intelligent citizens of the new republic resulted in a great boom in college founding, and the majority of the new colleges retained the colonial idea of a prime duty to produce Christian gentlemen—"defenders of the faith" certainly, if not actually ministers of Christianity. Fighting against secular encroachment by the states, the colleges saw themselves as an educational bulwark against over-emphasis on secular matters. The Dartmouth College case was indeed a landmark in this fight to preserve denominational integrity. The emotional reaction of post-1800 America against liberal and deistic notions in religion and morals ("French radicalism"), which reaction amounted to a second "Great Awakening" with all of the emotionality and renovation of the first, served to preserve the power of orthodox Christianity in higher education. By 1840, the country had some seventy-eight colleges, almost all of which were founded under religious sponsorship. The emphasis was placed on education for devout and moral church members—not for intellectual students of the arts, sciences, and human-

---

These in turn determine that people's behavioral and perceptual pattern. In the grammar, syntax, and word usage of a language, the *Weltanschauung* and character of its users is metalinguistically expressed. On the point generally, see: Benjamin Whorf, *Collected Papers on Metalinguistic,* (Washington, Foreign Service Institute, 1952). As Erich Fromm has noted, even the usage of verbs and nouns in a language is a significant clue to that people's mode of perception. See: Erich Fromm, *Beyond the Chains of Illusion* (New York: Simon and Schuster [Credo Series], 1962), pp. 118-119.

ities. Most certainly, piety overshadowed any notions of a free inquiry and pursuit of truth.

It was not until the 1860's and after, with the formation of the new land-grant state universities, that higher education began to reflect the needs of the new commercial and secular society of the nineteenth century. But in this period of nationalism with the expressed need to consolidate the new nation, it would appear that a non-intellectual, non-speculative education was precisely the sort to accomplish this moral retrenchment. The nation, after all, had undergone a revolution with all of the accompanying disruption of social life and thought. It was a time for putting together a solid national foundation upon which future generations could build with a feeling that they were not erecting a structure resting upon a bubble that might at any moment burst. There is, as is often noted, a time and a place for everything. Just how appropriate a climate for innovation and intellectual activity is presented by a country that has just recently come into being? Is "progress" a continual upward lineal movement, or does it require periodic plateaus of relative stability, times of evaluation and consolidation? Is progress "onward and upward," per se, an end in itself or a means to greater ends? Is the actual movement of progress itself the value, or the goal to which it attains?

Without espousing the highly debatable conclusion of Hegel that the historical "is" may be identified with the dialectically determined "ought," might it be suggested that the essentially non-intellectual educational atmosphere of the time in question seems to have been quite "appropriate" for the needs of that time?

The education of the National era may possibly be damned as failing to support reform or experimentation in its own province. (Some of these experimental ideas are included in the readings section.) One can, however, realistically think of experimental innovation only when one has an established base to fall back on if the experiment is unsuccessful. The cautious attitude of education during the National period may be defended on the grounds that, realistically, the society was unprepared for radical experimentation.

With regard to education's close allegiance to the social, political, and economic status quo and its disregard of reforming movements in these spheres, it might be pointed out that the most important educational accomplishment of the period—the common school—was achieved only *because* education was allied with political and social leaders. Horace Mann had learned well the lesson that Jackson taught: real freedom is not the absence of restraint but the power to effect choice. Using political methods in a realistic appeal to the powers that controlled effective choice, Mann was able to generate the means to actualize his dream of a common school. Noble aims are one thing, putting them into reality quite another, as many reformers have learned. Nobility of purpose remains just that unless joined to power to effect the purpose. The great educational achievement was the common school, to demand more of the period is perhaps unreasonable.

In any event, the frame of the uniquely American educational ladder was firmly outlined during this period. There were, quite obviously, missing rungs on this ladder if it was to actualize fully the basic Jeffersonian-Lockean principles of equality. A great Civil War was fought during the period, essentially a physical confrontation of the two diverse strains with regard to the meaning of equality and the legal nature of the Jeffersonian proclamation. As subsequent events clearly show, the Filmerian-patriarchal assumptions of the living law of the South were not eradicated, either by defeat in battle or by legislative action in Congress. The war did, however, force the issue with respect to one of the missing rungs on the educational ladder—a rung had to be provided for the newly freed slaves in a country that was not equipped for their presence in the society.

In summary, it may be fairly stated that the period, in spite of its limitations and problems, accomplished a great deal educationally. Perhaps more importantly, it established a viable frame and foundation for future generations to build upon. They are, in fact, still building.

SECTION 1

E Pluribus Unum

Forged by the flame of revolution and tempered in the campfires of a hundred campaigns, the bond that had united the New England Yankee and the Southern planter in common cause had proved sufficiently viable to withstand the combined assault of British arms, the desertions of "summer patriots," and the mendacity of war profiteers.

But how long would this bond last when the swords of war were replaced by the plows of peace, when revolutionary comradeship and common purpose existed only as the vague memories of aging men? Would the bond prove to be transitory—born of the immediacy of a crisis and incapable of surviving its resolution? If so, what then were the chances for the survival of this new nation? This was the primary problem that faced the leaders of the new nation in the immediate post-Revolutionary War years.

The solution was obvious. Although the cohesive power generated by revolutionary commitment could not be maintained indefinitely, it could be replaced by a cohesive force of equal magnitude. Such a force must be of a similar essence. i.e., transindividualistic, but not dependent upon perpetual crisis for its sustenance. The new force would be generated by the creation of a national spirit, a uniquely "American" spirit. This spirit must be so firmly rooted in the institutions and thought patterns of the society that it would be manifest in a national solidarity and identification. As the task was clear, so too was the instrument for its fulfillment—education.

Illustrated by some of the following readings, the process of "Americanization" was very much in the foreground of the educational proposals and activities of the period. From a "National University" to an "American Geography" the theme is dominant and pervasive, even complete to warnings against the dangers of possible contamination by exposure to European ideologies, manners, and patterns of thought. This somewhat xenophobic reaction is perhaps still evident in our society, in our distrust of foreigners and in our reluctance to learn foreign languages.

In addition to the nationalistic drive of the early part of the era, the ideals of the Enlightenment were also present. However, Enlightenment ideals of liberty, fraternity, equality, and the belief in the perfectibility and progress of man took different forms in different countries; and the American version was again distinctive. The excessive egalitarian zeal of the French Revolution was not the American pattern; the American rarely tended to excesses except perhaps in his Americanism. Americans, in adapting the principles of the Enlightenment, were more influenced by Locke than by Rousseau. Equality, in Locke's judgment, did not imply any sort of radical "leveling," except in the political area.* The majority of Americans viewed the activities of the French revolutionaries with alarm, lumping their excesses under the generic (and pejorative) heading of "French Radicalism." American notions of equality were quite limited in scope and were generally meliorated by a Calvinistic skepticism regarding man's ultimate perfectibility.

Man was equal before the law, or, if one was more Calvinistically inclined, equal in his depravity. Hence, he should be allowed to compete equally in life. Obviously, however, some were going to be more successful than others due to factors such as intellect, in which there was clearly no equality. This was, in the American perspective of the Enlightenment, the nature of things. Education, then, could not (as for Helvétius, for example) cure all social ills and guarantee man's perfection. It could, however, certainly improve man and enable him to exercise his (Lockean) right of competitive equality. Some would, however, always be more equal than others, as one of George Orwell's disturbing pigs observed about 150 years later in *Animal Farm* (1945).

One of the essential themes of this period was the accentuation of the uniquely "American" ideal. The idea of a national university was a popular one in certain circles, supported by Benjamin Rush and others. The following selection indicates the feelings of the first U.S. president on the subject of a national university. Washington was willing to go beyond mere approval, as the second selection clearly demonstrates.

---

* "Because equality is conceived of by Locke as the equal right of all men to freedom, Lockean equality is not an instrument of leveling in any area other than the political. . . . In areas outside of politics Lockean doctrine calls for competitive equality." S. A. Lakoff, *Equality in Political Philosophy* (Cambridge, Mass.: Harvard Universtiy Press, 1964), p. 100.

32. To Congress on a National University, 1796

George Washington

I have heretofore proposed to the consideration of Congress the expediency of establishing a National University, and also a Military Academy. The desirability of both these institutions has so constantly increased with every new view I have taken of the subject, that I cannot omit the opportunity of one for all recalling your attention to them.

The assembly to which I address myself, is too enlightned not to be fully sensible how much a flourishing state of the arts and sciences contributes to national prosperity and reputation. True it is, that our country, much to its honor, contains many seminaries of learning highly respectable and useful; but the funds upon which they rest are too narrow to command the ablest professors, in the different departments of liberal knowledge, for the institution contemplated, though they would be excellent auxiliaries.

Amongst the motives to such an institution, the assimiliation of the principles, opinions, and manners of our countrymen, by the common education of a portion of our youth from every quarter, well deserves attention. The more homogeneous our citizens can be made in these particulars, the greater will be our prospect of permanent union; and a primary object of such a national institution should be, the education of our youth in the science of government. In a republic, what species of knowledge can be equally important, and what duty more pressing on its legislature, than to patronize a plan for communicating it to those, who are to be the future guardians of the liberties of the country?

The institution of a military academy is also recommended by cogent reasons. However pacific the general policy of a nation may be, it ought never to be without an adequate stock of military knowledge for emergencies. The first would impair the energy of its character, and both would hazard its safety, or expose it to greater evils when war could not be avoided. Besides that war might often not depend upon its own choice. In proportion as the observance of pacific maxims might exempt a nation from the necessity of practising the rules of the military art, ought to be its care in preserving and transmitting, by proper establishments, the knowledge of that art. Whatever argument may be drawn from particular examples, superficially viewed, a thorough examination of the subject will evince, that the art of war is at once comprehensive and complicated; that

Reprinted from Jared Sparks, ed., *The Writings of George Washington,* XII (Boston: Little, Brown and Co., 1885), pp. 71-72.

it demands much previous study; and that the possession of it, in its most improved and perfect state, is always of great moment to the security of a nation. This, therefore, ought to be a serious care of every government; and for this purpose, an academy, where a regular course of instruction is given, is an obvious expedient, which different nations have successfully employed.

33. Gift of Shares in the Potomac Company for the National University, 1799

George Washington

I give and bequeath, in perpetuity, the 50 shares which I hold in the Potomac Company (under the aforesaid acts of the legislature of Virginia), toward the endowment of a university, to be established within the limits of the District of Columbia, under the auspices of the General Government, if that Government should incline to extend a fostering hand toward it; and, until such a seminary is established, and the funds arising on these shares shall be required for its support, my further will and desire is, that the profit accruing therefrom shall, whenever dividends are made, be laid out in purchasing stock in the Bank of Columbia, or some other bank, at the discretion of my executors, or by the Treasurer of the United States for the time being, under the direction of Congress; provided that honorable body should patronize the measure; and the dividends proceeding from the purchase of such stock are to be vested in more stock, and so on, until a sum adequate to the accomplishment of the object is obtained; of which I have not the smallest doubt before many years pass away, even if no aid or encouragement is given by legislative authority, or from any other source.

The great American nationalist and spelling authority, Noah Webster, was one of the more outspoken exponents of a distinctly American education. In the following article, which appeared in *The American*

Reprinted from Jared Sparks, ed., *The Writings of George Washington*, XII (Boston: Little, Brown and Co., 1885), pp. 72.

Magazine of May, 1788, Webster attacks the practice of sending children abroad to be educated and of importing teachers from Europe.

34. Dangers of a Foreign Education

Noah Webster

. . . Before I quit this subject, I beg leave to make some remarks on a practice which appears to be attended with important consequences; I mean that of sending boys to Europe for an education, or sending to Europe for teachers. That this was right before the revolution will not be disputed; at least so far as national attachments were concerned; but the propriety of it ceased with our political relation to Great Britain.

In the first place, our honor as an independent nation is concerned in the establishment of literary institutions, adequate to all our own purposes; without sending our youth abroad, or depending on other nations for books and instructors. It is very little to the reputation of America to have it said abroad, that after the heroic achievements of the late war, this independent people are obliged to send to Europe for men and books to teach their children A B C.

But in another point of view, a foreign education is directly opposite to our political interests and ought to be discountenanced, if not prohibited.

Every person of common observation will grant, that most men prefer the manners and the government of that country where they are educated. Let ten American youths be sent, each to a different European kingdom, and live there from the age of twelve to twenty, & each will give the preference to the country where he has resided.

The period from twelve to twenty is the most important in life. The impressions made before that period are commonly effaced; those that are made during that period *always* remain for many years, and *generally* thro' life.

Ninety-nine persons of a hundred, who pass that period in England or France, will prefer the people, their manners, their laws, and their government to those of their native country. Such attachments are injurious, both to the happiness of the men, and to the political interests of their own country. As to private happiness, it is universally known how much pain a man suffers by a change of habits in living. The customs of Europe are and ought to be different from ours; but when a man has been bred in one country, his attachments to its manners make them in a great measure, necessary to his happiness; on changing his residence, he must therefore

Reprinted from Noah Webster, *The American Magazine*, May, 1788, pp. 307-373.

break his former habits, which is always a painful sacrifice; or the discordance between the manners of his own country and his habits, must give him incessant uneasiness; or he must introduce, into a circle of his friends, the manners in which he was educated. All these consequences may follow at the same time, and the last, which is inevitable, is a public injury. The refinement of manners in every country should keep pace exactly with the increase of its wealth—and perhaps the greatest evil America now feels is, an improvement of taste and manners which its wealth cannot support.

A foreign education is the very source of this evil—it gives young gentlemen of fortune a relish for manners and amusements which are not suited to this country; which, however, when introduced by this class of people, will always become fashionable.

But a corruption of manners is not the sole objection to a foreign education; An attachment to a *foreign* government, or rather a want of attachment to our *own,* is the natural effect of a residence abroad, during the period of youth. It is recorded of one of the Greek cities, that in a treaty with their conquerors, it was required that they should give a certain number of *male children* as hostages for the fulfilment of their engagements. The Greeks absolutely refused, on the principle that these children would imbibe the ideas and embrace the manners of foreigners, or lose their love for their own country: But they offered the same number of *old* men, without hesitation. This anecdote is full of good sense. A man should always form his habits and attachments in the country where he is to reside for life. When these habits are formed, young men may travel without danger of losing their patriotism. A boy who lives in England from twelve to twenty, will be an *Englishman* in his manners and his feelings; but let him remain at home till he is twenty, and form his attachments, he may then be several years abroad, and still be an *American.*[1] There may be exceptions to this observation; but living examples may be mentioned, to prove the truth of the general principle here advanced, respecting the influence of habit.

It may be said that foreign universities furnish much better opportunities of improvement in the sciences than the American. This may be true, and yet will not justify the practice of sending young lads from their own country. There are some branches of science which may be studied to much greater advantage in Europe than in America, particularly chymistry. When these are to be acquired, young gentlemen ought to spare no pains to attend the best professors. It may, therefore, be useful, in some cases, for students to cross the atlantic to *complete* a course of studies; but it is

[1] Cicero was twenty-eight years old when he left Italy to travel into Greece and Asia. "He did not stir abroad," sayd Dr. Middleton, "till he had completed his education at home; for nothing can be more pernicious to a nation, than the necessity of a foreign one." Life of Cicero—Vol. 1, p. 48.

not necessary for them to go early in life, nor to continue a long time. Such instances need not be frequent even now; and the necessity for them will diminish in proportion to the future advancement of literature in America.

It is, however, much questioned whether, in the ordinary course a study, a young man can enjoy greater advantages in Europe than in America. Experience inclines me to raise a doubt, whether the danger to which a youth must be exposed among the sons of dissipation abroad, will not turn the scale in favor of our American colleges. Certain it is, that four fifths of the great literary characters in America never crossed the Atlantic.

But if our universities and schools are not so good as the English or Scotch, it is the business of our rulers to improve them—not to endow them merely; for endowments alone will never make a flourishing seminary—but to furnish them with professors of the first abilities and most assiduous application, and with a complete apparatus for establishing theories by experiments. Nature has been profuse to the Americans, in genius, and in the advantages of climate and soil. If this country, therefore, should long be indebted to Europe for opportunities of acquiring any branch of science in perfection, it must be by means of a criminal neglect of its inhabitants.

The difference in the nature of the American and European governments, is another objection to a foreign education. Men form modes of reasoning or habits of thinking on political subjects, in the country where they are bred—these modes of reasoning may be founded on fact in all countries—but the same principles will not apply in all governments, because of the infinite variety of national opinions and habits. Before a man can be a good Legislator, he must be intimately acquainted with the temper of the people to be governed. No man can be thus acquainted with a people, without residing amongst them and mingling with all companies. For want of this acquaintance, a Turgot and a Price may reason most absurdly upon the constitutions of the American states; and when any person has been long accustomed to believe in the propriety or impropriety of certain maxims or regulations of government, it is very difficult to change his opinions, or to persuade him to adapt this reasoning to new and different circumstances . . .

It is therefore of infinite importance that those who direct the councils of a nation, should be educated in that nation. Not that they should restrict their personal acquaintance to their own country, but their first ideas, attachments and habits should be acquired in the country which they are to govern and defend. When a knowledge of their own country is obtained, and an attachment to its laws and interests deeply fixed in their hearts, then young gentlemen may travel with infinite advantage and perfect safety. I wish not therefore to discourage travelling, but, if possible, to render it more useful to individuals and to the community. My meaning is, that *men* should travel, and not *boys*.

But it is time for the Americans to change their usual route, and travel thro a country which they never think of, or think beneath their notice.— I mean the United States.

While these States were a part of the British Empire, our interest, our feelings, were those of English men—our dependence led us to respect and imitate their manners—and to look up to them for our opinions. We little thought of any national interest in America—and while our commerce and government were in the hands of our parent country, and we had no common interest, we little thought of improving our acquaintance with each other or of removing prejudices, and reconciling the discordant feelings of the inhabitants of the different Provinces. But independence and union render it necessary that the citizens of different States should know each others characters and circumstances—that all jealousies should be removed —that mutual respect and confidence should succeed—and a harmony of views and interests be cultivated by a friendly intercourse. . . .

Americans, unshackle your minds, and act like independent beings. You have been children long enough, subject to the control, and subservient to the interest of a haughty parent. You have now an interest of your own to augment and defend—you have an empire to raise and support by your exertions—and a national character to establish and extend by your wisdom and virtues. To effect these great objects, it is necessary to frame a liberal plan of policy, and to build it on a broad system of education. Before this system can be formed and embraced, the Americans must *believe* and *act* from the belief, that it is dishonorable to waste life in mimicking the follies of other nations, and basking in the sunshine of foreign glory.

George Washington added his voice to condemn the practice of European education and to suggest that the time was ripe for a plan for universal education in these United States.

It is with indescribable regret, that I have seen the youth of the United States migrating to foreign countries, in order to acquire the higher branches of erudition, and to obtain a knowledge of the Sciences. Altho' it would be injustice to many to pronounce the certainty of their imbibing maxims, not congenial with republicanism; it must nevertheless be admitted, that a serious danger is encountered, by sending abroad among other political systems those, who have not well learned the value of their own.

Reprinted from John C. Fitzpatrick, ed., *The Writings of George Washington* (Washington: Government Printing Office 1940), 34, pp. 149-150.

The time is therefore come, when a plan of Universal education ought to be adopted in the United States. . . .

As noted earlier, Washington was a bit premature with this suggestion of universal education in the United States. The extension of federal governmental activity beyond the minimal bounds set by the Constitution was not a popular idea with the common man, who tended generally to feel his problem was to keep the government out of his life, not find areas in which it could extend its power. Further, as noted, education was still commonly associated in the minds of many with the church. The churches and religious organizations were convinced that education should remain generally within their province, in order to insure a godly and moral populace. The had no desire to repeat the excesses and atheistic revelry of the French Revolution, and they saw church-connected education as a means to thwart the importation of "French radicalism."

One demurrer against the extension of educational endeavor was filed by a William Manning of Massachusetts. This now famous essay, entitled "The Key of Libberty," expressed the anti-intellectualism of the early national period of American history. Portions of the "Key of Libberty" constitute the following selection.

35. The Key of Libberty

William Manning

To all the Republicans, Farmers, Mecanicks, and Labourers In Amarica your Canded attention is Requested to the Sentiments of a Labourer

Learning & Knowledg is assential to the preservation of Libberty & unless we have more of it amongue us we Cannot Seporte our Libertyes Long.

I am not a Man of Larning my selfe for I neaver had the advantage of six months schooling in my life. I am no travelor for I neaver was 50 Miles from whare I was born in no direction, & I am no grate reader of antiant history for I always followed hard labour for a living. But I always thought it My duty to search into & see for my selfe in all maters that consansed me

From William Manning, *The Key of Libberty*. . . . , February, 1798. Reprinted in *William and Mary Quarterly*, 3rd Series, XIII, January, 1956.

as a member of society, & when the war began between Brittan & Amarica I was in the prime of Life & highly taken up with Liberty & a free Government. I See almost the first blood that was shed in Concord fite & scores of men dead, dying & wounded in the Cause of Libberty, which caused serious sencations in my mind.

But I believed then & still believ it is a good cause which we aught to defend to the very last, & I have bin a Constant Reader of publick Newspapers & closely attended to men & measures ever sence, through the war, through the operation of paper money, framing Constitutions, makeing & constructing Laws, & seeing what selfish & contracted ideayes of interests would influence the best picked men & bodyes of men.

I have often thought it was imposable ever to seport a free Government, but firmly believing it to be the best sort & the ondly one approved off by heaven it was my unweryed study & prayers to the almighty for many years to find out the real cause & a remidy and I have for many years bin satisfyed in my own mind what the causes are & what would in a grate measure prove a reamidy provided it was carried into efect. . . .

. . . . .

The Reasons why a free government has always failed is from the unreasonable demands & desires of the few. They cant bare to be on a leavel with their fellow cretures, or submit to the determinations of a Lejeslature whare (as they call it) the Swinish Multitude are fairly represented, but sicken at the eydea, & are ever hankering & striving after Monerca or Aristocracy whare the people have nothing to do in maters of government but to seport the few in luxery & idleness.

For these & many other reasons a large majority of those that live without Labour are ever opposed to the prinsaples & operation of a free Government, & though the hole of them do not amount to one eighth part of the people, yet by their combinations, arts & skeems have always made out to destroy it soner or later, which I shall indeavour to prove by considering—

. . . . .

ON THE IGNORANCE OF THE MANY

Solomon said, Train up a Child in the way he should go, & when he is old he will not depart from it. And it is as true that if a child is trained up in the way he should not go, when he is old he will keep to it. It is the universal custom & practis of monorcal & dispotick government to train up their subjects as much in ignorance as they can in matters of government, & to teach them to reverance & worship grate men in office, & to take for truth what ever they say without examining for themselves.

Consiquently when ever Revolutions are brought about & free governments established it is by the influence of a few leeding men, who after they have obtained their object (like other men) can neaver receiv compensation & honours anough from the people for their services, & the people being brought up from their yuths to reverance & respect such men they go on old ways & neglect to search & see for themselves & take care of their own interists. Also being naturally very fond of being flattered, they redily hear to measures proposed by grate men who they are convinced have done them good services. This is the prinsaple ground on which the few work to Destroy a free government.

ON THE COMBINATIONS OF THE FEW

In a free government the few, finding their scheems & vues of interest borne down by the many, to gain the power they cant constitutionally obtain, Always indeavour to git it by cunning & corruption, contious at the same time that userpation when once began the safty of the userper consists ondly in grasping the hole. To efect this no cost nor pains is spared, but they first unite their plans & scheems by asotiations, conventions, & coraspondances with each other. The Marchents asotiate by themselves, the Phitisians by themselves, The Ministers by themselves, the Juditial & Executive Officers are by their professions often called together & know each others minds, & all letirary men & the over grown rich, that can live without labouring, can spare time for consultation. All being bound together by common interest, which is the stronges bond of union, join in their secret corraspondance to counter act the interests of the many & pick their pockets, which is efected ondly for want of the means of knowledg amongue them.

ON LARNING

Larning is of the gratest importance to the seport of a free government, & to prevent this the few are always crying up the advantages of costly collages, national acadimyes & grammar schooles, in ordir to make places for men to live without work, & so strengthen their party. But are always opposed to cheep schools & woman schools, the ondly or prinsaple means by which larning is spred amongue the Many.

ON KNOWLEDGE

The gratest & best meens of obtaining the knowledge nesecary for a free man to have, is by the Liberty of the Press, or publick Newspapers. To counter act and destroy this priviledge the few spare no pains to make them as costly as posable & to contradict everything in them that favours the interests of the Many, putting Darkness for Light, & Light for Darkness, falsehood for truth, & truth for falsehood, &cc. . . .

ON DOCTORS

The Doctors have established their Meditial Societyes & have both their State & County Meetings, by which they have so nearly enielated Quacary of all kinds, that a poor man cant git so grate cures of them now for a ginna, as he could 50 years ago of an old Squaw for halfe a pint of Rhum. The bisness of a Midwife could be purformed 50 years ago for halfe a doller & now it costs a poor man 5 hole ones. . . .

ON LITERARY MEN & COLEDGES

The true prinsaples of Republicanisam & a free government may be taught to the Uths in some of our Coleges & Acadimies for aught I know, but it is evident that other political prinsaples are admited in many of them, or we should not be stunded with Exhibitions in favour of Monocyes & runing down Republican prinsaples as we often be. One thing is prity cartain, that the Schollers are taught to keep up the dignity of their professions, for if we apply for a preacher or a School Master, we are told the price So Much, & they cant go under, for it is agreed upon & they shall be disgrased if they take less, let their abilityes for the servis be what they will. . . .

ON LAWYERS

The Lawyers have established their Bar Meetings & become the most formidable & influential ordir of any in the Government, & though they are nither Juditial nor Executive officers, but a kind of Mule ordir, ingendered by, & many times overawing both. This ordir of men git their living intirely from the quarrils follyes disputes & destreses of the Many & the intricacy of our Laws, & it is from the arts & doings of these men, that the Juditial & Executive officers are furnished with the chief of their bisness & imploy. Consiquently they are bound together by the strongest bonds of union. . . .

ON LARNING

No person who is a frind to Libberty will be against a large expence in Larning, but it aught to be promoted in the cheepest & best manner possable, which in my oppinnion would be:—For every State to maintain as many Coledges in conveniant parts thereof as would be attended upon to give the highest Degrees of Larning, & for every County to keep as many Grammer Schools or Acadimics in conveniant parts thereof as would be attended too by both sects summer & winter, & no student or scholer to pay anything for tuition, and for the County Schooles to pay a purticular attention to teaching the Inglish langueg & qualifying its scholors to teach & govern Common Schools for little children.

And for Every Town to be obliged to keep as Much as six weeks of wrighting school in the winter & twelve weeks of a woman school in the summer in every parte of the town. So that none should be thronged with two many schollers, nor none have too far to travel, & every person be obliged to send his children to school, for the publick are as much interested in the Larning of one child as an other.

If this method of Larning was established we should soone have a plenty of school masters & mistrises as cheep as we could hire other labour, & Labour & Larning would be conected together & lesen the number of those that live without work. Also we should have a plenty of men to fill the highest offices of State for less than halfe we now give. But insted of this mode of Larning the few are always striving to oblige us to maintain grait men with grate salleryes & to maintain Grammer Schools in every town to teach our Children a b c all which is ondly to give imploy to gentlemens sons & make places for men to live without worke. For their is no more need of a mans haveing a knowledge of all the languages to teach a Child to read write & cifer than their is for a farmer to have the marinors art to hold plow. . . .

The American should know his own country and know it well. Such a thesis was held by many during this period, none more insistently than Jedidiah Morse, the great pioneer of American geography. As Morse indicates in the following preface to his *The American Geography* (second edition, 1792), prior geographies had been compiled by Europeans. These were generally based on second-hand information and contained an amazing collection of errors. Frequently, too, it may be noted, these earlier geographies were demonstrations of the remarkable degree of inventiveness and sheer fantasy of their compilers. Such works, however, were not appropriate for the citizens of a new nation. As Webster was hard at work delineating an *American* language and usage, so Morse was presenting an *American* geography.

36. An American Geography

Jedidiah Morse

So imperfect are all the accounts of America hitherto published, even by those who once exclusively professed the best means of information, that from them very little knowledge of this country can be acquired. Europeans have been the sole writers of American Geography, and have too often suffered fancy to supply the place of facts, and thus have led their readers into errors, while they professed to aim at removing their ignorance. But since the United States have become an independent nation, and have risen into Empire, it would be reproachful for them to suffer this ignorance to continue; and the rest of the world have a right now to expect authentic information. To furnish this has been the design of the author of the following work; but he does not pretend that this design is completed, nor will the judicious and candid expect it, when they consider that he has trodden, comparatively, an unbeaten path—that he has had to collect a vast variety of materials—that these have been widely scattered—and that he could derive but little assistance from books already published. Four years have been employed in this work, during which period, the Author has visited the several states in the Union, and maintained an extensive correspondence with men of Science; and in every instance has endeavored to derive his information from the most authentic sources; he has also submitted his manuscripts to the inspection of Gentlemen in the states which they particularly described, for their correction. It is possible, notwithstanding, and indeed very probable, that inaccuracies may have crept in; but he hopes there are none of any great importance, and that such as may be observed, will not be made the subject of severe censure, but ascribed to some pardonable cause. He flatters himself, however, that the work now offered to the public, will be found to be as accurate, complete and impartial as the present state of American Geography and History could furnish. After all, like the Nation of which it treats, it is but

Reprinted from Jedidiah Morse, *The American Geography*, second edition, 1792.

an infant, and as such solicits the fostering care of the country it describes; it will grow and improve as the nation advances towards maturity, and the Author will gratefully acknowledge every friendly communication which will tend to make it perfect.

In the prosecution of the work, he has aimed at utility rather than originality, and of course, when he has met with publications suited to his purpose, he has made a free use of them; and he thinks it proper here to observe, that, to avoid unnecessary trouble, he has frequently used the words as well as the ideas of the writers, although the reader has not been particularly apprized of it. . . .

Nearly everyone, however, was convinced of the necessary connection between education and the preservation of the ideals that had launched the new nation. This idea may be seen in the following excerpts from various state constitutions. Note the continued belief in education as a necessary influence to prevent "vice and immorality" and to encourage virtue in the citizens of the new nation. Probably the most famous statement of this belief is found in the Ordinance of 1787: "Religion, morality, and knowledge being necessary to good government and the happiness of mankind, schools and the means of education shall forever be encouraged.*"

The sentiment of this famous Northwest Ordinance of 1787 is reflected in such state constitutions as that of Vermont (1787). New Hampshire, too, echoed the conviction that education was necessary for both democracy and virtue.

Pennsylvania went so far as to insist that education be extended to the poor (gratis).

37. Section 38 of the Vermont State Constitution of 1787

Sec. 38. Laws for the encouragement of virtue, and prevention of vice and immorality, ought to be constantly kept in force, and duly executed;

Reprinted from Benjamin Perley Poore, *The Federal and State Constitutions, Colonial Charters, and Other Organic Laws of the United States,* 2 Vols. (Washington: Government Printing Office, 1878).

* Ordinance of 1787, Article III, Reprinted in full in Benjamin Perley Poore, *The Federal and State Constitutions, Colonial Charters, and Other Organic Laws of the United States,* 2 Vols. (Washington: Government Printing Office, 1878).

and a competent number of schools ought to be maintained in each town for the convenient instruction of youth; and one or more grammar schools be incorporated, and properly supported in each county in this State. And all religious societies, or bodies of men, that may be hereafter united or incorporated, for the advancement of religion and learning, or for other pious and charitable purposes, shall be encouraged and protected in the enjoyment of the privileges, immunities, and estates, which they in justice ought to enjoy under such regulations as the General Assembly of this State shall direct.

38. Section 83 of the New Hampshire State Constitution of 1784 and 1792

Sec. 83. Knowledge and learning generally diffused through a community being essential to the preservation of a free government, spreading the opportunities and advantages of education through the various parts of the country being highly conducive to promote this end, it shall be the duty of the legislatures and magistrates, in all future periods of this government, to cherish the interest of literature and the sciences, and all seminaries and public schools; to encourage private and public institutions, rewards and immunities for the promotion of agriculture, arts, sciences, commerce, trade, manufactures, and natural history of the country; to countenance and inculcate the principles of humanity and general benevolence, public and private charity, industry and economy, honesty and punctuality, sincerity, sobriety, and all social affections and generous sentiments among the people.

39. Sections 1 and 2 of the Pennsylvania State Constitution of 1790 and 1838

Sec. 1. The legislature shall, as soon as conveniently may be, provide, by law, for the establishment of schools throughout the State, in such manner that the poor may be taught *gratis.*

Both of the above selections are reprinted from Benjamin Perley Poore, *The Federal and State Constitutions, Colonial Charters, and Other Organic Laws of the United States,* 2 Vols. (Washington: Government Printing Office, 1878).

Sec. 2. The arts and sciences shall be promoted in one or more seminaries of learning.

The recognition of the obligation of a state to provide for such items as education which, strictly speaking, went beyond mere protection of temporal interests and political rights, may possibly be traced to the provision in the Massachusetts Constitution of 1780, in large part the work of John Adams. In Chapter 6, Section II, of this document, under the heading "The Encouragement of Literature, etc.," Adams spelled out this extension of the obligation of the state. The clauses therein were later incorporated into other state constitutions but are all (according to Charles Francis Adams) "manifestly taken from this source. . . ."

40. The Encouragement of Literature

John Adams

Wisdom and knowledge, as well as virtue, diffused generally among the body of the people, being necessary for the preservation of their rights and liberties, and as these depend on spreading the opportunities and advantages of education in the various parts of the country and among the different orders of the people, it shall be the duty of the legislators and magistrates in all future periods of this commonwealth to cherish the interests of literature and sciences and all seminaries of them—especially the University of Cambridge, public schools and grammar schools in the towns—to encourage private societies and public institutions, rewards and immunities for the promotion of agriculture, arts, sciences, commerce, trades, manufactures, and a natural history of the country; to countenance and inculcate the principles of humanity and general benevolence, public and private charity, industry and frugality, honesty and punctuality in their dealings, sincerity, good humor, and all social affections and generous sentiments among the people. . . .

From *The Political Writings of John Adams,* edited by John A. Peer, Jr., copyright ©, 1954, by The Liberal Arts Press, Inc., reprinted by permission of the Liberal Arts Press Division of The Bobbs-Merrill Company, Inc., p. 103.

One of the major educational theories that prevailed during the early national period was that institutions of higher learning should be controlled by the state. Obviously, there were two ways in which this end could be realized. The states could either make state universities of the existing colonial colleges, or they could establish new state institutions themselves. The former method seemed the simpler and cheaper, and it was the first to be tried. In 1816, the New Hampshire State Legislature passed a bill making Dartmouth College a state university. The board of trustees of Dartmouth, however, (being staunch Federalists) sharply disagreed with this Jeffersonian notion of a state system of education and brought suit in the state supreme court to regain control of the school. Their appeal being therein denied, they hired the eloquent Daniel Webster to present their appeal to the U.S. Supreme Court.

With U.S. Chief Justice John Marshall writing the decision, the U.S. Supreme Court revised the state ruling and declared the legislation making Dartmouth a state university to be unconstitutional.

Marshall's decision had far-reaching effects for higher education. Blocking the states from one method of gaining control of higher education, it forced them to act on the other, i.e., to build their own state universities. Furthermore, of course, the Dartmouth College case guaranteed the integrity of private institutional charters from state negation, thus stimulating their further growth and support by private donors. The Dartmouth case may be followed in the next sequence of readings, which include the message of New Hampshire Governor, William Plumer, to his legislature requesting enactment of a bill to make Dartmouth a state school, a letter from Jefferson to Plumer supporting his idea, and portions of the famous decision by Chief Justice John Marshall of the U.S. Supreme Court.

41. Message to the New Hampshire Legislature

William Plumer

There is no system of government, where the general diffusion of knowledge is so necessary as in a Republic. It is therefore not less the duty than the

Reprinted from William Plumer, *New Hampshire Patriot* (Concord), June 11, 1816.

interest of the State to patronize and support the cause of literature and the sciences. So sensible were our ancestors of this, that they early made provision for schools, academies and a college, the good effects of which we daily experience. But all literary establishments, like every thing human, if not duly attended to, are subject to decay; permit me therefore to invite your consideration to the state and condition of Dartmouth college, the head of our learned institutions. As the State has contributed liberally to the establishment of its funds, and as our constituents have a deep interest in its prosperity, it has a strong claim to our attention. The charter of that college was granted December 30th, 1769, by John Wentworth, who was then governor of New Hampshire under the authority of the British king. As it emanated from royalty, it contained, as was natural it should, principles congenial to monarchy. Among others it established trustees, made seven a quorum, and authorized a majority of those present to remove any of its members which they might consider unfit or incapable, and the survivors *to perpetuate the board by themselves electing others to supply vacancies*. This last principle is hostile to the spirit and genius of a free government. Sound policy therefore requires that the mode of election should be changed, and that trustees in future should be elected by some other body of men. To increase the number of trustees, would not only increase the security of the college, but be a mean of interesting more men in its prosperity. If it should be made in future the duty of the President, annually in May, to report to the Governor a full and particular account of the state of the funds, their receipts and expenditures, the number of students and their progress, and generally the state and condition of the college, and the governor to communicate this statement to the legislature in their June session; this would form a check upon the proceedings of the trustees, excite a spirit of attention in the officers and students of the college, and give to the legislature such information as would enable them to act with greater propriety upon whatever may relate to that institution.

The college was formed for the public good, not for the benefit or emolument of its trustees; and the right to amend and improve acts of incorporation of this nature, has been exercised by all governments, both monarchical and republican. Sir Thomas Gresham established a fund to support lecturers in Gresham college in London, upon the express condition that the lecturers should be unmarried men, and upon their being married their interest in the fund should absolutely cease; but the British parliament in the year 1768, passed a law removing the college to another place, and explicitly enacted that if the lecturers were married, or should marry, they should receive their fees and stipend out of the fund, any restriction or limitation in the will of the said Gresham to the contrary notwithstanding. In this country a number of the States have passed laws that made material changes in the charters of their colleges. And in this State acts of incorporation of a similar nature have frequently been amended and changed by the legislature. By the several acts incorporating towns their limits were established; but whenever the legislature judged that the public good required a town to be made into two, they have made the division, and in some instances against the remonstrance of a majority of its inhabitants. In the charter of Dartmouth college it is expressly provided that the president, trustees, professors, tutors and other officers shall take the oath of allegiance to the British king; but if the laws of the United States, as well as those of New-Hampshire, abolished by implication that part of the charter, much more might they have done it directly and by express words. These facts shew the authority of the legislature to interfere upon this subject; and I trust you will make such further provisions as will render this important institution more useful to mankind. . . .

WILLIAM PLUMER.

State of New-Hampshire,
June 6, 1816.

42. Reply to Governor Plumer on the Dartmouth College Case, 1816

Thomas Jefferson

MONTICELLO, July 21, 1816.

I thank you, Sir, for the copy you have been so good as to send me, of your late speech to the legislature of your State, which I have read a second time with great pleasure, as I had before done in the public papers. It is replete with sound principles, and truly republican. Some articles, too, are worthy of peculiar notice. The idea that institutions established for the use of the nation cannot be touched nor modified, even to make them answer their end, because of rights gratuitously supposed in those employed to manage them in trust for the public, may perhaps be a salutary provision against the abuses of a monarch, but is most absurd against the nation itself. Yet our lawyers and priests generally inculcate this doctrine, and suppose that preceding generations held the earth more freely than we do;

Reprinted from Andrew A. Lipscomb and A. E. Bergh, eds., *The Writings of Thomas Jefferson,* XV (Washington: Thomas Jefferson Memorial Association, 1903), pp. 46-47.

had a right to impose laws on us, unalterable by ourselves, and that we, in like manner, can make laws and impose burdens on future generations, which they will have no right to alter; in fine, that the earth belongs to the dead and not the living. I remark also the phenomenon of a chief magistrate recommending the reduction of his own compensation. This is a solecism of which the wisdom of our late Congress cannot be accused. I, however, place economy among the first and most important of republican virtues, and public debt as the greatest of the dangers to be feared. We see in England the consequences of the want of it, their laborers reduced to live on a penny in the shilling of their earnings, to give up bread, and resort to oatmeal and potatoes for food; and their landholders exiling themselves to live in penury and obscurity abroad, because at home the government must have all the clear profits of their land. In fact, they see the fee simple of the island transferred to the public creditors, all its profits going to them for the interest of their debts. Our laborers and landholders must come to this also, unless they severely adhere to the economy you recommend. I salute you with entire esteem and respect.

43. Supreme Court Decision Sustaining the Dartmouth College Charter

John Marshall

This is an action of trover, brought by the trustees of Dartmouth College against William H. Woodward, in the State Court of New Hampshire, for the book of records, corporate seal, and other corporate property, to which the plaintiffs allege themselves to be entitled. . . .

The title of the plaintiffs originates in a charter dated the 13th day of December, in the year 1769, incorporating twelve persons therein mentioned, by the name of "The Trustees of Dartmouth College," granting to them and their successors the usual corporate privileges and powers, and authorizing the trustees, who are to govern the college, to fill up all vacancies which may be created in their own body.

The defendant claims under three acts of the legislature of New Hampshire, the most material of which was passed on the 27th of June, 1816, and is entitled, "an act to amend the charter, and enlarge and improve the corporation of Dartmouth College." Among other alterations in the charter,

Reprinted from *The Trustees of Dartmouth College v. Woodward,* 4 Wheaton 518: 4 Legal Ed., 629 (1819).

this act increases the number of trustees to twenty-one, gives the appointment of the additional members to the executive of the state, and creates a board of overseers, with power to inspect and control the most important acts of the trustees. This board consists of twenty-five persons. The president of the senate, the speaker of the house of representatives, of New Hampshire, and the Governor and Lieutenant-Governor of Vermont, for the time being, are to be members *ex officio*. The board is to be completed by the Governor and council of New Hampshire, who are also empowered to fill all vacancies which may occur. The acts of the 18th and 26th of December are supplemental to that of the 27th of June, and are principally intended to carry that act into effect.

The majority of the trustees of the college have refused to accept this amended charter, and have brought this suit for the corporate property, which is in possession of a person holding by virtue of the acts which have been stated.

It can require no argument to prove that the circumstances of this case constitute a contract. An application is made to the crown for a charter to incorporate a religious and literary institution. In the application, it is stated that large contributions have been made for the object, which will be conferred on the corporation as soon as it shall be created. The charter is granted, and on its faith the property is conveyed. Surely in this transaction every ingredient of a complete and legitimate contract is to be found.

The points for consideration are:

1. Is this contract protected by the constitution of the United States?
2. Is it impaired by the acts under which the defendant holds? . . .

The parties in this case differ less on general principles, less on the true construction of the constitution in the abstract, than on the application of those principles to this case, and on the true construction of the charter of 1769. This is the point on which the cause essentially depends. If the act of incorporation be a grant of political power, if it create a civil institution to be employed in the administration of the government, or if the funds of the college be public property, or if the state of New Hampshire, as a government, be alone interested in its transactions, the subject is one in which the legislature of the state may act according to its own judgment, unrestrained by any limitation of its power imposed by the constitution of the United States.

But if this be a private eleemosynary institution, endowed with a capacity to take property for objects unconnected with government, whose funds are bestowed by individuals on the faith of the charter; if the donors have stipulated for the future disposition and management of those funds in the manner prescribed by themselves, there may be more difficulty in the case, although neither the persons who have made these stipulations nor those for whose benefit they were made, should be parties to the cause. Those who are no longer interested in the property, may yet retain such an interest in the preservation of their own arrangements as to have a right to insist that those arrangements shall be held sacred. Or, if they have themselves disappeared, it becomes a subject of serious and anxious inquiry, whether those whom they have legally empowered to represent them forever may not assert all the rights which they possessed, while in being; whether, if they be without personal representatives who may feel injured by a violation of the compact, the trustees be not so completely their representatives, in the eye of the law, as to stand in their place, not only as respects the government of the college, but also as respects the maintenance of the college charter. . . .

. . . Dartmouth College is really endowed by private individuals, who have bestowed their funds for the propogation of the Christian religion among the Indians, and for the promotion of piety and learning generally. From these funds the salaries of the tutors are drawn; and these salaries lessen the expense of education to the students. It is, then, an eleemosynary, and, as far as respects its funds, a private corporation.

Do its objects stamp on it a different character? Are the trustees and professors public officers, invested with any portion of political power, partaking in any degree in the administration of civil government, and performing duties which flow from the sovereign authority?

That education is an object of national concern, and a proper subject of legislation, all admit. That there may be an institution founded by government, and placed entirely under its immediate control, the officers of which would be public officers, amenable exclusively to government, none will deny. But is Dartmouth College such an institution? Is education altogether in the hands of government? Does every teacher of youth become a public officer, and do donations for the purpose of education necessarily become public property, so far that the will of the legislature, not the will of the donor, becomes the law of the donation? These questions are of serious moment to society, and deserve to be well considered.

. . . . .

From this review of the charter, it appears that Dartmouth College is an eleemosynary institution, incorporated for the purpose of perpetuating the application of the bounty of the donors, to the specified objects of that bounty; that its trustees or governors were originally named by the founder, and invested with the power of perpetuating themselves; that they are not public officers, nor is it a civil institution, participating in the administration of government; but a charity school, or a seminary of education, incorporated for the preservation of its property, and the perpetual application of that property to the objects of its creation. . . .

Almost all eleemosynary corporations, those which are created for the promotion of religion, of charity, or of education, are of the same character. The law of this case is the law of all. In every literary or charitable institution, unless the objects of the bounty be themselves incorporated, the whole legal interest is in trustees, and can be asserted only by them. The donors, or claimants of the bounty, if they can appear in court at all, can appear only to complain of the trustees. In all other situations, they are identified with, and personated by, the trustees; and their rights are to be defended and maintained by them. Religion, Charity, and Education, are, in the law of England, legatees or donees, capable of receiving bequests or donations in this form. They appear in court, and claim or defend by the corporation. Are they of so little estimation in the United States that contracts for their benefit must be excluded from the protection of words which, in their natural import, include them? Or do such contracts so necessarily require new-modeling by the authority of the legislature that the ordinary rules of construction must be disregarded in order to leave them exposed to legislative alteration?

All feel that these objects are not deemed unimportant in the United States. The interest which this case has excited proves that they are not. The framers of the constitution did not deem them unworthy of its care and protection. They have, though in a different mode, manifested their respect for science, by reserving to the government of the Union the power "to promote the progress of science and useful arts, by securing for limited times to authors and inventors the exclusive right to their respective writings and discoveries." They have so far withdrawn science, and the useful arts, from the action of the state governments. Why, then, should they be supposed so regardless of contracts made for the advancement of literature as to intend to exclude them from provisions made for the security of ordinary contracts between man and man? No reason for making this supposition is perceived.

If the insignificance of the object does not require that we should exclude contracts respecting it from the protection of the constitution, neither, as we conceive, is the policy of leaving them subject to legislative alteration so apparent as to require a forced construction of that instrument in order to effect it. These eleemosynary institutions do not fill the place, which would otherwise be occupied by government, but that which would otherwise remain vacant. They are complete acquisitions to literature. They are donations to education; donations which any government must be disposed rather to encourage than to discountenance. It requires no very critical examination of the human mind to enable us to determine that one great inducement to these gifts is the conviction felt by the giver, that the disposition he makes of them is immutable. It is probable that no man ever was, and that no man ever will be, the founder of a college, believing at the time that an act of incorporation constitutes no security for the institution; believing that it is immediately to be deemed a public institution, whose funds are to be governed and applied, not by the will of the donor, but by the will of the legislature. All such gifts are made in the pleasing, perhaps delusive hope, that the charity will flow forever in the channel which the givers have marked out for it. If every man finds in his own bosom strong evidence of the universality of this sentiment, there can be but little reason to imagine that the framers of our constitution were strangers to it, and that, feeling the necessity and policy of giving permanence and security to contracts, of withdrawing them from the influence of legislative bodies, whose fluctuating policy, and repeated interferences, produced the most perplexing and injurious embarrassments, they still deemed it necessary to leave these contracts subject to those interferences. The motives for such an exception must be very powerful, to justify the construction which makes it. . . .

SECTION 2

The Character of Education in the New Republic

In order to get an overview of the society of America and its dominant educational characteristics during this period, it is sometimes helpful to take cognizance of the impressions of some of the non-American visitors to our shores. How did the American appear to his European cousins who came to observe him in his new habitat as the citizen of a new nation?

The American, by and large, was eager to learn, and he impressed foreign observers with his easy acceptance of new ideas and thoughts. This trait was especially noted by two Hungarian visitors, Francis and Theresa Pulszky, in their study, *White, Red, Black; Sketches of*

American Society . . . . (1853). They compared the British and American characters in this respect, and this comparison they extended to education.

44. The Generosity of Americans

Francis and Theresa Pulszky

THE Americans, unlike their English brothers, take care of the education of all the white children of the free States, and endeavor to do the same in the South, and not only in the cities, but also in the rural districts. The American government in the States and in Washington does not rest on the exclusive influence of the wealthier classes, but on the education of the people at large. Contrary to English custom, it is the State, not the Church, which provides for the schools; yet secular education has not impaired the religiosity of the people.

. . . . .

But with the English there is a class less intent on making money, and sometimes generous in spending, viz., the old aristocracy, which has inherited the accumulated riches of many generations. In America there is no such class; to favor the eldest son is not countenanced either by laws or by customs of the people; equal partition amongst the children is the law and the habit of the country. Wealth, therefore, changes hands rapidly. And yet the great bulk of Americans, though covetous of gain, are, on the whole, more generous than the English. To those who doubt this fact we point to the enormous amount of the numerous and continuous gifts and contributions for churches, hospitals, colleges, libraries, and charitable institutions of every description. The lower classes in America are better educated than in England; they are better off, and kind-heartedness and generosity are always characteristic with those who earn their livelihood by their labors and not by their capital. Moreover, the democratic institutions of universal suffrage and the frequent elections make the wealthy classes dependent on the working people for attaining honors; with universal suffrage individual liberty is impossible; one way, therefore, to get popularity is the establishment of institutions for the public.

. . . . .

The English nation is eminently conservative. It has attained the highest position to which it has aspired; it has now only to maintain it, in politics and in literature. New ideas, and even new words, are disliked in England;

Reprinted from Francis and Theresa Pulszky, *White, Red, Black; Sketches of American Society.* . . . (New York: Redfield, 1853), Vol. II, pp. 243-244, 248.

society is settled, and fears to be disturbed; the most necessary reforms are carried slowly, and with timorous hands. In America, the spirit of progress is bold, and often encroaching; with the exception of the Southern society, it changes its aspect incessantly; new ideas easily get a fair chance of being practically tried; the public at large does not shrink from testing at once different solutions of a political problem, and the sovereignty of the States affords great opportunity for it. New words are coined by the dozen; the old oak of the Anglo-Norman language still sprouts here as sprightly as it did in England three centuries ago, and though many of the leaves will soon wither and fall, others will remain as verdant as those which adorn the cisatlantic branches of the mighty stem.

Adam de Gurowski made a similar comparison with regard to the American desire to learn which follows in Selection 45.

In spite of these tendencies, the European generally found the American mind to be of a markedly practical and non-speculative type. One visitor, Edward Dicey of England, in his *Six Months in the Federal States* (1863) was markedly struck by the amazing uniformity of American society. This he attributed to American education and its universal diffusion throughout the country. In essence, everyone has learned the same sort of things in the same sort of language. Consequently, he found, everyone thinks in about the same sort of way. His comments are particularly interesting in this regard (see Selection 46).

Another important aspect of American society, one which impressed Francis Grund, was the tremendous influence of morality and religion in the country (see Selection 47).

45. The American Eagerness to Learn

Adam G. de Gurowski

Not less salient and peculiar than the public spirit, and created by the same or similar causes, is the characteristic of the American mind manifested in the thirst for knowledge, for information. It imperatively urges the individual with a pertinacity and generality not to be met with in any

Reprinted from Adam G. de Gurowski, *America and Europe* (New York: D. Appleton and Co., 1857), pp. 63-64.

other nation on the globe, to satisfy this noble mental irritation, to satisfy it by sacrifices of the time and means, whether large or small, at his disposal. It is thus the most brilliantly projecting feature, and an individual property of this people. Not the wealthy, not the better circumstanced are principally the expression of these urgings, but it is rather special to the laborious masses. Not outward worldly leisure produces or evokes it, but an inward impulse. That is one of the cardinal differences between American and European populations. This craving results from the radical recognition of equality of rights in every individual, inspiring him with self-consciousness, with self-respect, and opening before him the bright horizon of nobler purposes and aims. It is not a transmission by blood, nor the result of certain liberal concessions, called in Europe liberal institutions. In the English people, the nearest kindred to the majority of Americans, and living under liberal institutions, this spontaneity is not awakened, and the mass still gropes its way in a self-contented ignorance.

Neither is this craving incited by an admonition, exercised from above, by the efforts of a government, by the prevalent suggestions or example of a so-called superior stratum of society. This American phenomenon strengthens the faith that the human race is to bask in floods of light, that enlightenment is the essence of man's nature, although its effusion may have been benumbed for uncounted ages. This characteristic trait redeems at once the broadest and most truly democratic comprehension of a people from the cavils heaped on it by the apostles of an absolute supreme authority, which, according to their assertions, is to hover providentially above the masses, to take the initiative and to direct their mental development.

46. The Uniformity of American Society

Edward Dicey

In a moral as opposed to a material point of view, the most striking feature about American society is its uniformity. Everybody, as a rule, holds the same opinions about everything, and expresses his views, more or less, in the same language. These views are often correct, almost invariably intelligent and creditable to the holders. But still, even at the risk of hearing paradoxes defended, you cannot help wishing, at times, for a

Reprinted from Edward Dicey, *Six Months in the Federal States* (London: Macmillan and Co., 1863), pp. 167-169.

little more of originality. I believe that this monotony in the tone of American talk and opinion arises from the universal diffusion of education. Everybody is educated up to a certain point, and very few are educated above it. They have all learned the same lessons under the same teachers, and, in consequence, share the same sentiments to a degree which it is difficult for an Englishman to appreciate beforehand. This monotony is infinitely more striking in the men than in the women. Ninety-nine American lads in a hundred go through exactly the same system of training. Up to eighteen or nineteen, they are carefully, if not very deeply, grounded in all the branches of a good ordinary English education. Then they go into business, and from that time their intellectual self-culture ceases. Unless they happen to travel, they have very little time for reading anything except the newspapers. The women pursue their education even after marriage, and are in consequence better read and more intellectual in their tastes than English ladies. In the long run, however, the national tone of mind is always derived from the male sex, and therefore the prevalent tone of America is not that of a highly educated society. I do not mean to say, for one moment, that there are not hundreds and thousands of men of really first-class education in the Northern States. On the contrary, some of the most thoroughly educated men it has been my lot to meet with have been Americans. I am speaking of the mass, not of individuals. This opinion of mine, if it is correct, explains a fact which otherwise would seem discouraging: I mean the small share taken by educated men—in our sense of the word—in American politics. The truth is that if America were governed to any great extent by politicians of classical education, the country would not be fairly represented by its rulers. It is not the case that the fact of a gentleman having received a refined culture is any disqualification to him in the eyes of the constituencies. On the other hand, it is a very small recommendation. I do not deny that this is, in itself, an evil; but the true nature of the evil is not that men of education are disqualified from entering a political career in America, but that they form so small a class that they possess no political influence. Just in the same way, there is no doubt that, relatively to the period, there were more highly educated men in the Union half a century ago than there are now. The early settlers in any new country bring with them a higher degree of individual culture than they can impart to their children. In the same ratio, however, that the education of the individual decreases, the average education of the mass increases, and, on the whole, the general tone of the nation gains in consequence.

47. Influence of Morality and Religion in the U.S.

Francis Grund

Whatever contributes to confirm a people in the habitual exercise of freedom is an additional guarantee of its continuance; and whatever has been instrumental in procuring that freedom, or is associated with it in their minds, must be preserved with religious care, lest liberty itself should suffer in their estimation. This is the case with the doctrines of Christianity in the United States. Religion has been the basis of the most important American settlements; religion kept their little community together; religion assisted them in their revolutionary struggle; it was religion to which they appealed in defending their rights, and it was religion, in fine, which taught them to prize their liberties. It is with the solemnities of religion that the Declaration of Independence is yet annually read to the people from the pulpit, or that Americans celebrate the anniversaries of the most important events in their history. It is to religion they have recourse whenever they wish to impress the popular feeling with anything relative to their country; and it is religion which assists them in all their national undertakings. The Americans look upon religion as a promoter of civil and political liberty; and have, therefore, transferred to it a large portion of the affection which they cherish for the institutions of their country. In other countries, where religion has become the instrument of oppression, it has been the policy of the liberal party to diminish its influence; but in America its promotion is essential to the constitution.

Religion presides over their councils, aids in the execution of the laws, and adds to the dignity of the judges. Whatever is calculated to diminish its influence and practice has a tendency to weaken the government, and is, consequently, opposed to the peace and welfare of the United States. It would have a direct tendency to lessen the respect for the law, to bring disorder into their public deliberations, and to retard the administration of justice.

The deference which the Americans pay to morality is scarcely inferior to their regard for religion, and is, in part, based upon the latter. The least solecism in the moral conduct of a man is attributed to his want of religion, and is visited upon him as such. It is not the offense itself, but the outrage on society, which is punished. They see in a breach of morals a direct violation of religion; and in this, an attempt to subvert the political institutions of the country. These sentiments are all-powerful in checking

Reprinted from Francis J. Grund, *The Americans in Their Moral, Social, and Political Relations* (Boston: Marsh, Copen and Lyons, 1837), pp. 164-165.

the appearance of vice, even if they are not always sufficient to preclude its existence.

One of the most striking aspects of the new American culture was apparently (to judge by its frequent inclusion in European travel narratives) its decidedly commercial orientation. The urge towards material progress, economic success, and the aquisition of wealth seemed to many visitors to be almost the single-minded obsession of early Americans. This entrepreneurial spirit of individual enterprise was the result of the old Protestant ethic in secularized form germinating in the hospitable and rich soil of a democratic society.

The educational reflection of this character trait of the American was evident in several ways. Representative of the connection of education with the encouragement of industrial enterprise, the legislature of the state of Illinois recommended the following provision for the creation of industrial universities to Congress in 1853.

48. Recommendation to Create Industrial Universities

Illinois State Legislature

Whereas, the spirit and progress of this age and country demand the culture of the highest order of intellectual attainment in theoretic and industrial science; and

Whereas, it is impossible that our commerce and prosperity will continue to increase without calling into requisition all the elements of internal thrift arising from the labors of the farmer, the mechanic, and the manufacturer, by every fostering effort within the reach of the government; and

Whereas, a system of Industrial Universities, liberally endowed in each state of the union, co-operative with each other, and with the Smithsonian Institute at Washington, would develop a more liberal and practical education among the people, tend to more intellectualize the rising generation and eminently conduct to the virtue, intelligence and true glory of our common country; therefore be it

Reprinted by permission as quoted in Edmund J. James, *The Origin of the Land Grant Act of 1862 and Some Account of Its Author, Jonathan B. Turner* (Urbana: Univ. of Illinois Press, 1910), pp. 16-17.

Resolved, by the House of Representatives, the Senate concurring herein, That our Senators in Congress be instructed, and our Representatives be requested, to use their best exertions to procure the passage of a law of Congress donating to each state in the Union an amount of public lands not less in value than five hundred thousand dollars, for the liberal endowment of a system of Industrial Universities, one in each state in the Union, to co-operate with each other, and with the Smithsonian Institute at Washington, for the more liberal and practical education of our industrial classes and their teachers; a liberal and varied education, adapted to the manifold wants of a practical and enterprising people, and a provision for such educational facilities being in manifest concurrence with the intimations of the popular will, it urgently demands the united efforts of our strength.

Resolved, That the Governor is hereby authorized to forward a copy of the foregoing resolutions to our Senators and Representatives in Congress, and to the Executive and Legislature of each of our sister States, inviting them to co-operate with us in this meritorious enterprise.

American concern for education in its rural areas was expressed as early as 1787 in an article appearing in *The Columbia Magazine, or Monthly Miscellany*. This article suggested a plan for education with special reference to country life in sparsely settled regions. It motivated Dr. John de la Howe of South Carolina to provide for the creation of such a manual labor school in 1796, which was the first of its type in the United States and is still in operation.

49. Plan for Establishing Schools in a New Country, Where the Inhabitants are Thinly Settled, and Whose Children are to be Educated With a Special Reference to a Country Life

John de la Howe

Take any number of settlers, we will suppose sixty families, collected in a village, and they will be able to support a schoolmaster, and easily maintain their children at school: for twenty shillings a year, paid by each

Reprinted from *The Columbia Magazine, or Monthly Miscellany*, April, 1789, pp. 356-359.

family, will make up a competent salary for the master, and the children will be cloathed and fed at home.

But if sixty families are dispersed over a large tract of country, from twenty to forty miles in extent, how shall their children receive the benefits of education? The master's salary, it is true, can be paid as in the former case; but few parents will be disposed to incur the heavy expense of sending their children from home, and boarding them at a distant school. Hence, in such a scattered settlement, general ignorance will ensue; and the people consequently degenerate into vice, irreligion and barbarism. —To remedy evils of such magnitude will be difficult; perhaps it will be thought impracticable: to attempt it, however, will be laudable; and all those who have the dearest interests of society at heart, will give the measure their support.

If by charitable donations, or by grants of the state, adequate funds could be formed, to defray the expenses of the board and tuition of such children, the evils before mentioned would be remedied: but such funds are not to be hoped for: and if they could be obtained, it might well be doubted whether that would be the best mode of educating children destined for a laborious country life. There the boys are to be the future farmers, and the girls the farmers' wives. If both could, in early life, be well instructed in the various branches of their future employments, they would make better husbands, better wives, and more useful citizens. And if the mode of communicating such instruction could at the same time enable them largely to contribute to their own support, another important advantage would be gained.—These reflections have given rise to the following PLAN OF EDUCATION for a Country Life.

1. Let three or four hundred acres of land be appropriated for the use of a school: let it consist of a meadow, tillage and wood land, in convenient proportions.

2. Let a skilful and industrious manager be provided, who shall himself be a complete farmer, and have two labourers, one acquainted with farming, the other with gardening, to assist him.

3. Let the farm be completely stocked, and all the requisite carriages and husbandry utensils provided: such tools as are designed for boys, to be made of sizes suited to their strength.

4. Let the necessary buildings be erected for a school, a boarding house, a barn and work-shop. These may be very plain and cheap, and at the same time very comfortable. The necessary furniture and tools must also be provided.

5. A school master and a schoolmistress must be chosen with much circumspection. The latter will be the housekeeper.

6. A cook will be necessary; and she should know how to dress the plain, wholesome food of the country, in the best manner.

7. The childrens' beds and bedding, cloaths and materials for cloathing must be provided by their parents.

The necessary foundations being thus laid, the school and farm may be conducted agreeably to the following regulations.

1. No boy or girl under eight years of age should be admitted.

2. Both boys and girls should be taught to read, write and cypher. The boys should also be instructed in every useful branch of husbandry and gardening, and the girls in every kind of work necessary for farmers' wives to know and practice.

3. For the purpose of working, let the boys be divided into such a number of classes as shall be judged convenient, distributing equal proportions of the larger and smaller boys to each class. Whenever the nature of the work to be done will admit of it; let equal portions of it be assigned to the several classes, in order to excite their emulation, to excel in industry and skill: and for this reason each portion of land should be cultivated, through a whole season, by the same class to which it was first allotted.—It will be obvious to direct the several boys in the same class, to perform such parts of the general labours required of it, as shall be adapted to their several capacities and strength.

4. All the boys may be taught the methods of making and rearing nurseries of the most useful kind of fruit trees, shrubs and bushes, and of improving the former by grafting and budding. Each boy should have an equal portion of land allotted to him, on which he should raise a nursery; and when he has finished his course of education, should be allowed to take home with him all the trees, shrubs and bushes he has reared and cultivated; excepting only such a proportion as shall be requisite for supplying the school-farm. In like manner he should be allowed to take home with him a collection of useful garden seeds. In this way the most valuable fruits and plants would in a few years be spread and cultivated through the whole settlement.

5. When orchards shall be grown, they may be instructed in the art of making and fermenting cyder, so as to produce a soft and pleasant liquor.

6. A small brewery may be erected on the farm, and all the boys taught to malt barley and oats; and both boys and girls may be taught the art of brewing, so far, at least, as the same might be practiced in every farmer's family.—Perhaps by extending the plan of the malthouse and brewery, they might be able to supply that wholesome and nourishing liquor, good beer, to a great part of the settlement; and thus the use of pernicious, distilled liquors be superseded. Malt, at least, might thus be furnished, and yield a small revenue towards supporting the school.

7. The management of cattle will make a necessary branch of their education; and the modern method of managing bees will well deserve their attention.

8. Tending the cattle, and providing fuel and fencing stuff, will be the principal employments of the winter. But the boys may also make the wood-work of all those utensils of husbandry which will be requisite for the ensuing session. The elder boys will be capable of handling axes, and all the other tools used in those employments.

9. The girls will be taught to sew, to knit, to spin, to cook, to make beds, to clean house, to make and mend their own cloaths, to make the boys cloaths when cut out, and to mend them—to milk cows, and to make butter and cheese.

10. That they may learn to cook and perform all other household work, they should be divided into classes, in the same manner in which the boys were classed, and assist the house keeper and cook, a week at a time, in rotation.

11. A collection of children, from eight to fourteen or fifteen years of age, thus regularly employed, on a good farm, would be nearly able to maintain themselves; and if the expences of their schooling can thus be reduced as low, or nearly as low, as when, in ordinary cases, they live at home, the great obstacle to their education will be removed.

12. The winter will be the season most favourable for the literary instruction of the children; as then they will have but few necessary avocations; perhaps no more than will occasion that degree of exercise which the preservation of their health may require. But their learning need not be wholly interrupted in the summer. Every morning the boys may spend two hours at school, and be ready to go in the field to work by eight or nine o'clock. And when they go out, the girls may enter, and also spend two hours at school. Again at one o'clock (if they dine at noon) the boys may attend the school, continuing there an hour and an half, or two hours; and the girls may succeed them, as in the forenoon, attending the school a like length of time. Thus the same master might every day teach both girls and boys; and yet, in the whole, not to be confined above seven or eight hours in a day.—An hour every evening might be allowed the children, to amuse themselves in innocent sports.

13. The employments of a country life are so congenial to the human heart, the master of this rural academy could hardly forbear to engage in them, in the intervals between school hours. He would naturally be led to read the best authors on agriculture and rural affairs, and to get some acquaintance with botany. He would study theories, tracing useful practices back to their principles; and thus be able to communicate to the elder

boys, or youth, a degree of scientific knowledge of the very important art of which, in the field, they daily learned the practice.

14. I hardly need mention, what ought to be an indispensable part of education in every literary institution, That the children at this rural academy would be taught the plainest and most important principles of religion and morality.

15. It is to be presumed that the abler farmers would continue their children at school till they should be fourteen or fifteen years old. These children of both sexes, might make further advances in learning. They might study geography, and read some instructive histories, particularly the history of the United States, and a few of the best English moral writers, in prose and verse. At the same time they might learn so much of book-keeping as would be useful in the country; and the boys might be taught geometry, practical surveying, and the principles of mechanics.

16. Perhaps some useful manufactories might be established, in which the children, both male and female, might be very serviceable.

Such an institution as that here sketched out, need not be confined to frontier settlements; tho' the first idea of it was suggested by a reflection on their situation. Rural schools, or academies, upon such a plan, would perhaps be the most useful that could be established in the country towns and counties of this and every other state in America. Numerous advantages would result from them. I will hint at a few.

1. The children would be taught the plainest and most useful principles and rules of religion and morality.

2. They would be well and uniformly educated in the most necessary learning, and in the most important arts of civil life, *husbandry* and *domestic economy*.

3. They would acquire habits of industry.

4. Their manners and behaviour would be formed, and rendered mild and agreeable.

5. A few successive sets of scholars thus educated, returning to their several homes, would quite change the face of the country, in point of cultivation, and introduce a pleasing change in the knowledge, manners of the people, and abolish the invidious distinction of citizens and clowns.

Note particularly the five points or advantages suggested for such an educational scheme. The combination of morality, utility and industry is particularly good as a summation of the American view of education and its role in American society.

The idea of a manual labor school was also proposed by the Committee on Education of the Pennsylvania State Legislature in 1833. This group suggested that not only were such schools cheaper to maintain and promoters of democracy, but they would also spur intellectual development. Their proposal follows in Selection 50.

The working man, himself, was concerned with the education of his children. In Philadelphia, the Working Men of Philadelphia directed the questions in Selection 51 to certain legislature candidates in 1829.

The Boston Working Men's Party, in their official platform for 1830, also voiced their considerable concern with educational problems (see Selection 52).

50. Proposal of a Manual Labor School

Committee on Education of the Pennsylvania State Legislature

First, That the expense of education, when connected with manual labor judiciously directed, may be reduced at least one-half.

Second, That the exercise of about three hours' manual labor, daily, contributes to the health and cheerfulness of the pupil, by strengthening and improving his physical powers, and by engaging his mind in useful pursuits.

Third, That so far from manual labor being an impediment to the progress of the pupil in intellectual studies, it has been found that in proportion as one pupil has excelled another in the amount of labor performed, the same pupil has excelled the other, in equal ratio, in his intellectual studies.

Fourth, That manual labor institutions tend to break down the distinctions between rich and poor which exist in society, inasmuch as they give an almost equal opportunity of education to the poor by labor, as is afforded to the rich by the possession of wealth.

Fifth, That pupils trained in this way are much better fitted for active life, and better qualified to act as useful citizens, than when educated in any other mode,—that they are better as regards physical energy, and better intellectually and morally.

Reprinted from J. P. Wickersham, *A History of Education in Pennsylvania* (Lancaster: Inquirer Publishing Co., 1886), p. 306.

51. Questions on Candidates' Views on Education

Working Men of Philadelphia

SIR: The Delegates of the Working Men for the city, having placed your name in the list of fourteen, (from which seven will be chosen) as a candidate for the State Legislature; they are desirous (through the medium of the undersigned committee) to obtain your views in relation to the following subjects:

First. An equal and general system of Education.

Second. The banking system, and all other exclusive monopolies, considered with regard to the good or ill effects produced upon the productive classes by their operations.

Third. Lotteries, whether a total abolishment of them is not essential to the moral as well as pecuniary interest of society. Upon the important subject of Education we wish most distinctly to understand whether you do, or do not consider it essential to the welfare of the rising generation, "That an open school and competent teachers for every child in the state, from the lowest branch of an infant school to the lecture rooms of practical science, should be established, and those who superintend them to be chosen by the people."

Our object in soliciting your views, sir, upon these several important points, is to enable us in the discharge of our duty, as delegates, to select such men for the Legislature, as are willing as well as competent, to legislate upon subjects which the Working Men of the city consider of the greatest importance, not only to themselves but the community at large. If your views should be in accordance with the interests of those we have the honor to represent, we request you to allow us to place your name on our Ticket. We are very respectfully, Sir, your obedient servants, JOHN THOMASON, THOMAS TAYLOR, WILLIAM ENGLISH, JOHN ASHTON, JR., BENJ. MIFFLIN, *Committee.*

N.B. An immediate answer is particularly requested.

New York Free Enquirer, October 7, 1829. Reprinted in John R. Commons *et. al.,* eds., *A Documentary History of American Industrial Society* (Cleveland: A. H. Clark Co., 1910-1911), V, pp. 93-94.

52. 1830 Platform

Boston Working Men's Party

1. That we are determined by all fair and honorable means, to exalt the character, and promote the cause, of those who, by their productive industry, add riches to the state, and strength to our political institutions.

2. That we exclude from our association none, who, by their honest industry, render an equivalent to society for the means of subsistence which they draw therefrom.

3. That we regard all attempts to degrade the working classes as so many blows aimed at the destruction of popular virtue—without which no human government can long subsist.

4. That we view with abhorrence every attempt to disturb the public peace by uniting with political doctrines any question of religion or anti-religion.

5. That the establishment of a liberal system of education, attainable by all, should be among the first efforts of every lawgiver who desires the continuance of our national independence.

6. That provision ought to be made by law for the more extensive diffusion of knowledge, particularly in the elements of those sciences which pertain to mechanical employments, and to the politics of our common country.

7. That, as we hold to the natural and political equality of all men, we have a right to ask for laws which shall protect every good citizen from oppression, contumely and degradation.

8. That we are opposed to monopolies, under whatever guise they may be imposed on the community—whether in the shape of chartered institutions for private gain; or in that of taxes, levied, nominally for the public good, on the many for the advantage of the few.

9. That we regard the multiplication of statutes, and the mysterious phraseology in which they are ordinarily involved, as actual evils, loudly demanding correction.

10. That the people have a right to understand every law made for their government, without paying enormous fees for having them expounded by attorneys—by those perhaps who were instrumental in their construction, and in rendering them incomprehensible, even to themselves.

11. That every representative chosen to declare the sentiments of the

Boston Courier, August 28, 1830. Reprinted in John R. Commons *et. al.*, eds., *A Documentary History of American Industrial Society* (Cleveland: A. H. Clark Co., 1910-1911), V, pp. 188-189.

people, is bound to obey the popular voice, and to express it, or resign his trust forthwith.

12. That we are resolved to advocate, as one of our leading objects, the entire abrogation of all laws authorizing the imprisonment of the body for debt—at least until poverty shall be rendered criminal by law.

13. That we will endeavor by all practicable means to obtain a reform in our militia system.

14. That for the purpose of securing these objects, we will adopt a system of social discipline: hereby organizing ourselves under the title of Working Men of Boston.

15. That, for the furtherance of this plan, we recommend that a general meeting of our brethren and friends in the city, be held at an early day, for the purpose of selecting two delegates from each Ward, and two from South Boston, in order to constitute a General Executive Committee.

Education provided for the Negro in the ante-bellum South was far different from that provided for the working man in the North.

In the colonial era various religious agencies such as the Anglican Society for the Propagation of the Gospel in Foreign Parts had been active in efforts to educate the Negro, as well as the Indian. Although most of these organized efforts were abandoned after the Revolution, southern slave holders generally looked with favor on education, that is, literacy, for the slave for religious reasons, that he might be familiar with Christian doctrine and the Bible. Even this limited degree of schooling for the slave was proscribed after about 1830 as a result of several violent slave uprisings in the South and the fear of increasing violence. One southern state followed another in enacting prohibitions on schooling for Negroes. The following Act of the General Assembly of the Commonwealth of Virginia in 1831 is typical of these laws.

53. Limitations on Education of the Slave

5. *Be it further enacted,* That if any white person or persons assemble with free negroes or mulattoes, at any school-house, church, meeting-

Reprinted from *Acts Passed at a General Assembly of the Commonweath of Virginia, 1830-31* (Richmond, 1831), pp. 107-108.

house, or other place for the purpose of instructing such free negroes or mulattoes to read or write, such person or persons shall, on conviction thereof, be fined in a sum not exceeding fifty dollars, and moreover may be imprisoned at the discretion of the jury, not exceeding two months.

6. *Be it further enacted,* That if any white person, for pay or compensation, shall assemble with any slaves for the purpose of teaching and shall teach any slave to read or write, such person, or any white person or persons contracting with such teacher, so to act, who shall offend as aforesaid, shall, for such offence, be fined at the discretion of a jury, in a sum not less than ten, nor exceeding one hundred dollars, to be recovered on any information or indictment.

The responsibility for the religious instruction of the Negro, however, continued to rest on the white slave holder. Chancellor William Harper of the State of South Carolina, a leader of pro-slavery thought in the years preceding the war, seemed to find a solution in informal, non-school, religious instruction for the Negro.

54. Informal Education of Slaves

William Harper

Odium has been cast upon our legislation, on account of its forbidding the elements of education to be communicated to slaves. But, in truth, what injury is done to them by this? He who works during the day with his hands, does not read in intervals of leisure for his amusement, or the improvement of his mind—or the exceptions are so very rare, as scarcely to need the being provided for. Of the many slaves whom I have known capable of reading, I have never known one to read any thing but the Bible, and this task they impose on themselves as matter of duty. Of all methods of religious instruction, however, this, of reading for themselves, would be the most inefficient—their comprehension is defective, and the employment is to them an unusual and laborious one. There are but very

Reprinted from *Pro-Slavery Argument; As Maintained by the Most Distinguished Writers of the Southern States, Containing the Several Essays, on the Subject, of Chancellor Harper, Governor Hammond, Dr. Simms, and Professor Dew* (Charleston: Walker, Richards and Company, 1852), pp. 36-38.

few who do not enjoy other means more effectual for religious instruction. There is no place of worship opened for the white population, from which they are excluded. I believe it a mistake, to say that the instructions there given are not adapted to their comprehension, or calculated to improve them. If they are given as they ought to be—practically, and without pretension, and are such as are generally intelligible to the free part of the audience, comprehending all grades of intellectual capacity,—they will not be unintelligible to slaves. I doubt whether this be not better than instruction, addressed specially to themselves—which they might look upon as a device of the master's, to make them more obedient and profitable to himself. Their minds, generally, show a strong religious tendency, and they are fond of assuming the office of religious instructors to each other; and perhaps their religious notions are not much more extravagant than those of a large portion of the free population of our country. I am not sure that there is a much smaller proportion of them, than of the free population, who make some sort of religious profession. It is certainly the master's *interest* that they should have proper religious sentiments, and if he fails in his duty towards them, we may be sure that the consequences will be visited not upon them, but upon him.

If there were any chance of their elevating their rank and condition in society, it might be matter of hardship, that they should be debarred those rudiments of knowledge which open the way to further attainments. But this they know cannot be, and that further attainments would be useless to them. Of the evil of this, I shall speak hereafter. A knowledge of reading, writing, and the elements of arithmetic, is convenient and important to the free laborer, who is the transactor of his own affairs, and the guardian of his own interests—but of what use would they be to the slave? These alone do not elevate the mind of character, if such elevation were desirable.

Outside the South, in the regions of free labor, the typical American reluctance to accept charity, his cult of individual self-reliance, is well delineated by contemporary writers. There were, however, provisions for education for the poor in America. Pennsylvania, for example, made legal provision for such education in its state constitution.

New York City newspaper readers on May 18, 1805, read a proposal (Selection 56) for providing education to those poor children who were not being educated under the auspices of religious and benevolent societies already operating.

55. Pennsylvania's Constitutional Provisions for Schools for the Poor, 1802

Whereas, by the first section of the seventh article of the Constitution of this Commonwealth it is directed "That the Legislature shall as soon as conveniently may be, provide by law for the establishment of schools throughout the State, in such manner as that the poor may be taught gratis," Therefore,

Section I. Be it enacted, etc. That from and after the passing of this act the Guardians and Overseers of the poor of the City of Philadelphia, the District of Southwark and townships and Boroughs within this Commonwealth, shall ascertain the names of all those children whose parents or guardians they shall judge to be unable to pay for their schooling, to give notice in writing to such parent or guardian that provision is made by law for the education of their children or the children under their care, and that they have a full and free right to subscribe at the usual rates and send them to any school in their neighborhood, giving notice thereof as soon as may be to the Guardians or Overseers of the term for which they have subscribed, the number of scholars and the rate of tuition, and in those Townships where there are no guardians or overseers of the poor, the Supervisors of the Highways shall perform the duties herein required to be done by the Guardians or Overseers of the poor.

Section II. And be it further enacted by the authority aforesaid, That every Guardian or Overseer of the poor, or Supervisor of the Highways, as the case may be, in any township or place where any such child or children shall be sent to school as aforesaid, shall enter in a book the name or names, age and length of time such child or children shall have been so sent to school, together with the amount of schooling, school-books and stationery, and shall levy and collect in the same way and manner and under the same regulations as poor taxes or road taxes are levied and collected, a sufficient sum of money from their respective townships, boroughs, wards or districts, to discharge such expenses together with the sum of five per cent for their trouble.

Section III. And be it further enacted by the authority aforesaid, That the Guardians or Overseers of the poor for the time being, or Supervisors

Reprinted from J. P. Wickersham, *A History of Education in Pennsylvania* (Lancaster: Inquirer Publishing Co., 1886), pp. 263-64.

of the Highways as the case may be, shall use all diligence and prudence in carrying this act into effect, and shall settle their accounts in the same way and manner as by the existing laws of the State, the Guardians, Overseers of the poor, and Supervisors of the poor, and Supervisors of the Highways are authorized and required to settle their accounts.

Section IV. And it be further enacted by the authority aforesaid, That this act shall continue in force for the term of three years, and from thence to the end of the next sitting of the General Assembly and no longer.

56. The New York Free School Society, 1805

Address of the Trustees of the "Society for Establishing a Free School in the City of New York, for the Education of such Poor Children as do not Belong to, or are not Provided for by, any Religious Society."

While the various religious and benevolent societies in this city, with a spirit of charity and zeal which the precepts and example of the Divine Author of our religion could alone inspire, amply provide for the education of such poor children as belong to their respective associations, there still remains a large number living in total neglect of religious and moral instruction, and unacquainted with the common rudiments of learning, essentially requisite for the due management of the ordinary business of life. This neglect may be imputed either to the extreme indigence of the parents of such children, their intemperance and vice, or to a blind indifference to the best interests of their offspring. The consequences must be obvious to the most careless observer. Children thus brought up in ignorance, and amidst the contagion of bad example, are in imminent danger of ruin; and too many of them, it is to be feared, instead of being useful members of the community, will become the burden and pests of society. Early instruction and fixed habits of industry, decency, and order, are the surest safeguards of virtuous conduct; and when parents are either unable or unwilling to bestow the necessary attention on the education of their children, it becomes the duty of the public, and of individuals, who have the power, to assist them in the discharge of this important obligation. It is in vain that laws are made for the punishment of crimes, or that good men attempt to stem the torrent of irreligion and vice, if the evil is not

Reprinted from W. O. Bourne, *History of the Public School Society of the City of New York* (New York: Wood, 1870), pp. 6-8.

checked at its source; and the means of prevention, by the salutary discipline of early education, seasonably applied. It is certainly in the power of the opulent and charitable, by a timely and judicious interposition of their influence and aid, if not wholly to prevent, at least to diminish, the pernicious effects resulting from the neglected education of the children of the poor.

Influenced by these considerations, and from a sense of the necessity of providing some remedy for an increasing and alarming evil, several individuals, actuated by similar motives, agree to form an association for the purpose of extending the means of education to such poor children as do not belong to, or are not provided for, by any religious society. After meetings, numerously attended, a plan of association was framed, and a Memorial prepared and addressed to the legislature, soliciting an Act of Incorporation, the better to enable them to carry into effect their benevolent design. Such a law the Legislature, at their last session, was pleased to pass; and at a meeting of the Society, under the Act of Incorporation, on the sixth instant, thirteen Trustees were elected for the ensuing year.

The particular plan of the school, and the rules for its discipline and management, will be made known previous to its commencement. Care will be exercised in the selection of teachers, and, besides the elements of learning usually taught in schools, strict attention will be bestowed on the morals of the children, and all suitable means be used to counteract the disadvantages resulting from the situation of their parents. It is proposed, also, to establish, on the first day of the week, a school, called a Sunday School, more particularly for such children as, from peculiar circumstances, are unable to attend on the other days of the week. In this, as in the Common School, it will be a primary object, without observing the peculiar forms of any religious Society, to inculcate the sublime truths of religion and morality contained in the Holy Scriptures.

This Society, as will appear from its name, interferes with no existing institution, since children already provided with the means of education, or attached to any other Society, will not come under its care. Humble gleaners in the wide field of benevolence, the members of this Association seek such objects only as are left by those who have gone before, or are fellow-laborers with them in the great work of charity. They, therefore, look with confidence for the encouragement and support of the affluent and charitable of every denomination of Christians; and when they consider that in no community is to be found a greater spirit of liberal and active benevolence than among the citizens of New York, they feel assured that adequate means for the prosecution of their plan will be easily obtained. In addition to the respectable list of original subscriptions, considerable funds will be requisite for the purchase or hire of a piece of ground, and the erection of a suitable building for the school, to pay the teachers, and to defray other charges incident to the establishment. To accomplish this design, and to place the Institution on a solid and respectable foundation, the Society depends on the voluntary bounty of those who may be charitably disposed to contribute their aid in the promotion of an object of great and universal concern.

In spite of all good intentions, however, education was simply being overwhelmed by the sheer numbers to be educated, particularly in the rapidly growing rural-industrial complexes. One solution to this problem was to utilize Sunday (for the children who were forced to work the other six days of the week) for education. The Sunday School, unlike its modern counterpart, was originally an attempt to teach the rudiments of the three R's to working children.

A method that had been tried in England to deal with the massive number of pupils received a warm welcome as a possible solution to similar problems in America. This was the *monitorial* system of Joseph Lancaster (to pass over the disputed question of Lancaster's claim to originality of this method). Briefly, this system delegated responsibility from master to certain advanced pupils (monitors) to teach the lesson of the day. Aided by these monitors, one teacher could handle from 50 to 1,000 pupils. This was thought particularly expedient for the education of the poor, though the monitorial system was not wholly confined to charity schools. As the following introduction to a Lancasterian teaching manual shows, rural Americans were quite eager to try this British import.

The reading which follows (Selection 57) is an editorial comment appearing in *The Raleigh Register* of April 1, 1814, which indicates the support that the monitorial system received at this time in America. Lancaster himself came to America and lectured to interested groups on his monitorial system.

57. A Manual of the System of Teaching Reading, Writing, Arithmetic, and Needle-Work In the Elementary Schools of the British and Foreign School Society Also Lessons Adapted to the Lancastrian System of Education

When the rapid increase of our population is compared with the means of procuring Education, it is much to be feared, that at no distant period, a large proportion of the people, in many sections of the United States, will be destitute of this important blessing, unless private benevolence or public provision should apply the remedy. The Lancastrian System, as detailed in the above Manual, presents the best mode yet discovered of spreading the benefits of Education, either in the hands of individual Tutors or School Societies: under these impressions, the Philadelphia Society believe they cannot better fulfill the purpose of their Association, than by extending the knowledge of the System, and offering the means which the Lessons afford of carrying it into complete operation.

The views of the Society, however, in their publication, are not confined to Charity Schools: every citizen is interested; because the effects of the general introduction of this System will be the same as the creation or gift of a vast capital to be expended in Education: Its economy brings it within reach of the poor man's means; and to parents in moderate circumstances it will prove a saving of money, as well as a saving of time to their children. Nor are the most wealthy above the benefits which will flow from the general introduction of this System; its morality and the peculiar and happy fitness of all its details, to the capacities and feelings of children, no less than its economy, entitle it to the approbation and support of everyone who is interested in the welfare of the rising generation.

58. Editorial

The Raleigh Register

We congratulate our fellow-citizens on the prospect of establishing in the Preparatory School of our Academy, the highly approved mode of

Selection 57 is from a copy held by the American Antiquarian Society, Worcester, Massachusetts. Reprinted in Edgar W. Knight and Clifton L. Hall, eds., *Readings in American Educational History* (New York: Appleton-Century-Crofts, 1951), p. 136.

Selection 58 is from *The Raleigh Register,* April 1, 1814. Reprinted in Edgar W. Knight and Clifton L. Hall, eds., *Readings in American Educational History* (New York: Appleton-Century-Crofts, 1951), p. 135.

teaching children the first rudiments of Learning, invented by the celebrated Joseph Lancaster of London, by which one man can superintend the instruction of any number of scholars from 50 to 1000. At the monthly meeting of the trustees of the Academy on Saturday last, a favorable Report was made by a committee who had been appointed to consider this subject, from which it appeared, that when this plan shall be introduced, the children of all such parents in the city and neighborhood as are unable to pay their tuition, may be taught without additional expense, so that this institution will answer all the purposes of a free school.

The Report was unanimously concurred with, and a subscription immediately opened for effecting the object, which Mr. Glendenning generously headed with $50. Nearly $200. were subscribed by the Trustees present; and there is no doubt but a sufficient fund will be immediately raised for sending a fit person to the District of Columbia (where there is a school of this kind in operation under the direction of one of Mr. Lancaster's pupils), to receive the necessary instruction, and return hither for the purpose of undertaking the contemplated School, which it is proposed shall open with the ensuing year. Benevolent individuals who are willing to give aid to this plan for disseminating the benefits of education amongst the poorer classes of the community, are requested to place their names to the subscription paper, which is in the hands of Wm. Peace, Esq., Treasurer of the Academy.

SECTION 3

Character and Curriculum

From common school to college, at every level of education in early nineteenth-century America, the building of character was a major force in curriculum. Inculcation in the young of the virtues of honesty, sobriety, hard work, and the like was clearly far more important than mere excellence in the pursuit of learning. An aspect of the stress on character in education was the ardent denominationalism of the era, for example, the revivalist movement of the 1820's and 1830's which amounted to a second "Great Awakening." This denominational enthusiasm, especially strong in the South and West, had considerable impact on education, not only in curriculum offerings, but in the vast number of academies and colleges founded to represent a special religious point of view.

At the elementary school level, religious groups often became embroiled in struggles to get tax support for their particular schools. But the eventual trend among the supporters of the public common schools was toward agreement on the teaching of character in the "Protestant ethic" sense as a proper common denominator of denominations. Even the colleges and academies were becoming by mid-century less dogmatically sectarian and more inclined to stress the general traditional values and virtues through higher learning.

The everpresent religious impulse in teaching is illustrated in the following statement by the Middlesex County, Connecticut, Visitors and Overseers of Schools, *Code of Regulations,* which outlines a proper day in the common school.

59. A Day in School in Middlesex County, Connecticut, 1799

I. *General.* Instructors and scholars, shall punctually attend their schools, in due season, and the appointed number of hours.

The whole time of instructors and scholars shall be entirely devoted to the proper business and duties of the school.

Every scholar shall be furnished with necessary books for his instruction. In winter, effectual provision ought to be made for warming the schoolhouse, in season, otherwise the forenoon is almost lost.

The Bible—in selected portions—or the New Testament, ought, in Christian schools, to be read by those classes who are capable of reading decently, at the opening of the school before the morning prayer. If this mode of reading be adopted, it will remove every objection of irreverence, and answer all the purposes of morality, devotion, and reading. Some questions may be very properly proposed and answered by the master or scholars; and five minutes, thus spent, would be very profitable exercise of moral and other instruction.

Proper lessons, and fully within the scholar's power to learn, ought to be given to every class, each part of the day. These daily lessons ought to be faithfully learned and recited to the master, or his approved monitors.

One lesson in two or more days may be a review of the preceding lessons

From Visitors and Overseers of Schools, *Code of Regulations,* May 7, 1799. Given in *American Annals of Education,* VII (January, 1837), pp. 17-20.

of those days, and one lesson in each week a review of the studies of that week. The sum of this review, fairly written or noted in the book studied, may be carried by the scholars, each Saturday, to their respective parents or guardians.

Scholars equal in knowledge ought to be classed together. Those whose progress merits advancement should rise to a higher class, and those who decline by negligence should be degraded.

2. *School hours and work.* The hours of school ought, as much as possible, to be appropriated in the following, or a similar manner, viz:

IN THE MORNING, the Bible may be delivered to the head of each class, and by them to the scholars capable of reading decently or looking over. This reading, with some short remarks, or questions, with the morning prayer, may occupy the *first half hour.* The *second,* may be employed in hearing the morning lessons, while the younger classes are preparing to spell and read. The *third half hour* in attention to the writers. The *fourth* in hearing the under classes read and spell. The *fifth* in looking over and assisting the writers and cipherers. The *sixth* in hearing the under classes spell and read the second time; and in receiving and depositing pens, writing and reading books.

In all exercises of reading the teacher ought to pronounce a part of the lessons, giving the scholars a correct example of accent and emphasis, pauses, tones, and cadence. In all studies, the scholars ought to be frequently and critically observed. The teacher's eye on all his school is a great preservative of dilligence and order.

IN THE AFTERNOON, the *first* half hour may be employed in spelling together, repeating grammar, rules of arithmetic, and useful tables, with a clear, and full, but soft voice, while the instructor prepares pens, writing books, &c. The *second* and *third* half hours in hearing the under classes and assisting the writers and cipherers. The *fourth* in hearing the upper classes read. The *fifth* in hearing the under classes read, and spell the second time. The *sixth* in receiving and depositing the books &c, as above.

That the school be closed with an evening prayer, previous to which the scholars shall repeat a psalm or hymn—and also the Lord's prayer.

Saturday may be wholly employed in an orderly review of the studies of the week, excepting one hour appropriated to instruction in the first principles of religion and morality; and in repeating, together, the ten commandments. That the Catechism usually taught in schools be divided, by the master, into four sections, one of which shall be repeated successively on each Saturday.

Common-school textbooks especially reflected the heavily didactic style of teaching of the era. The most widely used of these was Noah Webster's famous Blue-back speller which had many editions and bindings from the 1780's to the mid-nineteenth century. Webster in his preface stated that the reading lessons were planned "to combine, with the familiarity of objects, useful truth, and practical principles"; and so they were.

60. From the Blue-Back Speller

Noah Webster

A good child will not lie, swear, nor steal.—He will be good at home, and ask to read his book; when he gets up he will wash his hands and face clean; he will comb his hair and make haste to school; he will not play by the way as bad boys do.

As for those boys and girls that mind not their books, and love not the church and school, but play with such as tell lies, curse, swear and steal, they will come to some bad end, and must be whipt till they mend their ways.

January begins the year, and the first day of that month is called New Year's day. Then people express to each other their good wishes, and little boys and girls expect gifts of little books, toys and plums.

There are five stages of human life, infancy, childhood, youth, manhood, and old age. The infant is helpless; he is nourished with milk—when he has teeth he begins to eat bread, meat, and fruit, and is very fond of cakes and plums. The little boy chuses some plaything that will make a noise, a hammer, a stick or a whip. The little girl loves her doll and learns to dress it. She chuses a closet for her baby-house, where she sets her doll in a little chair, by the side of a table, furnished with tea-cups as big as a thimble.

As soon as boys are large enough, they run away from home, grow fond of play, climb trees to rob birds' nests, tear their clothes, and when they come home their parents often chastise them.—O how the rod makes their legs smart. These are naughty boys, who love play better than their books.

. . . . .

Of the BOY *that stole* APPLES.

AN old Man found a rude Boy upon one of his trees stealing Apples, and

From a Webster Speller dated 1789. Reprinted courtesy Rutgers University Library.

desired him to come down; but the young Sauce-box told him plainly he would not. Won't you? said the old Man, then I will fetch you down; so he pulled up some tufts of Grass and threw at him; but this only made the Youngster laugh, to think the old Man should pretend to beat him down from the tree with grass only.

FABLE I.—*Of the* Boy *that stole* APPLES.

Well, well, said the old Man, if neither words nor grass will do, I must try what virtue there is in Stones: so the old Man pelted him heartily with stones, which soon made the young Chap hasten down from the tree and beg the old Man's pardon.

MORAL

If good words and gentle means will not reclaim the wicked, they must be dealt with in a more severe manner.

Varieties of spelling books and readers illustrate the same pious, didactic style in the readings. Textbook authors, moreover, appear to have borrowed indiscriminately from their competitors (a practice not unknown in modern times of course), so that certain popular stories and poems may reappear again and again.

61. Emerson's Second-class Reader

You are old, Father William, the young man cried,
   The few locks which are left you are gray;
You are hale, Father William, a hearty old man;
   Now tell me the reason, I pray.

In the days of my youth, Father William replied,
   I remembered that youth would fly fast,
And abused not my health and my vigor at first,
   That I never might need them at last.

. . .

62. Alexander's Spelling Book

WHY should I join with them in play,
   In whom I've no delight;
Who curse and swear, but never pray.
   Who call ill names, and fight?

From Emerson's *The Second-class Reader,* dated 1833. Reprinted courtesy Rutgers University Library.
From Alexander's *Spelling Book,* dated 1810. Reprinted courtesy Rutgers University Library.

I hate to hear a wanton song;
　　The words offend my ears;
I should not dare defile my tongue
　　With language such as theirs.

Againſt EVIL COMPANY.

My God, I hate to walk or dwell
　　With sinful children here;
Then let me not be sent to hell,
　　Where none but sinners are.

THIS is the day when Christ arose
　　So early from the dead;
Why should I keep my eyelids clos'd,
　　And waste my hours in bed?

Today with pleasure christians meet,
　　To pray, and hear thy word;
And I will go with cheerful feet
　　To learn thy will, O Lord.

I'll leave my sport and read and pray,
　　And so prepare for heaven;
O may I love this blessed day,
　　The best of all the seven.

Along with the literary materials in the readers and spellers available to the common-school scholars was usually also sketchy historical and geographic writing. The famous McGuffey reader, for example, far the most popular of the series books from around the middle of the century to the 1890's, offered a vast range of American historical lore but managed to avoid mention of the Civil War entirely. Somewhat more thorough study in history and geography became available during the nineteenth century in several textbooks written primarily to offer a consciously American point of view in these areas. Jedidiah Morse first published his *Geography Made Easy* in 1784, and it had many editions and many imitators in years to come. The Reverend C. A. Goodrich, whose "Peter Parley" reader had had wide success, published a *History of the United States* in 1822 for school use. It was followed a decade later by Noah Webster's *History*, which included "a brief Account of our [English] Ancestors, from the dispersion at Babel, to their Migration to America," as an introduction to American history down to the adoption of the Constitution. The patriotic spirit of these popular histories and geographies included as well the pious tone of the spellers, a combination well suited to the common schools of America in the National period.

63. The First American Geography

Jedidiah Morse

The *Andes,* in South America, stretch along the Pacific Ocean, from the Isthmus of Darien to the Straits of Magellan. The height of Chimborazo, the most elevated point in this vast chain of mountains is 20,280 feet, above 5000 feet higher than any other mountain in the known world.

North America has no remarkably high mountains. The most considerable are those known under the general name of the *Allegany Mountains*. These stretch along in many broken ridges under different names from Hudson's River to Georgia. The *Andes* and the *Allegany Mountains* are probably the same range interrupted by the Gulf of Mexico.

Who were the first people of America? And whence did they come? The Abbe Clavigero gives his opinion in the following conclusions:—

"The Americans descended from different nations, or from differ-

From Morse's *Geography Made Easy,* dated 1815. Reprinted courtesy Rutgers University Library.

ent families dispersed after the confusion of tongues. No person will doubt the truth of this, who has any knowledge of the multitude and great diversity of the American languages. In Mexico alone *thirty-five* have already been discovered.

But how did the inhabitants and animals originally pass to America?

The quadrupeds and reptiles of the new world passed there by land. This fact is manifest from the improbability and inconsistency of all other opinions.

This necessarily supposes an ancient union between the equinoxial countries of America and those of Africa, and a connexion of the northern countries of America with Europe on the E. and Asia on the W. The beasts of cold climes passed over the northern isthmuses, which probably connected Europe, America, and Asia; and the animals and reptiles peculiar to hot countries passed over the isthmus that probably connected S. America with Africa. Various reasons induce us to believe that there was formerly a tract of land which united the most eastern part of Brazil to the most western part of Africa; and that all the space of land may have been sunk by violent earthquakes, leaving only some traces of it in that chain of islands of which Cape de Verd, Ascension, and St. Matthew's Island make a part. In like manner, it is probable, the northwestern part of America was united to the northeastern part of Asia, and the northeastern parts of America to the northwestern parts of Europe, by Greenland, Iceland, etc.

Like the common school, the academy was regarded as an important guarantor of traditional morality. Piety and virtue were primary educational ends, as may be seen in the following charter of the Phillips Andover Academy in 1780.

64. Phillips Andover Academy Charter

Whereas, the education of youth has ever been considered by the wise and good, as an object of the highest consequence to the safety and happiness of a people; as at that period the mind easily receives and retains impressions, is formed with peculiar advantage to piety and virtue, and directed to the pursuit of the most useful knowledge; and, whereas the

Reprinted from *Acts and Laws of Massachusetts*, 1780, pp. 327-329.

Honorable Samuel Phillips of Andover, in the County of Essex, Esq., and the Honorable John Phillips of Exeter, in the County of Rockingham, and State of New Hampshire, Esq., on the first day of April, in the year of our Lord one thousand seven hundred and seventy eight, by a legal instrument of that date, gave, granted, and assigned to the Honorable William Phillips, Esquire, and others, therein named, and to their heirs, divers lots and parcels of land, in said Instrument described, as well as certain other estate, to the use and upon the trust following, namely, that the rents, profits, and interest thereof, be forever laid out and expended by the Trustees in the said Instrument named, for the support of a Public Free School or Academy, in the town of Andover:—and, whereas the execution of the generous and important design of the grantors aforesaid will be attended with very great embarrassments, unless, by an act of incorporation, the Trustees, mentioned in the said Instrument, and their successors, shall be authorized to commence and prosecute actions at law, and transact such other matters in their corporate capacity, as the interest of the said Academy shall require.

ACADEMY ESTABLISHED

1. Be it therefore enacted by the Council and the House of Representatives in General Court assembled, and by the authorship of the same; that there be and hereby is established in the Town of Andover, and County of Essex, an Academy, by the name of *Phillips Academy,* for the purpose of promoting piety and virtue, and for the education of youth, in the English, Latin, and Greek languages, together with Writing, Arithmetic, Music, and the Art of Speaking; also practical Geometry, Logic and Geography, and such other of the liberal Arts and Sciences, or Languages, as opportunity may hereafter permit, and as the Trustees, herein after provided, shall direct.

The academy was a widely varied institution of middle schools throughout the states, and, hence, its curriculum was enormously varied in its offerings in the differing schools. The catalog statement of the academy in New Brunswick, New Jersey, the Rutgers College Grammar School, is illustrative of an academically oriented institution, yet one offering a broad range of studies.

65. Rutgers College Grammar School

Rev. DeWitt Ten Broeck Reiley, A. M., Rector.
R. I. Woodruff, Principal.

LOCATION

This institution is located in New Brunswick on the avenue adjoining the Campus of Rutgers College. It is in close proximity to good boarding-houses, play-grounds, etc., and is within two minutes walk of the railroad depot, at which trains arrive at all hours of the day. Many scholars avail themselves of this, and live at home, while they come daily to New Brunswick at the hours of recitation.

The pupils who board in town are under the care of the Rector, who gives personal attention to their conduct and comfort in the houses where they board. For the purpose of furnishing more ample accommodations for boarding pupils, and of providing them with the care and oversight which they require, the Rector has purchased an extensive dwelling and grounds within a few minutes' walk of the Grammar School. The grounds contain eight acres of land, and the dwelling is large and convenient. This will be opened for boarding pupils at the beginning of the academic year, in September 1869, and will be in the immediate charge of the Rector. It will have the advantages of a healthy location, delightful play-grounds, and the seclusion necessary for study.

Before the opening of the next academic year it is designed also to make improvements and enlargements in the Grammar School Building, which will adapt it to the increased number of pupils, and to the advancing demands of education.

GRADING AND STUDIES

This school is graded into five classes, and the course extends through five years. Boys of twelve years of age are admitted into the lowest, but scholars are admitted into the school at any time, and are assigned to the classes for which they are qualified. The instruction given to the two lowest classes is such as is necessary to every one who would acquire a sound

Reprinted from *Catalogue of the Officers and Students of Rutgers College, New Brunswick, New Jersey, 1868-69* (New Brunswick, 1868), pp. 56-58, courtesy of Rutgers University Library.

EDUCATION. After leaving the fourth class, each scholar chooses the Classical or the Business Course. In the former are three classes, through which he passes in order to enter College.

In the *Business Course,* there are two classes, the instruction in which is intended to furnish the best practical knowledge of business that is possible to obtain in the time allowed, and thus fit the student for active commercial life. The scholar who finishes the Business Course, is also ready to enter the Scientific Department of the College.

In the rudimentary branches of Reading, Writing, Spelling, Grammar and Arithmetic, the effort is made to ensure a thorough drilling. Geography is taught with the aid of globes, maps and map-drawing. Declamation and Composition are regular exercises in all the classes.

In addition to the elementary studies, the members of the Business Classes receive instruction in Book-keeping, Commercial Law, History, Physiology, Natural History, Constitution of the United States, Natural Philosophy and the German Language. Special attention is devoted to Natural Science, which is made available even to the lower classes, by lectures on Technology, Natural History and other cognate branches. German and French are both taught to the classes, the former without extra charge.

In the classes preparing for College all the means which experienced teachers have been able to devise are employed to impart sound scholarship. The character of the Classical course in the institution is indicated by the standing in College of those who have been prepared in it. By drilling in Grammar, by written and free translations, by the study of Mythology, Ancient Geography and History, the pupil is advanced at the same time in a knowledge of the languages, and of the literature and philosophy of the classic ages.

In Mathematics the College class is carried through six books of Plane Geometry, and to Quadratic Equations in Algebra. They have also the benefit of lectures on Natural History and instruction in collecting and classifying specimens.

Two public examinations of all the classes in the school is held during the year, the first at the end of the first session, and the second at the end of the year. In addition to these, semi-monthly examinations are held in the studies of the classes.

ATTENDANCE

The hours of attendance are from 8.30 A. M. to 1.30 P. M.; during which there is a recess of fifteen minutes. For absence, tardiness or failures in recitations, written excuses are expected from parents or guardians. PUNC-

TUALITY is required not merely because necessary to all school progress, but as an invaluable habit in life.

The school year begins September 7, 1868, and closes June 23, 1869. Recesses are allowed on general public holidays and during Christmas week.

TERMS

TUITION.—English Branches, . $12 per quarter of ten weeks.
Latin, including the above, . 15 " "
Greek, . " " 17 " "
Incidentals, . . 1 per session.

The tuition is to be paid at the beginning of each session, in sums proportioned to the length of the session. No deduction for absence, unless occasioned by protracted sickness. There is no extra charge except for French.

In the higher learning in America of the national era, the education of the Christian gentleman was the foremost aim, and in this sense the curriculum of the college carried forward the character-building aims of common school and academy. In the college curriculum the study of "moral philosophy" was the crown of the classical curriculum, the essential education of the Christian gentleman. Illustrative of this spirit is the charter of the first state university in the United States, that of Georgia in 1785. Although first to be chartered, Georgia was not the first state university to be built; the honor here goes to the University of North Carolina which first opened its doors in 1795.

66. Charter of The University of Georgia

An act for the more full and complete establishment of a public seat of learning in this State.

As it is the distinguishing happiness of free governments, that civil order should be the result of choice, and not necessity, and the common wishes of the people become the laws of the land, their public prosperity, and even

Reprinted from R. and G. Watkins, *A Digest of the Laws of the State of Georgia* (Philadelphia: 1800), pp. 299-302.

existence, very much depends upon suitably forming the minds and morals of their citizens. Where the minds of the people in general are viciously disposed and unprincipled, and their conduct disorderly, a free government will be attended with greater confusions, and with evils more horrid than the wild uncultivated state of nature: It can only be happy where the public principles and opinions are properly directed, and their manners regulated. This is an influence beyond the sketch of laws and punishments, and can be claimed only by religion and education. It should therefore be among the first objects of those who wish well to the national prosperity, to encourage and support the principles of religion and morality, and early to place the youth under the forming hand of society, that by instruction they may be moulded to the love of virtue and good order. Sending them abroad to other countries for their education will not answer these purposes, is too humiliating an acknowledgment of the ignorance or inferiority of our own, and will always be the cause of so great foreign attachments, that upon principles of policy it is not admissible.

This country, in the times of our common danger and distress, found such security in the principles and abilities which wise regulations had before established in the minds of our countrymen, that our present happiness, joined to pleasing prospects, should conspire to make us feel ourselves under the strongest obligation to form the youth, the rising hope of our land, to render the like glorious and essential services to our country.

And whereas, for the great purpose of internal education, divers allotments of land have, at different times, been made, particularly by the legislature at their sessions in July, one thousand seven hundred and eighty-three; and February, one thousand seven hundred and eighty-four all of which may be comprehended and made the basis of one general and complete establishment: THEREFORE *the representatives of the freemen of the State of Georgia, in General assembly met, this twenty-seventh day of January, in the year of our Lord one thousand seven hundred and eighty-five, enact, ordain, and declare, and by these presents it is* ENACTED, ORDAINED, AND DECLARED.

An early example of the college curriculum is found in this announcement of the opening of the Indiana State Seminary in 1824, the institution which later became Indiana University.

The traditionally prescribed curriculum found an eloquent defense in a statement written by the Yale faculty in response to the threatening experimental ideas in curriculum current at the University of Virginia and elsewhere (see Selection 75) in the 1820's. The Yale Report of 1828 had a wide influence in bolstering the traditional conservative view that the classical curriculum of the residential college for the education of the Christian gentleman, was the right means and proper mission of the higher learning.

67. Advertisement for the Opening of Indiana State Seminary

The trustees of this institution are authorized to inform the public that the seminary buildings are now in a state of preparation, and will be ready for the reception of students by the first Monday of April, next, at which time the first session will commence under the Superintendency of the Rev'd BAYARD HALL, whom the trustees have engaged as a teacher. Mr. Hall is a gentleman whose classical attainments are perhaps not inferior to any in the western country; and whose acquaintance with the most approved methods of instruction in some of the best Universities in the United States and whose morals, manners and address, render him in every way qualified to give dignity and character to the institution.

There will be two sessions of five months each, in the year.

The admission fee for each scholar at the commencement of every session will be two dollars and fifty cents, making the expense of tuition for a year the sum of five dollars.

Good boarding can be had in respectable families, either in town or country at convenient distances, and on moderate terms, not exceeding $1.25 cents per week.

The institution will for the present be strictly classical, and each scholar will be required to furnish himself with a supply of classical books, of which the following are recommended, and will be needed from term to term:

Rose's Latin Grammar, latest edition.
Colloquies of Corderius.
Selectae Veteri.
Selectae Profanis.
Caesar.
Virgil, & Mair's introduction.
Valpy's Grammar, latest edition.
Testament.
Graeca Minora.

From *The Indiana Republican* (Madison), January 7, 1824. Reprinted in Edgar W. Knight and Clifton L. Hall, eds., *Readings in American Educational History* (New York: Appleton-Century-Crofts, 1951), pp. 237-238.

None of these books are to be accompanied with an English translation, but this remark is not intended to extend to such editions as have notes in English; which indeed for beginners are preferable.

The choice of Lexicons in either language is kept discretionary with the students: Ainsworth's in Latin and Scrurevelius' in Greek are however recommended. Other books than those specified, as progress in the languages is made, will hereafter be necessary; but these only at present need be procured. The whole number of students according to the different degrees of improvement, will be distributed into several classes in which the books just enumerated are to be employed.

The seminary buildings are erected on an elevated situation affording a handsome view of Bloomington, the county seat of Monroe County, and also a commanding prospect of the adjacent country, which is altogether pleasant and well calculated for rural retreats; and as regards the healthiness of the situation, we hazard nothing in the assertion, that it cannot be excelled by any western country.

Joshua O. Howe
John Ketcham
Jonathan Nichols
Samuel Dobbs
William Lowe
D. H. Maxwell

Bloomington, Jan. 7, 1824.

68. The Yale Report of 1828

From different quarters, we have heard the suggestion, that our colleges must be *new-modelled;* that they are not adapted to the spirit and wants of the age; that they will soon be deserted, unless they are better accommodated to the business character of the nation. As this point may have an important bearing upon the question immediately before the committee, we would ask their indulgence, while we attempt to explain, at some length, the nature and object of the present plan of education at the college.

We shall in vain attempt to decide on the expediency of retaining or altering our present course of instruction, unless we have a distinct apprehension of the *object* of a collegiate education. A plan of study may be well

Reprinted from "Original Papers in Relation to a Course of Literal Education," *The American Journal of Science and the Arts,* XV, January 1829, pp. 300-303, 313, 317-320.

adapted to a particular purpose, though it may be very unsuitable for a different one. Universities, colleges, academical, and professional seminaries, ought not to be all constituted upon the same model; but should be so varied as to attain the ends which they have severally in view.

What then is the appropriate object of a college? It is not necessary here to determine what it is which, in every case, entitles an institution to the *name* of a college. But if we have not greatly misapprehended the design of the patrons and guardians of this college, its object is to LAY THE FOUNDATION of a SUPERIOR EDUCATION: and this is to be done, at a period of life when a substitute must be provided for *parental superintendence*. The ground work of a thorough education, must be broad, and deep, and solid. For a partial or superficial education, the support may be of looser materials, and more hastily laid.

The two great points to be gained in intellectual culture, are the *discipline* and the *furniture* of the mind; expanding its powers, and storing it with knowledge. The former of these is, perhaps, the more important of the two. A commanding object, therefore, in a collegiate course, should be, to call into daily and vigorous exercise the faculties of the student. Those branches of study should be prescribed, and those modes of instruction adopted, which are best calculated to teach the art of fixing the attention, directing the train of thought, analyzing a subject proposed for investigation; following, with accurate discrimination, the course of argument; balancing nicely the evidence presented to the judgment; awakening, elevating, and controlling the imagination; arranging, with skill, the treasures which memory gathers; rousing and guiding the powers of genius. All this is not to be effected by a light and hasty course of study; by reading a few books, hearing a few lectures, and spending some months at a literary institution. The habits of thinking are to be formed, by long continued and close application. The mines of science must be penetrated far below the surface, before they will disclose their treasures. If a dexterous performance of the manual operations, in many of the mechanical arts, requires an apprenticeship, with diligent attention for years; much more does the training of the powers of the mind demand vigorous, and steady, and systematic effort.

In laying the foundation of a thorough education, it is necessary that *all* the important mental faculties be brought into exercise. It is not sufficient that one or two be cultivated, while others are neglected. A costly edifice ought not to be left to rest upon a single pillar. When certain mental endowments receive a much higher culture than others, there is a distortion in the intellectual character. The mind never attains its full perfection, unless its various powers are so trained as to give them the fair proportions which nature designed. If the student exercises his reasoning powers only, he will be deficient in imagination and taste, in fervid and impressive eloquence. If he confines his attention to demonstrative evidence, he will be unfitted to decide correctly, in cases of probability. If he relies principally on his memory, his powers of invention will be impaired by disuse. In the course of instruction in this college, it has been an object to maintain such a proportion between the different branches of literature and science, as to form in the student a proper *balance* of character. From the pure mathematics, he learns the art of demonstrative reasoning. In attending to the physical sciences, he becomes familiar with facts, with the process of induction, and the varieties of probable evidence. In ancient literature, he finds some of the most finished models of taste. By English reading, he learns the powers of the language in which he is to speak and write. By logic and mental philosophy, he is taught the art of thinking; by rhetoric and oratory, the art of speaking. By frequent exercise on written composition, he acquires copiousness and accuracy of expression. By extemporaneous discussion, he becomes prompt, and fluent, and animated. It is a point of high importance, that eloquence and solid learning should go together; that he who has accumulated the richest treasures of thought, should possess the highest powers of oratory. To what purpose has a man become deeply learned, if he has no faculty of communicating his knowledge? And of what use is a display of rhetorical elegance, from one who knows little or nothing which is worth communicating? Est enim scientia comprehendenda rerum plurimarum, sine qua verborum volubilitas inanis atque irridenda est. Cic. Our course, therefore, aims at a union of science with literature; of solid attainment with skill in the art of persuasion.

No one feature in a system of intellectual education, is of greater moment than such an arrangement of duties and motives, as will most effectually throw the student upon the *resources of his own mind*. Without this, the whole apparatus of libraries, and instruments, and specimens, and lectures, and teachers, will be insufficient to secure distinguished excellence. The scholar must form himself, by his own exertions. The advantages furnished by a residence at a college, can do little more than stimulate and aid his personal efforts. The *inventive* powers are especially to be called into vigorous exercise. However abundant may be the acquisitions of the student, if he has no talent at forming new combinations of thought, he will be dull and inefficient. The sublimest efforts of genius consist in the creations of the imagination, the discoveries of the intellect, the conquests by which the dominions of science are extended. But the culture of the inventive faculties is not the *only* object of a liberal education. The most gifted understanding cannot greatly enlarge the amount of science to which the wisdom of ages has contributed. If it were possible for a youth to have his faculties in the highest state of cultivation, without any of the knowledge which is derived from others, he would be but poorly fitted for the business of life. To the discipline of the mind, therefore, is to be added instruction. The analytic method must be combined with the synthetic. Analysis is most efficacious in directing the powers of invention; but is far too slow in its progress to teach, within a moderate space of time, the circle of the sciences.

In our arrangements for the communication of knowledge, as well as in intellectual discipline, such branches are to be taught as will produce a proper symmetry and balance of character. We doubt whether the powers of the mind can be developed, in their fairest proportions, by studying languages alone, or mathematics alone, or natural or political science alone. As the bodily frame is brought to its highest perfection, not by one simple and uniform motion, but by a variety of exercises; so the mental faculties are expanded, and invigorated, and adapted to each other, by familiarity with different departments of science.

A most important feature in the colleges of this country is, that the students are generally of an age which requires, that a substitute be provided for *parental superintendence*. When removed from under the roof of their parents, and exposed to the untried scenes of temptation, it is necessary that some faithful and affectionate guardian take them by the hand, and guide their steps. This consideration determines the *kind* of government which ought to be maintained in our colleges. As it is a substitute for the regulations of a family, it should approach as near to the character of parental control as the circumstances of the case will admit. It should be founded on mutual affection and confidence. It should aim to effect its purpose, principally by kind and persuasive influence; not wholly or chiefly by restraint and terror. Still, punishment may sometimes be necessary. There may be perverse members of a college, as well as of a family. There may be those whom nothing but the arm of law can reach.

. . . . .

But why, it is asked, should *all* the students in a college be required to tread in the *same steps?* Why should not each one be allowed to select those branches of study which are most to his taste, which are best adapted to his peculiar talents, and which are most nearly connected with his intended profession? To this we answer, that our prescribed course contains those subjects only which ought to be understood, as we think, by every one who aims at a thorough education. They are not the peculiarities of any profession or art. These are to be learned in the professional and practical schools. But the principles of science, are the common foundation of all high intellectual attainments. As in our primary schools, reading, writing, and arithmetic are taught to all, however different their pospects; so in a college, all should be instructed in those branches of knowledge, of which no one destined to the higher walks of life ought to be ignorant. What subject which is now studied here, could be set aside, without evidently marring the system. Not to speak particularly, in this place, of the ancient languages; who that aims at a well proportioned and superior education will remain ignorant of the elements of the various branches of the mathematics, or of history and antiquities, or of rhetoric and oratory, or natural philosophy, or astronomy, or chemistry, or mineralogy, or geology, or political economy, or mental and moral philosophy?

It is sometimes thought that a student ought not to be urged to the study of that for which he has *no taste or capacity*. But how is he to know, whether he has a taste or capacity for a science, before he has even entered upon its elementary truths? If he is really destitute of talent sufficient for these common departments of education, he is destined for some narrow sphere of action. But we are well persuaded, that our students are not so deficient in intellectual powers, as they sometimes profess to be; though they are easily made to believe, that they have no capacity for the study of that which they are told is almost wholly useless. . . .

We well know that the whole population of the country can never enjoy the benefit of a thorough course of education. A large portion must be content with the very limited instruction in our primary schools. Others may be able to add to this the privilege of a few months at an academy. Others still, with higher aims and more ample means, may afford to spend two or three years, in attending upon a partial course of study, in some institution which furnishes instruction in any branch or branches selected by the pupil or his parents.

The question is then presented, whether the college shall have all the variety of classes and departments which are found in academies; or whether it shall confine itself to the single object of a well proportioned and thorough course of study. It is said that the public now demand, that the doors should be thrown open to all; that education ought to be so modified, and varied, as to adapt it to the exigencies of the country, and the prospects of different individuals; that the instruction given to those who are destined to be merchants, or manufacturers, or agriculturalists, should have a special reference to their respective professional pursuits.

The public are undoubtedly right, in demanding that there should be appropriate courses of education, accessible to all classes of youth. And we rejoice at the prospect of ample provision for this purpose, in the improvement of our academies, and the establishment of commercial high-schools, gymnasia, lycea, agricultural seminaries, &c. But do the public insist, that every college shall become a high-school, gymnasium, lyceum, and academy? Why should we interfere with these valuable institutions? Why wish to take their business out of their hands? The college has its appropriate object, and they have theirs. What advantage would be gained by attempting to blend them all in one? When in almost all our schools, and academies, and professional seminaries, the standard of education has been enlarged and elevated, is this a time for the college to *lower* its standard? Shall we fall back, and abandon the ground which, for thirty years past, we have been striving so hard to gain? Are those who are seeking only a partial education to be admitted into the college, merely for the purpose of associating its *name* with theirs? of carrying away with them a collegiate *diploma,* without incurring the fearful hazard of being over-educated? Why is a degree from a college more highly prized, than a certificate from an academy, if the former is not a voucher of a superior education? When the course of instruction in the one, is reduced to the level of that in the other; to be graduated at either, will be equally honorable. What is the characteristic difference between a college and an academy? Not that the former teaches more branches than the latter. There are many academies in the country, whose scheme of studies, at least upon paper, is more various than that of the colleges. But while an academy teaches a little of every thing, the college, by directing its efforts to one uniform course, aims at doing its work with greater precision, and economy of time; just as the merchant who deals in a single class of commodities, or a manufacturer who produces but one kind of fabrics, executes his business more perfectly, than he whose attention and skill are divided among a multitude of objects.

If our treasury were overflowing, if we had a *surplus fund,* requiring us to look out for some new object on which to expend it, there might perhaps be no harm in establishing a department for a brief and rapid course of study, so far connected with the college, as to be under the superintendence of the same board of trust. But it ought to be as distinct from the four classes of undergraduates, as is the medical or law school. All the means which are now applied to the proper collegiate department, are barely sufficient, or rather are insufficient, for the object in view. No portion of our resources, or strength, or labor, can be diverted to other purposes, without impairing the education which we are attempting to give. A London university, commencing with a capital of several hundred thousand dollars, and aiming to provide a system of instruction for the youth in a city whose population is more than a million, may well establish its higher and inferior courses, its scientific and practical departments, its professional, mercantile, and mechanical institutions. But shall a college, with an income of two or three thousand a year from funds, affect to be at once a London university? Should we *ever* become such an institution, our present undergraduate course, ought still to constitute one distinct branch of the complicated system of arrangements.

But might we not, by making the college more accessible to different descriptions of persons, enlarge our *numbers,* and in that way, increase our income? This might be the operation of the measure, for a very short time, while a degree from the college should retain its present value in public estimation; a value depending entirely upon the character of the education which we give. But the moment it is understood that the institution has descended to an inferior standard of attainment, its reputation will sink to a corresponding level. After we shall have become a college in *name only,* and in reality nothing more than an academy; or half college, and half academy; what will induce parents in various and distant parts of the country, to send us their sons, when they have academies enough in their own neighborhood? There is no magical influence in an act of incorporation, to give celebrity to a literary institution, which does not command respect for itself, by the elevated rank of its education. When the college has lost its hold on the public confidence, by depressing its standard of merit, by substituting a partial, for a thorough education, we may expect that it will be deserted by that class of persons who have hitherto been drawn here by high expectations and purposes. Even if we should *not* immediately suffer in point of *numbers,* yet we shall exchange the best portion of our students, for others of inferior aims and attainments.

As long as we can maintain an elevated character, we need be under no apprehension with respect to numbers. Without character, it will be in vain to think of retaining them. It is a hazardous experiment, to act upon the plan of gaining numbers first, and character afterwards. . . .

SECTION 4

Educational Reforms

The struggle for the reform of education during the national period worked toward a system of schools reaching from elementary to higher learning institutions linked in what came to be called the American "ladder" of education. The framework of the ladder was created in the establishment of the free, public common school, in the publicly-supported high school, and in the expanded college which included the practical and professional in its offerings. In a broad sense the struggle was for the democratization of American education; more accurately, it was an effort to bring into being new educational institutions more in accord with the democratizing changes in the society. Yet, at the same time educational reform movements helped to form and to spread democratic thinking itself.

The effort to establish free, public common schools, the essential base of the ladder, had its beginnings and some of its early successes in Massachusetts with the work of James G. Carter, the first of the chief state school officers. His many writings in the cause of popular education include these comments in 1824 entitled "This Wretched Mockery," concerning education in Massachusetts.

69. This Wretched Mockery

James G. Carter

The pilgrims of Plymouth set the first example not only to our own country, but to the civilized world, of a system of free schools, at which were educated together, not by compulsion, but from mutual choice, all classes of the community—the high, the low, the rich, and the poor—a system, by which the state so far assumed the education of the youth, as to make all property responsible for the support of common schools for the instruction of all children. This institution was indeed the foster child, and has justly been the pride, of Massachusetts and of New England. Its influences were strong, and they still are strong, upon the moral and political character of the people. . . .

If the policy of the legislature in regard to free schools for the last twenty years be not changed, the institution which has been the glory of New England will, in twenty years more, be extinct. If the State continue to relieve itself of the trouble of providing for the instruction of the whole people, and to shift the responsibility upon the towns, and the towns upon the districts, and the districts upon individuals, each will take care of himself and his own family as he is able, and as he appreciates the blessing of a good education. The rich will, as a class, have much better instruction than they now have, while the poor will have much worse or none at all. The academies and private schools will be carried to much greater

Reprinted from "Essays on Popular Education," *Old South Leaflets,* VI, No. 135, pp. 201, 220.

perfection than they have been, while the public free schools will become stationary or retrograde, till at length they will be thrown for support upon the gratuitous and of course capricious and uncertain efforts of individuals; and then, like the lower schools of the crowded cities of Europe, they will soon degenerate into mere mechanical establishments, such as the famous *seminaries* of London, Birmingham, and Manchester, of which we hear so much lately, not for rational, moral, and intellectual instruction of human beings, but for training young animals to march, sing, and draw figures in sand—establishments in which the power of one man is so prodigiously multiplied that he can overlook, direct, and control the intellectual exercises of a thousand! And this wretched mockery of education they must be right glad to accept as a charity instead of inheriting as their birthright as good instruction as the country affords.

Horace Mann carried forward Carter's work as chief state school officer in Massachusetts from 1837 to 1848. By nature inclined to reform through persuasion, Mann's famous Annual Reports during his twelve years in office are masterpieces of persuasive argument on behalf of the common-school cause. The Twelfth Annual Report, of which excerpts are included here, is a most eloquent summing-up of his thought and work.

70. Twelfth Annual Report

Horace Mann

Under the Providence of God, our means of education are the grand machinery by which the "raw material" of human nature can be worked up into inventors and discoverers, into skilled artisans and scientific farmers, into scholars and jurists into the founders of benevolent institutions, and the great expounders of ethical and theological science. By means of early education, those embryos of talent may be quickened, which will solve the difficult problems of political and economical law; and by them, too, the genius may be kindled which will blaze forth in the Poets of Humanity. Our

Horace Mann, *Twelfth Annual Report of the Board of Education together with the Twelfth Annual Report of the Secretary of the Board* (Boston: Dutton and Wentworth, 1849). From a Facsimile Edition printed by the National Education Association, 1951.

schools, far more than they have done, may supply the Presidents and Professors of Colleges, and Superintendents of Public Instruction, all over the land; and send, not only into our sister states, but across the Atlantic, the men of practical science, to superintend the construction of the great works of art. Here, too, may those judicial powers be developed and invigorated, which will make legal principles so clear and convincing as to prevent appeals to force; and, should the clouds of war ever lower over our country, some hero may be found,—the nursling of our schools, and ready to become the leader of our armies, ...

INTELLECTUAL EDUCATION, AS A MEANS OF REMOVING POVERTY, AND SECURING ABUNDANCE

Another cardinal object which the government of Massachusetts, and all the influential men in the State should propose to themselves, is the physical well-being of all the people,—the sufficiency, comfort, competence, of every individual, in regard to food, raiment, and shelter. And these necessaries and conveniences of life should be obtained by each individual for himself, or by each family for themselves, rather than accepted from the hand of charity, or extorted by poor-laws. It is not averred that this most desirable result can, in all instances, be obtained; but it is, nevertheless, the end to be aimed at. True statesmanship and true political economy, not less than true philanthropy, present this perfect theory as the goal, to be more and more closely approximated by our imperfect practice. The desire to achieve such a result cannot be regarded as an unreasonable ambition; for, though all mankind were well-fed, well-clothed, and well-housed, they might still be but half-civilized. . . .

According to the European theory, men are divided into classes,—some to toil and earn, others to seize and enjoy. According to the Massachusetts theory, all are to have an equal chance for earning, and equal security in the enjoyment of what they earn. The latter tends to equality of condition; the former to the grossest inequalities. Tried by any Christian standard of morals, or even by any of the better sort of heathen standards, can any one hesitate, for a moment, in declaring which of the two will produce the greater amount of human welfare; and which, therefore, is the more comfortable to the Divine will? The European theory is blind to what constitutes the highest glory, as well as the highest duty, of a State. . . .

I suppose it to be the universal sentiment of all those who mingle any ingredient of benevolence with their notions on Political Economy, that vast and overshadowing private fortunes are among the greatest dangers to which the happiness of the people in a republic can be subjected. Such fortunes would create a feudalism of a new kind; but one more oppressive and unrelenting than that of the Middle Ages. The feudal lords in England, and on the continent, never held their retainers in a more abject condition of servitude, than the great majority of foreign manufacturers and capitalists hold their operatives and laborers at the present day. The means employed are different, but the similarity in results is striking. What force did then, money does now. The villein of the Middle Ages had no spot of earth on which he could live, unless one were granted to him by his lord. The operative or laborer of the present day has no employment, and therefore no bread, unless the capitalist will accept his services. The vassal had no shelter but such as his master provided for him. Not one in five thousand of English operatives, or farm laborers, is able to build or own even a hovel; and therefore they must accept such shelter as Capital offers them. The baron prescribed his own terms to his retainers; those terms were peremptory, and the serf must submit or perish. The British manufacturer or farmer prescribes the rate of wages he will give to his workpeople; he reduces these wages under whatever pretext he pleases; and they too have no alternative but submission or starvation. In some respects, indeed, the condition of the modern dependant is more forlorn than that of the corresponding serf class in former times. Some attributes of the patriarchal relation did spring up between the lord and his lieges, to soften the harsh relations subsisting between them. Hence came some oversight of the condition of children, some relief in sickness, some protection and support in the decrepitude of age. But only in instances comparatively few, have kindly offices smoothed the rugged relation between British Capital and British Labor. The children of the work-people are abandoned to their fate; and, notwithstanding the privations they suffer, and the dangers they threaten, no power in the realm has yet been able to secure them an education; and when the adult laborer is prostrated by sickness, or eventually worn out by toil and age, the poor-house, which has all along been his destination, becomes his destiny.

Now two or three things will doubtless be admitted to be true, beyond all controversy, in regard to Massachusetts. By its industrial condition, and its business operations, it is exposed, far beyond any other state in the Union, to the fatal extremes of overgrown wealth and desperate poverty. Its population is far more dense than that of any other state. It is four or five times more dense than the average of all the other states, taken together; and density of population has always been one of the proximate causes of social inequality. According to population and territorial extent, there is far more capital in Massachusetts,—capital which is movable, and instantaneously available,—than in any other state in the Union; and probably both these qualifications respecting population and territory could be omitted without endangering the truth of the assertion. . . .

Now, surely, nothing but Universal Education can counter-work this tendency to the domination of capital and the servility of labor. If one class possesses all the wealth and the education, while the residue of society is ignorant and poor, it matters not by what name the relation between them may be called; the latter, in fact and in truth, will be the servile dependants and subjects of the former. But if education be equably diffused, it will draw property after it, by the strongest of all attractions; for such a thing never did happen, and never can happen, as that an intelligent and practical body of men should be permanently poor. Property and labor, in different classes, are essentially antagonistic; but property and labor, in the same class, are essentially fraternal. The people of Massachusetts have, in some degree, appreciated the truth, that the unexampled prosperity of the State,—its comfort, its competence, its general intelligence and virtue,—is attributable to the education, more or less perfect, which all its people have received; but are they sensible of a fact equally important?—namely, that it is to this same education that two thirds of the people are indebted for not being, to-day, the vassals of as severe a tyranny, in the form of capital, as the lower classes of Europe are bound to in the form of brute force.

Education, then, beyond all other devices of human origin, is the great equalizer of the conditions of men—the balance-wheel of the social machinery. I do not here mean that it so elevates the moral nature as to make men disdain and abhor the oppression of their fellow-men. This idea pertains to another of its attributes. But I mean that it gives each man the independence and the means, by which he can resist the selfishness of other men. It does better than to disarm the poor of their hostility towards the rich; it prevents being poor. Agrarianism is the revenge of poverty against wealth. The wanton destruction of the property of others, —the burning of hay-ricks and corn-ricks, the demolition of machinery, because it supersedes hand-labor, the sprinkling of vitriol on rich dresses, —is only agrarianism run mad. Education prevents both the revenge and the madness. On the other hand, a fellow-feeling for one's class or caste is the common instinct of hearts not wholly sunk in selfish regards for person, or for family. The spread of education, by enlarging the cultivated class or caste, will open a wider area over which the social feelings will expand; and, if this education should be universal and complete, it would do more than all things else to obliterate factitious distinctions in society.

The main idea set forth in the creeds of some political reformers, or revolutionizers, is, that some people are poor *because* others are rich. This idea supposes a fixed amount of property in the community, which, by fraud or force, or arbitrary law, is unequally divided among men; and the problem presented for solution is, how to transfer a portion of this property from those who are supposed to have too much, to those who feel and know that they have too little. At this point, both their theory and their expectation of reform stop. But the beneficent power of education would not be exhausted, even though it should peaceably abolish all the miseries that spring from the coëxistence, side by side, of enormous wealth and squalid want. It has a higher function. Beyond the power of diffusing old wealth, it has the prerogative of creating new. It is a thousand times more lucrative than fraud; and adds a thousand fold more to a nation's resources than the most successful conquests. Knaves and robbers can obtain only what was before possessed by others. But education creates or develops new treasures,—treasures not before possessed or dreamed of by any one. . . .

If a savage will learn how to swim, he can fasten a dozen pounds' weight to his back, and transport it across a narrow river, or other body of water of moderate width. If he will invent an axe, or other instrument, by which to cut down a tree, he can use the tree for a float, and one of its limbs for a paddle, and can thus transport many times the former weight, many times the former distance. Hollowing out his log, he will increase, what may be called, its tonnage,—or, rather, its *poundage*,— and, by sharpening its ends, it will cleave the water both more easily and more swiftly. Fastening several trees together, he makes a raft, and thus increases the buoyant power of his embryo water-craft. Turning up the ends of small poles, or using knees of timber instead of straight pieces, and grooving them together, or filling up the interstices between them, in some other way, so as to make them water-tight, he brings his rude raft literally into *ship-shape*. Improving upon hull below and rigging above, he makes a proud merchantman, to be wafted by the winds from continent to continent. But, even this does not content the adventurous naval architect. He frames iron arms for his ship; and, for oars, affixes iron wheels, capable of swift revolution, and stronger than the strong sea. Into iron-walled cavities in her bosom, he puts iron organs of massive structure and strength, and of cohesion insoluble by fire. Within these, he kindles a small volcano; and then, like a sentient and rational existence, this wonderful creation of his hands cleaves oceans, breasts tides, defies tempests, and bears its living and jubilant freight around the globe. Now, take away intelligence from the ship-builder, and the steamship,—that miracle of human art,—falls back into a floating log; the log itself is lost; and the savage swimmer, bearing his dozen pounds on his back, alone remains.

And so it is, not in one department only, but in the whole circle of human labors. The annihilation of the sun would no more certainly be followed by darkness, than the extinction of human intelligence would plunge the race at once into the weakness and helplessness of barbarism. To have created such beings as we are, and to have placed them in this world, without the light of the sun, would be no more cruel than for a government to suffer its laboring classes to grow up without knowledge. . . .

For the creation of wealth, then,—for the existence of a wealthy people and a wealthy nation,—intelligence is the grand condition. The number of improvers will increase, as the intellectual constituency, if I may so call it, increases. In former times, and in most parts of the world even at the present day, not one man in a million has ever had such a development of mind, as made it possible for him to become a contributor to art or science. Let this development precede, and contributions, numberless, and of inestimable value, will be sure to follow. That Political Economy, therefore, which busies itself about capital and labor, supply and demand, interest and rents, favorable and unfavorable balances of trade; but leaves out of account the element of a wide-spread mental development, is nought but stupendous folly. The greatest of all the arts in political economy is, to change a consumer into a producer; and the next greatest is to increase the producer's producing power;—an end to be directly attained, by increasing his intelligence. . . .

MORAL EDUCATION

Moral education is a primal necessity of social existence. The unrestrained passions of men are not only homicidal, but suicidal; and a community without a conscience would soon extinguish itself. Even with a natural conscience, how often has Evil triumphed over Good! From the beginning of time, Wrong has followed Right, as the shadow the substance. As the relations of men became more complex, and the business of the world more extended, new opportunities and new temptations for wrong-doing have been created. With the endearing relations of parent and child, came also the possibility of infanticide and parricide; and the first domestic altar that brothers ever reared was stained with fratricidal blood. Following close upon the obligations to truth, came falsehood and perjury, and closer still upon the duty of obedience to the Divine law, came disobedience. With the existence of private relations between men, came fraud; and with the existence of public relations between nations, came aggression, war, and slavery. . . .

Even so, like a weltering flood, do immoralities and crimes break over all moral barriers, destroying and profaning the securities and the sanctities of life. Now, how best shall this deluge be repelled? What mighty power, or combination of powers, can prevent its inrushing, or narrow the sweep of its ravages?

The race has existed long enough to try many experiments for the solution of this greatest problem ever submitted to its hands; and the race has experimented, without stint of time or circumscription of space, to mar or modify legitimate results. Mankind have tried despotisms, monarchies, and republican forms of government. They have tried the extremes of anarchy and of autocracy. They have tried Draconian codes of law; and, for the lightest offences, have extenguished the life of the offender. They have established theological standards, claiming for them the sanction of Divine authority, and the attributes of a perfect and infallible law; and then they have imprisoned, burnt, massacred, not individuals only, but whole communities at a time, for not bowing down to idols which ecclesiastical authority had set up. These and other great systems of measures have been adopted as barriers against error and guilt; they have been extended over empires, prolonged through centuries, and administered with terrible energy; and yet the great ocean of vice and crime overleaps every embankment, pours down upon our heads, saps the foundations under our feet, and sweeps away the securities of social order, of property, liberty, and life.

At length, these experiments have been so numerous, and all of them have terminated so disastrously, that a body of men has risen up, in later times, powerful in influence, and not inconsiderable in numbers, who, if I may use a mercantile phrase, would abandon the world as a total loss;— who mock at the idea of its having a benevolent or even an intelligent Author or Governor; and who, therefore, would give over the race to the dominion of chance, or to that of their own licentious passions, whose rule would be more fatal than chance.

But to all doubters, disbelievers, or despairers, in human progress, it may still be said, there is one experiment which has never yet been tried. It is an experiment which, even before its inception, offers the highest authority for its ultimate success. Its formula is intelligible to all; and it is as legible as though written in starry letters on an azure sky. It is expressed in these few and simple words:—*"Train up a child in the way he should go, and when he is old he will not depart from it."* This declaration is positive. If the conditions are complied with, it makes no provision for a failure. Though pertaining to morals, yet, if the terms of the direction are observed, there is no more reason to doubt the result, than there would be in an optical or a chemical experiment.

But this experiment has never yet been tried. Education has never yet been brought to bear with one hundredth part of its potential force, upon the natures of children, and, through them, upon the character of men, and of the race. In all the attempts to reform mankind which have hitherto been made, whether by changing the frame of government, by aggravating or softening the severity of the penal code, or by substituting a government-created, for a God-created religion;—in all these attempts, the infantile and youthful mind, its amenability to influences, and the enduring and self-operating character of the influences its receives, have been almost wholly unrecognized. Here, then, is a new agency, whose powers are but just beginning to be understood, and whose mighty energies, hitherto, have been but feebly invoked; and yet, from our experience, limited and imperfect as it is, we do know that, far beyond any other earthly instrumentality, it is comprehensive and decisive. . . .

RELIGIOUS EDUCATION

Grave charges have been made against us, that our purpose was to exclude religion; and to exclude that, too, which is the common exponent of religion,—the Bible,—from the Common Schools of the State; or, at least, to derogate from its authority, and destroy its influence in them. Whatever prevalence a suspicion of the truth of these imputations may have heretofore had, I have reason to believe that further inquiry and examination have done much to disabuse the too credulous recipients of so groundless a charge. Still, amongst a people so commendably sensitive on the subject of religion, as are the people of Massachusetts, any suspicion of irreligious tendencies, will greatly prejudice any cause, and, so far as any cause may otherwise have the power of doing good, will greatly impair that power.

It is known, too, that our noble system of Free Schools for the whole people, is strenuously opposed;—by a few persons in our own State, and by no inconsiderable numbers in some of the other states of this Union;—and that a rival system of "Parochial" or "Sectarian Schools," is now urged upon the public by a numerous, a powerful, and a well-organized body of men. It has pleased the advocates of this rival system, in various public addresses, in reports, and through periodicals devoted to their cause, to denounce our system as irreligious and anti-Christian. They do not trouble themselves to describe what our system is, but adopt a more summary way to forestall public opinion against it, by using general epithets of reproach, and signals of alarm.

In this age of the world, it seems to me that no student of history, or observer of mankind, can be hostile to the precepts and the doctrines of the Christian religion, or opposed to any institutions which expound and exemplify them; and no man who thinks, as I cannot but think, respecting the enduring elements of character, whether public or private, can be willing to have his name mentioned while he is living, or remembered when he is dead, as opposed to religious instruction, and Bible instruction for the young. In making this final Report, therefore, I desire to vindicate my conduct from the charges that have been made against it;

The very terms, *Public School,* and *Common School,* bear upon their face, that they are schools which the children of the entire community may attend. Every man, not on the pauper list, is taxed for their support. But he is not taxed to support them as special religious institutions; if he were, it would satisfy, at once, the largest definition of a Religious Establishment. But he is taxed to support them, as a *preventive* means against dishonesty, against fraud, and against violence; on the same principle that he is taxed to support criminal courts as a *punitive* means against the same offences. He is taxed to support schools, on the same principle that he is taxed to support paupers; because a child without education is poorer and more wretched than a man without bread. He is taxed to support schools, on the same principle that he would be taxed to defend the nation against foreign invasion, or against rapine committed by a foreign foe; because the general prevalence of ignorance, susperstition, and vice, will breed Goth and Vandal at home, more fatal to the public well-being, than any Goth or Vandal from abroad. And, finally, he is taxed to support schools, because they are the most effective means of developing and training those powers and faculties in a child, by which, when he becomes a man, he may understand what his highest interests and his highest duties are; and may be, in fact, and not in name only, a free agent. The elements of a political education are not bestowed upon any school child, for the purpose of making him vote with this or that political party, when he becomes of age; but for the purpose of enabling him to choose for himself, with which party he will vote. So the religious education which a child receives at school, is not imparted to him, for the purpose of making him join this or that denomination, when he arrives at years of discretion, but for the purpose of enabling him to judge for himself, according to the dictates of his own reason and conscience, what his religious obligations are, and whither they lead. But if a man is taxed to support a school, where religious doctrines are inculcated which he believes to be false, and which he believes that God condemns; then he is excluded from the school by the Divine law, at the same time that he is compelled to support it by the human law. This is a double wrong. It is politically wrong, because, if such a man educates his children at all, he must educate them elsewhere, and thus pay two taxes, while some of his neighbors pay less than their due proportion of one; and it is religiously wrong, because he is constrained, by human power, to promote what he believes the Divine Power forbids. The principle involved in such a course is pregnant with all tyrannical consequences. It is broad enough to sustain any claim of ecclesiastical domination, ever made in the darkest ages of the world. Every religious persecution, since the time of Constantine, may find its warrant in it, and can be legitmately defended upon it. If a man's estate may be taken from him to pay for teaching a creed which he believes to be false, his children can be taken from him to be taught the same creed; and he, too, may be punished to any extent, for not voluntarily surrendering both his estate and his offspring. If his children can be compulsorily taken and taught to believe a creed which the parent disbelieves, then the parent can be compulsorily taken and made to subscribe the same creed. And, in regard to the extent of the penalties which may be invoked to compel conformity, there is no stopping-place between taking a penny and inflicting perdition. It is only necessary to call a man's reason and conscience and religious faith, by the name of recusancy, or contumacy, or heresy, and so to inscribe them on the statute book; and then the non-conformist or dissenter may be subdued by steel, or cord, or fire; by anathema and excommunication in this life, and the terrors of end-less perdition in the next. Surely, that system cannot be an irreligious, an anti-Christian, or an un-Christian one, whose first and cardinal principle it is, to recognize and protect the highest and dearest of all human interests, and of all human rights. . . .

It is still easier to prove that the Massachusetts school system is not anti-Christian nor un-Christian. The Bible is the acknowledged expositor of Christianity. In strictness, Christianity has no other authoritative expounder. This Bible is in our Common Schools, by common consent. Twelve years ago, it was not in all the schools. Contrary to the genius of our government, if not contrary to the express letter of the law, it had been used for sectarian purposes,—to prove one sect to be right, and others to be wrong. Hence, it had been excluded from the schools of some towns, by an express vote. But since the law and the reasons on which it is founded, have been more fully explained and better understood; and since sectarian instruction has, to a great extent, ceased to be given, the Bible has been restored. I am not aware of the existence of a single town in the State, in whose schools it is not now introduced, either by a direct vote of the school committee, or by such general desire and acquiescence, as supersede the necessity of a vote. In all my intercourse, for twelve years, whether personal or by letter, with all the school officers in the State, and with tens of thousands of individuals in it, I have never heard an objection made to the use of the Bible in school, except in one or two instances; and, in those cases, the objection was put upon the ground, that daily familiarity with the book, in school, would tend to impair a reverence for it.

If the Bible, then, is the exponent of Christianity; if the Bible contains the communications, precepts, and doctrines, which make up the religious system, called and known as Christianity; if the Bible makes known those truths, which, according to the faith of Christians, are able to make men wise unto salvation; and if this Bible is in the schools, how can it be said that Christianity is excluded from the schools; or how can it be said that the school system, which adopts and uses the Bible, is an anti-Christian, or an un-Christian system? If that which is the acknowledged exponent and basis of Christianity is in the schools, by what tergiversation in language, or paralogism in logic, can Christianity be said to be shut out from the schools? If the Old Testament were in the schools, could a Jew complain, that Judaism was excluded from them? If the Koran were read regularly and reverently in the schools, could a Mahomedan say that Mahomedanism was excluded? Or, if the Mormon Bible were in the schools, could it be said that Mormonism was excluded from them?

Is it not, indeed, too plain, to require the formality of a syllogism, that if any man's creed is to be found in the Bible, and the Bible is in the schools, then that man's creed is in the schools? This seems even plainer than the proposition, that two and two make four;—that is, we can conceive of a creature so low down in the scale of intelligence, that he could not see what sum would be produced by adding two and two together, who still could not fail to see, that, if a certain system, called Christianity, were contained in, and inseparable from, a certain book called the Bible, then wherever the Bible might go, there the system of Christianity must be. . . .

And further; our law explicit and solemnly enjoins it upon all teachers, without any exception, "to exert their best endeavors, to impress on the minds of children and youth committed to their care and instruction, the principles of piety, justice, and a sacred regard to truth, love to their country, humanity and universal benevolence, sobriety, industry, and frugality, chastity, moderation, and temperance, and those other virtues which are the ornament of human society, and the basis upon which a republican constitution is founded." Are not these virtues and graces part and parcel of Christianity? In other words, can there be Christianity without them? While these virtues and these duties towards God and man, are inculcated in our schools, any one who says that the schools are anti-Christian or un-Christian, expressly affirms that his own system of Christianity does not embrace any one of this radiant catalogue; that it rejects them all; that it embraces their opposites!

And further still; our system makes it the express duty of all the "resident ministers of the Gospel" to bring all the children within the moral and

Christian inculcations above enumerated; so that he who avers that our system is an anti-Christian or an un-Christian one, avers that it is both anti-Christian and un-Christian for a "minister OF THE GOSPEL to promote, or labor to diffuse, the moral attributes and excellences," which the statue so earnestly enjoins.

This topic invites far more extended exposition; but this must suffice. In bidding an official Farewell to a system, with which I have been so long connected, to which I have devoted my means, my strength, my health, twelve years of time, and, doubtless, twice that number of years from what might otherwise have been my term of life, I have felt bound to submit these brief views in its defence. In justice to my own name and memory; in justice to the Board of which I was originally a member, and from which I have always sought counsel and guidance; and in justice to thousands of the most wise, upright, and religious-minded men in Massachusetts, who have been my fellow-laborers in advancing the great cause of Popular Education, under the auspices of this system, I have felt bound to vindicate it from the aspersions cast upon it, and to show its consonance with the eternal principles of equity and justice. I have felt bound to show, that, so far from its being an irreligious, an anti-Christian, or an un-Christian system, it is a system which recognizes religious obligations in their fullest extent; that it is a system which invokes a religious spirit, and can never be fitly administered without such a spirit; that it inculcates the great commands, upon which hang all the law and the prophets; that it welcomes the Bible, and therefore welcomes all the doctrines which the Bible really contains, and that it listens to these doctrines so reverently, that, for the time being, it will not suffer any rash mortal to thrust in his interpolations of their meaning, or overlay the text with any of the "many inventions" which the heart of man has sought out. It is a system, however, which leaves open all other means of instruction,—the pulpits, the Sunday schools, the Bible classes, the catechisms, of all denominations,—to be employed according to the preferences of individual parents. It is a system which restrains itself from teaching, that what it does teach is all that needs to be taught, or that should be taught; but leaves this to be decided by each man for himself, according to the light of his reason and conscience; and on his responsibility to that Great Being, who, in holding him to an account for the things done in the body, will hold him to the strictest account for the manner in which he has "trained up" his children.

Such, then, in a religious point of view, is the Massachusetts system of Common Schools. Reverently, it recognizes and affirms the sovereign rights of the Creator; sedulously and sacredly it guards the religious rights of the creature; while its seeks to remove all hinderances, and to supply all furtherances to a filial and paternal communion between man and his Maker. In a social and political sense, it is a *Free* school system. It knows no distinction of rich and poor, of bond and free, or between those who, in the imperfect light of this world, are seeking, through different avenues, to reach the gate of heaven. Without money and without price, it throws open its doors, and spreads the table of its bounty, for all the children of the State. Like the sun, it shines, not only upon the good, but upon the evil, that they may become good; and, like the rain, its blessings descend, not only upon the just, but upon the unjust, that their injustice may depart from them and be known no more.

Each state had its Carters and Manns, its leaders in the struggle for the common school, who agreed on aims but differed often in style and method for bringing about change. In Pennsylvania, Thaddeus Stevens was at the forefront of the school-reform movement, not, however, as a school official but as a state legislator and later as a congressman. His speech on behalf of free schools to the Pennsylvania state legislature in 1835 illustrates his particular approach, one more of imposition than of persuasion.

71. On Behalf of Free Schools in Pennsylvania, 1835

Thaddeus Stevens

Mr. Speaker: I will briefly give you the reasons why I shall oppose the a repeal of the school law.

This law was passed at the last session of the legislature with unexampled unanimity, but one member of this house voting against it. It has not yet come into operation, and none of its effects have been tested by experience in Pennsylvania. The passage of such a law is enjoined by the constitution; and has been recommended by every governor since its adoption. Much to his credit, it has been warmly urged by the present executive in his annual messages delivered at the opening of the legislature. To repeal it now, before its practical effects have been discovered, would argue that it contained some glaring and pernicious defect, and that the

Reprinted from *Report of the United States Commissioner of Education for 1898-1899*, pp. 518-21.

last legislature acted under some strong and fatal delusion, which blinded every man of them to the interests of the Commonwealth. I will attempt to show that the law is salutary, useful and important, and that consequently the last legislature acted wisely in passing and the present would act unwisely in repealing it; that, instead of being oppressive to the people, it will lighten their burdens, while it elevates them in the scale of human intellect.

It would seem to be humiliating to be under the necessity, in the nineteenth century, of entering into a formal argument, to prove the utility, and, to free governments, the absolute necessity of education. More than two thousand years ago the Deity, who presided over intellectual endowments, ranked highest for dignity, chastity, and virtue among the goddesses worshipped by cultivated pagans. And I will not insult this house or our constituents by supposing any course of reasoning necessary to convince them of its high importance. Such necessity would be degrading to a Christian age, a free republic.

If an elective Republic is to endure for any great length of time, every elector must have sufficient information, not only to accumulate wealth and take care of his pecuniary concerns, but to direct wisely the legislature, the ambassadors, and the Executive of the nation—for some part of all these things, some agency in approving or disapproving of them, falls to every freeman. If then, the permanency of our Government depends upon such knowledge, it is the duty of government to see that the means of information be diffused to every citizen. This is a sufficient answer to those who deem education a private and not a public duty—who argue that they are willing to educate their own children, but not their neighbor's children. . . . The amendment which is now proposed as a substitute for the school law of last session, is, in my opinion, of a most hateful and degrading character. It is a reenactment of the pauper law of 1809. It proposes that the assessors shall take a census, and make a record of the poor. This shall be revised, and a new record made by the county commissioners, so that the names of those who have the misfortune to be poor men's children shall be forever preserved, as a distinct class, in the archives of the country! The teacher, too, is to keep in his school a pauper book, and register the names and attendance of poor scholars; thus pointing out and recording their poverty in the midst of their companions. Sir, hereditary distinctions of rank are sufficiently odious; but that which is founded on poverty is infinitely more so. Such a law should be entitled "An act for branding and marking the poor, so that they may be known from the rich and proud." Many complain of this tax, not so much on account of its amount, as because it is for the benefit of others and not themselves. This is a mistake; it is for their own benefit, inasmuch as it perpetuates the Government and insures the due administration of the laws under which they live, and by which their lives and property are protected. Why do they not urge the same objection against all other taxes? The industrious, thrifty, rich farmer pays a heavy county tax to support criminal courts, build jails, and pay sheriffs and jail keepers, and yet probably he never has, and never will have, any personal use of either. He never gets the worth of his money by being tried for a crime before the court, by being allowed the privilege of the jail on conviction, or receiving an equivalent from the sheriff or his hangman officers! He cheerfully pays the tax which is necessary to support and punish convicts, but loudly complains of that which goes to prevent his fellow-being from becoming a criminal, and to obviate the necessity of those humiliating institutions.

This law is often objected to, because its benefits are shared by the children of the profligate spendthrift equally with those of the most industrious and economical habits. It ought to be remembered that the benefit is bestowed, not upon the erring parents, but the innocent children. Carry out this objection and you punish children for the crimes or misfortunes of their parents. You virtually establish castes and grades founded on no merit of the particular generation, but on the demerits of their ancestors; an aristocracy of the most odious and insolent kind—the aristocracy of wealth and pride.

It is said that its advantages will be unjustly and unequally enjoyed, because the industrious, money-making man keeps his whole family constantly employed, and has but little time for them to spend at school; while the idle man has but little employment for his family, and they will constantly attend school. I know, sir, that there are some men, whose whole souls are so completely absorbed in the accumulation of wealth, and whose avarice so increases with success, that they look upon their very children in no other light than as instruments of gain—that they, as well as the ox and the ass within their gates, are valuable only in proportion to their annual earnings. And, according to the present system, the children of such men are reduced almost to an intellectual level with their co-laborers of the brute creation. This law will be of vast advantage to the offspring of such misers. If they are compelled to pay their taxes to support schools, their very meanness will induce them to send their children to them to get the worth of their money. Thus it will extract good out of the very penuriousness of the miser. Surely a system which will work such wonders, ought to be as greedily sought for, and more highly prized, than that coveted alchemy which was to produce gold and silver out of the blood and entrails of vipers, lizards, and other filthy vermin.

Why, sir, are the colleges and literary institutions of Pennsylvania now, and ever have been, in a languishing and sickly condition? Why, with a fertile soil and genial climate, has she, in proportion to her population, scarcely one-third as many collegiate students as cold, barren New England? The answer is obvious; she has no free schools. Until she shall have you may in vain endow college after college; they will never be filled, or filled only by students from other States. In New England free schools plant the seeds and the desire of knowledge in every mind, without regard to the wealth of the parent or the texture of the pupil's garments. When the seed, thus universally sown, happens to fall on fertile soil, it springs up and is fostered by a generous public until it produces its glorious fruit. Those who have but scanty means and are pursuing a collegiate education, find it necessary to spend a portion of the year in teaching common schools; thus imparting the knowledge which they acquire, they raise the dignity of the employment to a rank which it should always hold, honorable in proportion to the high qualifications necessary for its discharge. Thus devoting a portion of their time to acquiring the means of subsistence, industrious habits are forced upon them and their minds and bodies become disciplined to a regularity and energy which is seldom the lot of the rich. It is no uncommon occurrence to see the poor man's son, thus encouraged by wise legislation far outstrip and bear off the laurels from the less industrious heirs of wealth. Some of the ablest men of the present and past days never could have been educated, except for that benevolent system. Not to mention any of the living, it is well known that that architect of an immortal name, who plucked "the lightning from heaven and the sceptre from tyrants," was the child of free schools. Why shall Pennsylvania now repudiate a system which is calculated to elevate her to that rank in the intellectual, which, by the blessing of Providence, she holds in the natural world? To be the keystone of the arch, the "very first among her equals?" I am aware, sir, how difficult it is for the great mass of people, who have never seen this system in operation, to understand its advantages. But is it not wise to let it go into full operation and learn its results from experience? Then, if it prove useless or burdensome, how easy to repeal it. I know how large a portion of the community can scarcely feel any sympathy with, or understand the necessity of the poor; or appreciate the exquisite feelings which they enjoy when they see their children receiving the boon of education, and rising in intellectual superiority above the clogs which hereditary poverty had cast upon them. It is not wonderful that he whose far acres have descended to him, from father to son in unbroken succession, should never have sought for the surest means of alleviating it. Sir, when I reflect how apt hereditary wealth, hereditary influence, and perhaps as a consequence, hereditary pride are to close the avenues and steel the heart against the wants and the rights of the poor, I am induced to thank my Creator for having from early life bestowed upon me the blessings of poverty. Sir, it is a blessing, for if there be any human sensation more ethereal and divine than all others, it is that which feelingly sympathizes with misfortune.

The extension of the common school upward had its early beginnings in 1821 with the organization in Boston of the English Classical School, the name of which was changed within a few years to the English High School. In the course of the following fifty years the institution of the high school spread to every town and city in America, offering free secondary-level instruction to the graduates of the public elementary school. The curriculum of the public school, however, was in general modeled after the college-preparatory studies of the academies, and in this regard the high school was not so much an extension of the common school as it was a tuition-free replacement of the prestigious classical academy. The following is an outline of Cincinnati public high school offerings in 1856.

72. A Sketch of Woodward High School in Cincinnati, 1856

The System of Common Schools in Cincinnati was established in 1828-29 under a special act of the Legislature, by which a tax of $7000. was annually imposed for the building of school-houses, and a like amount, in addition to the state appropriation, for the support of schools. Under this act schoolhouses were erected, in point of location, size, and internal convenience, greatly in advance of the then generally received notions as to school architecture.

In 1834 the system was greatly extended, and in 1845 the trustees were authorized to establish schools of different grades, and in 1850 to appoint a superintendent.

In 1847 a central high school was organized, and in 1852 the Woodward Fund and the Hughes Fund, amounting to $300,000, and yielding

Reprinted from *American Journal of Education*, IV, 1858, pp. 520-525.

over $5000. (the Woodward estate, in 1856, yielded $4510.), were united for the purpose of sustaining two schools of this grade.

In 1853 a building was erected for the accommodation of the Hughes High School, at an expense, including lot, of about $40,000, and in 1856, in an opposite section of the city, another building, at a cost of $50,000, for the Woodward High School. The latter, built in the Tudor style of architecture, was of brick and three stories high, with a high basement. The basement contained two Philosophical Rooms, 27⅔ x 42⅔ feet in size; and four furnaces. The first and second floors were alike and contained four classrooms each, while the third floor was given over to a Lecture Hall, 68⅔ x 83⅔ feet in size, a large platform, and two small ante rooms. The building was warmed by four hot-air furnaces, and lighted by gas.

The course of study and textbooks for both schools, as prescribed by the school board in January, 1856, was as follows:

FIRST YEAR

First Session

English Grammar, Brown or Pinneo, completed
English History, Goodrich or Markham, completed
Ray's Algebra, to Sec. 172

Second Session

Weld's Latin Lessons, to Part II.
Fitch's Physical Geography
Andrews' and Stoddard's Latin Grammar
Ray's Algebra, to Sec. 305
Physical Geography (3 lessons)
Reading (2 lessons)

(Five lessons in each of the above weekly)

Once a Week During the Year

Lectures, by the Principal, on Morals and Manners
Aids to Composition, completed
Composition and Declamation, by sections, each once in three weeks
Reading and Vocal Music
Penmanship, if needed

SECOND YEAR

First Session

Weld's Latin Lessons, to History
Andrews' and Stoddard's Latin Grammar
Geometry, Davies' Legendre, to

Second Session

Weld's Latin Lessons, completed
Andrews and Stoddard, completed
Geometry, Davies' Legendre, to Book IX

Book V
Gray's Natural Philosophy, to Pneumatics

Gray's Natural Philosophy, completed

(Five lessons in each of the above weekly)

Once a Week During the Year

Reading, Elemental Sounds
Rhetoric and Vocal Music
Composition and Declamation, by sections

THIRD YEAR

First Session

Silliman's Chemistry, to Sec. 282
Algebra and Spherics, Ray's and Davies' Legendre completed
Andrews' Caesar or Sallust, 50 Sections (3d)
German or French (3 days)

Second Session

Silliman's Chemistry, to Vegetable Chemistry
Davies' Trigonometry, completed
Cooper's Virgil's Aeneid, 3 books (3d)
German or French (3 days)

Once a Week Throughout the Year

Constitution of the United States
Hedge's Logic
Reading, Rhetoric, and Vocal Music
Composition and Declamation, by sections

FOURTH YEAR

First Session

Cutter's Physiology & Hygiene
McIntire's Astronomy
Gray and Adams' Geology
Folsom's Cicero, 3 Orations (3 days)
Moral Philosophy (1 day)
German or French (3 days)

Second Session

Davies' Navigation and Surveying
Weber's General History
Wayland's Mental Philosophy
Evidences of Christianity (1 day)
German or French (3 days)

Once a Week Throughout the Year

Critical Readings, Vocal Music
Compositions, by sections
Original Addresses, by sections

COLLEGE CLASS

For those preparing to enter college, the following may be substituted for the regular studies of the fourth year,

> Virgil's Aeneid, six books
> Caesar or Sallust, completed
> Cicero's Orations, six
> Crosby's Greek Grammar
> Felton's Greek Reader

The question of democracy in secondary education was considered at length by George S. Boutwell in 1857 in a speech to the American Institute of Instruction entitled "The Relative Merits of Public High Schools and Endowed Academies."

73. The Relative Merits of Public High Schools and Endowed Academies

George S. Boutwell

The distinguishing difference between the advocates of endowed schools and of free schools is this: those who advocate the system of endowed academies go back in their arguments to one foundation, which is, that in education of the higher grades the great mass of the people are not to be trusted. And those who advocate a system of free education in high schools put the matter where we have put the rights of property and liberty, where we put the institutions of law and religion—upon the public judgment. And we will stand there. If the public will not maintain institutions of learning, then, I say, let institutions of learning go down. If I belong to a state which cannot be moved from its extremities to its centre, and from its centre to its extremities, for the maintenance of a system of public instruction, then, in that respect, I disown that state; and if there be one state in this Union whose people cannot be aroused to maintain a system of public instruction, then they are false to the great leading idea of American principles, and of civil, political, and religious liberty.

Reprinted from George S. Boutwell, *Thoughts on Educational Topics and Institutions* (Boston, Phillip Sampson and Co., 1859), pp. 152-163.

It is easy to enumerate the advantages of a system of public education, and the evils—I say evils—of endowed academies, whether free or charging payment for tuition. Endowed academies are not, in all respects, under all circumstances, and everywhere, to be condemned. In discussing this subject, it may be well for me to state the view that I have of the proper position of endowed academies. They have a place in the educational wants of this age. This is especially true of academies of the highest rank, which furnish an elevated and extended course of instruction. To such I make no objection, but I would honor and encourage them. Yet I regard private schools, which do the work usually done in public schools, as temporary, their necessity as ephemeral, and I think that under a proper public sentiment they will soon pass away. They cannot stand,—such has been the experience in Massachusetts,—they cannot stand by the side of a good system of public education. Yet where the population is sparse, where there is not property sufficient to enable the people to establish a high school, then an endowed school may properly come in to make up the deficiency, to supply the means of education to which the public wealth, at the present moment, is unequal. Endowed institutions very properly, also, give a professional education to the people. At this moment we cannot look to the public to give that education which is purely professional. But what we do look to the public for is this: to furnish the means of education to the children of the whole people, without any reference to social, pecuniary, political, or religious distinctions, so that every person may have a preliminary education sufficient for the ordinary business of life.

It is said that the means of education are better in an endowed academy, or in an endowed free school, than they can be in a public school. What is meant by *means* of education? I understand that, first and chiefly, as extraneous means of education, we must look to a correct public sentiment, which shall animate and influence the teacher, which shall give direction to the school, which shall furnish the necessary public funds. An endowed free academy can have none of these things permanently. Take, for example, the free school established at Norwich by the liberality of thirty or forty gentlemen, who contributed ninety thousand dollars. What security is there that fifty years hence, when the educational wants of the people shall be changed, when the population of Norwich shall be double or treble what it is now, when science shall make greater demands, when these forty contributors shall have passed away, this institution will answer the wants of that generation? According to what we know of the history of this country, it will be entirely inadequate; and, though none of us may live to see the prediction fulfilled or falsified, I do not hesitate to say that the school will ultimately prove a failure, because it is founded in a mistake.

Then look and see what would have been the state of things if there had been public spirit invoked to establish a public high school, and if the means for its support had been raised by taxation of all the people, so that the system of education would have expanded according to the growth of the city, and year by year would have accommodated itself to the public wants and public zeal in the cause. Though these means seem now to be ample, they will by and by be found too limited. The school at Norwich is encumbered with regulations; and so every endowed institution is likely to be, because the right of a man to appropriate his property to a particular object carries with it, in the principles of common law, and in the administration of the law, in all free governments, the right to declare, to a certain extent, how that property shall be applied. . . .

And then look further, and see how, under a system of public instruction, you can build up, from year to year, in the growth of the child, a system according to his wants. Private instruction cannot do this. What do we do where we have a correct system? A child goes into a primary school. He is not to go out when he attains a certain age. He might as well go out when he is of a certain height; there would be as much merit in one case as in the other. But he is advanced when he has made adequate attainments. Who does not see that the child is incited and encouraged and stimulated by every sentiment to which you should appeal? And, then, when he has gone up to the grammar school, we say to him, "You are to go into the high school when you have made certain attainments." And who is to judge of these attainments? A committee appointed by the people, over whom the people have some ultimate control. And in that control they have security for two things: first, that the committee shall not be suspected of partiality; and secondly, that they shall not be actually guilty of partiality. In the same manner, there is security for the proper connection between the high school and the schools below. But in the school at Norwich—of which I speak because it is now prominent—you have a board of twenty-five men, irresponsible to the people. They select a committee of nine; that committee determines what candidates shall be transferred from the grammar schools to the high school. May there not be suspicion of partiality? If a boy or girl is rejected, you look for some social, political, or religious influence which has caused the rejection, and the parent and child complain. Here is a great evil; for the real and apparent justice of the examination and decision by which pupils are transferred from one school to another is vital to the success of the system.

There is another advantage in the system of public high schools, which I imagine the people do not always at first appreciate. It is, that the private school, with the same teachers, the same apparatus, and the same means, cannot give the education which may be, and usually is, furnished in the public schools. This statement may seem to require some considerable support. We must look at facts as they are. Some people are poor; I am sorry for them. Some people are rich, and I congratulate them upon their good fortune. But it is not so much of a benefit, after all, as many think. It is worth something in this world, no doubt, to be rich; but what is the result of that condition upon the family first, the school afterwards, and society finally? It is, that some learn the lesson of life a little earlier than others; and that lesson is the lesson of self-reliance, which is worth more than—I will not say a knowledge of the English language—but worth more than Latin or Greek. If the great lesson of self-reliance is to be learned, who is more likely to acquire it early,—the child of the poor, or the child of the rich; the child who has most done for him, or the child who is under the necessity of doing most for himself? Plainly, the latter. Now, while a system of public instruction in itself cannot be magnified in its beneficial influences to the poor and to the children of the poor, it is equally beneficial to the rich in the facility it affords for the instruction of their children. Is it not worth something to the rich man, who cannot, from the circumstances of the case, teach self-reliance around the family hearth, to send his child to school to learn this lesson with other children, that he may be stimulated, that he may be provoked to exertions which he would not otherwise have made? For, be it remembered that in our schools public sentiment is as well marked as in a college, or a town, or a nation; that it moves forward in the same way. And the great object of a teacher should be to create a public sentiment in favor of virtue. There should be some pioneers in favor of forming a correct public sentiment; and when it is formed it moves on irresistibly. It is like the river made up of drops from the mountain side, moving on with more and more power, until everything in its waters is carried to the destined end.

So in a public school. And it is worth much to the man of wealth that there may be, near his own door, an institution to which he may send his children, and under the influence of which they may be carried forward. For, depend upon it, after all we say about schools and institutions of learning, it is nevertheless true of education, as a statesman has said of the government, that the people look to the school for too much. It is not, after all, a great deal that the child gets there; but, if he only gets the ability to acquire more than he has, the schools accomplish something. If you give a child a little knowledge of geography or arithmetic, and have not developed the power to accomplish something for himself, he comes to but little in the world. But put him into the school,—the primary, grammar, and high school, where he must learn for himself,—and he will be fitted for the world of life into which he is to enter. . . .

The duty of the public is to provide means for the education of all. To do that, we need the political, social, and moral power of all, to sustain teachers and institutions of learning; and endowed or free schools, depending upon the contributions of individuals, can never, in a free country, be raised to the character of a system. If you rob the public schools of the influence of our public-spirited men, if they take away a portion of their pupils from them, our system is impaired. It must stand as a whole, educating the entire people, and looking to all for support, or it cannot be permanently maintained.

Men of vision, such as Boutwell, could speak of the public schools "educating the entire people," but the reality in the post-Civil War years was that the classical college-preparatory curriculum of the high school limited the benefits of secondary schooling to the few, to the privileged few, in the opinion of many. The immigrant child, the Negro, and the lower classes in general of the time could find no place in the proper studies of the high school. Why, it was asked, should tax monies be expended for the educational advancement of those already privileged members of society in secondary schools? The question was brought in a precedent-setting test case in the Michigan courts, and a ruling, which came to be called the Kalamazoo Decision, was rendered in 1876 by the Michigan Supreme Court.

74. The Kalamazoo Decision

The bill in this case is filed to restrain the collection of such portion of the school taxes assessed against complainants for the year 1872, as have been voted for the support of the high school in that village, and for the payment of the salary of the superintendent. While, nominally, this is the end sought to be attained by the bill, the real purpose of the bill is wider and vastly more comprehensive than this brief statement would indicate, inasmuch as it seeks a judicial determination of the right of school authorities, in what are called union school districts of the state, to levy taxes upon the general public for the support of what in this state are known as high schools, and to make free by such taxation the instruction of children in other languages than the English.

·   ·   ·   ·   ·   ·   ·   ·   ·   ·   ·   ·   ·

Reprinted from *Charles E. Stuart et al. vs. School District No. 1 of the Village of Kalamazoo,* 30, Michigan, p. 69.

The more general question which the record presents we shall endeavor to state in our own language, but so as to make it stand out distinctly as a naked question of law, disconnected from all considerations of policy or expediency, in which light alone we are at liberty to consider it. It is, as we understand it, that there is no authority in this state to make the high schools free by taxation levied on the people at large. The argument is that while there may be no constitutional provision expressly prohibiting such taxation, the general course of legislation in the state and the general understanding of the people have been such as to require us to regard the instruction in the classics and in the living modern languages in these schools as in the nature not of practical and therefore necessary instruction for the benefit of the people at large, but rather as accomplishments for the few, to be sought after in the main by those best able to pay for them, and to be paid for by those who seek them, and not by general tax. And not only has this been the general state policy, but this higher learning of itself, when supplied by the state, is so far a matter of private concern to those who receive it that the courts ought to declare it incompetent to supply it wholly at the public expense. This is in substance, as we understand it, the position of the complainants in this suit.

When this doctrine was broached to us, we must confess to no little surprise that the legislation and policy of our state were appealed to against the right of the state to furnish a liberal education to the youth of the state in schools brought within the reach of all classes. We supposed it had always been understood in this state that education, not merely in the rudiments, but in an enlarged sense, was regarded as an important practical advantage to be supplied at their option to rich and poor alike, and not as something pertaining merely to culture and accomplishment to be brought as such within the reach of those whose accumulated wealth enabled them to pay for it. As this, however, is now so seriously disputed, it may be necessary, perhaps, to take a brief survey of the legislation and general course, not only of the state, but of the antecedent territory, on the subject. . . .

[Included here is a review of the educational history of the State, from the Ordinance of 1787 to the new state constitution of 1850.]

The instrument [the constitution of 1850] submitted by the convention to the people and adopted by them provided for the establishment of free schools in every school district for at least three months in each year, and for the university. By the aid of these we have every reason to believe the people expected a complete collegiate education might be obtained. . . . The inference seems irresistible that the people expected the tendency towards the establishment of high schools in the primary-school districts would continue until every locality capable of supporting one was supplied. And this inference is strengthened by the fact that a considerable number of our union schools date their establishment from the year 1850 and the two or three years following.

.   .   .   .

If these facts do not demonstrate clearly and conclusively a general state policy, beginning in 1817 and continuing until after the adoption of the present constitution, in the direction of free schools in which education, and at their option the elements of classical education, might be brought within the reach of all the children of the state, then, as it seems to us, nothing can demonstrate it. We might follow the subject further and show that the subsequent legislation has all concurred with this policy, but it would be a waste of time and labor. We content ourselves with the statement that neither in our state policy, in our constitution, or in our laws, do we find the primary-school districts restricted in the branches of knowledge which their officers may cause to be taught, or the grade of instruction that may be given, if their voters consent in regular form to bear the expense and raise the taxes for the purpose.

Thomas Jefferson's vision of reformed and expanded higher education in America was of a university made up of faculties in a broad variety of studies, both general and professional, with major concern for the pursuit of new knowledge in all areas. This expanded idea of a university, far beyond the college advocated in the Yale Report, culminated in the founding of the University of Virginia in 1825, though a half century passed before the intellectually oriented university became a reality in American higher learning.

75. Letter to Peter Carr

Thomas Jefferson

Monticello, September 7th, 1814.

Dear Sir,—On the subject of the academy or college proposed to be established in our neighborhood, I promised the trustees that I would prepare for them a plan, adapted, in the first instance, to our slender funds, but

Reprinted from Nathaniel Francis Cabell, ed., *Early History of the Universtiy of Virginia as Contained in the Letters of Thomas Jefferson and Joseph C. Cabell* (Richmond: J. W. Randolph, 1856), pp. 384-390.

susceptible of being enlarged, either by their own growth or by accession from other quarters.

I have long entertained the hope that this, our native State, would take up the subject of education, and make an establishment, either with or without incorporation into that of William & Mary, where every branch of science, deemed useful at this day, should be taught in its highest degree. With this view, I have lost no occasion of making myself acquainted with the organization of the best seminaries in other countries, and with the opinions of the most enlightened individuals, on the subject of the sciences worthy of a place in such an institution. In order to prepare what I have promised our trustees, I have lately revised these several plans with attention; and I am struck with the diversity of arrangement observable in them —no two alike. Yet, I have no doubt that these several arrangements have been the subject of mature reflection, by wise and learned men, who, contemplating local circumstances, have adapted them to the condition of the section of society for which they have been framed. I am strengthened in this conclusion by an examination of each separately, and a conviction that no one of them, if adopted without change, would be suited to the circumstances and pursuit of our country. The example they have set, then, is authority for us to select from their different institutions the materials which are good *for us,* and, with them, to erect a structure, whose arrangement shall correspond with our own social condition, and shall admit of enlargement in proportion to the encouragement it may merit and receive. As I may not be able to attend the meetings of the trustees, I will make you the depository of my ideas on the subject, which may be corrected, as you proceed, by the better view of others, and adapted, from time to time, to the prospects which open upon us, and which cannot be specifically seen and provided for.

In the first place, we must ascertain with precision the object of our institution, by taking a survey of the general field of science, and marking out the portion we mean to occupy at first, and the ultimate extension of our views beyond that, should we be enabled to render it, in the end, as comprehensive as we would wish.

1. ELEMENTARY SCHOOLS

It is highly interesting to our country, and it is the duty of its functionaries, to provide that every citizen in it should receive an education proportioned to the condition and pursuits of his life. The mass of our citizens may be divided into two classes—the laboring and the learned. The laboring will need the first grade of education to qualify them for their pursuits

and duties; the learned will need it as a foundation for further acquirements. A plan was formerly proposed to the Legislature of this State for
laying off every county into hundreds or wards of five or six miles square,
within each of which should be a school for the education of the children
of the ward, wherein they should receive three years' instruction gratis,
in reading, writing, arithmetic, as far as fractions, the roots and ratios,
and geography. The Legislature, at one time, tried an ineffectual expedient
for introducing this plan, which having failed, it is hoped they will some
day resume it in a more promising form.

2. GENERAL SCHOOLS

At the discharging of the pupils from the elementary schools, the two
classes separate—those destined for labor will engage in the business of
agriculture, or enter into apprenticeships to such handicraft art as may be
their choice; their companions, destined to the pursuits of science, will
proceed to the college, which will consist, 1st, of General Schools; and 2d,
of Professional Schools. The General Schools will constitute the second
grade of education.

The learned class may still be subdivided into two sections; 1, Those
who are destined for learned professions, as a means of livelihood; and 2,
The wealthy, who, possessing independent fortunes, may aspire to share
in conducting the affairs of the nation, or to live with usefulness and respect
in the private ranks of life. Both of these sections will require instruction in
all the higher branches of science; the wealthy to qualify them for either
public or private life; the professional section will need those branches,
especially, which are the basis of their future profession, and a general
knowledge of the others, as auxiliary to that, and necessary to their standing and associating with the scientific class. All the branches, then, of useful
science, ought to be taught in the general schools, to a competent extent,
in the first instance. These sciences may be arranged into three departments,
not rigorously scientific, indeed, but sufficiently so for our purposes. These
are, I, Language; II, Mathematics; III, Philosophy.

I. *Language.* In the first department, I would arrange a distinct science.
1, Languages and History, ancient and modern; 2, Grammar; 3, Belles
Lettres; 4, Rhetoric and Oratory; 5, A school for the deaf, dumb and blind.
History is here associated with languages, not as a kindred subject, but on a
principle of economy, because both may be attained by the same course of
reading, if books are selected with that view.

II. *Mathematics.* In the department of mathematics, I should give place
distinctly, 1, Mathematics pure; 2, Physico-Mathematics; 3, Physic; 4,

Chemistry; 5, Natural History, *to wit:* Mineralogy; 6, Botany; and 7, Zoology; 8, Anatomy; 9, the Theory of Medicine.

III. *Philosophy.* In the Philosophical department, I should distinguish, 1, Ideology; 2, Ethics; 3, the Law of Nature and Nations; 4, Government; 5, Political Economy.

But, some of these terms being used by different writers, in different degrees of extension, I shall define exactly what I mean to comprehend in each of them.

I. 3. Within the term of Belles Lettres I include poetry and composition generally, and Criticism.

II. 1. I consider pure Mathematics as the science of, I, Numbers, and II, Measure in the abstract; that of numbers comprehending Arithmetic, Algebra and Fluxions; that of Measure (under the general appellation of Geometry) comprehending Trigonometry, plane and spherical, conic sections, and transcendental curves.

II. 2. Physico-Mathematics treat of physical subjects by the aid of mathematical calculation. These are Mechanics, Statics, Hydrostatics, Hydrodynamics, Navigation, Astronomy, Geography, Optics, Pneumatics, Acoustics.

II. 3. Physics, or Natural Philosophy, (not entering the limits of Chemistry,) treat of natural substances, their properties, mutual relations and action. They particularly examine the subjects of motion, action, magnetism, electricity, galvanism, light, meteorology, with an &c. not easily enumerated. These definitions and specifications render immaterial the question whether I use the Generic terms in the exact degree of comprehension in which others use them; to be understood is all that is necessary to the present object.

3. PROFESSIONAL SCHOOLS

At the close of this course the students separate; the wealthy retiring, with a sufficient stock of knowledge, to improve themselves to any degree to which their views may lead them, and the professional section to the professional schools, constituting the third grade of education, and teaching the particular sciences which the individuals of this section mean to pursue, with more minuteness and detail than was within the scope of the general schools for the second grade of instruction. In these professional schools each science is to be taught in the highest degree it has yet attained. They are to be the

1st *Department,* the fine arts, to wit: Civil Architecture, Gardening, Painting, Sculpture, and the theory of Music; the

2d *Department,* Architecture, Military and Naval; Projectiles, Rural Economy, (comprehending Agriculture, Horticulture and Veterinary,) Technical Philosophy, the practice of Medicine, Materia Medica, Pharmacy and Surgery. In the

3d *Department,* Theology and Ecclesiastical History; Law, Municipal and Foreign.

To these professional schools will come those who separated at the close of their first elementary course, to wit:

The lawyer to the school of law.

The ecclesiastic to that of theology and ecclesiastical history.

The physician to those of the practice of medicine, materia medica, pharmacy and surgery.

The military man to that of military and naval architecture and projectiles.

The agricultor to that of rural economy.

The gentleman, the architect, the pleasure gardener, painter and musician to the school of fine arts.

And to that of technical philosophy will come the mariner, carpenter, ship-wright, pump maker, clock maker, machinist, optician, metallurgist, founder, cutler, druggist, brewer, vintner, distiller, dyer, painter, bleecher, soap maker, tanner, powder maker, salt maker, glass maker, to learn as much as shall be necessary to pursue their art understandingly, of the sciences of geometry, mechanics, statics, hydrostatics, hydraulics, hydrodynamics, navigation, astronomy, geography, optics, pneumatics, acoustics, physics, chemistry, natural history, botany, mineralogy and pharmacy.

The school of technical philosophy will differ essentially in its functions from the other professional schools. The others are instituted to ramify and dilate the particular sciences taught in the schools of the second grade on a general scale only. The technical school is to abridge those which were taught there too much *in extenso* for the limited wants of the artificer or practical man. These artificers must be grouped together, according to the particular branch of science in which they need elementary and practical instruction; and a special lecture or lectures should be prepared for each group—and these lectures should be given in the evening, so as not to interrupt the labors of the day. The school, particularly, should be maintained wholly at the public expense, on the same principles with that of the ward schools. Through the whole of the collegiate course, at the hours of recreation on certain days, all the students should be taught the manual exercise, military evolutions and manœuvres, should be under a standing organization as a military corps, and with proper officers to train and command them. . . .

On this survey of the field of science, I recur to the question, what portion of it we mark out for the occupation of our institution? With the first grade of education we shall have nothing to do. The sciences of the second grade are our first object; and, to adapt them to our slender beginnings, we must separate them into groups, comprehending many sciences each, and greatly more, in the first instance, than ought to be imposed on, or can be competently conducted by a single professor permanently. They must be subdivided from time to time, as our means increase, until each professor shall have no more under his care than he can attend to with advantage to his pupils and ease to himself. In the further advance of our resources, the professional schools must be introduced, and professorships established for them also. For the present, we may group the sciences into professorships, as follows, subject, however, to be changed, according to the qualifications of the persons we may be able to engage.

I. Professorship.
Language and History, ancient and modern. Belles Lettres,
Rhetoric and Oratory.
II. Professorship.
Mathematics pure—Physico-Mathematics. Physics—
Anatomy—Medicine—Theory.
III. Professorship.
Chemistry—Zoology—Botany—Mineralogy.
IV. Professorship.
Philosophy.

The organization of the branch of the institution which respects its government, police and economy, depending on principles which have no affinity with those of its institution, may be the subject of separate and subsequent consideration.

With this tribute of duty to the Board of Trustees, accept the assurance of my great esteem and consideration.

TH: JEFFERSON.

"Democracy's college," the land-grant college movement of the post-Civil War years, in many ways represents the culmination of the democratization of American education, the completion of the higher learning rungs of the American education ladder. Much of the work was done by Jonathan Baldwin Turner of Illinois and others like him in the years just prior to the war, men who envisioned a great advancement of society through higher learning extended with some practical revisions to the "industrial classes." Turner's "Plan for an Industrial University for the State of Illinois," written in 1851, summarizes his thinking in higher education as well as much of the thinking that was contained in the Morrill Act of 1862.

76. Plan for an Industrial University for Illinois

Jonathan Baldwin Turner

The whole history of education, both in Protestant and Catholic countries, shows that we must begin with the higher institutions, or we can never succeed with the lower; for the plain reason, that neither knowledge nor water will run up hill. No people ever had, or ever can have, any system of common schools and lower seminaries worth anything, until they first founded their higher institutions and fountains of knowledge from which they could draw supplies of teachers, &c., for the lower. We would begin, therefore, where all experience and common sense show that we must begin, if we would effect anything worthy of an effort.

In this view of the case, the first thing wanted in this process is a NATIONAL INSTITUTE OF SCIENCE, to operate as the great central luminary of the national mind, from which all minor institutions should derive light and heat, and toward which they should, also, reflect back their own. This primary want is already, I trust, supplied by the Smithsonian Institute, endowed by James Smithson, and incorporated by the U. S. Congress, at Washington, D.C.

To co-operate with this noble Institute, and enable the industrial classes to realize its benefits in practical life, we need a *University for the Industrial Classes* in each of the States, with their consequent subordinate institutes, lyceums, and high schools, in each of the counties and towns.

The objects of these institutes should be to apply existing knowledge directly and efficiently to all practical pursuits and professions in life, and to extend the boundaries of our present knowledge in all possible practical directions.

PLAN FOR THE STATE UNIVERSITY

There should be connected with such an institution, in this State, a sufficient quantity of land of variable soil and aspect, for all its needful annual experiments and processes in the great interests of Agriculture and Horticulture.

Reprinted from J. B. Turner, "Plan for an Industrial University for the State of Illinois," in *Industrial Universities for the People*, Second edition: (Chicago: Robert Fergus, 1854), pp. 20-33.

Buildings of appropriate size and construction for all its ordinary and special uses; a complete philosophical, chemical, anatomical, and industrial apparatus; a general cabinet, embracing everything that relates to, illustrates or facilitates any one of the industrial arts; especially all sorts of animals, birds, reptiles, insects, trees, shrubs, and plants found in this State and adjacent States.

Instruction should be constantly given in the anatomy and physiology, the nature, instincts, and habits of animals, insects, trees, and plants; their laws of propagation, primogeniture, growth, and decay, disease and health, life and death, on the nature, composition, adaptation, and regeneration of soils; on the nature, strength, durability, preservation, perfection, composition, cost, use, and manufacture of all materials of art and trade; on political, financial, domestic, and manual economy, (or the saving of labor of the hand,) in all industrial processes; on the true principles of national, constitutional, and civil law; and the true theory and art of governing and controlling, or directing the labor of men in the State, the family, shop, and farm; on the laws of vicinage, or the laws of courtesy and comity between neighbors, as such, and on the principles of health and disease in the human subject, so far at least as is needful for household safety; on the laws of trade and commerce, ethical, conventional, and practical; on book-keeping and accounts; and, in short, in all those studies and sciences, of whatever sort, which tend to throw light upon any art or employment, which any student may desire to master, or upon any duty he may be called to perform; or which may tend to secure his moral, civil, social, and industrial perfection, as a man.

No species of knowledge should be excluded, practical or theoretical; unless, indeed, those specimens of "organized ignorance" found in the creeds of party politicians and sectarian ecclesiastics should be mistaken by some for a species of knowledge.

Whether a distinct classical department should be added or not, would depend on expediency. It might be deemed best to leave that department to existing colleges as their more appropriate work, and to form some practical and economical connection with them for that purpose; or it might be best to attach a classical department in due time to the institution itself.

To facilitate the increase and practical application and diffusion of knowledge, the professors should conduct, each in his own department, a continued series of *annual experiments*.

For example, let twenty or more acres of each variety of grain, (each acre accurately measured,) be annually sown, with some practical variation on each acre, as regards the quality and preparation of the soil, the kind and quantity of seed, the time and mode of sowing or planting, the time, and modes, and processes of cultivation and harvesting, and an accurate account kept of all costs, labor, &c., and of the final results. Let analogous experiments be tried on all the varied products of the farm, the fruit yard, the nursery, and the garden; on all modes of crossing, rearing, and fattening domestic animals, under various degrees of warmth and of light, with and without shelter; on green, dry, raw, ground, and cooked food, cold and warm; on the nature, causes, and cure of their various diseases, both of those on the premises and of those brought in from abroad, and advice given, and annual reports made on those and all similar topics. . . .

As regards the PROFESSORS, they should, of course, not only be men of the most eminent practical ability in their several departments, but their connexion with the institution should be rendered so fixed and stable, as to enable them to carry through such designs as they may form, or all the peculiar benefits of the system would be lost.

Instruction, by lectures or otherwise, should be given mostly in the coldest months of the year; leaving the professors to prosecute their investigations, and the students their necessary labor, either at home or on the premises, during the warmer months.

The institution should be open to all classes of students above a fixed age, and for any length of time, whether three months or seven years, and each taught in those particular branches of art which he wishes to pursue, and to any extent, more or less. And all should pay their tuition and board bills, in whole or in part, either in money or necessary work on the premises —regard being had to the ability of each.

Among those who labor, medals and testimonials of merit should be given to those who perform their task with most promptitude, energy, care, and skill; and all who prove indolent or ungovernable, excluded at first from all part in labor, and speedily, if not thoroughly reformed, from the institution itself; and here again let the law of nature instead of the law of rakes and dandies be regarded, and the true impression ever made on the mind of all around, that WORK ALONE IS HONORABLE, and indolence certain disgrace if not ruin.

At some convenient season of the year, the Commencement, or ANNUAL FAIR of the University, should be holden through a succession of days. On this occasion the doors of the institution, with all its treasures of art and resources of knowledge, should be thrown open to all classes, and as many other objects of agricultural or mechanical skill, gathered from the whole State, as possible, and presented by the people for inspection and premium on the best of each kind; judgment being rendered, in all cases, by a committee wholly disconnected with the institution. On this occasion, all the professors, and as many of the pupils as are sufficiently advanced, should be constantly engaged in lecturing and explaining the divers objects and interests of their departments. In short, this occasion should be made the great annual GALA-DAY of the Institution, and of all the industrial classes, and all other classes in the State, for the exhibition of their products and their skill, and for the vigorous and powerful diffusion of practical knowledge in their ranks, and a more intense enthusiasm in its extension and pursuit.

As matters now are, the world has never adopted any efficient means for the application and diffusion of even the practical knowledge which does exist. True, we have fairly got the primer, the spelling book, and the newspaper abroad in the world, and we think that we have done wonders; and so, comparatively, we have. But if this is a wonder, there are still not only wonders, but, to most minds, inconceivable miracles, from new and unknown worlds of light, soon to burst forth upon the industrial mind of the world.

Here, then, is a general, though very incomplete outline of what such an institution should endeavor to become. Let the reader contemplate it as it will appear when generations have perfected it, in all its magnificence and glory; in its means of good to man, to *all men* of *all classes;* in its power to evolve and diffuse practical knowledge and skill, true taste, love of industry, and sound morality—not only through its apparatus, experiments, instructions, and annual lectures and reports, but through its thousands of graduates, in every pursuit in life, teaching and lecturing in all our towns and villages; and then let him seriously ask himself, is not such an object worthy of at least an effort, and worthy of a state which God himself, in the very act of creation, designed to be the first agricultural and commercial State on the face of the globe?

Who should set the world so glorious an example of educating their sons worthily of their heritage, their duty, and their destiny, if not the people of such a State? In our country, we have no aristocracy, with the inalienable wealth of ages and constant leisure and means to perform all manner of useful experiments for their own amusement; but we must create our nobility for this purpose, as we elect our rulers, from our own ranks, to aid and serve, not to domineer over and control us. And this done, we will not only beat England, and beat the world in yachts, and locks, and reapers, but in all else that contributes to the well being and true glory of man.

I maintain that, if every farmer's and mechanic's son in this State could now visit such an institution but for a single day in the year, it would do him more good in arousing and directing the dormant energies of mind, than all the cost incurred, and far more good than many a six months of professed study of things he will never need and never want to know.

The most natural and effectual mental discipline possible for any man, arises from setting him to earnest and constant thought about the things he daily does, sees, and handles, and all their connected relations and interests. The final object to be attained with the industrial class, is to make them THINKING LABORERS; while of the professional class we should desire to make LABORIOUS THINKERS: the production of goods to feed and adorn the body being the final end of one class of pursuits; and the production of thought, to do the same for the mind, the end of the other. But neither mind nor body can feed on the offals of preceding generations. And this constantly recurring necessity of re-production leaves an equally honorable, though somewhat different, career of labor and duty open to both, and, it is readily admitted, should and must vary their modes of education and preparation accordingly.

It may do for the man of books to plunge at once amid the catacombs of buried nations and languages, to soar away to Greece, or Rome, or Nova-Zemba, Kamtschatka, and the fixed stars, before he knows how to plant his own beans, or harness his own horse, or can tell whether the functions of his own body are performed by a heart, stomach, and lungs, or with a gizzard and gills.

But for the man of work thus to bolt away at once from himself and all his pursuits in after-life, contravenes the plainest principles of nature and common sense. No wonder such educators have ever deemed the liberal culture of the industrial classes an impossibility; for they have never tried nor even conceived of any other way of educating them, except that by which they are rendered totally unfit for their several callings in after-life. How absurd it would seem to set a clergyman to plowing, and studying the depredations of blights, insects, the growing of crops, &c., &c., in order to give him habits of thought and mental discipline for the pulpit; yet this is not half as ridiculous, in reality, as the reverse absurdity of attempting to educate the man of work in unknown tongues, abstract problems and theories, and metaphysical figments and quibbles.

Some, doubtless, will regard the themes of such a course of education as too sensuous and gross to lie at the basis of a pure and elevated mental culture. But the themes themselves cover all possible knowledge, and all modes and phases of science, abstract, mixed, and practical. In short, the field embraces all that God has made, and all that human art has done; and if the created universe of God and the highest art of man are too gross for our refined uses, it is a pity the "morning stars and the sons of God" did not find it out as soon as the blunder was made. But, in my opinion, these topics are of quite as much consequence to the well-being of man and the healthful development of mind, as the concoction of the final nostrum in medicine, or the ultimate figment in theology and law, conjectures about the galaxy or the Greek accent; unless, indeed, the pedantic professional trifles of one man in a thousand are of more consequence than the daily vital interests of all the rest of mankind.

But can such an institution be created and endowed? Doubtless it can be done, and done at once, if the industrial classes so decide. The fund given to this State by the General Government, expressly for this purpose, is amply sufficient, without a dollar from any other source; and it is a mean, if not an illegal, perversion of this fund, to use it for any other purpose. It was given to the people, the whole people, of this State; not for a class, a party, or sect, or conglomeration of sects; not for common schools, or family schools, or classical schools; but for "An University," or Seminary, of a high order, in which should of course be taught all those things which every class of the citizens most desire to learn—their own duty and business for life. This, and this alone, is an University in the true, original sense of the term. And if an institution which teaches all that is needful only for the three professions of law, divinity, and medicine, is, therefore, an University, surely one which teaches all that is needful for all the varied professions of human life is far more deserving of the name and the endowments of an University. . . .

Doubtless, objections can be urged against this plan, and all others than can be proposed. Most of them may be at once anticipated, but there is not space enough to notice them here. Some, for example, cherish an ardent and praiseworthy desire for the perfection of our common schools, and desire still longer to use that fund for that purpose. But no one imagines that it can long be kept for that use; and if it could, I think it plain that the lower schools of all sorts would be far more benefited by it here than in any other place it could be put.

Others may feel a little alarm, when, for the first time in the history of the world, they see the millions throwing themselves aloof from all political and ecclesiastical control, and attempting to devise a system of liberal education for themselves; but on mature reflection we trust they will approve the plan; or, if they are too old to change, their children will.

I shall enter upon no special pleas in favor of this plan of disposing of our State fund. I am so situated in life that it cannot possibly do me any personal good, save only in the just pride of seeing the interests of my brethren of the industrial class cared for and promoted, as in such an age and such a State they ought to be. If they want the benefit of such an institution they can have it. If they do not want it, I have not another word to say. In their own will, alone, lies their own destiny, and that of their children.

Respectfully submitted,

J. B. TURNER.

SECTION 5

Transcendentalists, Romantics, and Reformers

The movement in American thought known as Transcendentalism, though essentially localized in New England and brief in its duration even there, nevertheless exerted a strong influence in our country. It left in its wake a deep impression which marked ideas and institutions. Although the number of adherents to this way of thought were limited, they made up in quality what they lacked in quantity. When since has this country seen or heard the like of Emerson, Thoreau, Parker, Channing, and Alcott? Like a brief though intense white hot flame, transcendentalism as a way of life and thought illuminated and permeated American minds for but a short time. The after-image of the flame, however, remained indelibly impressed on the American heritage.

As a philosophy, transcendentalism is directly traceable to Immanual Kant, but to say this is really to say very little. Kant, after all, was not Emerson, nor was he the intellectual heir of New England thought. It is to New England, not to Germany that one must go to understand the transcendentalists; to the Concord of Emerson and Thoreau, not to the Königsberg of Kant. As to the substance of the transcendental thought, the reader must be referred to its eloquent spokesmen—Henry David Thoreau, the inimitable bachelor of nature; Ralph Waldo Emerson, scholar, teacher and philosopher; and Bronson Alcott, mystic and educator. For the benefit of those who have not made the acquaintance of these remarkable men, a brief definition of transcendentalism by Emerson will illuminate them:

> The transcendentalist adopts the whole connection of spiritual doctrine. He believes in miracles, in the perpetual openness of the human

mind to new influx of light and power; he believes in inspiration and
ecstasy. He wishes that the spiritual principle should be suffered to
demonstrate itself to the end, in all possible applications to the state of
man, without the admission of anything unspiritual, that is, anything
positive, dogmatic, personal.

The reader is duly warned, however, that defining and labeling, so dear
to contemporary hearts, is quite contradictory to transcendentalism
—to make the attempt is rather like attempting to squeeze a shadow
into a box. It is to be hoped that this definition satisfies no reader, that
he is left with questions, and that he will seek to answer his question
by further reading and thought.

With regard to the place of this transcendentalism in the subject of
education, Emerson's statement as to his belief in "the perpetual openness of the human mind to new influx of light and power" may be taken
as a starting point, for here is the transcendentalists' philosophy of
education. The transcendentalist was not only a contemplator, he was
a doer. Above all else, he was a teacher, although sometimes (like
Thoreau) his best teaching was done far away from schools. As a
teacher (in the more usual sense), few of the transcendentalists were
more active than Bronson Alcott, a philosopher who accepted without
qualification the primacy and pre-eminence of the soul. Alcott was not
a learned man; his readings were poetical and meditative rather than
intellectual. He found his nourishment in the speculative thinkers of
ancient Greece, in Plato, and above all in Pythagoras. As Emerson
noted in his journal for 1848 (Vol. VII, p. 493), "I was accustomed
to characterize Alcott, in England, by saying that he was the one man
I had met who could read Plato without surprise." Alcott himself
testified as to his regard for Pythagoras as an educator in the following
selection.

77. Pythagoras

Bronson Alcott

Of the great educators of antiquity, I esteem Pythagoras the most eminent and successful; everything of his doctrine and discipline comes com-
mended by its elegance and humanity, and justifies the name he bore of
the golden-souled Samian, and founder of Greek culture. He seems to have

Reprinted from O. B. Frothingham, *Transcendentalism in New England* (New
York: Putnam, 1880), pp. 251-252.

stood in providential nearness to human sensibility, as if his were a maternal relation as well, and he owned the minds whom he nurtured and educated. The first of philosophers, taking the name for its modesty of pretension, he justified his claim to it in the attainments and services of his followers; his school having given us Socrates, Plato, Pericles, Plutarch, Plotinus, and others of almost equal fame, founders of states and cultures. . . . He was reverenced by the multitude as one under the influence of divine inspiration. He abstained from all intoxicating drinks, and from animal food, confining himself to a chaste nutriment; hence his sleep was short and undisturbed; his soul vigilant and pure; his body in state of perfect and invariable health. He was free from the superstitions of his time, and pervaded with a deep sense of duty towards God, and veneration for his divine attributes and immanency in things. He fixed his mind so intently on the attainment of wisdom, that systems and mysteries inaccessible to others were opened to him by his magic genius and sincerity of purpose. The great principle with which he started, that of being a seeker rather than a possessor of truth, seemed ever to urge him forward with a diligence and activity unprecedented in the history of the past, and perhaps unequalled since. He visited every man who could claim any degree of fame for wisdom or learning; whilst the rules of antiquity and the simplest operations of nature seemed to yield to his researches; and we moderns are using his eyes in many departments of activity into which pure thought enters, being indebted to him for important discoveries alike in science and metaphysics.

Alcott declined to join the Brook Farm community or the community of Adin Ballow at Milford and supported himself by manual labor in Concord. He considered his primary mission as one of education, which he conceived as the process of drawing out souls of children (or adults). The educational process, for Alcott, was primarily spiritual—to entice the indwelling diety to shine forth. As Emerson stated in his journal in 1848 (Vol. VII, p. 499):

> Alcott declares that a teacher is one who can assist the child in obeying his own mind, and who can remove all unfavorable circumstances. He believes that from a circle of twenty well-selected children he could draw in their conversation everything that is in Plato, and as much better in form than is in Plato. . . .

78. On a Child's Acquirements

Bronson Alcott

To conceive a child's acquirements as originating in nature, dating from his birth into his body, seems an atheism that only a shallow metaphysical theology could entertain in a time of such marvellous natural knowledge as ours. "I shall never persuade myself," says Synesius, "to believe my soul to be of like age with my body." And yet we are wont to date our birth, as that of the babes we christen, from the body's advent, so duteously inscribed in our family registers, as if time and space could chronicle the periods of the immortal mind, and mark its longevity by our chronometers. Only a God could inspire a child with the intimations seen in its first pulse-plays; the sprightly attainments of a single day's doings afford the liveliest proofs of an omniscient Deity, revealing His attributes in the motions of the little one! . . . . Were the skill for touching its tender sensibilities, calling forth its budding gifts, equal to the charms the child has for us, what noble characters would graduate from our families—the community receiving its members accomplished in the personal graces, the state its patriots, the church its saints, all glorifying the race.

The initial experiment with an Alcott type school was made in 1825, in Cheshire, Connecticut. This school aimed at the elevation of the individual mind. In place of long benches (forms) then in general usage in schools, single desks were used. Blackboards as well as a library, evening entertainments, and light gymnastic exercises were introduced into the school. Students were treated with gentleness and were encouraged to keep individual diaries.

Knowledge was made as attractive as possible. The similarity of the practices of the Cheshire School with those of Pestalozzi is rather striking; however, Alcott apparently hit upon his ideas independently of the great Swiss educator.

In 1834, Boston was the scene of another Alcott style educational experiment in a school kept in the Masonic Temple. Such luminaries

Reprinted from O. B. Frothingham, *Transcendentalism in New England* (New York: Putnam, 1880), p. 252.

as Margaret Fuller, Mrs. Nathaniel Hawthorne, and Elizabeth Peabody
were involved in this project. In order to enlist the sentiments of honor
and shame in the behavioral conduct of his students, Alcott adopted the
notion of vicarious punishment—the innocent bearing pain for the
guilty—the master for the pupil. He established the practice of setting
aside some time for question and answer sessions with pupils, addressed
to their "higher faculties," and gave a series of "Conversations on the
Gospels." This last practice was subject to continued attack in the
newspapers, and, arousing the ire of conservatives, the attack resulted
in pressure being brought to close the school. In April, 1839, the
school closed its doors. Both Alcott and his ideas, however, survived.
So impressed were some with Alcott's notion that the English Pestalozzian, James P. Graves, named the school he founded near London,
Alcott House, after the American educator.

In 1859, Alcott was chosen superintendent of schools for Concord,
Massachusetts. His educational thoughts are well expressed in a series
of three reports which he made on needs and conditions of the Concord
schools. Portions of these reports are given in the following selection.

79. Reports on Concord Schools

Bronson Alcott

The school is the primary interest of the community. Every parent naturally desires a better education for his children than he received himself,
and spends liberally of his substance for this pleasure; wisely hoping to
make up his deficiencies in that way, and to complement himself in their
better attainments; esteeming these the richest estate he can leave, and the
fairest ornaments of his family name.

Especially have I wished to introduce the young to the study of their
minds, the love of thinking; often giving examples of lessons in analysis
and classification of their faculties. I think I may say that these exercises
have given much pleasure, and have been found profitable alike to the
teacher and the children. In most instances, I have closed my visits by
reading some interesting story or parable. These have never failed of gaining
attention, and in most cases, prompt responses. I consider these readings
and colloquies as among the most profitable and instructive of the superintendent's labors.

Reprinted from O. B. Frothingham, *Transcendentalism in New England* (New
York: Putnam, 1880), pp. 275-281.

The graceful exercise of singing has been introduced into some of the schools. It should prevail in all of them. It softens the manners, cultivates the voice, and purifies the taste of the children. It promotes harmony and good feelings. The old masters thought much of it as a discipline. "Let us sing" has the welcome sound of "Let us play,"—and is perhaps the child's prettiest translation of "Let us pray,"—admitting him soonest to the intimacy he seeks.

Conversations on words, paraphrases and translations of sentences, are the natural methods of opening the study of language. A child should never be suffered to lose sight of the prime fact that he is studying the realities of nature and of the mind through the picture books of language. Any teaching falling short of this is hollow and a wrong done to the mind.

For composition, let a boy keep his diary, write his letters, try his hand at defining from a dictionary and paraphrasing, and he will find ways of expressing himself simply as boys and men did before grammars were invented.

Teaching is a personal influence for the most part, and operating as a spirit unsuspected at the moment. I have wished to divine the secret source of success attained by any, and do justice to this; it seemed most becoming to regard any blemishes as of secondary account in the light of the acknowledged deserts. We require of each what she has to give, no more. Does the teacher awaken thought, strengthen the mind, kindle the affections, call the conscience, the common sense into lively and controlling activity, so promoting the love of study, the practice of the virtues; habits that shall accompany the children outwards into life? The memory is thus best cared for the end of study answered; the debt of teacher to parents, of parents to teacher discharged, and so the State's bounty best bestowed.

A little gymnasticon, a system of gestures for the body might be organized skilfully and become part of the daily exercises in our schools. Graceful steps, pretty musical airs, in accompaniment of songs—suiting the sentiment to the motions, the emotions, ideas of the child—would be conducive to health of body and mind alike. We shall adopt dancing presently as a natural training for the manners and morals of the young.

Conversation is the mind's mouth-piece, its best spokesman; the leader elect and prompter in teaching; practised daily, it should be added to the list of school studies; an art in itself, let it be used as such, and ranked as an accomplishment second to none that nature or culture can give. Certainly the best we can do is to teach ourselves and children how to talk. Let conversation displace much that passes current under the name of recitation; mostly sound and parrotry, a repeating by rote not by heart, unmeaning sounds from the memory and no more. "Take my mind a moment," says the teacher, "and see how things look through that prism," and the pupil sees prospects never seen before or surmised by him in that lively perspective.

. . . . .

Perhaps we are correcting the old affection for flogging at some risk of spoiling the boys of this generation. Girls have always known how to cover with shame any insult of that sort, but the power of persuasion comes slow as a promptitude to supersede its necessity. Who deals with a child, deals with a piece of divinity obeying laws as innate as those he transgresses, and which he must treat tenderly, lest he put spiritual interests in jeopardy. Punishment must be just, else it cannot be accepted as good, and least of all by the wicked and weak.

The accomplished teacher combines in himself the art of teaching and of ruling; power over the intellect and the will, inspiration and persuasiveness. And this implies a double consciousness in its possessor that carries forward the teaching and ruling together; noting what transpires in motive as in act; the gift that in seeing controls. It is the sway of presence and of mien; a conversion of the will to his wishes, without which other gifts are of little avail.

Be sure the liveliest dispensations, the holiest, are his (the unruly boy's) —his as cordially as ours, and sought for as kindly. We must meet him where he is. Best to follow his bent if bent beautifully; else bending him gently, not fractiously, lest we snap or stiffen a stubbornness too stiff already. Gentleness now; the fair eye, the conquering glances straight and sure; the strong hand, if you must, till he fall penitent at the feet of Persuasion; the stroke of grace before the smiting of the birch; for only so is the conquest complete, and the victory the Lord's. If she is good enough she may strike strong and frequent, till thanks come for it; but who is she, much less he, that dares do it more than once, nor repents in sorrow and shame for the strokes given? Only 'the shining ones' may do it for good.

It is difficult to reach the sources of ignorance and consequent crime in a community like ours, calling itself free, and boasting of its right to do what it will. But freedom is a social not less than an individual concern, and the end of the State is to protect it. The first object of a free people is the preservation of their liberties. It becomes, then, their first duty to assume the training of all the children in the principles of right knowledge and virtue, as the only safeguard of their liberties. We cannot afford to wait at such hazards. The simplest humanities are also the least costly, and the nearest home. We should begin there. The State is stabbed at the hearthside and here liberty and honor are first sold. It is injured by family neglect, and should protect itself in securing its children's virtue against their parents' vices; for, by so doing, can it alone redeem its pledges to humanity and its citizens' liberties. A virtuous education is the greatest alms it can bestow on any of its children.

The magnum opus of transcendental educational thought may very well have been the famous oration given by Ralph Waldo Emerson before the Phi Beta Kappa Society at Cambridge, August 31, 1837. Titled "The American Scholar" this has become one of the best known of Emerson's essays. It would be well to emphasize the word "American" in the title of this essay, for Emerson began his oration by pointing out that "our day of dependence, our long apprenticeship to the learning of other lands, draws to a close." Emerson viewed the division by the gods of Man into men as sort of a division of labor "just as the hand was divided into fingers, the better to answer its end." In the delegation of function, the scholar is the intellect. Properly functioning, he is "Man Thinking"; in the degenerate state he may become merely a thinker or, worse yet, "the parrot of other mens' thinking."

Although the primary influence upon the mind is nature, and Emerson notes that the ancient Delphic wisdom of "know thyself" becomes one with "the modern precept," "study nature," the mind of the scholar is also influenced by the mind of the past.

Although a bookworm does not qualify as a scholar for Emerson, he does, of course, admit the necessity of some reading for a wise man. History and exact science, claimed Emerson, must be learned by laborious reading. Colleges, too, have a place in the development of the scholar; they teach him "elements."

When the colleges aim to drill and not to create or "set the hearts of their youth on flame," they will recede in public importance "whilst they grow richer every year."

The scholar is not to be a totally reclusive person vegetating in non-activity but a man of action, a doer. Although action is necessarily subordinate in the nature of scholarly endeavors, it is nonetheless essential. Without it, said Emerson, "he is not yet man." The "preamble of thought, the transition through which it passes from the unconscious to the conscious is action."

The scholar needs courage and confidence, for he is obligated by his function as scholar to hear and set forth the pronouncements of Reason on men and events.

Finally, after so brilliantly stating his faith in the scholar as ". . . that man who must take up into himself all the ability of the time, all the contributions of the past, all the hopes of the future," Emerson summed up his oration in the last paragraph of Selection 80.

80. From "The American Scholar"

Ralph Waldo Emerson

II. The next great influence into the spirit of the scholar is the mind of the Past—in whatever form, whether of literature, of art, of institutions, that mind is inscribed. Books are the best type of the influence of the past, and perhaps we shall get at the truth—learn the amount of this influence more conveniently—by considering their value alone.

The theory of books is noble. The scholar of the first age received into him the world around; brooded thereon; gave it the new arrangement of his own mind, and uttered it again. It came into his life; it went out from him truth. It came to him short-lived actions; it went out from him immortal thoughts. It came to him business; it went from him poetry. It was dead fact; now, it is quick thought. It can stand, it can go. It now endures, it now flies, it now inspires. Precisely in proportion to the depth of mind from which it issued, so high does it soar, so long does it sing.

Or, I might say, it depends on how far the process had gone, of transmuting life into truth. In proportion to the completeness of the distillation, so will the purity and imperishableness of the product be. But none is quite perfect. As no air-pump can by any means make a perfect vacuum, so neither can any artist entirely exclude the conventional, the local, the perishable from his book, or write a book of pure thought, that shall be as efficient, in all respects, to a remote posterity, as to contemporaries, or rather to the second age. Each age, it is found, must write its own books; or rather, each generation for the next succeeding. The books of an older period will not fit this.

Yet hence arises a grave mischief. The sacredness which attaches to the act of creation, the act of thought, is transferred to the record. The poet chanting was felt to be a divine man: henceforth the chant is divine also. The writer was a just and wise spirit; henceforward it is settled the work is perfect; as love of the hero corrupts into worship of his statue. Instantly

Reprinted from Ralph Waldo Emerson, *Nature, Addresses, and Lectures* (Boston: Houghton Mifflin, 1855), pp. 89-92, 98-99, 102-104, 113-115.

the book becomes noxious: the guide is a tyrant. The sluggish and perverted mind of the multitude, slow to open to the incursions of Reason having once so opened, having once received this book, stands upon it, and makes an outcry if it is disparaged. Colleges are built on it. Books are written on it by thinkers, not by Man Thinking; by men of talent, that is, who start wrong, who set out from accepted dogmas, not from their own sight of principles. Meek young men grow up in libraries, believing it their duty to accept the views which Cicero, which Locke, which Bacon, have given; forgetful that Cicero, Locke, and Bacon were only young men in libraries when they wrote these books.

Hence, instead of Man Thinking, we have the bookworm. Hence the book-learned class, who value books, as such; not as related to nature and the human constitution, but as making a sort of Third Estate with the world and the soul. Hence the restorers of readings, the emendators, the bibliomaniacs of all degrees.

Books are the best of things, well used; abused, among the worst. What is the right use? What is the one end which all means go to effect? They are for nothing but to inspire. I had better never see a book than to be warped by its attraction clean out of my own orbit, and made a satellite instead of a system. The one thing in the world, of value, is the active soul. This every man is entitled to; this every man contains within him, although in almost all men obstructed and as yet unborn. The soul active sees absolute truth and utters truth, or creates. In this action it is genius; not the privilege of here and there a favorite, but the sound estate of every man. In its essence it is progressive. The books, the college, the school of art, the institution of any kind, stop with some past utterance of genius. This is good, say they—let us hold by this. They pin me down. They look backward and not forward. But genius looks forward: the eyes of man are set in his forehead, not in his hindhead: man hopes: genius creates. Whatever talents may be, if the man create not, the pure efflux of the Deity is not his;—cinders and smoke there may be, but not yet flame. There are creative manners, there are creative actions, and creative words; manners, actions, words, that is, indicative of no custom or authority, but springing spontaneous from the mind's own sense of good and fair.

. . . . .

Of course, he who has put forth his total strength in fit action has the richest return of wisdom. I will not shut myself out of this globe of action, and transplant an oak into a flowerpot, there to hunger and pine; nor trust the revenue of some single faculty, and exhaust one vein of thought, much like those Savoyards, who, getting their livelihood by carving shepherds, shepherdesses, and smoking Dutchmen, for all Europe, went out one day to the mountain to find stock, and discovered that they had whittled up the last of their pine trees. Authors we have, in numbers, who have written out their vein, and who, moved by a commendable prudence, sail for Greece or Palestine, follow the trapper into the prairie, or ramble round Algiers, to replenish their merchantable stock.

If it were only for a vocabulary, the scholar would be covetous of action. Life is our dictionary. Years are well spent in country labors; in town; in the insight into trades and manufactures; in frank intercourse with many men and women; in science; in art; to the one end of mastering in all their facts a language by which to illustrate and embody our perceptions. I learn immediately from any speaker how much he has already lived, through the poverty or the splendor of his speech. Life lies behind us as the quarry from whence we get tiles and copestones for the masonry of today. This is the way to learn grammar. Colleges and books only copy the language which the field and the work yard made.

But the final value of action, like that of books, and better than books, is that it is a resource. That great principle of Undulation in nature, that shows itself in the inspiring and expiring of the breath; in desire and satiety; in the ebb and flow of the sea; in day and night; in heat and cold; and, as yet more deeply ingrained in every atom and every fluid, is known to us under the name of Polarity—these "fits of easy transmission and reflection," as Newton called them, are the law of nature because they are the law of spirit.

. . . . .

These being his functions, it becomes him to feel all confidence in himself, and to defer never to the popular cry. He and he only knows the world. The world of any moment is the merest appearance. Some great decorum, some fetish of a government, some ephemeral trade, or war, or man, is cried up by half mankind and cried down by the other half, as if all depended on this particular up or down. The odds are that the whole question is not worth the poorest thought which the scholar has lost in listening to the controversy. Let him not quit his belief that a popgun is a popgun, though the ancient and honorable of the earth affirm it to be the crack of doom. In silence, in steadiness, in severe abstraction, let him hold by himself; add observation to observation, patient of neglect, patient of reproach, and bide his own time—happy enough if he can satisfy himself alone that this day he has seen something truly. Success treads on every right step. For the instinct is sure, that prompts him to tell his brother what he thinks. He then learns that in doing down into the secrets of his own mind he has descended into the secrets of all minds. He learns that he who has mastered any law in his private thoughts, is master to that extent of all men whose language he speaks, and of all into whose language his own can be translated. The poet, in utter solitude remembering his spontaneous thoughts and recording them, is found to have recorded that which men in crowded cities find true for them also. The orator distrusts at first the fitness of his frank confessions, his want of knowledge of the persons he addresses, until he finds that he is the complement of his hearers—that they drink his words because he fulfills for them their own nature; the deeper he dives into his privatest, secretest presentiment, to his wonder he finds this as the most acceptable, most public, and universally true. The people delight in it; the better part of every man feels, This is my music; this is myself.

. . . . .

If there be one lesson more than another which should pierce his ear, it is, The world is nothing, the man is all; in yourself is the law of all nature, and you know not yet how a globule of sap ascends; in yourself slumbers the whole of Reason; it is for you to know all; it is for you to dare all. Mr. President and Gentlemen, this confidence in the unsearched might of man belongs by all motives, by all prophecy, by all preparation, to the American Scholar. We have listened too long to the courtly muses of Europe. The spirit of the American freeman is already suspected to be timid, imitative, tame. Public and private avarice make the air we breathe thick and fat. The scholar is decent, indolent, complaisant. See already the tragic consequence. The mind of this country, taught to aim at low objects, eats upon itself. There is no work for any but the decorous and the complaisant. Young men of the fairest promise, who begin life upon our shores, inflated by the mountain winds, shined upon by all the stars of God, find the earth below not in unison with these, but are hindered from action by the disgust which the principles on which business is managed inspire, and turn drudges, or die of disgust, some of them suicides. What is the remedy? They did not yet see, and thousands of young men as hopeful now crowding to the barriers for the career do not yet see, that if the single man plant himself indomitably on his instincts, and there abide, the huge world will come round to him. Patience—patience; with the shades of all the good and great for company; and for solace and perspective of your own infinite life; and for work the study and the communication of principles, the making those instincts prevalent, the conversion of the world. Is it not the chief disgrace in the world, not to be an unit;—not to be reckoned one character;—not to yield that peculiar fruit which each man was created to bear, but to be reckoned in the gross, in the hundred, or the thousand, of the party, the section, to which we belong; and our opinion predicted geographically as the north, or the south? Not so, brothers and friends—please God, ours shall not be so. We will walk on our own feet; we will work with our own hands; we will speak our own minds. The study of letters shall be no longer a name for pity, for doubt, and for sensual indulgence. The dread of man and the love of man shall be a wall of defense and a wreath of joy around all. A nation of men will for the first time exist, because each believes himself inspired by the Divine Soul which also inspires all men.

From the journals kept by Emerson, one may harvest a great bounty of transcendentalist wisdom. These briefly encapsulated bits of wisdom at times rival the aphorisms of Nietzsche in their crystalline clarity and directness. The journal or diary was very much a part of the transcendentalist tradition (it will be recalled that Alcott included the keeping of a diary by his students as part of his educational practice). In a sense, it is in their journals that one encounters the real Emerson and Thoreau, and the reading of these journals is a pleasant and rewarding glimpse into the minds of their authors. The following few examples of his thoughts on education have been culled from Emerson's journal. Note that the numbers in parentheses following these excerpts refer to the year in the 1800's in which the item was entered in the journal, his age at that time, the number of the volume in which it appears and the page number, respectively.

81. From the Journal

Ralph Waldo Emerson

Sad it was to see the death-cold convention yesterday morning, as they sat shivering, a handful of pale men and women in a large church, for it seems the Law has touched the business of Education with the point of its pen, and instantly it has frozen stiff in the universal congelation of society. An education in things is not. We all are involved in the condemnation of words, an age of words. We are shut up in schools and college recitation rooms for ten or fifteen years, and come out at last with a bellyful of words and do not know a thing. We cannot use our hands, or our legs, or our eyes, or our arms. We do not know an edible root in the woods. We cannot tell our course by the stars, nor the hour of the day by the sun. It is well if we can swim and skate. We are afraid of a horse, of a cow, of a dog, of a cat, of a spider. Far better was the Roman rule to

Reprinted from Ralph Waldo Emerson, *Collected Works* . . . (Boston: Houghton Mifflin, 1893).

teach a boy nothing that he could not learn standing. ('39-36-V 250, 251)

Don't let them eat their seed-corn; don't let them anticipate, antedate, and be young men, before they have finished their boyhood. Let them have the fields and woods, and learn their secret and the base- and football, and wrestling, and brickbats, and suck all the strength and courage that lies for them in these games; let them ride bareback, and catch their horse in his pasture, let them hook and spear their fish, and shin a post and a tall tree, and shoot their partridge and trap the woodchuck, before they begin to dress like collegians and sing in serenades, and make polite calls.

('56-52-IX 40, 41)

The great difference between educated men is that one class acknowledge an ideal standard and the other class do not. We demand of an intellectual man, be his defects what they may, and his practice what it may, faith in the possible improvement of man. ('38-35-V 24)

Out upon scholars with their pale, sickly, etiolated indoor thoughts. Give me the out-of-door thoughts of sound men—the thoughts, all fresh, blooming. ('55-51-VII 532)

A scholar is a man with this inconvenience, that, when you ask him his opinion of any matter, he must go home and look up his manuscripts to know. ('55-52-VIII 557)

I am convinced that if a man will be a true scholar, he shall have perfect freedom. The young people and the mature hint at odium, and aversion of faces to be presently encountered in society. I say, No: I fear it not. No scholar need fear it. ('38-35-V 30)

The teacher should be the complement of the pupil; now, for the most part, they are Earth's diameters wide of each other. A college professor should be elected by setting all the candidates loose on a miscellaneous gang of young men taken at large from the street. He who could get the ear of these youths after a certain number of hours, or of the greatest number of these youths, should be professor. Let him see if he could interest these rowdy boys in the meaning of a list of words. ('46-43-VII 224)

But it is plain that the adults' education should be undertaken. When our Republic, O Plato! shall begin, the education shall not end with the youth, but shall be as vigorously continued in maturity. ('49-46-VII 57)

The scholar is a man of no more account in the street than another man; as the sound of a flute is not louder than the noise of a saw. But as the tone of the flute is heard at a greater distance than any noise, so the fame of the scholar reaches farther than the credit of the banker. ('42-38-VI 166)

The things taught in colleges and schools are not an education, but the means of education. ('31-28-II 404)

Books are to be read, and every library should be a circulating library.

('31-28-II 407)

For my report on the Greek Committee I must not forget to insert my opinion on examinations—that whenever one is on trial, two are on trial; the examiner is instructed whenever the pupil is examined. ('68-65-X 259)

Education aims to make the man prevail over the circumstance. ('40-37-V 441)

Knowledge is the straight Line; *Wisdom* is the power of the straight line, or the Square; *Virtue* is the power of the Square; or the Solid. ('45-42-VII 114)

It may, perhaps, be inferred from what has preceded that the transcendentalists were idle dreamers and useless people who withdrew from the world and affairs to contemplate nature or something equally impractical. Doubtless, the transcendental philosophy did produce such individuals, but their performance must not be confused with the legitimate fruit of transcendentalism which was an earnest seeking and aspiration for the betterment of humanity. Just as it is rather unwise to summarize the philosophy of Epicurus as "eat, drink, and be merry," similarly one would miss the true heart of the transcendental movement to observe that they were simply a group of neurotic nature-worshippers of a romantic cast.

One of the genuine attempts at creative and practical reform that drew strength from the transcendental movement was the Brook Farm experiment in cooperative living. With his optimistic view of the potential of the human spirit, the transcendentalist was a natural reformer. He simply could not be satisfied with the status quo, for every idea that he held dear told him that man qua man could be so much more than he was. In method, transcendentalist reform took the form of individual regeneration and spiritual awakening. His reforming was "commensurate with human existence; a tendency towards prefection of being." He was more concerned with *internal* reform through the re-kindling of the dormant spark of individual human spirit and dignity than with external human circumstances.

With his primary assumption of human dignity and individual worth, the transcendentalist was generally an anti-slavery man; he saw the same humanity in slave as in master, without division by perceptual external differences such as skin pigment.

Educational reform was motivated by a belief in the latent capacity of all, and transcendentalist education was simply education directed to drawing out that capacity, as the school of Alcott clearly demonstrates. First and foremost was the assumption and conviction of the supreme dignity of the individual. Because of this, the transcendentalist could not support reform that did not proceed from this assumption, although it might superficially better the motival or external circumstances of individuals. Thus, the socialism of Fourier was generally rejected because it negated self-determination of the individual and made him merely a creature of circumstance. The Brook Farm community of 1841, established in West Roxbury, Massachusetts, was not shaped by the doctrines of St. Simon, Proudhon, or Fourier. Brook Farm was actually an attempt to establish a new social order based on respect for the dignity and aspirations of man. This may be clearly seen in the following reading, the preamble to the constitution of the Brook Farm community, or as it was officially named, "The Brook-Farm Association for Industry and Education."

The Association provided its members with certain guarantees, which are ennumerated in Article III of the Brook Farm constitution.

In 1844, the Brook-Farm Association connected itself with the New York socialists, who followed Fourier, a move which eventually resulted in the demise of the Brook Farm ideal in 1847 when the Association was disbanded.

82. Constitution of the Brook Farm Community

In order more effectually to promote the great purposes of human culture; to establish the external relations of life on a basis of wisdom and purity; to apply the principles of justice and love to our social organization in accordance with the laws of Divine Providence; to substitute a system of brotherly cöoperation for one of selfish competition; to secure to our children and those who may be entrusted to our care, the benefits of the highest physical, intellectual and moral education, which in the progress of knowledge the resources at our command will permit; to institute an attractive, efficient, and productive system of industry; to prevent the exercise of worldly anxiety, by the competent supply of our necessary wants; to diminish the desire of excessive accumulation, by making the acquisition

Reprinted from O. B. Frothingham, *Transcendentalism in New England* (New York: Putnam, 1880), pp. 159, 161.

of individual property subservient to upright and disinterested uses; to guarantee to each other forever the means of physical support, and of spiritual progress; and thus to impart a greater freedom, simplicity, truthfulness, refinement, and moral dignity, to our mode of life;—we the undersigned do unite in a voluntary Association, and adopt and ordain the following articles of agreement, to wit:

ARTICLE III.

GUARANTIES.

SEC. 1.   The Association shall provide such employment for all its members as shall be adapted to their capacities, habits, and tastes; and each member shall select and perform such operations of labor, whether corporal or mental, as shall be deemed best suited to his own endowments and the benefit of the Association.

SEC. 2.   The Association guarantees to all its members, their children and family dependents, house-rent, fuel, food, and clothing, and the other necessaries of life, without charge, not exceeding a certain fixed amount to be decided annually by the Association; no charge shall ever be made for support during inability to labor from sickness or old age, or for medical or nursing attendance, except in case of shareholders, who shall be charged therefor, and also for the food and clothing of children, to an amount not exceeding the interest due to them on settlement; but no charge shall be made to any members for education or the use of library and public rooms.

SEC. 3.   Members may withdraw from labor, under the direction of the Association, and in that case, they shall not be entitled to the benefit of the above guaranties.

SEC. 4.   Children over ten years of age shall be provided with employment in suitable branches of industry; they shall be credited for such portions of each annual dividend, as shall be decided by the Association, and on the completion of their education in the Association at the age of twenty, shall be entitled to a certificate of stock to the amount of credits in their favor, and may be admitted as members of the Association.

One of the more interesting movements in educational reform to which the transcendentalists lent their support was that of the American Lyceum. For those who may not be familiar with this facet of American education, the following selection of a proposed constitution for the Lyceum will provide its rationale. This proposal was written by Josiah Holbrook, the founder of the movement, and it appeared in the *American Journal of Education* in 1828.

83. Proposed Constitution for the American Lyceum

Josiah Holbrook

American Lyceum. The undersigned agree to associate under the name —————, Branch of the American Lyceum, and adopt the following articles for their constitution.

Article 1. The objects of the lyceum are the improvement of its members in useful knowledge, and the advancement of popular education, by introducing uniformity and improvements in common schools, by becoming auxiliary to a board of education.

Article 2. To effect these objects, they will procure a cabinet, consisting of books, apparatus for illustrating the sciences, and a collection of minerals, and will hold meetings for discussions, dissertations, illustrating the sciences, or other exercises which shall be thought expedient.

Article 3. Any person may be a member of the lyceum, by paying into the treasury annually, 2 dollars; and 20 dollars paid at any one time will entitle a person, his or her heirs, or assigns, to membership forever. Persons under 18 years of age will be entitled to all the privileges of the society, except of voting, for one-half of the annual sum above named.

Article 4. The officers of this branch of the lyceum shall be a president, vice-president, treasurer, recording and corresponding secretaries, 3 or 5 curators, and 3 delegates, to be appointed by ballot on the first Wednesday of September annually.

Article 5. The president, vice-president, treasurer, and secretaries will perform the duties usually implied in those offices. The curators will have charge of the cabinet and all other property of the lyceum not appertaining to the treasury, and will be the general agents to do any business for the society under their direction. The delegates will meet delegates from branches of the lyceum in this county semiannually, to adopt regulations for their general and mutual benefit, or to take measures to introduce uniformity and improvements into common schools, and to diffuse useful and practical knowledge generally through the community, particularly to form and aid a board of education.

Article 6. To raise the standard of common education, and to benefit the juvenile members of the lyceum, a portion of the books procured shall be

Reprinted from *American Journal of Education,* Vol. III, pp. 503.

fitted to young minds; and teachers of schools may be permitted to use for the benefit of their pupils who are members of the lyceum, the apparatus and minerals under such restrictions as the association shall prescribe.

Article 7. The president or any five members will have power at any time to call a special meeting, which meeting shall be legal, if notice shall be given according to the direction in the By-Laws.

Article 8. The lyceum will have power to adopt such regulations and by-laws as shall be necessary for the management and use of the cabinet, for holding meetings, or otherwise for their interest.

Article 9. The foregoing articles may be altered or amended by vote of two-thirds present, at any legal meetings; said alteration or amendment having been proposed at a meeting, not less than four weeks previous to the one at which it is acted upon.

This emphasis upon self-culture and improvement was quite congenial to the transcendentalist credo. Indeed, transcendentalists like Emerson were popular speakers at the various Lyceums throughout the country, and many of Emerson's essays were originally talks to these groups. The same group of Lyceum members and transcendental philosophers were also, as the proposed constitution indicates, supporters of the common-school movement in the United States.

The great concern of the Lyceums with education may be seen in Selection 84 which lists subjects presented for discussion in the Lyceums.

84. Proposed Subjects for Discussion

1. What are the greatest desiderata in relation to the improvement of common schools?

2. What are the most eligible and practical means of advancing and perfecting the science of instruction?

3. To what extent is the monitorial system advisable and practicable in common schools?

4. What is the most eligible plan of promoting education, by legislative enactments?

5. Ought manual labor schools to be encouraged, and upon what general plan?

Reprinted from *American Annuals of Education,* Vol. I, p. 376.

6. Should every boy who can devote his whole time to study until the age of 16 be put to the study of Latin and Greek, and if not, to what class should these languages be restricted?

7. To what extent may lectures be useful in common schools?

8. To what extent can the natural sciences be advantageously introduced into common schools?

9. The object and usefulness of town and district Lyceums?

10. What should be the object of county and state Lyceums, and how should they be formed?

REFERENCES

Crane, Theodore Rawson (ed.). *The Colleges and the Public, 1787-1862*. New York: Teachers College, Columbia University, 1963.

Cremin, Lawrence A. *The American Common School*. New York: Teachers College, Columbia University, 1951.

Cremin, Lawrence A. (ed.). *The Republic and the School: Horace Mann on the Education of Free Men*. New York: Teachers College, Columbia University, 1957.

DeTocqueville, Alexis. *Democracy in America*. New York: Mentor, 1956.

Harris, William T., and Sanborn, Franklin B. A. *Bronson Alcott: His Life and Philosophy*. Boston: Roberts Bros., 1893.

Kiefer, Monica M. *American Children Through Their Books, 1700-1835*. Philadelphia: University of Pennsylvania Press, 1948.

Knight, Edgar W. *A Documentary History of Education in the South Before 1860*. 5 vols. Chapel Hill: University of North Carolina Press, 1949-1953.

Lee, Gordon C. (ed.). *Crusade Against Ignorance: Thomas Jefferson on Education*. New York: Teachers College, Columbia University, 1961.

Monroe, Will S. *History of the Pestalozzian Movement in the United States*. Syracuse: C. W. Bardeen, 1907.

Monroe, Will S. *The Educational Labors of Henry Barnard*. Syracuse: C. W. Bardeen, 1893.

Reisner, E. H. *Nationalism and Education Since 1789*. New York: Macmillan Co., 1922.

Reisner, E. H. *The Evolution of the Common School*. New York: Macmillan Co., 1935.

Thursfield, Richard E. *Henry Barnard's American Journal of Education*. Baltimore: Johns Hopkins Press, 1945.

PART 3

An Era of Expansion and Reform
1877-1960

I THE LATE NINETEENTH CENTURY

UNLIKE Minerva from the brow of Zeus, progressive education did not (contrary to the notions of a great many people who should know better) spring fully formed from the brain of John Dewey. The era of progress and reform which began in the latter decades of the nineteenth century was a generalized and a multiphasic movement that affected all facets of American intellectual, social, and political life. A specialized manifestation of this general movement developed in the field of education as well as in the other social institutions of our land. So active indeed was this reforming spirit in the educational area that for many people to this day it is the educational aspect of the progressive era that epitomizes the period. This educational aspect, its pluralistic strands rather loosely gathered together under the label of "Progressive Education," has doubtlessly precipitated more controversy, frayed tempers, vicious attacks, and ardent defenses than any other phase of American educational history.

Bearing in mind that the progressive educational movement was a special form of a whole generalized national movement for progress and reform, an attempt to trace some of its origins and roots should prove profitable.

Origins of Progressive Education

The progressive era had its origins to a large degree in the demographic fact that by the late nineteenth century the American civilization had been quite thoroughly transformed from a rural-agricultural to an urban-industrial organization. If the basically humanitarian essence of the American *Weltanschauung* was to be perpetuated in the light of the transformed socio-economic and demographic make-up of the American scene, a radical re-appraisal of American institutions was needed. The social cohesion and stability intrinsically engendered by a small-town, agrarian civilization was shattered radically by the economic and social upheaval that took work out of the home/family complex and into the industrial/factory milieu. Vast numbers of workers, necessary to appease the well-nigh insatiable manpower demands of industry, moved into the cities, where, augmented by waves of immigrants, they created industrial slums and ghettos with frightening rapidity. These later immigrants who came to America to work, to build, and to sweat out long hours under shameful conditions in underpaid positions of labor were of a different type from earlier migrants. They were non-Nordic people of diverse linguistic stocks and non-Protestant religious backgrounds, mainly of East European or Mediterranean origins, and they could not "melt" into American society with the ease of their predecessors. Without some definite effort, they would remain isolated from the mainstream of American culture until they died.

The transmission of the culture had been traditionally the major function of the formal and informal educational system. Social stability, cohesion, and security had been supplied by the informal education of the family. The family, however, had itself been transformed by its new urban-industrial setting. It was impossible, under the new socio-economic conditions, for the family to effectively carry out its informal educational tasks. Clearly the burden had to be taken up by the formal educational institution, but the schools were neither oriented nor equipped for this new task. The complexities and requirements of the new society could not be met by a formal school system oriented to a society that was receding rapidly into the pages of history. The common schools and the traditional approaches to education were hopelessly inadequate to cope with the new American society. To many, the transformed society obviously required an equally transformed school system in order to carry out its expanded and changed mission.

The school had to be re-formed, re-oriented, re-designed to meet the increased and different educational demands of an urban-industrial civilization. It would have to take over many educational tasks previously informally performed by the family. It would have to take on the responsibility of "Americanizing" immigrants whose racial, religious, and linguistic backgrounds were sharply at variance with American culture.

The movement towards educational re-forming was supplemented and spurred by several other factors as well as the simple fact of a transformed cultural milieu.

American political concerns during the period were evolving in a definite fashion from the abstract to the concrete. The transition from the abstract statements of basic equality proclaimed in the Declaration of Independence, noble but rather vague as to concrete practice, to the more specific efforts to ensure equality of the Jacksonians represented, itself, an evolutionary expanse. Jeffersonian-Jacksonian democracy, which had in part produced the American common school, underwent yet another re-interpretation in the eyes of some during the late nineteenth and early twentieth centuries. The classical-liberal enunciation of freedom (defined essentially as the lack of restraint) seemed to run counter to a positive affirmation of the equality of all men. To use a rather far-fetched illustration, it is one thing to be free to purchase a Mercedes-Benz automobile in the sense that there are no legal restraints precluding this purchase. Obviously, however, it is quite another matter to be "free" to make this purchase in the sense of freedom that would include the concrete power of effective choice. For the classical-liberal, the latter implication would not be included in a definition of freedom. Now this is not to imply that what one might call the "new liberal" interpretation of freedom would assert that all men should have an expensive foreign car. What is implied, however, is that freedom should be augmented by egalitarianism in certain basic areas of effective choice. In other words, the power of effective choice in certain areas should be insured by an extraneous agency for all citizens. This agency was generally the federal government. This new interpretation of the concrete guarantee of certain freedoms (defined as effective choice) was simply a further extension or evolution of the Jefferson-Jackson democratic tradition. Its legitimacy is still debated, of course, but during the progressive era the new interpretation found several persuasive spokesmen, and the functions of government were extended far beyond the deliberately minimal areas assigned by the classical-liberal tradition.

Education as well was thought of by some as being in need of extension in effort and sphere. Schooling was one of the areas that should be insured as an effective choice for all children.

It has been noted that this transformation of the democratic tradition was evolutionary. This term is particularly appropriate, for during this era the social interpretation of the Darwinian evolutionary theory played an important role in the movement towards concrete reform and progress.

From an argument supporting the social status quo, laissez-faire, classical-liberal society of the survival of the fittest as a law of nature, Darwinism was turned into an argument for active, planned social reform.

Disagreeing with William Graham Sumner's "Conservative" Social Darwinism, certain social theorists, such as Lester Ward and Albion Small, saw evolution as clear evidence for the role of man as the innovator and reformer of his environment and institutions. Man, they argued, by reason of his faculty of reason, could solve rather than simply accept the problems of his life. This "Reform" Darwinism therefore, stressed the position of man, not as one who could only accept and adapt to his environment but as one who could apply his reason to create a better environment. Advancement and progress of man and society through the proper application of reason was the optimistic interpretation of the "Reform" Darwinists. Clearly, this meant more schools, a greater extension of educational opportunity. A curriculum should be oriented towards teaching not the glories of the past but the proper and effective use of the mind of man, with which he could guide the course of events to a glorious future. Progress was not inevitable of course, but it was certainly within the realm of possibility for man; widespread and properly oriented education could extend this into the realm of the probable. From the rather pessimistic (or at best static) social message of "Conservative" Darwinism, the theory of evolution became a dynamic and positive voice for directed social reform and for the reasoned, deliberate improvement of man's environment and institutions.

Social Darwinism of the "reform" variety was given a formal philosophic structure with the development of the indigenous American philosophy called *Pragmatism*. As a philosophy built upon a conception of the mind viewed as an instrument or tool to be used in the service of man, Pragmatism provided the technical philosophic background for active reform. As a theory of truth and value that found the only criterion of the "rightness" of either in the examined consequences of action, Pragmatism was uniquely suited for a time that was more interested in concrete action and results than in abstract speculation. Translated into educational theory by William James, John Dewey, and others, Pragmatism demanded an education with no arbitrarily and inflexibly set *a priori* goals; rather, these men saw education reflecting the basic evolutionary principle of constant change and novelty. As education cannot claim to see into the future (with the exception of the belief that it will be different from the present), to educate as if it could would be fallacious. What education could and should do, however, would be to act as stimulus to growth, to the building of a better future. Ideas must be tested, acted upon. Their consequences must be evaluated and utilized for future action to meet the continually changing conditions of life. This necessitated an impetus toward and freedom for experimentation in the classroom for a closer working relationship of teacher and pupil. Study of the past for its own sake was useless. As a guide to understanding the present, however, study of the past was a legitimate undertaking. The Pragmatists did not disregard the old curriculum and subject matter *in toto;* rather, they approached these matters from a different perspective and point of view. Subject matter was all around; it would be found in the life situation of the pupil, in the here and now. History, for example, in the hands of scholars like Becker, Robinson, and Beard was studied from a "problems" point of view. What light could it throw on present conditions and happenings? History, as anything else, must prove its worth, not on the grounds of intrinsic value because of academic tradition but by the Pragmatic criterion of actual present worth.

To trace many of the indirect sources of the progressivist reforms in education, it would be necessary to take note of several European contributions in educational theory and reformist tradition. The *Émile* of the French *philosophe* Jean-Jacques Rousseau had been discussed in America since colonial times, and, indeed, it was a veritable manifesto for educationalists who wanted to treat the child as a unique individual of intrinsic worth. Traditionally, education from ancient times onward had tended to treat the state of childhood as an unfortunate but necessary evil on the way to adult maturity. The "child-ishness" of the child was neither attractive nor sacred—it was simply something to be overcome as quickly (although not always as painlessly) as possible. Adult standards would not be compromised. The child would be dressed as a miniature adult and expected to act like one. To borrow a happy Augustinian phrase, the child was to be rapidly cured of his "pernicious blythsomeness."

With the *Émile* of Rousseau, however, the child *qua* child received recognition as a unique and essentially "good" individual. Child-nature was to be respected as an entity of intrinsic worth, to be protected from the debilitating and corrupting influence of the adult world. The child was to perfect himself in an environment that was oriented not to an adult world but to the special world of the child. This was the romantic vision of the proper school, based not upon adult fiat but upon a knowledge of the nature of the child.

With the subsequent ramification of this general thesis by educators in the Rousseauean tradition, such as Pestalozzi and Froebel, the world of the child was sanctified in and of itself. No longer was it to be simply an adult world writ small. There was, to be sure, a tendency for the pendulum to swing just as far towards a sanctification of a sort of sacred and pure state of a romanticized concept of childhood as it had previously swung in the opposite direction. Johann Heinrich

Pestalozzi, one of the world's greatest teachers of children, was one of the first educators to insist upon a thorough study of child developmental processes and psychology. He and others became convinced that learning for the child was vitally related to the environment in which it took place. Such an environment had to be carefully considered and specially prepared by the educator. Children, considered as individuals rather than as a abstract aggregate mass, obviously learned at different rates of speed and had different needs and interests. The educator had to take all this into consideration if he was to successfully carry out his task. This demanded an increased sensitivity and appreciation of child-nature on the part of the teacher.

Influenced by sense-realism, Pestalozzi developed a new pedagogical methodology. Called the "object lesson," the Pestalozzian method based learning upon the concrete objectification of knowledge, utilizing actual objects rather than abstract descriptions of objects of knowledge. Why lecture the child about a tree when he can be introduced to its component parts—see, savor, and handle leaves and branches? Pestalozzian naturalistic pedagogy was introduced into the United States by Edward A. Sheldon, and it became the basis of teacher education at Oswego (New York) Normal School. Sheldon's graduates spread the gospel throughout the country, although the reduction of the Pestalozzian object method to a drill manual effectively destroyed its value as a creative teaching method. In the hands of an uninspired teacher, the object lesson could become as dry and removed from the reality of the child as any other lesson. Actually, Pestalozzian educational theory had been known in the United States during the time of Horace Mann's crusade for the common school, but it was Sheldon and his Oswego students who spread the doctrine widely to the educational rank and file.

To reduce these European influences to their basic components, it may be noted that the prevailing doctrinal influences included the view of education as a preparation for life, the stress upon instruction that dealt with objects rather than with abstractions of them, and the radical acceptance of the natural activity of child-play as both essential and instructive.

A more mystical interpretation of this general educative thesis, represented by the ideas of Friedrich Froebel, was imported to this country in 1857. This founder of the kindergarten movement in Germany approached education from the standpoint of a mystical idealism, stressing not only the concrete but the symbolic significance of object teaching. By the 1860's the kindergarten had become part of the lexicon of American education.

Later in the century, in the eighties and nineties, yet another German theorist, Johann Friedrich Herbart, exerted significant influence on American thinking in education. The Herbartian ideas seemed to such American interpreters as the McMurray brothers, Charles and Frank, to offer the possibility of a scientifically based pedagogy. A psychology oriented curriculum and teaching method in this view should open up the study of education as a university discipline subject to the rigors of scientific research, with the promise of eventual professionalization of pedagogy and pedagogues. The Herbartianism of the era, moreover, coincided with, as well as influenced, new efforts to study the mind of the child with deepened insight. The work of G. Stanley Hall and other psychologists of the "child-study movement" seemed to provide exciting possibilities for the reforming of education.

The background of this largely imported body of educational belief, from Rousseau to Herbart, provided ample precursory impetus towards educational reform in the United States.

As seen thus far, the progressive reform movement in education did not suddenly emerge on the American scene *de novo*. Its origins as a specialized segment of the general movement of reform for progress must be located in a variety of sources—educational, political, philosophic, and economic. From a purely educational standpoint, the framework for potential reform had been built in the early nineteenth century by the Manns and Barnards. It became the mission of the innovators of the late nineteenth and early twentieth centuries to fill the empty spaces in the ladder of a vast system of public education, a system which, when completed, would make this country a model for the whole world in the area of education.

To attempt to define fully the general term *Progressive Education* is perhaps to chase a will-of-the-wisp. Based upon multiple sources it took an amazing variety of forms, often somewhat contradictory in nature. In many respects the term labels an *attitude* towards education more than anything else. A changed view of the child which placed his needs and interests at the core of a curriculum naturally stressed the necessity of a thorough understanding of the child as a prerequisite to successful pedagogy. The redefined concept of the mind and intellect was to serve as a tool to solve the problems of humanity and society. Intellect was to be treated as an active process; ideas were to be tested in the arena of action. As Max Lerner has observed, the instrumental approach recognizes that ideas are used in behalf of a way of life and in the struggles for its achievement. When ideas are viewed instrumentally, the primary regard is for their validity and for the creative action that they will evoke through that validity. Finally, it was the school that was to be the nucleus of social reform; the progress of the individual and society would be effectively generated by an education articulated to real life, its problems, and areas for reform.

PROGRESSIVISM IN AMERICAN EDUCATION

What exactly was this *traditional school* that was to be so radically reformed by the progressive? In a sense, it must be admitted that the traditional school was, for the progressives, the epitome of all educational evil writ large. So large as to be, to a degree, a convenient strawman. In actual fact, the traditional school was simply a school that was attuned to an American society that no longer existed. Incapable of adapting to the tremendous transformation of the American society from a simple agrarian to a highly complex industrial culture, the schools simply ignored the new America that was being created around them. The progressive vision of change was to reform the schools to cope with the realities of the present. As has been noted, the framework for educational reform was present in America, having been built by the common-school pioneers and reformers.

First and foremost of the newly created realities with which the progressive reformers had to cope was the simple fact of the vastly enlarged population to be schooled. One source of this population explosion was the increased flow of immigrants. The other was a booming national birthrate, a biological attribute that had long been one of the nation's outstanding characteristics. To get some idea of immigration increases, it may be noted that between 1789 and 1829 the total immigration was roughly 400,000. By 1840 this trickle had increased to 1,713,251 and ten years later to 2,598,214. Industrial expansion that followed the termination of the Civil War attracted by the beginning of the twentieth century an influx of 5,246,613 immigrants. Indeed, between 1901 and 1910 the trickle had become a sizeable flow, for in that span some 9 million immigrants entered the country.[1] As noted above, the national backgrounds of these immigrants included southern and eastern Europe. Problems of assimilation into the American culture, minimal with earlier immigrants who, by and large, were of similar national background to the original settlers, were for the first time creating the necessity for definite efforts in the direction of conscious assimilation.

The homogeneity of the American village was replaced by the heterogeneous American city. Many of the new immigrants, linguistically and culturally isolated from the native American citizenry, congregated together in different areas of industrial cities, forming communities of cultural and national ghettos within industrial slums. Coupled with the native-born of the lower classes, who also contributed to the industrial slum population, this produced a vast number of children for whom the traditional school was simply inadequate. The progressive educators saw in this teeming unschooled mass a challenge to the school; their vision was an educational system that would meet not only the problem of the sheer weight of numbers, but also the new problems of democratic orientation and assimilation.

To meet the needs of the children of this age in terms of the realities of the age, the progressives saw the need for radical revision and expansion of the curriculum into areas heretofore unnecessary or provided for by institutions other than the school. Concerns with such things as the health (physical and mental) of the child became part of the school's task in progressive eyes. Vocational training (obviously

[1] V. T. Thayer, *Formative Ideas in American Education* (New York: Dodd, Mead & Co., 1965), pp. 65-66.

most of these children would have to work for a living in some industrial capacity) could no longer be provided by apprenticeship alone; again, the school had to step in to fill the gap. As Calvin Woodward of Washington University in St. Louis observed, the old style classical education yielded gentlemen, more often unfitted by their education than fitted by it to earn their daily bread. During the 1890's the concept of manual training enjoyed a tremendous vogue in the nation's schools, essentially to provide the trained technicians and noncommissioned officers in the army of industrial labor.

The changed attitudes towards the child, the learning process, and the curriculum all led inexorably towards the radical reformation of the school. The school should be a pleasant place, wherein the physical, mental, and social growth of the child could take place. In a very real sense it was to be a laboratory where ideas could be examined and acted upon and wherein their consequences could be evaluated—all to lead to the continual growth of the learner. School was to be a great adventure in learning, with the skillfull teacher available to guide the process. The classroom itself was to be transformed from a dull, monotonous, and depressing place of forced confinement into a place of light and beauty—healthy and conducive to the explorations of questioning eager minds.

The classroom was to be the arena of exploration. Why, it was reasoned, fill childish heads with dry and lifeless facts when all about the child is changing, pulsating, dynamic life? Education should not divorce itself from that life, or it would become itself lifeless and devoid of any real involvement with the learner. Education could not provide nice pat answers to the problems that the young learner would encounter in the future. If it was honest, education would have to admit that it probably could not even imagine what these problems would be, far less claim answers. What education could do, however, was to see that the young explorer was properly and adequately equipped for his journey through life. Basic equipment would include the habit of intelligent problem solving, using acquired knowledge as a lever to clarify other problematic areas so that the process of individual growth could go on. There must be that intangible feeling of being free to seek one's own solutions and answers which must permeate every classroom of the nation. To produce free thinking individuals, not recognizable replicas, must become the goal of the teacher. To accomplish this end, the role of the teacher itself must be transformed —from a martinet content to equate academic progress with the rote regurgitation of predigested trivia into a creative, experienced guide and intellectual assistant to the child's development as an individual. In short, the teacher must become a professional, not only as a master of subject matter but as an individual both sensitive to, and aware of, the child and the process whereby he learns. Courses in child development, in learning theory and educational psychology must figure in the preparation of a teacher. Indeed, the idea that any reasonably competent person with an adequate grasp of some academic discipline could, *ipso facto,* serve as a teacher was sharply called into doubt. The idea of special preparation for a teacher, apart from mere subject-matter mastery, created a veritable avalanche of "methods courses," "developmental courses," etc., in the curricula of the teachers colleges. The teacher was becoming an educator.

II   THE TWENTIETH CENTURY

THE PASSING OF THE PROGRESSIVE EDUCATION MOVEMENT

When one looks at some of the great concerns of the progressive educators—their insistence upon the recognition of individual differences, the stress upon psychological and developmental processes in schooling, the concern of the school with all classes of society, etc.—one wonders, perhaps, at the violent controversy they initiated. What, after all, is so alarming or even radical about such concerns? The lack of emotion generally surrounding these progressive concerns in today's educational climate of opinion makes it difficult for us to appreciate the crusading fervor and the bitter disputes that once accompanied each of them. It would be a rare teacher or parent today who would question the notion that a realization of the individual differences of pupils is essential to a well-run classroom. In effect, much of the progressive fire has been dampened, not by the logic of debate but by the simple process of time and the gradual acceptance of diverse elements of the progressive program. What to the progressive educator was a vital point, a nucleus of reform, has become part of the "conventional wisdom" of education. True, the sharp edges have become softened, the emotional appeal reduced. Nonetheless many of the progressive concerns have simply been quietly incorporated into the total educational picture. Certainly, there is little that remains that could arouse the emotional crusading spirit of the early progressives.

What then was really the result of the "Era of Progress" in education? Did it actually result in a radical transformation of the school? Was the vision of the educational reformers actually realized in concrete practice, or did it fade into compromise and superficial dissatisfactions?

Clearly many of the aims of progressive education were achieved in the nation's schools. The classrooms themselves were transformed into comfortable and generally nonthreatening places conducive to learning. Moveable furniture to a great degree replaced old stationary desks and seats; color and cleanliness became standard features. Children were permitted to move about and to engage in discussion to a greater degree than ever before. Textbooks became revitalized and deliberately geared to children's interests and abilities. Teachers became aware of psychological learning and developmental processes.

By and large, however, it has been the progressive *methodology* that has been incorporated (with modification) into the system of education. The real underlying vision of the progressive educators, that of the school as the key agent and instrument in the total reform of society, never came about. The external trappings of progressive education, the superficial innovations in pedagogical techniques, even the terminology, have to some extent passed into the "conventional wisdom" of American education.[2] The real reformation of the school, however, was never attained. Why, it must be asked, did this transformation stop short of its ultimate goal?

The answer is found, in part, within the peculiar framework of progressive education itself. Providing a lively stimulus towards the

[2] John Kenneth Galbraith's term, used in this context with effect by Lawrence A. Cremin, *The Transformation of the School* (New York: Knopf, 1961), pp. 328 ff.

professionalization of teachers, progressive education, with its stress on the uniqueness of the educator's role and necessary preparation, at the same time separated the teacher from his necessary ally in social reform—the concerned layman. More and more, education became the province of the educator; educational dialogue and discussion became limited to a closed clique of professionals who spoke in a jargon beyond the understanding of the interested non-professional. Cut off by his professional status from society in general, the new educationalist retreated more and more into the small in-group for his discussions. The support so necessary for real reform was cut off from education by its well-meaning practitioners, thus limiting the scope of their activities to purely pedagogical matters. The mass support of voters was lost to the movement.

This isolation of the educationalists further removed progressive education from the mainstream of political progressivism, making education a separate and unaligned aspect of overall progressive thought. In effect, progressive education became so particularized and professionalized that it effectively removed itself from the sources of power to effect reform and change to any large extent. This isolation had the result of producing a professional inbreeding among the progressive educators. They lost sight of the greater ends of social reform and became ensnared in their own professional rhetoric and esoteric terminology.

There was another fatal flaw contained within the fabric of the progressive theory that precluded any real success in the matter of radical reform. Progressive concern with the individual was based upon a concept of freedom that failed to provide for the mass organization necessary to produce change. Even the vision of the revitalization of the community through the school was a localized procedure, never visualized as reform on the mass scale that came to characterize twentieth-century efforts in this direction. The failure to align itself with the political power and mass organization necessary to effect total reforms proved to be a weakness in the progressive reform movement, which limited education reform to strictly operational matters.

Thus it was that the movement of progressive education, instead of spreading in ever widening circles of influence in society, tended to move in increasingly restricted spheres of influence, finally becoming a closed professional club of devotees isolated even from the rest of the academic profession, surrounded by a virtually inpenetrable air of mystique and overspecialized, often meaningless (except to the initiate) jargon.

As a movement, progressive education is a thing of the past, a matter for the historian. But, in our haste, let us not fail to render the honors that are justly due.[3] Perhaps the reforming crusade in education was, in the light of present knowledge of the complexities of social change, incredibly simplistic and naive. Perhaps much was done in the name of progressive education that approached the ludicrous and well deserved the bitter invective and satire that it called forth. It cannot be denied, however, that in spite of its weaknesses, the reforming movement called "Progressive Education" made a considerable contribution to the American educational scene. The reformers added a great deal to the classroom and to the school much of which is taken quite for granted today. In fact, much of that which characterizes contemporary educational thought and practice has its roots in progressive education.

Yet the great irony of the "passing of progressivism" remains that since progressive education never lived, that is, the vision of a transformed school and society never in reality accomplished in America, progressive education cannot be said to have died.

[3] For an interesting exploration of the point, cf. Paul Nash, "The Strange Death of Progressive Education," *Educational Theory,* XIV, 2 (April, 1964), pp. 65-75.

SECTION 1

The Expansion of American Education

The post-Civil War decades formed an era of vast expansion in American education in diversity of curriculum offerings, in numbers of students, and in some areas in the basic idea of the aim and function of education itself. The framework of the system of public instruction, the great American "ladder," that had been built by the reformers of the national era, began to be filled in and strengthened in these years by new reformers with new ideas. The years of the late nineteenth and early twentieth centuries brought the rise of mass education in America, with some notable exceptions—the "new immigrant" and the Negro in the North as well as the South. Furthermore the extension of education was formed in grades and patterns, from kindergarten to graduate school, that have remained to the present.

The direction of this expansion in education was guided in large measure by the benevolent hand of William T. Harris, a remarkable man who combined the wisdom of a philosopher with the organizational ability of an administrator. Harris was an idealist, a Hegelian, who founded and edited the *Journal of Speculative Philosophy;* yet he was for many years a successful superintendent of St. Louis schools, and later he served as United States Commissioner of Education. His approach to education, "the opening of the five windows of the soul," is illustrative of the idealistic thinking which predominated in theory of education during the latter decades of the nineteenth century, thinking that the progressive educators later came to call "traditionalist." Yet here is a concept of education that envisions an enormous expansion of American education in a progression of studies from elementary school to the university.

85. The Philosophy of Education

William T. Harris

. . . There are, then, three epochs of school education—elementary, secondary and higher. The first or elementary stage is the opening of the five windows of the soul. (1) Arithmetic is the foundation of our knowledge

of nature, by which we measure and count all things inorganic. When its
first principles are mastered the child begins to want to combine the organic
with the inorganic, and then we come to another window (2), that of
elementary geography. The distribution of animal and plant life is learned,
and the child begins to peep into the organization of things, the growth of
plants, and the formation of the continents and the earth. Thirdly, he learns
to read and write, and gets a glimpse into literature. The original colloquial
vocabulary learned at home, variously estimated at from 300 or 400 to
3,000 or 4,000 words, deals only with commonplace things. But the school
takes this colloquial vocabulary as a key and opens up the great reservoir
of literature in books, initiating him into a higher class of words, expressive
of fine shades of feeling and thought. Thus, to his own vocabulary are
added those of great writers, who have seen nature from a different point
of view, and presented their thoughts in gems of literary style. Literature
lifts up the pupil into the realms of human nature and discloses the motives
which govern the actions of men. Yet Spencer puts this last in his course
of study. After learning all science has to give, after learning one's trade
and the care of his body, he would then, if there is leisure, permit literature
and art. But literature is the greatest educator we have. It has made possible newspapers and periodicals and books, with pictures of human life
and of the motives governing our actions. The fourth window of the soul is
grammar, wherein we have a glimpse of the logical structure of the intellect
as revealed in language. The fifth window is history (that of his own country), wherein he sees revealed the aspirations of his countrymen, his own
nature, written out in colossal letters; and these five studies should make
the elementary education of the student. The secondary education takes up
human learning and continues it along the same lines, namely: 1, inorganic
nature; 2, organic nature; 3, literature (the heart); 4, grammar and logic
(the intellect); and 5, history (the will). Algebra deals with general numbers, while Arithmetic has definite numbers to operate with. Geometry and
physics continue inorganic nature, while natural history continues the study
already commenced in geography. Then come Greek and Latin, and here
is opened up a great field of study into the embryology of our civilization.
In the dead languages we have the three great threads running through the
history of human progress. The Greek, with its literature and aesthetic art
and its philosophy, showing the higher forms of human freedom in contrast
with the Egyptian, which showed only the struggle for freedom and never
the man separated from the animal and the inorganic world. The Roman,
with the continual gaze upon the will of man, seeks the true forms of con-

Reprinted from W. T. Harris, "The Philosophy of Education," Notes Supplementary
to the *Johns Hopkins University Studies in Historical and Political Science*, XI,
pp. 257-277 (an abstract of five lectures, 7 Jan. to 4 Feb., 1893).

tracts and treaties and corporations, whereby one man may combine with
another, and it essays the conquering of men and reducing them to obedience to civil law, not only external conquest but internal conquest as well.
The Hebrew thread is the religious one, which we recognize in the celebration of worship one day each week and in the various holy days. We
acknowledge this the most essential thread of our civilization. So, with the
secondary education we begin to get the embryology of our forms of life.
The higher or collegiate education is the comparative step of education.
Each branch is studied in the light of all the others. Natural science and
sociology are investigated; logic and mental philosophy; ethics and rhetoric;
as well as the philosophy of history and of literature, and the comparative
sciences, which furnish the light for the whole method of higher education.
The first, or elementary education, then, is but superficial, a mere inventory;
the secondary insists on some reflection on what has been learned; and the
third, or higher education, is the unity and comparison of all that has been
learned, so that each is explained by the whole. Give the child possession
of the embryology of civilization, and his insight into the evolution of
civilization is insured. Educators have adopted the course of study as it
exists, led by an unconscious or blind impulse.

Akin to the idealism of Harris in spirit, yet deriving its main inspiration from the romantic naturalism of Rousseau and Pestalozzi, was the
educational theory of Edward A. Sheldon and the "Oswego movement." Sheldon's work in the training of teachers at the New York
State Normal School at Oswego, based on the Pestalozzian "object-
lesson" method, had a wide influence on American elementary-school
instruction during these years. In the following passage Sheldon discusses the theory of the object lesson.

86. Object Teaching

Edward A. Sheldon

. . . Now, any proper system of education must be based upon philosophical principles, upon a knowledge of the natural order of development
of the being to be educated, in his mental, moral and physical constitution,

Reprinted from E. A. Sheldon, "Object Teaching," *American Journal of Education,*
XIV, 1894, p. 95.

and the corresponding appliances for promoting such growth; and no one can hope for success who does not clearly comprehend these principles. The first effort then on the part of teachers' should be to study *principles,* and then the *mode* of applying them. The reverse of this is the course now being pursued in this country. Teachers are endeavoring to imitate models from books, rather than making themselves first familiar with the principles upon which these methods are based, and then using these models as aids in applying them. The only remedy for this evil, as it seems to us, is the establishment of Training Schools for the *professional* education of teachers. Not schools in which the branches are taught, but where the whole aim and effort shall be to impart a *practical* knowledge of the science of education and the art of applying it. In these schools should be exhibited the highest excellence in the art of teaching. There should also be schools of practice where the students shall have abundant opportunity for applying the instruction they receive, and the methods they observe.

87. Two Specific Lessons

Edward A. Sheldon

LESSON ON ANIMALS

The Horse

Matter	*Method*
1. A horse has legs, body, head, eyes, ears, mane, tail, hoofs.	1. Present the picture; let the children name the parts when pointed to, and point to them when named.
2. A horse has a large round body, long thin legs, a long handsome tail, flowing mane, and upright pointed ears.	2. Lead the children to talk about the parts—give the terms required to express ideas—as handsome. Bring out pointed by comparing the two ends of a cut pencil. Which most resemble the ears of a horse? Why? Bring out upright by holding the pencil in different directions.

Reprinted by permission from N. H. Dearborn, *The Oswego Movement in American Education,* Contribution to Education, No. 183 (New York: Teachers College, Columbia University, 1925), pp. 162-163.

3. A horse can walk, trot, gallop, kick and neigh. Horse walks, trots, gallops. What else a horse can do with his legs. When he does this. What sound he makes. Terms given.

3. Lead the children to talk of any actions they have seen the horse perform. Let a boy show how.

4. Refer children to the uses of the horse.

4. A horse can draw a cart or carriage; can carry people on its back.

5. Let the children say who made the horse; how He likes us to treat it. Speak of its usefulness to us and lead the children to mention different ways in which they can show it kindness.

5. We should never treat the horse cruelly, but always be very gentle with him.

Lesson on Objects

Leather

1. Raw material and manufactured article. The children having stated from what substance leather is made, examine specimen of the raw material and manufactured article—are required to find the qualities of each. The teacher tabulating on the slate.

The skin of animals is:	*Leather is:*
Soft and moist	Soft and dry
Slightly tough	Very tough
When soft pliable, but when dry liable to crack	Flexible and elastic
Porous	Dense and waterproof
Perishable, decaying readily when wet or moist	Very durable
Fatty or oily	Without oil
Hairy	Without hair
Comparatively useless	Very useful

2. Process of manufacture. Children told that they have to discover what has to be done to such a substance as skin to change it into such a substance as leather.

3. Question on the state of the skin or hide when taken from the animal. Would have portions of flesh or fat attached to the inside. Why this must be taken away. Refer to the state of meat if kept for some time; would decay and occasion foul smells. Children may be told that fat and flesh could not

not be made into leather. Tell them that the first process consists of scraping the skin with a knife, and that this is termed fleshing.

4. What next must be done. Again compare the skin and leather. The first has hairs. The children may be told that leather can be made without removing the hair. This is sometimes done. But when we want leather without hair for shoes, gloves, etc., the hair must be removed at this point. Children to judge how this can be done. To mention any ways in which they have seen hair taken off skins; shaved, plucked or by scalding—but this is neither shaven, shorn or plucked, but the skins are soaked in troughs filled with lime water. This soaking so loosens the hair that it can be scraped off—the scraping is done with a knife and is called hairing.

In the 1880's, the thinking on education of the German philosopher, Johann Friedrich Herbart, was introduced to America through the writings of Charles DeGarmo, the brothers Frank and Charles A. McMurray, and others. The essential aim of education stated by the American Herbartians was a "moral and ethical revelation of the world." Yet their major influence on teaching and teacher education came from their search for a scientific, psychologic basis for education. The search led in one direction through the National Herbart Society (which later changed its name to the National Society for the Study of Education) toward the formation of a university discipline of "education." In another direction it led toward a teaching method, an organized, rigid procedure offered as the key to effective instruction in any area, the "Five Formal Steps."

88. The Elements of General Method

Charles A. McMurray

In projecting a general plan of popular education we are beholden to the prejudices of no man nor class of men. Not even the traditional prejudices of the great body of teachers should stand in the way of setting up the noblest ideal of education. Educational thinkers are in duty bound to free themselves from utilitarian notions and narrowness, and to adopt the

Reprinted from Charles A. McMurray, *The Elements of General Method: Based on the Principles of Herbart* (New York: Macmillan Co., 1903), pp. 14-19.

best platform that children by natural birthright can stand upon. They are called upon to find the best and to apply it to as many as possible. Let it be remembered that each child has a complete growth before him. His own possibilities, and not the attainments of his parents and elders, are the things to consider.

Shall we seek to avoid responsibility for the moral aim by throwing it upon the family and the church? But the more we probe into educational problems, the more we shall find the essential unity of all educational forces. The citadel of a child's life is his moral character, whether the home, the school, or the church build and strengthen its walls. If asked to define the relation of the school to the home, we shall quickly see that they are one in spirit and leading purpose, that instead of being separated they should be brought closer together.

In conclusion, therefore, shall we make moral character the clear and conscious aim of school education, and then subordinate school studies and discipline, mental training and conduct, to this aim? It will be a great stimulus to thousands of teachers to discover that this is the real purpose of school work, and that there are abundant means not yet used of realizing it. Having once firmly grasped this idea, they will find that there is no other having half its potency. It will put a substantial foundation under educational labors both theoretical and practical, which will make them the noblest of enterprises. Can we expect the public school to drop into such a purely subordinate function as that of intellectual training, to limit its influence to an almost mechanical action, the sharpening of the mental tools? Stated in this form, it becomes an absurdity.

Is it reasonable to suppose that the rank and file of our teachers will realize the importance of this aim in teaching, so long as it has no recognition in our public system of instruction? The moral element is largely present among educators as an instinct, but it ought to be evolved into a clear purpose with definite means of accomplishment. It is an open secret, in fact, that while our public instruction is obtensibly secular, having nothing to do directly with religion or morals, there is nothing about which good teachers are more thoughtful and anxious than about the means of moral influence. Occasionally some one from the outside attacks our public schools as without morals and godless, but there is no lack of stanch defenders on moral grounds. Theoretically and even practically, to a considerable extent, we are all agreed upon the supreme value of moral education. But there is a striking inconsistency in our whole position on the school problem. While the supreme value of the moral aim will be generally admitted, it has no open recognition in our school course, either as a principal or as a subordinate aim of instruction. Moral education is not germane to the avowed purposes of the public school. If it gets in at all, it is by the back door. It is incidental, not primary. The importance of making the leading aim of education clear and conscious to teachers, is great. If their conviction on this point is not clear, they will certainly not concentrate their attention and efforts upon its realization. Again, in a businesslike education, where there are so many important and necessary results to be reached, it is very easy and common to put forward a subordinate aim, and to lift it into undue prominence, even allowing it to swallow up all the energies of teacher and pupils. Owing to this diversity of opinion among teachers as to the results to be reached, our public schools exhibit a chaos of conflicting theory and practice, and a numberless of hobby-riders.

How to establish the moral aim in the centre of the school course, how to subordinate and realize the other educational aims while keeping this chiefly in view, how to make instruction and school discipline contribute unitedly to the formation of vigorous moral character, and how to unite home, school, and other life experiences of a child in perfecting the one great aim of education—these are some of the problems whose solution will be sought. . . .

That the other justifiable aims of education, such as physical training, mental discipline, orderly habits, gentlemanly conduct, practical utility of knowledge, liberal culture, and the free development of individuality, will not be weakened by placing the moral aim in the forefront of educational motives, we are convinced.

Herbart has stated the moral aim of education at the beginning of his "Outlines of Educational Doctrine," Lange and De Garmo, pp. 7 and 8, as follows:—

"The term 'virtue' expresses the whole purpose of education. Virtue is the idea of inner freedom which has developed into an abiding actuality in an individual. Whence, as inner freedom is a relation between insight and volition, a double task is at once set before the teacher. It becomes his business to make actual each of these two factors separately, in order that a later permanent relationship may result.

"But even here, at the outset, we need to bear in mind the identity of morality with the effort put forth to realize the permanent actuality of the harmony between insight and volition. To induce the pupil to make this effort is a difficult achievement; at all events, it becomes possible only when the twofold training mentioned above is well under way. It is easy enough, by the study of the example of others, to cultivate theoretical acumen. The moral application to the pupil himself, however, can be made, with hope of success, only in so far as his inclinations and habits have taken a direction in keeping with his insight."

· · · · ·

The Herbart school stands for certain progressive ideas which, while not exactly new, have, however, received such a new infusion of life-giving blood that the vague formulæ of theorists have been changed into the definite, mandatory requirements and suggestions of real teachers. The fact that a pedagogical truth has been vaguely or even clearly stated a dozen times by prominent writers, is no reason for supposing that it has ever had any vital influence upon educators. The history of education shows conclusively that important educational ideas can be written about and talked about for centuries without finding their way to any great extent into the schoolrooms. What we now need in education is definite and well-grounded theories and plans, backed up by honest and practical execution.

The Herbartians have patiently submitted themselves to thoroughgoing tests in both theory and practice. After years of experiment and discussion, they have come forward with certain propositions of reform which are designed to infuse new life and meaning into educational labors.

The first proposition is to make the foundation of education immovable by resting it upon growth in moral character, as the purpose which serious teachers must put first. The selection of studies and the organization of the school course follow this guiding principle.

The second is permanent, many-sided interest. The life-giving power which springs from the awakening of the best interests in the two great realms of real knowledge should be felt by every teacher. Though not entirely new, this idea is better than new, because its deeper meaning is clearly brought out, and it is rationally provided for by the selection of interesting materials and by marking out an appropriate method of treatment. All knowledge must be infused with feelings of interest, if it is to reach the heart and work its influence upon character by giving impulse to the will.

Thirdly, the idea of organized unity, or concentration, in the mental stores gathered by children, in all their knowledge and experience, is a thought of such vital meaning in the effort to establish unity of character, that, when a teacher once realizes its import, his effort is toned up to great undertakings.

Fourthly, the culture epochs give a suggestive bird's-eye view of the historical meaning of education, and of the rich materials of history and literature for supplying suitable mental food to children. They help to realize the ideas of interest, concentration, and apperception.

Apperception is the practical key to the most important problems of education, because it compels us to keep a sympathetic eye upon the child in his moods, mental states, and changing phases of growth; to build hourly upon the only foundation he has, his previous acquirements and habits.

Finally, the Herbartians have grappled seriously with that great and comprehensive problem, the common school course. The obligation rests upon them to select the materials and to lay out a course of study which embodies all their leading principles in a form suited to children and to our school conditions.

One of the several influential committees organized by the National Education Association during these years was the Committee of Ten, which was charged with studying and making recommendations regarding secondary-school curriculum. Under the chairmanship of Charles W. Eliot, President of Harvard, the committee reported in 1893, creating a storm of controversy. The recommendations on college admission which seemed to be the heart of the report especially came under bitter attack from the Herbartians and other "moderns." This section of the report is included here and is followed by a critique written by G. Stanley Hall, who was a leading theorist in educational psychology of the era.

89. Report of the Committee of Ten

One of the subjects which the Committee of Ten were directed to consider was requirements for admission to college; and particularly they were expected to report on uniform requirements for admission to colleges, as well as on a uniform secondary school programme. Almost all the Conferences have something to say about the best mode of testing the attainments of candidates at college admission examinations; and some of them, notably the Conferences on History and Geography, make very explicit declarations concerning the nature of college examinations. The improvements desired in the mode of testing the attainments of pupils who have pursued in the secondary schools the various subjects which enter into the course will be found clearly described under each subject in the several Conference reports; but there is a general principle concerning the relation of the secondary schools to colleges which the Committee of Ten, inspired and guided by the Conferences, feel it their duty to set forth with all possible distinctness.

The secondary schools of the United States, taken as a whole, do not exist

Reprinted from National Educational Association, "Report of the Committee of Ten." Published for the NEA by The American Book Company, 1894, pp. 51-53.

for the purpose of preparing boys and girls for colleges. Only an insignifi-
cant percentage of the graduates of these schools go to colleges or scientific schools. Their main function is to prepare for the duties of life that
small proportion of all the children in the country—a proportion small in
number, but very important to the welfare of the nation—who show
themselves able to profit by an education prolonged to the eighteenth year,
and whose parents are able to support them while they remain so long at
school. There are, to be sure, a few private or endowed secondary schools
in the country, which make it their principal object to prepare students for
the colleges and universities; but the number of these schools is relatively
small. A secondary school programme intended for national use must
therefore be made for those children whose education is not to be pursued
beyond the secondary school. The preparation of a few pupils for college
or scientific school should in the ordinary secondary school be the incidental, and not the principal object. At the same time, it is obviously desirable
that the colleges and scientific schools should be accessible to all boys or
girls who have completed creditably the secondary school course. Their
parents often do not decide for them, four years before the college age,
that they shall go to college, and they themselves may not, perhaps, feel
the desire to continue their education until near the end of their school
course. In order that any successful graduate of a good secondary school
should be free to present himself at the gates of the college or scientific
school of his choice, it is necessary that the colleges and scientific schools
of the country should accept for admission to appropriate courses of their
instruction the attainments of any youth who has passed creditably through
a good secondary school course, no matter to what group of subjects he may
have mainly devoted himself in the secondary school. As secondary school
courses are now too often arranged, this is not a reasonable request to prefer
to the colleges and scientific schools; because the pupil may now go through
a secondary school course of a very feeble and scrappy nature—studying
a little of many subjects and not much of any one, getting, perhaps, a little
information in a variety of fields, but nothing which can be called a thorough
training. Now the recommendations of the nine Conferences, if well carried
out, might fairly be held to make all the main subjects taught in the secondary schools of equal rank for the purposes of admission to college or
scientific school. They would all be taught consecutively and thoroughly,
and would all be carried on in the same spirit; they would all be used for
training the powers of observation, memory, expression, and reasoning;
and they would all be good to that end, although differing among themselves
in quality and substance. . . . A college might say,—We will accept for admission any groups of studies taken from the secondary school programme,
provided that the sum of the studies in each of the four years amounts to

sixteen, or eighteen, or twenty periods a week,—as may be thought best,—and provided, further, that in each year at least four of the subjects presented shall have been pursued at least three periods a week, and that at least three of the subjects shall have been pursued three years or more. For the purposes of this reckoning, natural history, geography, meteorology, and astronomy might be grouped together as one subject. Every youth who entered college would have spent four years in studying a few subjects thoroughly; and, on the theory that all the subjects are to be considered equivalent in educational rank for the purposes of admission to college, it would make no difference which subjects he had chosen from the programme—he would have had four years of strong and effective mental training. The Conferences on Geography and Modern Languages make the most explicit statement to the effect that college requirements for admission should coincide with high-school requirements for graduation. The Conference on English is of opinion "that no student should be admitted to college who shows in his English examination and his other examinations that he is very deficient in ability to write good English." This recommendation suggests that an ample English course in the secondary school should be required of all persons who intend to enter college. It would of course be possible for any college to require for admission any one subject, or any group of subjects, in the table, and the requirements of different colleges, while all kept within the table, might differ in many respects; but the Committee are of opinion that the satisfactory completion of any one of the four years' courses of study embodied in the foregoing programmes should admit to corresponding courses in colleges and scientific schools. They believe that this close articulation between the secondary schools and the higher institutions would be advantageous alike for the schools, the colleges, and the country.

90. On the Report of the Committee of Ten

G. Stanley Hall

Once beneficent, college entrance requirements, as now enforced in some parts of our country and in some respects, are almost an unmitigated curse to high schools, exploiting them against their normal interests and the purpose of the people who support them, and thus perverting their natural

Reprinted from G. Stanley Hall, *Adolescence: Its Psychology,* 2 vols. (New York: Appleton & Co., 1905), II, pp. 510-512.

development, enforcing artifacts of both method and matter, and sacrificing the interests of the vast majority who will never go to college.

This invasion and subjection has been rendered plausible even to its victims by three extraordinary fallacies. (a) The Committee of Ten "unanimously declare that every subject which is taught at all in a secondary school should be taught in the same way and to the same extent to every pupil so long as he pursues it, no matter what the probable destination of the pupil may be or at what point his education is to cease." This is a masterpiece of college policy. But in the first place this principle does not apply to the great army of incapables, shading down to those who should be in schools for dullards or subnormal children, for whose mental development heredity decrees a slow pace and early arrest, and for whom by general consent both studies and methods must be different. To refuse this concession to the wide range of individual differences is a specious delusion, which in a democracy may be perfectly honest. Difficulties must be omitted, the interest of the hour more appealed to, illustrations multiplied, and different beginnings, means, and goals early sought. Nor does this principle, of course, apply to geniuses. The school is not constructed for such. They go by leaps and find their own way. We must consider, then, only pupils that lie between these extremes. Again, this is unknown in other lands, where it would bring the direst confusion. European systems seem constructed on the converse principle that subjects should be approached in as many different ways as there are ultimate goals, while choices between academic and other careers are made before the teens, and methods and matter in the same topics diverge increasingly up the grades. The courses in English public secondary schools differ as much in method from those of the great endowed fitting schools as they do in matter. So the gymnasia and *Real* schools differ from each other, and both still more from the *Volk* schools, and as do the *lycée* and polytechnic schools in France, while text-books on the same subject are radically different. Besides the distinction between those destined for technical and professional careers and those who study for culture purposes, there are many species and varieties of difference. Again, in the vast number of monotechnic, polytechnic, commercial, and other courses, some of the departments of physics and chemistry, which are of immediate application, are emphasized. The horological school course emphasizes vibrations; the great lithograph school of Vienna lays stress upon light, and that in certain aspects; the schools of telegraphy, upon electricity; those of wine culture, upon the chemistry of fermentation; those of agriculture, upon the practical problems of chemistry involved in fertilization; secondary schools for art, upon the geometry connected with perspective; those for the lower order of engineering, upon mechanics; and so on indefinitely, all selecting those parts and principles, and even sub-aspects and methods, from the fields of these great sciences that lie nearest to and shed most light upon practise, and with comparatively little matter in common with some sciences. With all this precious development the principle of the Committee of Ten would make havoc, lacking as it does all proper conception of the magnitude of each science and its vast variety of approaches. In topics like astronomy and physics, even the question where to begin the mathematical side, how much stress to lay upon it, or whether to omit it entirely, like Tyndall, is largely a problem of destination.

Even in teaching modern languages there are recognized differences of both method and matter, whether the pupil needs to be taught chiefly and first to speak and hear the language or to read and command its literary resources. Geography might almost be called in its best modern development the introduction to various sciences, and I think there is now general agreement that much more stress should be laid upon it for those who finish their education early than for those who continue. So in English, children who leave school early have, as we saw above, an inalienable right to some knowledge, slight though it be, of the general moral lessons of the great masterpieces which those who go on have other means of attaining. Who would say that if a child has six months or one year to learn what the Latin or Greek world really means, he should begin as the pupil would who is to specialize in these topics later? Not only thus does this principle fail to recognize how vast as the mind itself the great departments of knowledge are, but how the pedagogic instinct almost inclines to the belief that there are perhaps almost as many ways of approach to them as there are minds, and that it would not be an insanely wild thesis for those not ignorant of the anthropology of youth to maintain that every individual mind has ideally its own best personal way of approach to every science, because each mind not only has, but is, its own method. There is especially the great fundamental distinction between those approaches that begin with practise, art, skill, and industry or for those who are motor-minded, into whom the great function of the teacher is to instil as much scientific knowledge and as many principles as can be made of practicable service, and the professional and the other culture groups who can follow a logical order. In looking over the text-books for these two kinds of minds or "destinations," one is struck with the very limited amount of subject-matter which is common, and also with the fact that these differences rest on fundamental differences of constitution, and that to force them into one mold would be wasteful, undemocratic, and pedagogically immoral. This principle ignores the fact that the average youth of high school age, and especially in the early teens, has not so far reached the age of reason that logical methods can be made supreme, but that genetic methods which cross-section it must also be largely relied on. Some need far more popular science or can not depart from utilities. But minds destined to high development grasp and follow the order and logic of science far earlier than others. In general the more vigorous and capable of high development is an adolescent mind, the less appeal is needed to this kind of interest—i.e., the smaller the mental area necessary to cultivate, to generate interest in the great spring of mind. The female intellect, in general, is far more in need of this, and develops specialized and abstract interest later than that of the average boy.

(*b*) Closely associated with this is the principle that "all subjects are of equal educational value if taught equally well." . . . [Here follows a discussion of the point]

(*c*) Another related surd that has acquired wide vogue and wrought only mischief is that fitting for college is essentially the same as fitting for life. . . . [Discussion follows]

These three so-called principles thus turn out to be only clever recruiting precepts, special pleas of able advocates holding briefs for the college rather than the judicial decisions of educational statesmanship. The strategists of this policy urge that social classes are favored by European schools, and that it is an American idea of unique value that every boy should as long as possible feel that he is on the high road to the bachelor's degree and will reach it, if he does not stop, just as we teach that he may become president, but they ignore the fact that there are as great differences in natural ability as those artificially created in any aristocracy, and that the very life of a republic depends on bringing these out, in learning how to detect betimes, and give the very best training to, those fittest for leadership. If all topics have equal culture value and fit equally well for life and college, every youth would naturally select whatever topics the college suggests, and every teacher woud adopt any methods it prescribes, for all other differences are obliterated. The growing preponderance of scholastic topics, the increase of high school classes in the first year, and the augmented subserviency of secondary teachers, who here find the uniformity so dear to the inert mind—because its ready-made scheme, supported by the most respectable pedagogic authority, relieves them from the vaster problems of local and all other adjustments—show the triumphs, and the growing percentages of those who drop out from loss of zest show the havoc wrought by these masterstrokes of college politics. The voters, who have lately so multiplied high schools, were at first pleased with the dignity of the fitting function that seemed to make academic life so accessible, but the people are slower and their interests less enlightened and less sharply defined. Their real voice has not yet been clearly heard, and their unformulated purpose has not yet been accomplished. It is an infinitely greater problem to fit for life than to fit for college, and requires far more thought and a larger accumulation of experiences. It was natural, therefore, that college interests, which are so simple and easy, should be the first on the ground and should come to power. The evils of this dominance are now so great and manifest that they must be transient.

In the span of twenty-five years from the Report of the Committee of Ten to the publication in 1918 of the Report of the Commission on the Reorganization of Secondary Education, certain remarkable changes in thinking regarding curriculum had come about. The Seven Cardinal Principles set down by the Commission reflected mainly the influence of Herbert Spencer and the Darwinian thinking during these years. Outlined in the Report was an education for the struggle of life, for the survival of the fit, both for the individual and, in the aggregate, for the nation. In the extension of aims in education, the Seven Cardinal Principles implied a considerable widening of the function of education into whole new areas of activity and new emphases in study. Here were aims that seemed to be in accord with the rise of mass education in America.

91. The Seven Cardinal Principles of Secondary Education, 1918

Secondary education should be determined by the needs of the society to be served, the character of the individuals to be educated, and the knowledge of educational theory and practice available. These factors are by no means static. Society is always in process of development; the character of the secondary-school population undergoes modification; and the sciences on which educational theory and practice depend constantly furnish new information. Secondary education, however, like any other established agency of society, is conservative and tends to resist modification. Failure to make adjustments when the need arises leads to the necessity for extensive reorganization at irregular intervals. The evidence is strong that such a comprehensive reorganization of secondary education is imperative at the present time.

1. *Changes in society.*—Within the past few decades changes have taken

Reprinted from *Cardinal Principles of Secondary Education* (Washington, Government Printing Office, 1918), Bulletin No. 35, 1918, Department of the Interior, Bureau of Education. A report of the Commission on the Reorganization of Secondary Education, pp. 7-11.

place in American life profoundly affecting the activities of the individual. As a citizen, he must to a greater extent and in a more direct way cope with problems of community life, State and National Governments, and international relationships. As a worker, he must adjust himself to a more complex economic order. As a relatively independent personality, he has more leisure. The problems arising from these three dominant phases of life are closely interrelated and call for a degree of intelligence and efficiency on the part of every citizen that can not be secured through elementary education alone, or even through secondary education unless the scope of that education is broadened.

The responsibility of the secondary school is still further increased because many social agencies other than the school afford less stimulus for education than heretofore. In many vocations there have come such significant changes as the substitution of the factory system for the domestic system of industry; the use of machinery in place of manual labor; the high specialization of processes with a corresponding subdivision of labor; and the break-down of the apprentice system. In connection with home and family life have frequently come lessened responsibility on the part of the children; the withdrawal of the father and sometimes the mother from home occupations to the factory or store; and increased urbanization, resulting in less unified family life. Similarly, many important changes have taken place in community life, in the church, in the State, and in other institutions. These changes in American life call for extensive modifications in secondary education.

2. *Changes in the secondary-school population.*—In the past 25 years there have been marked changes in the secondary-school population of the United States. The number of pupils has increased, according to Federal returns, from one for every 210 of the total population in 1889-90, to one for every 121 in 1899-1900, to one for every 89 in 1909-10, and to one for every 73 of the estimated total population in 1914-15. The character of the secondary-school population has been modified by the entrance of large numbers of pupils of widely varying capacities, aptitudes, social heredity, and destinies in life. Further, the broadening of the scope of secondary education has brought to the school many pupils who do not complete the full course but leave at various stages of advancement. The needs of these pupils can not be neglected, nor can we expect in the near future that all pupils will be able to complete the secondary school as full-time students.

At present only about one-third of the pupils who enter the first year of the elementary school reach the four-year high school, and only about one in nine is graduated. Of those who enter the seventh school year, only one-half to two-thirds reach the first year of the four-year high school.

Of those who enter the four-year high school about one-third leave before the beginning of the second year, about one-half are gone before the beginning of the third year, and fewer than one-third are graduated. These facts can no longer be safely ignored.

3. *Changes in educational theory.*—The sciences on which educational theory depends have within recent years made significant contributions. In particular, educational psychology emphasizes the following factors:

(*a*) *Individual differences in capacities and aptitudes among secondary-school pupils.* Already recognized to some extent, this factor merits fuller attention.

(*b*) *The reëxamination and reinterpretation of subject values and the teaching methods with reference to "general discipline."*—While the final verdict of modern psychology has not as yet been rendered, it is clear that former conceptions of "general values" must be thoroughly revised.

(*c*) *Importance of applying knowledge.*—Subject values and teaching methods must be tested in terms of the laws of learning and the application of knowledge to the activities of life, rather than primarily in terms of the demands of any subject as a logically organized science.

(*d*) *Continuity in the development of children.*—It has long been held that psychological changes at certain stages are so pronounced as to over-shadow the continuity of development. On this basis secondary education has been sharply separated from elementary education. Modern psychology, however, goes to show that the development of the individual is in most respects a continuous process and that, therefore, any sudden or abrupt break between the elementary and the secondary school or between any two successive stages of education is undesirable.

The foregoing changes in society, in the character of the secondary-school population, and in educational theory, together with many other considerations, call for extensive modifications of secondary education. Such modifications have already begun in part. The present need is for the formulation of a comprehensive program of reorganization, and its adoption, with suitable adjustments, in all the secondary schools in the Nation. Hence it is appropriate for a representative body like the National Education Association to outline such a program. This is the task entrusted by that association to the Commission on the Reorganization of Secondary Education.

Education in the United States should be guided by a clear conception of the meaning of democracy. It is the ideal of democracy that the individual and society may find fulfillment each in the other. Democracy sanctions neither the exploitation of the individual by society, nor the disregard of the interests of society by the individual. More explicitly—

The purpose of democracy is so to organize society that each member may develop his personality primarily through activities designed for the well-being of his fellow members and of society as a whole.

This ideal demands that human activities be placed upon a high level of efficiency; that to this efficiency be added an appreciation of the significance of these activities and loyalty to the best ideals involved; and that the individual choose that vocation and those forms of social service in which his personality may develop and become most effective. For the achievement of these ends democracy must place chief reliance upon education.

Consequently, education in a democracy, both within and without the school, should develop in each individual the knowledge, interests, ideals, habits, and powers whereby he will find his place and use that place to shape both himself and society toward ever nobler ends.

In order to determine the main objectives that should guide education in a democracy it is necessary to analyze the activities of the individual. Normally he is a member of a family, of a vocational group, and of various civic groups, and by virtue of these relationships he is called upon to engage in activities that enrich the family life, to render important vocational services to his fellows, and to promote the common welfare. It follows, therefore, that worthy home-membership, vocation, and citizenship, demand attention as three of the leading objectives.

Aside from the immediate discharge of these specific duties, every individual should have a margin of time for the cultivation of personal and social interests. This leisure, if worthily used, will recreate his powers and enlarge and enrich life, thereby making him better able to meet his responsibilities. The unworthy use of leisure impairs health, disrupts home life, lessens vocational efficiency, and destroys civic-mindedness. The tendency in industrial life, aided by legislation, is to decrease the working hours of large groups of people. While shortened hours tend to lessen the harmful reactions that arise from prolonged strain, they increase, if possible, the importance of preparation for leisure. In view of these considerations, education for the worthy use of leisure is of increasing importance as an objective.

To discharge the duties of life and to benefit from leisure, one must have good health. The health of the individual is essential also to the vitality of the race and to the defense of the Nation. Health education is, therefore, fundamental.

There are various processes, such as reading, writing, arithmetical computations, and oral and written expression, that are needed as tools in the affairs of life. Consequently, command of these fundamental processes, while not an end in itself, is nevertheless an indispensable objective.

And, finally, the realization of the objectives already named is dependent upon ethical character, that is, upon conduct founded upon right principles, clearly perceived and loyally adhered to. Good citizenship, vocational excellence, and the worthy use of leisure go hand in hand with ethical character; they are at once the fruits of sterling character and the channels through which such character is developed and made manifest. On the one hand, character is meaningless apart from the will to discharge the duties of life, and, on the other hand, there is no guarantee that these duties will be rightly discharged unless principles are substituted for impulses, however well-intentioned such impulses may be. Consequently ethical character is at once involved in all the other objectives and at the same time requires specific consideration in any program of national education.

This commission, therefore, regards the following as the main objectives of education: 1. Health. 2. Command of fundamental processes. 3. Worthy home-membership. 4. Vocation. 5. Citizenship. 6. Worthy use of leisure. 7. Ethical character.

The naming of the above objectives is not intended to imply that the process of education can be divided into separated fields. This can not be, since the pupil is indivisible.. Nor is the analysis all-inclusive. Nevertheless, we believe that distinguishing and naming these objectives will aid in directing efforts; and we hold that they should constitute the principal aims in education.

Those persons engaged most intensively in the Darwinian struggle for survival were the immigrants to America in the decades at the turn of the century, the "new immigrants." The humanitarian reformer Jacob Riis gives an accurate impression of the effect of the urban slum on the lives of children as well as the all too limited effect of existing schools. Riis, in the following passages, moreover, reflects the attitude and spirit typical of urban reformers of the era.

92. The Children of the Poor

Jacob A. Riis

Under the heading "Just One of God's Children," one of the morning newspapers told the story not long ago of a newsboy at the Brooklyn Bridge, who fell in a fit with his bundle of papers under his arm, and was carried into the waiting-room by the Bridge police. They sent for an ambu-

Reprinted from Jacob A. Riis, "The Children of the Poor" in Robert A. Woods, ed., *The Poor in Great Cities* (New York: Scribner, 1895), pp. 86-95; 99-103; 110-111; 114.

lance, but before it came the boy was out selling papers again. The reporters asked the little dark-eyed newswoman at the bridge entrance which boy it was.

"Little Maher it was," she answered.

"Who takes care of him?"

"Oh! no one but God," said she, "and he is too busy with other folks to give him much attention."

Little Maher was the representative of a class that is happily growing smaller year by year in our city. It is altogether likely that a little inquiry into his case could have placed the responsibility for his forlorn condition considerably nearer home, upon someone who preferred giving Providence the job to taking the trouble himself. There are homeless children in New York. It is certain that we shall always have our full share. Yet it is equally certain that society is coming out ahead in its struggle with this problem. In ten years, during which New York added to her population one-fourth, the homelessness of our streets, taking the returns of the Childrens Aid Society's lodging-houses as the gauge, instead of increasing proportionally has decreased nearly one-fifth; and of the Topsy element, it may be set down as a fact, there is an end.

If we were able to argue from this a corresponding improvement in the general lot of the poor, we should have good cause for congratulation. But it is not so. The showing is due mainly to the perfection of organized charitable effort, that proceeds nowadays upon the sensible principle of putting out a fire, viz., that it must be headed off, not run down. It is possible also that the Bowery lodging-houses attract a larger share of the half-grown lads with their promise of greater freedom, which is not a pleasant possibility. The general situation is not perceptibly improved. The menace of the Submerged Tenth has not been blotted from the register of the Potter's Field, and though the "twenty thousand poor children who would not have known it was Christmas," but for public notice to that effect, be a benevolent fiction, there are plenty whose brief lives have had little enough of the embodiment of Christmas cheer and good-will in them to make the name seem like a bitter mockery. If indeed, New York were not what she is; if it were possible to-morrow to shut her door against the immigration of the world and still maintain the conditions of to-day, I should confidently predict a steady progress that would leave little of the problem for the next generation to wrestle with. But that is only another way of saying "if New York were not New York." It is because she is New York that in reviewing our own miseries we have to take into account half the poverty, the ignorance, and the helplessness of the cities of the Old World, that is dumped at our door while the procession of the strong and of the able moves on. And that is what makes our problem.

.   .   .   .   .

I recall, not without amusement, one of the early experiences of a committee with which I was trying to relieve some of the child misery in the East Side tenements by providing an outing for the very poorest of the little ones, who might otherwise have been overlooked. In our anxiety to make our little charges as presentable as possible, it seems we had succeeded so well as to arouse a suspicion in our friends at the other end of the line that something was wrong, either with us or with the poor of which the patrician youngsters in new frocks and with clean faces, that came to them, were representatives. They wrote to us that they were in the field for the "slum children," and slum children they wanted. It happened that their letter came just as we had before us two little lads from the Mulberry Street Bend, ragged, dirty, unkempt, and altogether a sight to see. Our wardrobe was running low, and we were at our wits' end how to make these come up to our standard. We sat looking at each other after we had heard the letter read, all thinking the same thing, until the most courageous said it: "Send them as they are." Well, we did, and waited rather breathlessly for the verdict. It came, with the children, in a note by return train, that said: "Not *that* kind, please!" And after that we were allowed to have things our own way.

The two little fellows were Italians. In justice to our frightened friends, it should be said that it was not their nationality, but their rags, to which they objected; but not very many seasons have passed since the crowding of the black-eyed brigade of "guinnies," as they were contemptuously dubbed, in ever-increasing numbers into the ragged schools and the kindergartens, was watched with regret and alarm by the teachers, as by many others who had no better cause. The event proved that the children were the real teachers. They had a more valuable lesson to impart than they came to learn, and it has been a salutary one. To-day they are gladly welcomed. Their sunny temper, which no hovel is dreary enough, no hardship has power to cloud, has made them universal favorites, and the discovery has been made by their teachers that as the crowds pressed harder their school-rooms have marvellously expanded, until they embrace within their walls an unsuspected multitude, even many a slum tenement itself, cellar, "stoop," attic, and all. Every lesson of cleanliness, of order, and of English taught at the school is reflected into some wretched home, and rehearsed there as far as the limited opportunities will allow. No demonstration with soap and water upon a dirty little face but widens the sphere of these chief promoters of education in the slums. "By'm by," said poor crippled Pietro to me, with a sober look, as he labored away on his writing lesson, holding down the paper with his maimed hand, "I learn t' make an Englis' letter; maybe my fader he learn too." I had my doubts of the father. He sat watching Pietro with a pride in the achievement that was clearly proportionate to the struggle it cost, and mirrored in his own face every grimace and contortion the progress of education caused the boy. "Si! si!" he nodded eagerly; "Pietro he good-a boy; make Englis', Englis'!" and he made a flourish with his clay-pipe, as if he too were making the English letter that was the object of their common veneration.

Perhaps it is as much his growing and well-founded distrust of the middleman, whose unresisting victim he has heretofore been, and his need of some other link to connect him with the English-speaking world that surrounds him, as any personal interest in book-learning, that impels the illiterate Italian to bring his boy to school early and see that he attends it. Whatever his motive, the effect is to demonstrate in a striking way the truth of the observation that real reform of poverty and ignorance must begin with the children. In his case, at all events, the seed thus sown bears some fruit in the present as well as in the coming generation of toilers. The little ones, with their new standards and new ambitions, become in a very real sense missionaries of the slums, whose work of regeneration begins with their parents. They are continually fetched away from school by the mother or father to act as interpreters or go-betweens in all the affairs of daily life, to be conscientiously returned within the hour stipulated by the teacher who offers no objection to this sort of interruption, knowing it to be the best condition of her own success. One cannot help the hope that the position of trust in which the children are thus placed may, in some measure, help to mitigate their home-hardships. From their birth they have little else, though Italian parents are rarely cruel in the sense of abusing their offspring. It is the home itself that constitutes their chief hardship. Theirs are the poorest tenements, the filthiest hovels in the city. It is only when his years offer the boy an opportunity of escape to the street, that a ray of sunlight falls into his life; in his back-yard or in his alley it seldom finds him out. Thenceforward most of his time is spent there, until the school claims him. Since the sewing-machine found its way, with the sweater's mortgage, into the Italian slums also, his sweet-faced sister has been robbed to a large extent of even the freedom of the dump, where she used to pick cinders for her mother's kitchen fire, and she has taken her place among the wage-earners when not on the school-bench. Sickness, unless it be mortal, is no excuse from the drudgery of the tenement. When, recently, one little Italian girl, hardly yet in her teens, stayed away from her class in the Mott Street Industrial School so long that her teacher went to her home to look her up, she found the child in a high fever, in bed, sewing on coats with swollen eyes, though barely able to sit up.

. . . . .

Naturally the teaching of these children must begin by going backward. The process may be observed in the industrial schools, of which there are twenty-one scattered through the poor tenement districts, with a total enrolment of something over five thousand pupils.* A count made last October showed that considerably more than one-third were born in twelve foreign countries where English was not spoken, and that over ten per cent knew no word of our language. The vast majority of the rest were children of foreign parents, mostly German and Irish, born here. According to the location of the school it is distinctively Italian, Bohemian, Hebrew, or mixed, the German, Irish, and colored children coming in under this head and mingling without the least friction. Whatever its stamp of nationality, the curriculum is much the same. The start, as often as is necessary, is made with an object-lesson—soap and water being the elements and the child the object. The alphabet comes second on the list. Later on follow lessons in sewing, cooking, carpentry for the boys, and like practical "branches," of which the home affords the child no demonstration. The prizes for good behavior are shoes and clothing, the special inducement a free lunch in the dinner hour. Very lately a unique exercise has been added to the course in the schools, that lays hold of the very marrow of the problem with which they deal. It is called "saluting the flag," and originated with Colonel George T. Balch, of the Board of Education, who conceived the idea of instilling patriotism into the little future citizens of the Republic in doses to suit their childish minds. To talk about the Union, of which most of them had but the vaguest notion, or of the duty of the citizen, of which they had no notion at all, was nonsense. In the flag it was all found embodied in a central idea which they could grasp. In the morning the star-spangled banner was brought into the school, and the children were taught to salute it with patriotic words. Then the best scholar of the day before was called out of the ranks, and it was given to him or her to keep for the day. The thing took at once and was a tremendous success. . . .

The earliest notion of order and harmless play comes to the children through the kindergartens, to which access is now made easier every day. Without a doubt this is the longest step forward that has yet been taken in the race with poverty; for the kindergarten, in gathering in the children, is gradually but surely conquering also the street, with its power for mischief. Until it came, the street was the only escape from the tenement—a Hobson's choice, for it is hard to say which is the most corrupting. The opportunities rampant in the one were a sad commentary on the sure defilement of the other.

* These schools are established and managed by the Children's Aid Society, as a co-ordinate branch of the public-school system.

With the end of Reconstruction, the Negro was returned to an economic state of semi-slavery in the still agrarian South and to only a slightly better state in the urban centers of the North and the West. Though schooling for Negroes was limited indeed, where it did exist the "separate but equal" doctrine prevailed as in the southern school systems, or in "de facto" segregation, as it came to be called, elsewhere. The Negro educational leader, Booker T. Washington, offered at least hope for the betterment of the race in his thinking on education and in his work at the Tuskegee Institute in Alabama. Praised by both Negro and white, his system of industrial education attained wide influence over the years, though by the 1930's it came to be severely criticized by such groups as the NAACP as essentially a second-class education for second-class citizenship. The following passage illustrates Washington's basic ideas and attitudes toward the education of the Negro.

93. Negro Education Not a Failure

Booker T. Washington

Several persons holding high official position have said recently that it does not pay, from any point of view, to educate the Negro; and that all attempts at his education have so far failed to accomplish any good results. The Southern States, which out of their poverty are contributing rather liberally for the education of all the people, as does individual and organised philanthropy throughout the country, have a right to know whether the Negro is responding to the efforts they have made to place him upon a higher plane of civilisation.

Will it pay to invest further money in this direction? In seeking to answer this question, it is hardly fair to compare the progress of the American Negro with that of the American white man, who, in some unexplained way, got thousands of years ahead of the Negro in the arts and sciences of civilisation. But to get at the real facts and the real capability of the black man, compare for a moment the American Negro with the Negro in Africa, or the black man with the black man. In South Africa alone there are five million black people who have never been brought, through school or other agencies, into contact with a higher civilisation in a way to have their minds

Reprinted from Booker T. Washington, *Working with the Hands* (New York: Doubleday, Page & Co., 1904), pp. 231-233; 242-246.

or their ambitions strengthened or awakened. As a result, the industries of South Africa languish and refuse to prosper for lack of labour. The native black man refuses to labour because he has been neglected. He has few wants and little ambition, and these can be satisfied by labouring one or two days out of the seven. In the southern part of the United States there are more than eight millions of my race who, both by contact with the whites and by education in the home, in school, in church, have had their minds awakened and strengthened—have thus had their wants increased and multiplied many times. Hence, instead of a people in idleness, we have in the South a people who are anxious to work because they want education for their children; they want land and houses, and churches, books, and papers. In a word, they want the highest and best in our civilisation. Looked at, then, from the most material and selfish point of view, it has paid to awaken the Negro's mind, and there should be no limit placed upon the development of that mind.

Does the American Negro take advantage of opportunities to secure education? Practically no schoolhouse has been opened for the Negro since the war that has not been filled. Often hungry and in rags, making heroic sacrifices, the Negro youth has been determined to annihiliate his mental darkness. With all his disadvantages, the Negro, according to official records, has blotted out 55.5 per cent of his illiteracy since he became a free man, while practically 95 per cent of the native Africans are illiterate. After years of civilization and opportunity, in Spain, 68 per cent of the population are illiterate; in Italy, 38 per cent. In the average South American country about 80 per cent are illiterate, while after forty years the American Negro has only 44.5 per cent of illiteracy to his debit. I have thus compared the progress of my race, not with the highest civilised nations, for the reason that, in passing judgment upon us, the world too often forgets that, either consciously or otherwise, because of geographical or physical proximity to the American white man, we are being compared with the very highest civilisation that exists. But when compared with the most advanced and enlightened white people of the South, we find 12 per cent of illiteracy for them and only 44 per cent for our race. . . .

Years ago some one asked an eminent clergyman in Boston if Christianity is a failure. The Reverend doctor replied that it had never been tried. When people are bold enough to suggest that the education of the Negro is a failure, I reply that it has never been tried. The fact is that 44.5 per cent of the coloured people of this country to-day are illiterate. A very large proportion of those classed as educated have the merest smattering of knowledge, which means practically no education. Can the Negro child get an education in school four months and out of school eight months? Can the white child of the South who receives $4.92 per capita for education, or the black child who receives $2.21, be said to be given an equal chance in the battle of life, or has education been tried on them? The official records in Louisiana, for instance, show that less than one-fourth of the Negro children of school age attend any school during the year. This one-fourth was in school for a period of less than five months, and each Negro child of school age in the State had spent on him for education last year but $1.89, while each child of school age in the State of New York had spent on him $20.53. In the former slave States ninety per cent of the Negro children of school age did not attend school for six months during the year 1900.

Wherever the race is given an opportunity for education, it takes advantage of that opportunity, and the change can be seen in the improved material, educational, moral and religious condition of the masses. Contrast two townships, one in Louisiana, where the race has had little chance, with one in Farmville, Virginia, by means of the United States Bulletin of the Department of Labour. In the Louisiana township only 10 per cent attend school, and they attend for but four months in a year, and 71 per cent of the people are illiterate. And as a result of this ignorance and neglect, we find that only 50 per cent of the people living together as man and wife are legally married. Largely through the leadership of Hampton graduates, 56 per cent of the black children in Farmville, Virginia, attend either public or private school from six to eight months. There is only 39 per cent of illiteracy. Practically all the people living together as man and wife are legally married, and in the whole community only 15 per cent of the births are illegitimate.

But the vital point which I want to emphasise is the disposition of the Negro to exercise self-help in the building up of his own schools in connection with the State public school system. Wherever we send out from Tuskegee, or any of our Southern colleges, a Negro leader of proper character, he shows the people in most cases how to extend the school term beyond the few months provided for by the State. Out of their poverty the Southern States are making a tremendous effort to extend and improve the school term each year, but while this improvement is taking place, the Negro leaders of the character to which I have referred must be depended upon largely to keep alive the spark of education.

It now seems settled that the great body of our people are to reside for all time in the Southern portion of the United States. Since this is true, there is no more helpful and patriotic service than to help cement a friendship between the two races that shall be manly, honourable, and permanent. In this work of moulding and guiding a public sentiment that shall forever maintain peace and good-will between the races on terms commendable to each, it is on the Negro who comes out of our universities, colleges, and industrial schools that we must largely depend. Few people realise how, under the most difficult and trying circumstances, during the last forty years, it has been the educated Negro who counselled patience and self-control and thus averted a war of races. Every Negro going out from our institutions properly educated becomes a link in the chain that shall forever bind the two races together in all the essentials of life.

Finally, reduced to its last analysis, there are but two questions that constitute the problem of this country so far as the black and white races are concerned. The answer to the one rests with my people, the other with the white race. For my race, one of its dangers is that it may grow impatient and feel that it can get upon its feet by artificial and superficial efforts rather than by the slower but surer process which means one step at a time through all the constructive grades of industrial, mental, moral, and social development which all races have had to follow that have become independent and strong. I would counsel: We must be sure that we shall make our greatest progress by keeping our feet on the earth, and by remembering that an inch of progress is worth a yard of complaint. For the white race, the danger is that in its prosperity and power it may forget the claims of a weaker people; may forget that a strong race, like an individual, should put its hand upon its heart and ask, if it were placed in similar circumstances, how it would like the world to treat it; that the stronger race may forget that, in proportion as it lifts up the poorest and weakest, even by a hair's breadth, it strengthens and ennobles itself.

All the Negro race asks is that the door which rewards industry, thrift, intelligence, and character be left as wide open for him as for the foreigner who constantly comes to our country. More than this, he has no right to request. Less than this, a Republic has no right to vouchsafe.

The rise of mass education in state institutions of higher learning during the late nineteenth and early twentieth centuries was by any measure an impressive achievement. More than just adding new rungs to the American educational "ladder," higher education began to expand curriculum offerings and services in a variety of new directions. A view of this expansion of the college as a truly monumental accomplishment, particularly the state universities as the "crown of the school system of the State," is offered in Ellwood P. Cubberley's textbook interpretation of the history of American education, *Public Education in the United States,* the first edition of which was published in 1919.

94. The Expansion of the American College

Ellwood P. Cubberley

EXPANSION OF THE ORIGINAL COLLEGE

In [a preceding] Chapter we traced briefly the rise of the state university as the crown of the school system of the State, and the endowment by Congress, in 1862, of an entirely new type of higher instruction in the colleges of agriculture and mechanic arts. One of the earliest of these new institutions to become established, as well as one of the most heavily endowed, was Cornell University, in New York, opened in 1868. This institution, and the State University of Michigan, together rendered a very valuable pioneer service, during the quarter-century following the opening of Cornell, in marking out new lines of collegiate activity and new relationships between the colleges and the high schools beneath. At Cornell University instruction in science, agriculture, and engineering was placed on an entirely new footing, and the instruction in the older subjects of the college curriculum was both broadened and deepened. Michigan was one of the first state universities to free itself from the hampering influences of state politics on the one hand and sectarian influences on the other; to open its doors to women on the same terms as men (1870); to begin the development of instruction in history (1857), education (1879), and government (1881), with a view to serving the State; and to examine and accredit the high schools (1871) and receive pupils from accredited schools into its freshman class without examination.

Before 1850 the colleges usually offered but one course, based on Greek, Latin, and Mathematics, known as the classical course, and leading to the A.B. degree. Brown offered a parallel course, without Greek and emphasizing more modern studies, in 1851, leading to the Ph.B. degree. Harvard organized the Lawrence Scientific School, in 1851, with instruction in science, and leading to the B.S. degree, and Yale made a similar organization in the Sheffield Scientific School, in 1852. Dartmouth and Rochester also established courses for the B.S. degree in 1852, Michigan in 1853, and Columbia a course for the Ph.B. degree in 1864. By 1880 our

Reprinted by permission from Ellwood P. Cubberley, *Public Education in the United States* (Boston: Houghton Mifflin Co., 1919), pp. 431-434.

colleges were offering three or four parallel courses, much as the high schools did twenty years later. These led to different degrees—B.A., B.L., B.S., and Ph.B. Graduate instruction was also organized, and courses leading to the A.M., M.S., and Ph.D. degrees was in time provided. The first Ph.D. degree granted in the United States was by Yale, in 1851. Few others were granted by our universities before the opening of the first distinctively graduate university—Johns Hopkins, at Baltimore, in 1876.

CREATION OF NEW CHAIRS AND SCHOOLS

With the creation of new chairs to represent new subjects of study, or subdivisions of old subjects, which became common after about 1875, the next tendency was to reorganize the colleges by departments, such as Greek, Latin, English, history, mathematics, physics, biology, etc. This became the common form of organization for the larger universities after about 1890, and still continues. With the very rapid increase in the quantity of knowledge, and the subdivision of old subjects into many new chairs, the more recent tendency has been to re-group the university into a series of colleges and schools. To-day a large state university would include most or all of the following colleges, schools, or divisions, each subdivided into a number of departments or branches of knowledge, and often leading to separate degrees.

1. The college of liberal arts.
2. The college of engineering.
3. The college of agriculture.
4. The school of history and economics.
5. The school of pure science.
6. The school of education.
7. The school of household arts.
8. The school of fine arts.
9. The school of business administration.
10. The school of journalism.
11. The school of law.
12. The school of medicine.
13. The school of veterinary medicine.
14. The school of pharmacy.
15. The school of dentistry.
16. The school of forestry.
17. The school of mining.
18. The school of architecture.
19. The university-extension division.
20. The summer-session division.

SOCIAL SIGNIFICANCE OF THIS GREAT EXPANSION

All this rapid development and subdivision of the university into schools and colleges indicates the assumption of new service for the welfare of the State. That the State has appreciated the service has been shown by a university development previously unknown. Since about 1885, when the state universities began to turn their attention to serving and advancing the welfare of the State, university attendance and revenues have advanced by leaps and bounds. During the same period the stimulating competition of such privately-endowed universities as Harvard, Yale, Columbia, Johns Hopkins, Tulane, Chicago, and Stanford has also made itself felt. The growth in student enrollment may be seen from the figures, at different dates, for a dozen of our larger state universities, as given on the following page.

State University of	1885	1895	1905	1915
*California	197	1781	3294	6434
*Georgia	184	299	483	651
*Illinois	247	814	3597	5439
Iowa	234	1133	1560	2680
Michigan	524	2818	3832	5833
*Minnesota	54	2171	3633	4484
*Missouri	573	614	1892	3140
*Nebraska	142	1397	2728	3832
*Ohio	64	805	1835	4599
Texas	151	630	1235	2574
Washington	6	425	811	3249
*Wisconsin	313	1520	3010	5128

Coincident with this rapid increase in students, faculty-schools, and courses has been the greatest number and amount of gifts of money to our universities ever given to aid higher education in any land. Such gifts are evidence of the public appreciation of the valuable services to the State and Nation rendered by our colleges and universities, both publicly and privately endowed. The States, too, have put millions into the equipment and maintenance of these higher institutions, believing in them as creators of advanced public opinion and as training schools for the future leaders of the State. In a recent article in the *Atlantic Monthly*, President Pritchett wrote:

The rise of these great universities is the most epoch-making feature of our American civilization, and they are to become more and more the leaders, and the makers of our civilization. They are of the people. When a state university has gained solid ground, it means that the people of a whole state have turned their faces toward the light; it means that the

* The state agricultural college in these States is combined with the state university.

whole system of state schools has been welded into an effective agent for civilization. Those who direct the purposes of these great enterprises of democracy cannot be too often reminded that the highest function of a university is to furnish standards for a democracy.

One aspect of the expansion in higher education was the breakdown of the classical curriculum of the American college with the introduction of the "elective system." The new plan was originated at Harvard under the aegis of President Eliot. Discussion of this controversial break with the traditional idea of the college was carried on not only in the educational journals, but in the popular press generally. E. L. Godkin, editor of *The Nation,* a leading journal of the day, commented editorially on the elective question.

95. Yale and Harvard

E. L. Godkin

Yale College has apparently taken up the practice begun by Harvard of issuing an annual report, in which the president not only gives an account of the actual condition of the college, but briefly discusses various university problems. The appearance of the two reports simultaneously will hereafter furnish those who are interested in the higher education with materials for a very instructive comparison of what may be called the two rival methods in university administration. The prominent part which Harvard has taken in introducing the elective system and the system (among the higher classes at least) of voluntary recitation, makes her in a certain sense the representative of those who think that the true function of a university is simply to provide the means of learning for those who wish to learn, and that no part of the energy or ability of its instructors should be expended either in stimulating the stupid or inert, or in bringing to punitive justice those who neglect their opportunities.

Yale, on the other hand, has hitherto represented, and, if we may judge by President Porter's report, still represents, those who consider a university a place for general training, moral as well as intellectual, in which the professor should stand literally *in loco parentis,* and not only provide

Reprinted from "Yale and Harvard," *The Nation,* XXXIV (January 19, 1882), pp. 50-51.

the student with the means of instruction, but see that he gets it whether he likes it or not. The former is the European idea, and it is to the European type that Harvard is gradually approximating. The latter may be called the American idea, and in preaching it President Porter seeks to uphold what may be called the distinctively American college. There is nothing on the Continent exactly like the Yale view of the "college boy," and nothing in England except in the public schools. The relation of the professors to the students which President Porter upholds in the report before us, resembles nothing so much as the relation of the assistant master toward the boys at Eton, or Rugby, or Harrow. There could not be a better description of the role of the English assistant master, who teaches classics and mathematics in school hours, and afterward superintends the cricket and boating, than President Porter gives when he says that "the true and radical remedy" for the tendency in public schools and colleges to disregard "the plainest axioms of manners and morals," and to violate "the accepted axioms of courtesy and truth," is, first, to "hold the student to his duties in no mask or disguise," and then to introduce as "great variety into the student's life as practicable—making reasonable provision for attractive amusements and athletic activities."

Harvard, on the other hand, seems to aim more and more at leaving the student to take as much or as little of the advantages in the direction of learning which the place offers him as he pleases, and at withdrawing more and more from any charge of his morals and manners which is not necessary to the maintenance of public decency and good order. The elective system, in which the student picks out, within certain very wide limits, the course of study he will pursue, and the system of voluntary recitation, in which the student of the upper classes—also within certain very wide limits—uses attendance on recitations as an aid to his studies or not as he pleases, are leading features in a regime which takes for granted that a young man who goes to college begins life, and becomes his own master, to the same degree and in the same sense as a young man who gets a clerkship in the city, and leaves his parents in order to earn his bread. That this regime is found to give satisfaction we conclude from President Eliot's assertion that—

"Whoever reads the history of the development of the elective system, as it is recorded in the successive annual reports of the dean of the college faculty since 1870, will arrive at the well-grounded conviction that every extension of the system has been a gain to the individual student, to the college, and to every interest of education and learning; and will also see reason to believe that the time is not far distant when the few subjects still prescribed for all students will in their turn become elective."

We have called President Porter's idea of the duties of a university toward the undergraduates the American idea; but it is becoming every day more and more doubtful whether it will remain so, and for several reasons. One is that no large college seems to be able to play successfully the part either of the schoolmaster or parent. Yale has long plumed herself on being emphatically what religious parents would consider a "safe" college, or a college in which exemplary care was taken of the student's morals. Nevertheless, President Porter almost confesses that parents have begun to lose confidence in her from this point of view, and that those who wish to have their sons well looked after are beginning to prefer the smaller colleges; and apropos of this he reads his own staff a long lecture on the need of stricter discipline and closer attention to faith and morals. If Yale cannot succeed in the role of a guardian, no large college can. In fact, we venture to assert that, allowing for numbers and opportunity, the standard of conduct, or what may be called the tone, is—if there be any difference—higher among students in the colleges which allow them largest liberty than in the colleges which take most pains to exert a direct influence on character either by exhortation or fines and penalties. In managing all large bodies of young men by means of restraint, if the restraint be mild and easily evaded, it constitutes in itself, owing to one of the best-known peculiarities of human nature, a strong incentive to excess or disobedience. To be effective, therefore, it has to be overwhelmingly powerful and fortified by the sternest sanctions, such as those of military discipline. But no college can use any such discipline, and, therefore, every college which attempts to treat youths of eighteen as children through its rules fails lamentably in securing their enforcement. That a very large body of parents prefer colleges which promise large control of conduct is quite true. But if they are now finding out, as President Porter hints, that the large colleges at least cannot keep this promise, they are simply coming to a kind of knowledge which has long been within the reach of those who know anything of college life. There is no American college which, in order to provide adequate supervision of morals and manners on the parental theory, would not need double its present force of officers, and a very different kind of officers from those who now fill its chairs. The present professors would make poor policemen, or drill-sergeants, even if their time were not fully occupied with their duties as instructors.

Taking all this in connection with the dismal complaints of poverty which both universities make, we cannot help inclining to the belief that the American college of the future will belong rather to the European or Harvard type than to the present American or Yale one. No efficient seat of learning can, with any endowment which any American college now possesses or hopes to possess, undertake anything approaching to parental care of the students. They will all soon cease to promise anything of the kind. . . .

The idea of the university came to fruition in America at an institution organized in 1876, with an appropriate endowment, the Johns Hopkins University in Baltimore. Under the presidency of Daniel Coit Gilman the new university reached toward an expanded concept of the higher learning, toward new intellectual dimensions in education. Gilman recalled these formative years in 1902.

96. The Launching of a University

Daniel Coit Gilman

During the last half century American universities have grown up with surprising rapidity. It is not necessary to fix an exact date for the beginning of this progress. Some would like to say that the foundation of the Lawrence Scientific School in Harvard University, and, almost simultaneously, the foundation of the Sheffield School of Science in New Haven were initial undertakings. These events indicated that the two oldest colleges of New England were ready to introduce instruction of an advanced character, far more special than ever before, in the various branches of natural and physical science. An impulse was given by the passage of the Morrill Act, by which a large amount of scrip, representing public lands, was offered to any State that would maintain a college devoted to agriculture and the mechanic arts, without the exclusion of other scientific and literary studies. The foundation of Cornell University was of the highest significance, for it fortunately came under the guidance of one who was equally devoted to historical and scientific research, one whose plans showed an independence of thought and a power of organisation then without precedent in the field of higher education. The changes introduced in Harvard, under masterful leadership, when the modern era of progress began, had profound influence. The subsequent gifts of Johns Hopkins, of Rockefeller, of Stanford, of Tulane, promoted the establishment of new institutions, in sympathy with the older colleges, yet freer to introduce new subjects and new methods. The State universities of the Northwest and of the Pacific coast, as population and wealth increased, became an

Reprinted from D. C. Gilman, "The Launching of a University," *Scribners' Magazine*, XXXI (March, 1902), pp. 327-331.

important factor. These multiform agencies must all be carefully considered when an estimate is made of the progress of the last half-century.

I was a close observer of the changes which were introduced at Yale in the fifties and sixties, the grafting of a new branch—"a wild olive," as it seemed—upon the old stock. Then I had some experience, brief but significant, in California, as the head of the State University, at a time when it was needful to answer the popular cry that it should become chiefly a school of agriculture, and when it was important to show the distinction between a university and a polytechnic institute. Then came a call to the East and a service of more than a quarter of a century in the organisation and development of a new establishment. These are three typical institutions. Yale was a colonial foundation, wedded to precedents, where an effort was made to introduce new studies and new methods. California was a State institution, benefited by the so-called agricultural grant, where it was necessary to emphasise the importance of the liberal arts, in a community where the practical arts were sure to take care of themselves. Baltimore afforded an opportunity to develop a private endowment free from ecclesiastical or political control, where from the beginning the old and the new, the humanities and the sciences, theory and practice, could be generously promoted.

In looking over this period, remarkable changes are manifest. In the first place, science receives an amount of support unknown before. This is a natural consequence of the wonderful discoveries which have been made in respect to the phenomena and laws of nature and the improvements made in scientific instruments and researches. Educational leaders perceived the importance of the work carried on in laboratories and observatories under the impulse of such men as Liebig and Faraday. With this increased attention to science, the old-fashioned curriculum disappeared, of necessity, and many combinations of studies were permitted in the most conservative institutions. Absolute freedom of choice is now allowed in many places. Historical and political science has come to the front, and it is no longer enough to learn from a text-book wearisome lists of names and dates; reference must be made to original sources of information, or, at any rate, many books must be consulted in order to understand the progress of human society. Some knowledge of German and French is required of everyone. English literature receives an amount of attention never given to it in early days. Medicine is no longer taught by lectures only, but the better schools require continued practice in biological laboratories and the subsequent observation of patients in hospitals and dispensaries. The admission of women to the advantages of higher education is also one of the most noteworthy advances of the period we are considering.

The historian who takes up these and allied indications of the progress of American universities will have a difficult and an inspiring theme. It has been a delightful and exhilarating time in which to live and to work, to observe and to try. All the obstacles have not been overcome, some mistakes have been made, much remains for improvement, but on the whole the record of the last forty or fifty years exhibits substantial and satisfactory gains. The efforts of scholars have been sustained by the munificence of donors, and more than one institution now has an endowment larger than that of all the institutions which were in existence in 1850.

In the middle of the century the word "university" was in the air. It was cautiously used in Cambridge and New Haven, where a number of professional schools were living vigorous lives near the parental domicile, then called "the college proper," as if the junior departments were colleges improper. To speak of "our university" savoured of pretence in these old colleges. A story was told at Yale that a dignitary from a distant State introduced himself as chancellor of the university. "How large a faculty have you?" asked Dominie Day. "Not any," was the answer. "Have you any library or buildings?" "Not yet," replied the visitor. "Any endowment?" "None," came the monotonous and saddening negative. "What have you?" persisted the Yale president. The visitor brightened as he said, "We have a very good charter."

Among enlightened and well-read people, the proper significance of a university was of course understood. Students came home from Europe, and especially from Germany, with clear conceptions of its scope. Everett, Bancroft, Ticknor, Hedge, Woolsey, Thacher, Whitney, Child, Gould, Lane, Gildersleeve and others were familiar with the courses of illustrious teachers on the Continent. European scholars were added to the American faculties—Follen, Beck, Lieber, Agassiz, Guyot, and others also distinguished. But the American colleges had been based on the idea of an English college, and upon this central nucleus the limited funds and the unlimited energies of the times were concentrated, not indeed exclusively, but diligently. Any diversion of the concentrated resources of the treasury to "outside" interests, like law, medicine, and theology, was not to be thought of. Even now, one hears occasionally the question, "after all, what *is* the difference between a university and a college?" To certain persons, the university simply means the best place of instruction that the locality can secure. The country is full of praiseworthy foundations which ought to be known as high-schools or academies or possibly as colleges, but which appear to great disadvantage under the more pretentious name they have assumed. Just after the war the enthusiastic sympathy of the North for the enfranchised blacks led to the bestowal of the highest term in educational nomenclature upon the institutes where the freedmen were to be taught. Fortunately, Hampton and Tuskegee escaped this christening, but Fiske, Atlanta, and Howard foundations were thus named. It is nearer the truth to say that the complete university includes four faculties—the liberal arts or philosophy, law, medicine, and theology. Sometimes a university is regarded as the union, under one board of control, of all the highest institutions of a place or region. There is one instance,—the State of New York,—where the name "university" is given to a board which in a general way supervises all the degree-giving institutions in the State.

When the announcement was made to the public, at the end of 1873, that a wealthy merchant of Baltimore had provided by his will for the establishment of a new university, a good deal of latent regret was felt because the country seemed to have already more higher seminaries than it could supply with teachers, students, or funds. Another "college" was expected to join the crowded column, and impoverish its neighbours by its superior attractions. Fortunately, the founder was wise as well as generous. He used the simplest phrases to express his wishes; and he did not define the distinguished name that he bestowed upon his child, nor embarrass its future by needless conditions. Details were left to a sagacious body of trustees whom he charged with the duty of supervision. They travelled east and west, brought to Baltimore experienced advisers, Eliot, Angell, and White, and procured many of the latest books that discussed the problem of education. By and by they chose a president, and accepted his suggestion that they should give emphasis to the word "university" and should endeavour to build up an institution quite different from a "college," thus making an addition to American education, not introducing a rival. Young men who had already gone through that period of mental discipline which commonly leads to the baccalaureate degree were invited to come and pursue those advanced studies for which they might have been prepared, and to accept the inspiration and guidance of professors selected because of acknowledged distinction or of special aptitudes. Among the phrases that were employed to indicate the project were many which then were novel, although they are now the commonplaces of catalogues and speeches.

Opportunities for advanced, not professional, studies were then scanty in this country. In the older colleges certain graduate courses were attended by a small number of followers—but the teachers were for the most part absorbed with undergraduate instruction, and could give but little time to the few who sought their guidance. . . .

As the day has now come when there is almost a superfluity of advanced courses, let me tell some of the conditions which brought the Johns Hopkins foundations into close relations with these upward and onward movements.

Before a university can be launched there are six requisites: An idea;

capital, to make the idea feasible; a definite plan; an able staff of co-adjutors; books and apparatus; students. On each of these points I shall briefly dwell, conscious of one advantage as a writer—conscious, also, of a disadvantage. I have the advantage of knowing more than anyone else of an unwritten chapter of history; the disadvantage of not being able or disposed to tell the half that I remember.

"The idea of the university" was a phrase to which Cardinal Newman had given currency in a remarkable series of letters in which he advocated the establishment of a Catholic foundation in Dublin. At a time when ecclesiastical or denominational colleges were at the front, and were considered by many people the only defensible places for the education of young men, his utterances for academic freedom were emancipating; at a time when early specialisation was advocated, his defence of liberal culture was reassuring. The evidence elicited by the British university commissions was instructive, and the writings of Mark Pattison, Dr. Appelton, Matthew Arnold, and others were full of suggestions. Innumerable essays and pamphlets had appeared in Germany discussing the improvements which were called for in that land of research. The endeavours of the new men at Cambridge and New Haven, and the instructive success of the University of Virginia, were all brought under consideration. Under these favourable circumstances, *Zeitgeist* they may be called, the Johns Hopkins was founded upon the idea of a university as distinct from a college.

The capital was provided by a single individual. No public meeting was ever held to promote subscriptions or to advocate higher education; no speculation in land was proposed· no financial gains were expected; no religious body was involved, not even the Society of orthodox Friends, in which the founder had been trained, and from which he selected several of his confidential advisers. He gave what seemed at the time a princely gift; he supplemented it with an equal gift for a hospital. It was natural that he should also give his name. That was then the fashion. . . .

Given the idea and the funds, the next requisite was a plan. In my first interviews with the trustees, I was strongly impressed by their desire to do the very best that was possible under the circumstances in which they were placed. We quickly reached concurrence. Without dissent, it was agreed that we were to develop, if possible, something more than a local institution, and were at least to aim at national influence; that we should try to supplement, and not supplant, existing colleges, and should endeavour to bring to Baltimore, as teachers and as students, the ablest minds that we could attract. It was understood that we should postpone all questions of building, dormitories, commons, discipline, and degrees; that we should hire or buy in the heart of the city a temporary perch, and remain on it until we could determine what wants should be revealed, and until we could decide upon future buildings. We were to await the choice of a faculty before we matured any schemes of examination, instruction, and graduation. . . .

New Educational Theories

To discerning eyes, the ramshackle educational edifice that had been reared upon the foundation so painstakingly laid by Horace Mann and his followers bore little resemblance to the noble structure envisaged by its architects and planners. The educational picture during the 1870's and 1880's was a bleak one indeed. Relieved by only a few isolated specks of animating color, it must be largely painted in drab and somber hues, depressing and uninspiring as a whole. It would have taken a gifted prophet indeed to have predicted that in a few short decades the educational picture would have undergone a complete metamorphosis, that the few specks of color would have spread, joined, and dominated the whole. This metamorphosis of the educational picture constituted what was, in essence, a revolution. It is generally entitled "The Progressive Movement," and it will be the purpose of this section of readings to present the thoughts, dreams, and hopes of some of its revolutionary leaders.

It is appropriate to begin with some of the ideas postulated by one of the earliest of those "bright specks of color" almost lost amid the generally barren educational landscape of the 1870's and 1880's. This color was generated by the dynamic Francis W. Parker. Called by John Dewey the "father of progressive education," Parker was an ex-Colonel (Civil War) who turned his hand to education. His work of educational reform in the schools of Quincy, Massachusetts, made the

"Quincy System" known throughout the world in educational circles.

In the summer of 1882, Col. Parker gave a series of talks on his educational ideas to a fascinated audience at the Martha's Vineyard Summer Institute. One of his audience, Lelia E. Patridge, reported on these talks in a book published in 1885 under the title *Notes of Talks on Teaching*.

Parker introduced at this institute many of the themes that would later become a part of the educational arsenal of progressive education. With regard to examinations, as an example, he stated the belief that the standard of examinations was the greatest obstacle in the way of real teaching. Pleading for educational reform, Parker told his listeners:

> Instead of stubbornly standing, and obstinately denying that there is no need of reform, and that all so-called new methods are worthless; let us honestly, earnestly, prayerfully study the great science of teaching. Let us learn, and courageously apply the truths that shall set us free; and the day will soon come when the teacher will lead society, and mould opinion.

For Parker, education of the character was the overarching aim of all education. In his final talk of the summer, Parker spelled out this aspect of his educational philosophy in some detail. As a summation of Parker's contributions and beliefs, it is a most valuable and enlightening piece.

97. On Teaching

Francis W. Parker

No matter how much educators may differ in regard to the means and methods of teaching, upon one point there is substantial agreement; viz. that the end and aim of all education, is the development of character. There is also, little or no difference of opinion, in regard to the elements that form the common ideal of character. Love of truth, justice, and mercy; benevolence, humility, energy, patience, and self-control, are recognized the world over, as some of the essentials that should govern human action. True character is recognized and felt, by all classes and conditions of society though they may be incapable of its analysis. Just as the lower

Reprinted from F. W. Parker, *Notes of Talks on Teaching,* reported by Lelia E. Patridge (New York: E. L. Kellogg & Co., 1885), pp. 166-167, 170, 173-176, 178-182.

types of intellect feel the power of the few masterpieces of art, without knowing its source.

All the knowledge and skill of an individual, all he thinks, knows, and does, is manifested in his character. Character is the summation of all these manifestations. Character is the expression of all that is in the mind, and it may be analyzed into habits. A habit is the tendency and desire to do that which we have repeatedly done before. A habit then, consists in doing, the primary foundation of which, is to be found in the possibilities for action that lie latent in the mind of the new-born child. The environment of the child, determines the kind, quality, and direction of its mental action. Education adapts the environment, by limiting it to those circumstances which lead the mind to act in the right manner, and in the right direction. The mother and teacher, be it through ignorance or knowledge, determine the doing of the child. The true teacher leads the child to do that which ought to be done. The famous principle of Comenius; "Things that have to be done, should be learned by doing them," includes in its category, the whole truth that should govern every parent and teacher in building the character of a child. Everything that may determine action, be it religious precepts, moral maxims, the best influences, or whatever of good may be brought to bear upon the child, find their limitations in what they inspire, and stimulate the child to do.

The opinion prevails among many teachers, that intellectual development, is, by its nature, separate and distinct from moral training. Of all the evils in our schools, this terrible mistake is productive of the greatest. The powers of the mind determine by their limitations all human action. There is no neutral ground. Every thing done has a moral, or immoral tendency. That is, doing, forms by repetition, a habit, and habits make up character. Let no one think that I am trenching on religious or theological grounds. I simply repeat what I have said before; the greatest truths of religion, the highest forms of morality, nature and art with all their beauty, can do no more than stimulate, inspire, direct, and fix mental action.

The true method of teaching, is the exact adaptation of the subject taught, or means of growth, to the learning mind. The mind can best grow, in only one way. If the adaptation of the subject to the mind is wrong, the action of the mind is impaired, and weakened, by ineffectual attempts to grasp it; and then the will of the teacher is obliged to come in, with artificial stimulants—to unhealthy mental action. Under such conditions, real essential happiness, that must come from the child's right emotions, is wanting; and the subject becomes in itself, an object of dislike and disgust to the child. Such teaching, I hold, must be, of its very nature, immoral. On the other hand, when the mind is in the full tide of healthy normal action, when it loves what it does, and does what it loves, the leading power of the teacher, in right directions, is enhanced to an incalculable degree. If the teacher knows the child, and her heart lies close to the child's heart, every motion of his mental and moral pulse, every desire to do wrong, or right, will always be felt by her. However much the teacher may desire to help the child, however strong her own moral or religious feelings may be, wrong methods, and misapplied teaching, stand as formidable barriers between herself and the child. Many a father who would have given his life for his boy, has, simply because he did not understand his child's nature, failed in his method of training, and driven the boy to ruin. The will of a parent, may deprive the child of the use of his reason so long, that when the controlling will is removed, the child finds himself weak, and helpless; a prey to any stronger will that may chose to master him.

Primary education consists, as I have said, in training the power of attention. The attractiveness of the object attended to, controls the will. The desire to attend, is thus aroused, making it possible for the mind to exert more and more power in such acts, until the reason comes in to govern the will, enabling the mind to concentrate itself whenever required.

There are two factors in education;—thought, and expression. Most teaching, is the training of the skill to express thought, with little or no regard to the thought itself. Precision is an indispensable mode of training skill in writing, drawing, position, and accurate ways of acting; but, when the training of precision is made the main motive of schoolwork; when the ways a child sits, places his feet, holds his hands, stares at a book, stands up, marches, utters a sentence, etc. are the be all and end all in the teacher's plan of work; then, precision invades the sacred realm of thought evolution, and the mind's power to act is crushed and crippled. I have seen schools of this description where the results would be grand, if the systematic clock-work-like operations were performed with puppets, instead of living human beings. Such training educates the willing followers of demagogues; prompt to march when the commanding boss gives the word.

Conceit is another outgrowth of this quantity ideal. The spectacle is a common one, of a young man, the model of his class, persistent and alert, possessed of a powerful verbal memory, which enables him to cram page after page of the text-book, distancing all competitors, carrying off all the class honors, and finally; armed with his sheepskin, [his Alma Mater's gracious indorsement of his wonderful attainments] confidently stepping out into the world, never questioning but that he will conquer in the new life, as easily as he did in the old. But the first spear-thrust of reality shivers his panoply of empty words, and leaves him defenceless, before the rigorous demands of an uncompromising world. "The long perspective of our life is truth, and not a show;" and I hold that sort of teaching, in the highest degree immoral, which crams the heads of our children, with the unusable pages of text-books, and then leads them to suppose that they are gaining real knowledge. By making quantity our ideal, we develop and foster conceit; and conceit is one of the most formidable barriers to true knowledge.

Inspire them to seek earnestly for the truth, and develop in them, one of the greatest of all human virtues—humility. "The meek shall inherit the earth," said the Great Teacher. He alone is really learning, who feels the immensity of the truth, and realizes that all he knows, or can know, in this world, is but as a drop to the great ocean of truth, that stretches boundless and fathomless into eternity. The teacher, above all others, should constantly be adding to his store of knowledge; and he who imagines that he has no more to learn in the art of teaching, is fit only to take his small place among other fossils.

Primary education consists, as I have repeatedly tried to show, in the development of the power of attention; and it will be plain to all, that the selection of the objects of thought and attention is a matter of the highest importance. The things presented must be pure, good, and beautiful, for that to which we attend, comes into the heart, and forms the basis of all our thinking and imagination; "Out of the heart the mouth speaketh." Where shall we look for the highest source of the good, the true, and the beautiful? To the thoughts of God in nature. The study of nature, is the best and highest foundation for morality, and a preparation for the revealed truth, that comes to the child later in life. Compare the drill upon hieroglyphics, empty words, and meaningless forms, with the observation of trees, flowers, animals, and the forms of earth. The one stimulates thought, and fills the mind with ideas of beauty; the other crowds the mind with useless, ugly forms that cannot, from their very nature, stimulate it to renewed action. A child's mind, filled with that which is pure, and good, has no room for wickedness and sin. The study of the natural sciences is one of the best means of bringing about this result. Did you ever observe the character of a boy who early fell in love with nature, and who spent his spare hours with plants, or animals, seeking for their haunts, watching their habits, and making collections for preservation? Such boys, so far as I have known, are genuinely good. They have neither the time, nor the inclination, for evil doing. The study of the thoughts of God in nature, filling the mind, as it does, with things of beauty, prepares the imagination for clear and strong conceptions of the higher and spiritual life.

Let no one misunderstand me, or imagine for a moment, that I mean to limit moral training to these subjects. Far from it. I am only trying to show, how all these things may be used in developing true character. Children learn very much by imitation. The teacher, whether good or bad, leaves his everlasting imprint on every child under his care. He can conceal nothing from the intuitional power of the child. Whatever you are, becomes immortal through the souls of your pupils. The precepts of a true teacher have immense weight; but the example has a still greater.

In my talk upon School Government, I said, that the end and aim of school education, is to train a child to work, to work systematically, to love work, and to put his brains into work. The clearest expression of thought, is expression in the concrete. Working with the hands, is one great means of primary development. It is also one of the very best means of moral training. From the first, every child has an intense desire to express his thought in some other way, than in language. Froebel discovered this, and founded the Kindergarten. No one can deny, that true Kindergarten training is moral training. Ideas and thoughts come into the mind, demanding expression. The use of that which is expressed, to the child, is the means it gives him, to compare his thought, with its concrete expression. The expression of the form made, compared with the ideal, stimulates to further trials. In making and building, is found the best means of training attention.

I wish to make a sharp distinction here, between *real work,* and *drudgery.* Real work is done on real things, producing tangible results, results that are seen and felt. Real work is adapted at every step to the child's power to do. Every struggle brings success, and makes better work possible. Drudgery, on the other hand, is the forced action of the mind upon that which is beyond mental grasp, upon words that cannot be apprehended, upon lessons not understood. Drudgery, consists, mainly, of the monotonous use of the verbal memory. There is no variety; not a bush or shrub along the pathway. This is the kind of study that produces ill-health. It is the straining of the mind upon disliked subjects, with the single motive, to gain applause, rewards, and diplomas. Thousands of nervous, earnest, faithful girls, spurred on by unwise parents, yearly lose their lives, or become hopeless invalids, in this costly and useless struggle. Real work stimulates every activity of mind and body. It furnishes the variety so necessary to interest, and is like true physical development that exercises every muscle and strengthens the whole man. Real work is always interesting, like real play. No matter how earnest the striving may be, it is followed by a glow of genuine pleasurable emotion.

There is great outcry against our schools and colleges, caused by the suspicion that they educate children to be above manual labor. This suspicion is founded upon fact, I am sorry to say; but the statement of the fact is not correct. Children are educated *below* manual labor. The vague, meaningless things they learn, are not adapted to real work; no effectual habits of labor are formed by rote-learning. The student's desire is too often, when he leaves school or college, to get a living by means of empty words. The world has little or no use for such rubbish. That man should gain his bread by the sweat of his brow, is a curse changed to the highest possible blessing. The clergyman, the lawyer, the physician, the teacher, need the benefit of an early training in manual labor, quite as much as the man who is to labor with his hands all his life. Manual labor is the foundation of clear thinking, sound imagination, and good health. There should be no real difference between the methods of our common schools, and the methods of training in manual labor schools. A great mistake has been made in separating them. All school work should be real work. We learn to do by doing. "Satan finds some mischief still, for idle hands to do." The direct influence of real work is, to absorb the attention in the things to be done; leaving no room in the consciousness for idleness, and its consequent vices. Out of real work, the child develops a motive, that directs his life work. Doing work thoroughly, has a great moral influence. One piece of work well done, one subject well mastered, makes the mind far stronger and better, than a smattering of all the branches taught in our schools. School work, and manual labor, have been for a long time divorced; I predict that the time is fast coming, when they will be joined in indissoluble bonds. The time too, is coming, when ministers will urge upon their hearers, the great importance of manual labor, as a means of spiritual growth. At no distant date, industrial rooms will become an indispensable part of every good school; the work of the head, and skill of the hand, will be joined in class-room, and workshop, into one comprehensive method of developing harmoniously the powers of body, mind, and soul. If you would develop morality in the child, train him to work.

In all that I have said, and whatever mistakes I have made, either in thought or expression, I have had but one motive in my heart, and that is, that the dear children of our common country, may receive at our hands, a development of intellectual, moral, and spiritual power, that will enable them to fight life's battle, to be thoughtful conscientious citizens, and prepare them for all that may come thereafter. Whatever we would have our pupils, we must be ourselves.

There were a few other bright spots on the educational canvas in the 1870's and 1880's besides the dynamic and insightful colonel.

Rural education was in a particularly sorry state, and demands for its renovation and reform came from the farmers through their Granges and Farmers Institutes. This attention to agricultural education was in actuality the rural phase of the more encompassing movement afoot in the land for vocational education.

This vocational education movement of the late nineteenth century had a dual aspect; it was pressed by both urban and rural educators. The schools were not meeting the socio-economic demands of a rapidly changing society—a familiar picture to the historian of education. Since the evolution of society was towards industrialization, antiquated, "bookish," overly intellect-oriented education was felt to be inadequate as a preparation for youth who would participate in the industrial growth of America. Manual, vocational training was seen by many as the key to the dilemma. On the rural scene, available education was viewed as equally impractical and unrealistic for a potential agriculturalist. Worse than that, it educated rural youth towards the cities—the agrarian myth was endangered by the increasing desertion of farms by improperly educated potential yeomen, who gravitated towards the big cities. Rural education must also be vocationally oriented, and the proper vocation was, of course, an agricultural one. Education would keep the youth on the farm and thus revitalize the rapidly disappearing agrarian way of life. Scientific agricultural courses, demonstration farms, agricultural clubs, special education for rural teachers—all were efforts in this direction. Legislative demands resulted in such federal laws as the Smith-Lever Act (Agricultural Extension Program) and the 1917 Smith-Hughes Act (federal support of agricultural, industrial, and trade subjects).

Another contributory source to the reform movement in education which would eventually coalesce into progressive educational reform came from social reformers. The social conscience of the country was awakened in the 1890's by writers like Jacob Riis and Jane Addams. Reform societies sprang up like desert plants after a rainfall, but it was the settlement movement that caught the fancy of America. This urban social reform movement aimed at nothing less than the humanization of a callous and dehumanizing industrial society. It moved into the neighborhoods to reconstruct the shattered slums into purposeful communities. Naturally, education played a large role in this regeneration of the neighborhood. Jane Addams, of Hull House fame, saw that the school must play its part in the humanization of the industrial monster by giving the slum child a sense of worth and human significance. The alienation of the worker from his work, precipitated by mass industry with its division of labor, was to be overcome by an education that would provide the young worker with a sense of dignity, a *raison d'être*. The properly educated worker would overcome the tyranny of the machine and assert his individual significance and worth in the face of the degrading production line. Obviously, education had to be changed—had to become as socially conscious as the settlement houses. Hence, another voice was added to the growing demand for a thorough overhaul of the schools.

The following selection is from *Democracy and Social Ethics* (1902), in which Jane Addams expresses some of her views regarding proper educational methods and orientation.

98. Education for Life

Jane Addams

As democracy modifies our conception of life, it constantly raises the value and function of each member of the community, however humble he may be. We have come to believe that the most "brutish man" has a value in our common life, a function to perform which can be fulfilled by no one else. We are gradually requiring of the educator that he shall free the powers of each man and connect him with the rest of life. We ask this not merely because it is the man's right to be thus connected, but because we have become convinced that the social order cannot afford to get along without his special contribution. Just as we have come to resent all hindrances which keep us from untrammelled comradeship with our fellows, and as we throw down unnatural divisions, not in the spirit of the eighteenth-century reformers, but in the spirit of those to whom social equality has become a necessity for further social development, so we are impatient to use the dynamic power residing in the mass of men, and demand that the educator free that power. We believe that man's moral idealism is the constructive force of progress, as it has always been; but because every human being is a creative agent and a possible generator of fine enthusiasm, we are sceptical of the moral idealism of the few and demand the education of the many, that there may be greater freedom,

Reprinted by permission of the publishers from Jane Addams, *Democracy and Social Ethics*, A. F. Scott, ed., (Cambridge, Mass.: Harvard University Press, 1964), pp. 178-181.

strength, and subtilty of intercourse and hence an increase of dynamic power. We are not content to include all men in our hopes, but have become conscious that all men are hoping and are part of the same movement of which we are a part.

Many people impelled by these ideas have become impatient with the slow recognition on the part of the educators of their manifest obligation to prepare and nourish the child and the citizen for social relations. The educators should certainly conserve the learning and training necessary for the successful individual and family life, but should add to that a preparation for the enlarged social efforts which our increasing democracy requires. The democratic ideal demands of the school that it shall give the child's own experience a social value; that it shall teach him to direct his own activities and adjust them to those of other people. We are not willing that thousands of industrial workers shall put all of their activity and toil into services from which the community as a whole reaps the benefit, while their mental conceptions and code of morals are narrow and untouched by any uplift which the consciousness of social value might give them.

We are impatient with the schools which lay all stress on reading and writing, suspecting them to rest upon the assumption that the ordinary experience of life is worth little, and that all knowledge and interest must be brought to the children through the medium of books. Such an assumption fails to give the child any clew to the life about him, or any power to usefully or intelligently connect himself with it.

As sad a sight as an old hand-loom worker in a factory attempting to make his clumsy machine compete with the flying shuttles about him, is a workingman equipped with knowledge so meagre that he can get no meaning into his life nor sequence between his acts and the far-off results.

Manufacturers, as a whole, however, when they attempt educational institutions in connection with their factories, are prone to follow conventional lines, and to exhibit the weakness of imitation. We find, indeed, that the middle-class educator constantly makes the mistakes of the middle-class moralist when he attempts to aid working people. The latter has constantly and traditionally urged upon the workingman the specialized virtues of thrift, industry, and sobriety—all virtues pertaining to the individual. When each man had his own shop, it was perhaps wise to lay almost exclusive stress upon the industrial virtues of diligence and thrift; but as industry has become more highly organized, life becomes incredibly complex and interdependent. If a workingman is to have a conception of his value at all, he must see industry in its unity and entirety; he must have a conception that will include not only himself and his immediate family and community, but the industrial organization as a whole. It is doubtless true that dexterity of hand becomes less and less imperative as the invention of machinery and subdivision of labor proceeds; but it becomes all the more necessary, if the workman is to save his life at all, that he should get a sense of his individual relation to the system. Feeding a machine with a material of which he has no knowledge, producing a product, totally unrelated to the rest of his life, without in the least knowing what becomes of it, or its connection with the community, is, of course, unquestionably deadening to his intellectual and moral life. To make the moral connection it would be necessary to give him a social consciousness of the value of his work, and at least a sense of participation and a certain joy in its ultimate use; to make the intellectual connection it would be essential to create in him some historic conception of the development of industry and the relation of his individual work to it.

Workingmen themselves have made attempts in both directions, which it would be well for moralists and educators to study. It is a striking fact that when workingmen formulate their own moral code, and try to inspire and encourage each other, it is always a large and general doctrine which they preach. They were the first class of men to organize an international association, and the constant talk at a modern labor meeting is of solidarity and of the identity of the interests of workingmen the world over. It is difficult to secure a successful organization of men into the simplest trades organization without an appeal to the most abstract principles of justice and brotherhood. As they have formulated their own morals by laying the greatest stress upon the largest morality, so if they could found their own schools, it is doubtful whether they would be of the mechanic institute type. Courses of study arranged by a group of workingmen are most naïve in their breadth and generality. They will select the history of the world in preference to that of any period or nation. The "wonders of science" or "the story of evolution" will attract workingmen to a lecture when zoölogy or chemistry will drive them away. The "outlines of literature" or "the best in literature" will draw an audience when a lecturer in English poetry will be solitary. This results partly from a wholesome desire to have general knowledge before special knowledge, and is partly a rebound from the specialization of labor to which the workingman is subjected. When he is free from work and can direct his own mind, he tends to roam, to dwell upon large themes. Much the same tendency is found in programmes of study arranged by Woman's Clubs in country places. The untrained mind, wearied with meaningless detail, when it gets an opportunity to make its demand heard, asks for general philosophy and background.

In a certain sense commercialism itself, at least in its larger aspect, tends to educate the workingman better than organized education does. Its interests are certainly world-wide and democratic, while it is absolutely undiscriminating as to country and creed, coming into contact with all climes and races. If this aspect of commercialism were utilized, it would in a measure counter balance the tendency which results from the subdivision of labor.

The most noteworthy attempt to utilize this democracy of commerce in relation to manufacturing is found at Dayton, Ohio, in the yearly gatherings held in a large factory there. Once a year the entire force is gathered together to hear the returns of the business, not so much in respect to the profits, as in regard to its extension. At these meetings, the traveling salesmen from various parts of the world—from Constantinople, from Berlin, from Rome, from Hong Kong—report upon the sales they have made, and the methods of advertisement and promotion adapted to the various countries.

Stereopticon lectures are given upon each new country as soon as it has been successfully invaded by the product of the factory. The foremen in the various departments of the factory give accounts of the increased efficiency and the larger output over former years. Any man who has made an invention in connection with the machinery of the factory, at this time publicly receives a prize, and suggestions are approved that tend to increase the comfort and social facilities of the employees.

In spite of the isolated pleas and efforts of individuals like Parker and Addams, in spite of the demands of farmers for more realistic rural education, education, by and large, was content to remain in the moribund and inadequate state into which it had decayed by the late nineteenth century. Voices crying in the wilderness were simply not enough to arouse the populace, and most educators were reasonably content with "business as usual." After all, rocking the boat was risky business. It was much easier and more comfortable to continue teaching *in vacuuo* and to restrict one's vision to the blackboard at hand. Clearly, what was needed was a loud voice that could speak to the large audience of the country—an artist who could paint in no uncertain hues the drab and uninspiring educational picture and place it before the eyes of the public. Such an individual was Dr. Joseph Mayer Rice.

Rice, fittingly enough, was neither educator nor journalist. He was, by profession, a pediatrician who had in the course of his medical work in New York City become interested in the problem of educa-

tion. Studying the subject for two years in Europe, he returned to his
native land in 1891 seeking an outlet for his educational ideas. From
the editor of *The Forum,* a New York monthly, Rice received a commission to prepare an extensive first-hand survey of the nation's
schools. From January to June of 1892, Rice traveled the country,
interviewing educators and observing the schools in operation. In
October of the same year the first of his articles appeared in *The
Forum,* and they continued in monthly installments until June of
1893. Rice minced no words. He had talked with some 1,200 teachers
in thirty-six cities, observing from thirty to thirty-five teachers at work
in each city in six to eight schools in each city. The results were generally shocking. Political manipulation, incompetent faculties, corrupt practices—all were documented and presented to the public in
the pages of *The Forum.* Mention was made, of course, of the exceptions (such as the Cook County Normal School run by the renowned
Colonel Parker), but the scandalous situation in the great majority of
our schools shocked a generally apathetic public. In his final article
for *The Forum,* Rice tried to answer the problem. The following
reading is a portion of that article.

99. Our Public School System: A Summary

Joseph M. Rice

The number of classes into which our schools can be divided is, in my
opinion, three. They are as follows:

In the first class I place those schools that are still conducted on the
antiquated notion that the function of the school consists primarily in crowding into the memory of the child a certain number of cut-and-dried facts,
ignoring the modern view that the aim of the school should be to develop the
child in all his faculties, intellectual, moral and physical. These schools
consequently represent education as it was before the time of the great
educators, when a science of education was unknown. In schools of this
order, the teachers are required to do nothing beyond securing certain
memoriter results. As such results can be obtained by any one who is able
to read, write and cipher, provided he is a good disciplinarian, it is only in
the class-rooms of those teachers who are sufficiently interested in their

Reprinted from Joseph M. Rice, "Our Public School System: A Summary, "*The
Forum,* Vol. XV, Mar-Aug 1893, pp. 507-518.

work to do more than is required of them that we find any evidence of the existence of a science of education. And, further, as in these schools the manner in which the growing mind acquires ideas is a mere side issue, the teacher makes no attempt to study the needs of the child and, consequently, no bond of sympathy forms between the pupil and the teacher, the attitude of the teacher toward the child being as a rule cold and unsympathetic, and at times actually cruel and barbarous. And as the mental food is given in the most indigestible and unpalatable form, learning is devoid of all pleasure, the school becomes a source of drudgery and childhood is robbed of its happiness.

But why do schools so thoroughly mechanical still exist in an enlightened age and in a country so progressive as ours? It is frequently claimed that the old education is more practical than the new, but this assertion is made in ignorance of facts. Indeed facts prove that more is accomplished in a given period by scientific than by mechanical teaching. And, further, that system of education that leads the child to observe and to think and to acquire manual dexterity while memorizing facts, is certainly more practical than the education whose aim is limited to leading the pupils simply to memorize facts. Again, it is claimed that in some localities the old system better answers the needs of the people than the new, and that the system of education must be regulated according to the needs of the individual community. In that case, the old system of education is applicable only to those communities where there is no necessity for the people either to observe or to reason. But where can such a community be found?

Again, we all know that in many of our cities the pupils will never receive more than three or four years of schooling, and we all agree that no pains should be spared to give such children at least some knowledge of the three R's before they begin their struggle for existence. But, as I have pointed out in previous articles, even in this the advocates of the mechanical reading, writing and arithmetic schools have no foundation upon which to base their argument. The children educated in our most scientific schools are much further advanced in reading and in the power to express their thoughts in writing at the end of the third school year than those brought up under a mechanical system, and they cipher at least as well.

It is not, therefore, because the old system of education is more practical than the new, or because it better answers the needs of the people, or because it accomplishes more in a given period, that in so many of our cities the science of education is ignored. The real causes for the existence of these miserable schools at the present stage of civilization are corruption and selfishness on the part of school officials, and unjustifiable ignorance, as well as criminal negligence, on the part of parents. It is in the cities where the school-board appoints such superintendents as will make able tools and fails to re-elect them when they are conscientious, in cities where it is not merit but friendship, business or politics that determines the appointment and discharge of teachers, in cities where the parents sit idly by while the members of the school-board use their children for selfish purposes, and with few exceptions in such cities only, that the science of education finds no room in the schools. In a few instances, the antiquated system of education appears to be entirely the result of misdirected and incompetent supervision. When the superintendents fail to instruct and inspire their teachers, or are unable to recognize the difference between scientific and unscientific instruction, the schools are, as a rule, mechanical. In these cases, the teachers are permitted, either through ignorance or carelessness, to fall into ruts out of which they never rise. To divorce the schools from politics does not in itself mean to raise the standard of the schools, but simply to remove the pressure from them so that it becomes possible for them to advance. When the schools are no longer under the baneful influence of politics, they will become, in nearly every instance, no more and no less than the superintendents make of them. A feature common to all the schools of the first class is that far too little, if anything, is done by the superintendents to inspire and instruct the teachers in their charge. In nearly all of them, the number of superintendents is too small, more than two hundred teachers being placed in charge of a supervising officer.

Among the schools of this order that I visited are those of Baltimore, Buffalo, Cincinnati, New York, Worcester, Mass., Milwaukee, St. Louis, Chicago, the Boston primary schools, and a few others. In Peoria, Ill., I visited only three schools. In one of them I found the spirit good. The other two, however, were distinctly of this order, the discipline being similar to that found in the schools of St. Louis, which, in my opinion, are the most barbarous schools in the country. In Brooklyn, the conditions are decidedly unfavorable, and, although I have not examined them closely, I feel at liberty, from what I have seen and heard of them, to inform those interested in the schools of that city that I have every reason to believe that they also belong to this class. Although the schools of the cities I have just mentioned differ to a considerable extent in regard to details, they do not vary much, in my opinion, in their general excellence. In all of them the vast majority of the teachers lack in professional spirit, and the instruction, regardless of subject, is, in the main, purely mechanical. The particular causes leading to the unfavorable condition of nearly all these schools, I have stated at length in previous articles.

The schools of the second class differ widely from those of the first in regard to their aim. While the aim of the first class of schools is simply to give the child a certain amount of information, that of the second class is the natural development of the child in all his faculties. In these schools the teachers are guided in their work by the nature of the child-mind, that is, by the laws of mental development. Consequently, it is not the text-books or the arbitrary will of the superintendent, but the laws of psychology that now become the ruling spirit of the schools. In thus reversing the order of things, the atmosphere of the school-room becomes entirely transformed. The teacher who endeavors to instruct in accordance with the nature of the mind is of necessity compelled to study the child, so that she may understand him and know how to minister to his needs. In this manner a true bond of sympathy forms between the teacher and the child. The attitude of the teacher now changes from that of lord and master to that of friend and guide. She is no longer cold and harsh, but loving and sympathetic, and the atmosphere of the school-room consequently changes from that of a prison or a factory to that of a refined and refining home. In schools of this nature the happiness of childhood is preserved, not only because the child is treated with kindness and consideration, but also because the work is interesting and, therefore, pleasurable. Further, while in the first class of schools the recitation-periods are devoted principally to hearing children recite lessons that they have studied by heart from text-books, in the second class such lesson-hearing is not tolerated, the teacher being obliged at least to attempt to devote these periods to actual teaching. In these schools, education is regarded as a science, and the teacher is in search of such light as will guide her in giving the child the benefit of progress. We find widely distributed among the teachers a truly progressive spirit, much enthusiasm and a desire to learn. In almost all instances the teachers of such schools constantly pursue professional studies under the guidance of the superintendent. And, lastly, owing to the fact that the child is treated with sympathy and the fact that the atmosphere of the school-room is charged with refining influence, it can scarcely be doubted that these schools exert unconsciously a favorable influence on the moral character of the child, a phase that is absolutely lacking in the first class of schools.

The typical schools of this class also vary considerably in regard to the details of the work, but, in my opinion, when considered in their totality, they do not vary to any appreciable extent in their general degree of excellence. They are all characterized by the fact that the efforts of the superintendents are directed primarily toward inspiring and instructing the teachers, mere school-inspection and the examination of classes being considered of only secondary importance. In all of them the spirit is excellent. These schools, however, have certain weak points which I shall mention while discussing the schools of the third class.

The schools that, in my opinion, are distinctively of this type are those of Washington, D. C., Yonkers, N. Y., Springfield, Mass., Jackson and Ionia, Mich., Quincy and Brookline, Mass., and others. In the schools of Washington, D. C., there is a complete system of manual training that does not skip a link from the kindergarten to the highest class of the high-school, and many of the features of this work are excellent. In Quincy and in Brookline, Mass., more has been done with the natural sciences than in the other schools of this class. In Springfield, the primary arithmetic is very interesting and thoughtful, and throughout the schools a feature has been made of the scientific teaching of geography. The schools of Ionia, Mich., are peculiar in so far as they are conducted on the departmental plan, each teacher instructing the children in only one subject. In Yonkers, N. Y., and in Jackson, Mich., I found the spirit excellent and the teachers earnest, but the curriculum rather narrow.

The schools that I have just mentioned have reached a distinctive stamp of a comparatively high order for the reason that they have been for some time laboring under very favorable conditions. They have for a number of years been well supervised and in large part free from politics. In a large number of the cities that I visited, I found the schools striving to break away from the old-fashioned methods and to accomplish what the typical schools of the second class have already accomplished. They have, however, for numerous reasons not yet reached the standard of the schools of the second class, being still in a transitional stage.

In Philadelphia, for example, the superintendents have for many years been endeavoring to raise the standard of the schools, but their efforts have as yet met with but little success because the schools are practically controlled by ward politicians who are doing all in their power to use the schools for their own selfish ends. The schools of Cleveland, Ohio, were in former years in good condition, but have since been ruined by the politicians. Last year a complete reorganization of the school-system of Cleveland was effected. It is not improbable that under Judge A. S. Draper, who was appointed their superintendent a short time ago, these schools will regain their former glory. The schools of Detroit appear to be laboring under the same difficulties as those of Cleveland. Detroit's training-school for teachers, however, appeared to me to be an excellent school. The schools of Davenport, Iowa, may be said to have crystallized on a lower plane than that of the typical schools of the second class. While in Davenport the methods are not entirely unscientific, the pupils are treated with undue rigidity and the spirit is not good. These schools appear to be suffering from a degree of conservatism that is altogether out of harmony with the progressive spirit of the West. Next, there are a number of cities whose schools, owing to the excellence of recently-appointed superintendents, are destined soon to reach a much higher than their present standard. Among these are the schools of Des Moines, Iowa, Lansing, Mich., and Moline, Ill. The spirit in these schools is excellent, and more scientific methods will be sure to follow. The schools of some cities never reach a distinctive character, for the reason that they are constantly changing their superintendents.

Besides the cities I have named, I visited a number that I do not feel at liberty to classify, because I did not follow them in all their lines of work. I was attracted to some of them with the object of observing special lines of work, and to others in the hope that I might succeed in finding hidden treasures. I visited Toronto, Canada, for the purpose of observing the reading, of which I had heard so much. Mr. Hughes, Inspector (Superintendent) of schools of that city, has given much attention to phonics. The results in reading, as well as in penmanship in the lower primary grades, are indeed remarkable. I found many of the children at the end of the fourth or fifth month of school-life able to read almost any new word without assistance, and to write from dictation, correctly and very rapidly, even words of several syllables. The penmanship of many of these little children is as good as that of the average adult. In Toronto the cheerfulness of the class-rooms is almost without a parallel.

The schools of the third class are, in spirit, similar to those of the second class, but they differ from them so considerably in their methods of instruction, and particularly in those followed in the primary grades, that they may, in my opinion, be regarded as having reached a higher stage of development. The difference in this, namely, that although in the second class of schools an attempt is made to teach scientifically, yet each branch of knowledge is still taught in large part independently, while in the third class of schools the walls between the various branches, to a considerable extent, disappear, an attempt being made to teach the subjects in their natural relations to each other. In the latter class of schools, the mind is no longer regarded as consisting of a number of independent compartments, one for penmanship, a second for reading, a third for arithmetic, a fourth for geography, etc., but the ideas gained regardless of subject are led to support each other, and they become clearer by being seen in the light of each other. In other words, the schools of the third class are characterized by the fact that they are conducted upon what is known as the principle of Unification. While in most of our schools several hours are devoted daily to the independent study of language in its various phases, namely, reading, penmanship, spelling and composition, in the schools conducted upon the principle of unification, language is regarded simply as a means of expression and not as a thing apart from ideas. Instruction in almost every branch now partakes of the nature of a language-lesson, the child being led to learn the various phases of language in large part incidentally, while acquiring and expressing ideas. From the start an attempt is made to devote most of the time either to gaining ideas or to rendering ideas more clear by expressing them in written language as well as with the pencil, the brush and other tools. . . .

As I have pointed out in the present article, the general educational spirit of the country is progressive, the schools of a large number of our cities now laboring in the right direction. . . . In closing, I will once more call attention to the fact that it is the duty of the public to lend all possible encouragement to those who are striving in the right direction. On the other hand, it is the duty of all parents, to take active steps toward crushing school officials who have fallen so low as to sell, for their own profit, not only the happiness of the little ones entrusted to their care while in the school, but also their opportunity to become developed into sound men and women, intellectually, morally and physically.

The reaction of the popular press to the work and suggestions of Rice was generally of a sympathetic nature. The professional journals of education, predictably enough, reacted in quite a different fashion. The following appraisal of Rice's work appeared in *Education*.

100. Editorial from Education

The *Forum* is publishing a series of critical articles on the public school systems of the leading American cities; having already disposed of Baltimore, Buffalo and Cincinnati. The writer is a certain Dr. Rice; who seems to have recently abandoned the work of physicking his patients for a course in pedagogy in Germany. Returning to New York, he announces that he has spent the past year in the examination of the public schools of our American cities, and is prepared, through the columns of this magazine, to diagnose the condition of each, administer purgatives, sedatives or tonics; even, if necessary, "heroic treatment," with appropriate surgery. So far he has found very little to praise, either in the schools or the educational public of these cities. The few pages devoted to Cincinnati, Ohio, illustrate his method; itself a pronounced illustration of the high critical type of amateur high educator that now seems in favor in the magazines. In this summary critique Mr. Rice appears to know nothing of the historical development

Reprinted from *Education*, XIII (1892-1893), pp. 245-246.

of popular education in Cincinnati; what it has done for one of the most cosmopolitan of our great American cities, or the ground it now covers in its municipal life. No one would suspect that the public school system of Cincinnati is one of the most complete in the country; offering free schooling to every child, from the primary to a very respectable free university; a teacher's training school, for twenty years past one of the best; two high schools, well known for solid work; a flourishing free public library, with free scholarships in promising schools of art, music and technology. Within the past twenty years the Cincinnati schools have attracted national observation for new departures in the use for moral training of rare extracts from English literature; the public celebration of Author's Days, and tree planting by the children. That all this has been done, as everywhere else, amid a storm of opposition from municipal and ecclesiastical politicians, some unfortunate changes in supervision and a steady disparagement of the public school system itself, by an influential class of citizens, aided by the press, is true. Mr. Rice has lamentably failed to see, and so has virtually slandered the true educational public, nowhere more intelligent, progressive and determined than in the Queen city. That an expert of this type should have mistaken the stupidity of a few incompetent teachers for the general method of instruction and evidently recorded the disparagement of a few dozen chronic grumblers against the school for a fair estimate of education in Cincinnati, is not remarkable. It is only a little more pronounced instance of a style of criticism affected by rising young magazine writers, fresh from European studies, and therefore competent to sit on high stools "sizing up" the American people.

Theoretical support for the reforming spirit was not long in making its appearance on the intellectual scene. One important theoretical adjunct to educational thought came from the social application of the biological theories of Charles Darwin. Social Darwinism's most influential spokesman to America was Herbert Spencer, whose writings enjoyed a tremendous following in this country during the 1870's and 1880's. Spencer's essays on education attempted to answer the question of what knowledge was of most worth. The Spencerian answer was an unequivocal vote for the study of science. The influence of the Spencerian emphasis upon scientific study was manifested in the 1893 N.E.A. Committee of Ten, whose recommendations were heavily weighted with scientific studies for the secondary school.

Spencer's interpretations of the social applications of evolutionary theory were even more influential. He saw man's relationship to history as one of adaptation to life's conditions; rather than being the molder of history, man is acted upon by history. Proper education, logically enough, became, for Spencer, education for adaptation—a preparation for life in a rather passive vein. Reforming efforts of men were self-delusionary, for change comes only through the infinitely gradual process of evolution which follows its own supra-human laws. Mind itself follows this evolutionary pattern in its development, claimed Spencer, and education as an agent for social reform and progress was a vain denial of the scientific laws of evolution. In line with this interpretation of Social Darwinism, Spencer held that efforts towards progressive reform were actually corrupting influences on the individualism of the populace. One must be allowed the freedom of demonstrating one's fitness for survival and not be supported by welfare reforms.

The Spencerian interpretation of Social Darwinism in America was underlined by the prolific writings of William Graham Sumner of Yale. Following the Spencerian mold, Sumner resisted the reforming efforts of the times, placing his faith rather in the slow working out of the natural and unimpeded processes of evolution. Laissez-faire individualist, anti-reformist, defender of the status quo, Sumner epitomized what has sometimes been aptly called "Conservative Darwinism." The following essay is illustrative of his thinking.

101. An Examination of a Noble Sentiment

William Graham Sumner

A noble sentiment is a very noble thing when it is genuine. A soul which would not throb in response to a noble sentiment, if it were genuine, would prove that it was base and corrupt. On the other hand, a noble sentiment, if it is not genuine, is one of the most corrupting things in the world. The habit of entertaining bogus sentiments of a plausible sound, deprives both mind and heart of sterling sense and healthful emotion. It is no psychological enigma that Robespierre, who was a hero of the eighteenth-century *sensibilité,* should have administered the Reign of Terror. People who

Reprinted by permission from A. G. Keller and M. R. Davie, eds., *Selected Essays of William Graham Sumner* (New Haven: Yale University Press, 1924), pp. 90-93.

gush are often most impervious to real appeals, and to genuine emotion. It therefore seems that we must be on our guard against pretended noble sentiments, as against very dangerous pitfalls, and test them to see whether they are genuine or not.

The sentiment which I now propose to examine is this: that we ought to see to it that everyone has an existence worthy of a human being, or to keep it in the form in which it is offered, a *menschenwürdiges Dasein*. It is a matter of accident that it is stated in German. A noble sentiment often loses poetry and transcendental solemnity to such an extent, when translated into everyday English, that it might seem like begging the question of its truth and value to translate it.

The first question is: what is an existence worthy of a human being? The hod-carrier, who is earning a dollar a day, will say that it is what he could get for a dollar and a half; the mechanic at two dollars will say that it would cost three; a man whose income is a thousand dollars will say that it costs fifteen hundred. I once heard a man, whose salary was twelve thousand dollars, speak of five thousand a year as misery. A *menschenwürdiges Dasein*, therefore, at the first touch gives us the first evidence of something wrong. It sounds like a concrete and definite thing, but it is not such; a *menschenwürdiges Dasein* is the most shifting and slippery notion which the human mind can try to conceive. In general it is about fifty per cent more than each one of us is getting now, which would, for a time, mean happiness, prosperity, and welfare to us all.

The next question is: for how many people must a *menschenwürdiges Dasein* be provided? The provision of such an existence is the first necessity which meets one of us when he comes to understand the world in which he lives,—that is, he has to earn his living,—for the exceptions, those who inherit a living, are so few that they may be disregarded by the rest of us on whom this proposed duty will fall. The task of earning a living is found, generally, to be a somewhat heavy one, chiefly for the reason, as shown in the former paragraph, that a man's definition of a decent living will not stay fixed long enough for him to realize it. As soon as he thinks that he sees his way to it he wants to marry; then he becomes responsible for the *menschenwürdiges Dasein* of a number of other persons. His whole energy, his whole life long, rarely suffices to do more than meet this obligation. Such is the fate of the man who tries to guarantee a *menschenwürdiges Dasein* to himself, his wife, and his children. But the man who is to be provided with such an existence, under the new arrangement proposed, will not have any such difficulty to contend with; he is to have a living secured to him by the state, or the social reformers, or somebody else. His wife and children will obviously have as good a claim to a *menschenwürdiges Dasein* as he; their support will therefore cause him no anxiety and no burden. Therefore this class of persons will increase with great rapidity. They are, of course, all those who have neglected or refused to win a *menschenwürdiges Dasein* for themselves; and whenever it is determined that somebody else shall give it to them, it is provided that their number shall multiply indefinitely and forever.

Furthermore, in all these propositions the fact is overlooked that no humanitarian proposition is valid unless it is applied to the whole human race. If I am bound to love my fellow-man, it is for reasons which apply to Laplanders and Hottentots just as much as to my neighbor across the street; our obligation to provide a *menschenwürdiges Dasein* is just as great toward Africans or Mongolians as toward Americans. It must certainly be as wide as all *Menschen,* that is, all human beings. There are millions of people on the globe whose mode of life, whose *Dasein,* is far below that of the most miserable wretch in the United States, never has been any better than it is, never will be any better as far ahead as anybody can see, and they cannot be said to be to blame for it. It is true that they do not know that they are badly off; they do not bother their heads about a *menschenwürdiges Dasein.* They do not work much and they are quite free from care—very much more so than the average American taxpayer. got it, just because they have not got it (and no other reason is alleged in connection with the proposition before us), then the persons to whom I have referred have a very much stronger claim, for they are very much farther away from it.

The next question is: what will be the effect on people of securing them a *menschenwürdiges Dasein?* Plainly it must be to pauperize them, that is, to take away all hope that they can ever win such an existence for themselves. If not, and if the proposition means only that we hope and strive to make our community as prosperous as possible, and to give everybody in it as good chances as possible, then that is just what we are trying to do now, to the best of our ability, and the proposal is only an impertinence; it interrupts and disturbs us without contributing anything to the matter in hand. Now it is one of the worst social errors to pauperize people; it demoralizes them through and through; it ruins their personal character and makes them socially harmful; it lowers their aims and makes sure that they will never have good ones; it corrupts their family life and makes sure that they will entail sordid and unworthy principles of action on their children. If any argument could be brought forward for an attempt to secure to everyone an existence worthy of a man, it would be that, in that way, everyone among us might be worthy to be a human being; but, whenever the attempt it made, the only result will be that those who get an existence worthy of a human being in that way are sure to be morally degraded below any admissible standard of human worth.

The next question is: who is to secure the *menschenwürdiges Dasein* to the aforesaid persons? Evidently it can only be those who have already, no one knows by what struggles and self-denial, won it for themselves. This proposition, like all the others of the class to which it belongs, proposes to smite with new responsibilities, instead of rewards, the man who has done what everyone ought to do. We are told what fine things would happen if every one of us would go and do something for the welfare of somebody else; but why not contemplate also the immense gain which would ensue if everybody would do something for himself? The latter is ever so much more reasonable than the former; for those who are now taking care of themselves have very little strength to spare, while those who are not now taking care of themselves might do a great deal more. The plan of securing to those who have not a *menschenwürdiges Dasein* that blessing, is a plan for leaving the latter at ease and putting more load on the former; to the society, therefore, it is doubly destructive, increasing its burdens and wasting its resources at the same time.

The next question is: what means are to be used to give a *menschen-würdiges Dasein* to everybody? To this there is no answer; we are left to conjecture. The most reasonable conjecture is that the proponents themselves do not know; they have not made up their minds; they have not really faced the question. A proposition to give everybody an existence worthy of a human being, without a specification of the measures by which it is proposed to do it, is like a proposition to make everybody handsome.

Our analysis has therefore shown that this noble sentiment is simply a bathos.

Sumner, however, was not the only American to focus sharply upon the social implications of Darwinism. One could, it soon appeared, begin with the same set of evolutionary data as did Spencer and Sumner and yet arrive at entirely opposite conclusions regarding its social application. Such an innovating mind belonged to Lester Frank Ward, a largely self-educated and unknown government paleontologist.

Ward reasoned that the Spencerian stress upon the evolutionary process as being guided solely by natures's law, inaccessible to the interference of mortal creature (and the laissez-faire doctrines that were the social corollaries to this process) was correct—up to a point. The point of departure from the Spencer-Sumner interpretation was, for Ward, the introduction of a new variable (itself an evolutionary product) into the scheme. This variable was that crowning glory of evolutionary development that had been enthroned by the Greek philosophers as the very essence of humanity—the rational mind of man. With mind on the scene, Ward claimed, the evolutionary process was no longer blind or removed from human ken or influence, it could be consciously and rationally directed towards social improvement.

Ward, therefore, represents the "Reform Darwinism," as opposed to the older "Conservative" variety. Education, for Ward, was the primary agent of social reform, the very backbone of human progress. The greater the diffusion of knowledge, the greater was the potentiality for human betterment and the purposeful direction of evolution to social good. Education should be universal and state supported (Spencer and Summer saw education as entirely a parental, not a societal, responsibility), for all had the capacity to become educated. Always self-conscious of his humble beginnings and status, Ward saw education as the great transcender and equalizer of class differences and barriers. Like Spencer, Ward tended to stress education in the sciences; unlike Spencer, however, he saw education as the primary human activity. The following reading is from Ward's two-volume *Dynamic Sociology,* a major portion of which is devoted to education.

102. Education as a Factor in Dynamic Sociology

Lester Frank Ward

The doctrine that education is an active factor in Dynamic Sociology is simply a corollary from the doctrine of evolution in general, which rests upon the power of the environment to mold the organism. For what is education but a quality of the environment? To deny its influence on society is to deny the influence of the environment upon the organism. In enforcing education we are dealing with minors, over all whose acts there must always be exercised more or less constraint. They are simply required to be in certain places at certain times, and to perform certain acts which are foreseen to be destined to benefit them and society in after years. Obedience to these requirements, no matter how unwillingly, can not fail to produce the result foreseen. The intellect and the faculties of the mind are affected by the external influences artificially supplied for the purpose,

Reprinted from Lester Frank Ward, *Dynamic Sociology* (New York: D. Appleton & Co., 1883, 2 vols.), II, pp. 632-633.

and the individual can not by any act of consciousness prevent them from being so affected. Adults are themselves subject to this purely mechanical law of education, and children are far more plastic and impressible than adults. No one can say that he would have been the same as he is had his education been different, or wanting entirely. No one can help becoming acquainted with truths that are thrust upon him and made to appeal to his faculties. Of course, open and conscious resistance to impressions, especially in adults, would tend somewhat to diminish their force and clearness. But this can never practically occur in education. Usually there is no resistance, and often the educational influences are agreeable. It should be the aim to render them still more so.

The problem of education is, therefore, reduced to this: whether the members of society shall continue to pass through life surrounded only by the natural and unorganized influences which every-where exist, by which they are indeed constantly acquiring knowledge, such as it is, and many conceptions which are not knowledge because they consist of erroneous inferences; whether they shall thus be left to form all kinds of undigested and unsystematized ideas, half of which are objectively unreal, and most of the remainder too narrow to be of any value, yet to which their conduct will rigidly correspond, producing its legitimate effect upon themselves and upon society; or, whether they shall be required to pass a portion of their early lives under a system of artificial circumstances, so regulated that the bulk of the influences which appeal to the senses and produce ideas will be both reliable and important, and from which, under no other than the normal operations of the mind, reliable and valuable knowledge must necessarily result, solid character be formed, and the highest ethical and dynamic actions be induced, exerting rigidly corresponding effects upon themselves and upon society. It is, in short, the question whether the social system shall always be left to nature, always be genetic and spontaneous, and be allowed to drift listlessly on, intrusted to the by no means always progressive influences which have developed it and brought it to its present condition, or whether it shall be regarded as a proper subject of art, treated as other natural products have been treated by human intelligence, and made as much superior to nature, in this only proper sense of the word, as other artificial productions are superior to natural ones.

Evolutionary theory made its impact on psychology as well as on sociology, and both would influence education. Far and away the most prolific writer and systematizer of evolutionary psychology was

Granville Stanley Hall. Hall was a spokesman of the idea (borrowed from biology) that ontogeny paralleled phylogeny. In less elegant expression, this simply means that he (along with Spencer, Herbart, and others) believed that the development of the individual human organism (ontogeny) recapitulated the entire evolution of the human race (phylogeny) from pre-savagery to civilization.

In its development through the various stages that paralleled (more or less) the stages of the evolution of the human race, the individual human organism had to live through each stage so that the mind (also an evolutionary product) would follow a process of normal growth. The educational implications of such a psychology are clear. Indeed, Hall's major criterion of judgement of a civilization was precisely the manner in which its children grew. Schools were judged by the extent to which they adapted themselves to the natural (evolutionary) growth of children. Hall is justly famed as the father of the "child-study" movement in America. The following selection demonstrates the relationship of psychology and education as Hall saw it.

103. The Ideal School Based on Child Study

G. Stanley Hall

I. The kindergarten age is from two or three to six or seven. Here, before the ideal school can be inaugurated, we need some work of rescue from the symbolists. Now the body needs most attention, and the soul least. The child needs more mother, and less teacher; more of the educated nurse, and less of the metaphysician. We must largely eliminate, and partly reconstruct, the mother-plays, while transforming and vastly enlarging the repertory of the gifts and occupations. We must develop the ideal nursery, playgrounds, and rooms, where light, air, and water are at their best. The influences of the new hygiene have been felt least here, where they are needed most. The neglect of these basal principles suggests that we have still among us those whose practice implies a belief that any old place is good enough to hatch out beautiful souls, provided only Froebelian orthodoxy of doctrine and method is steadfastly maintained. In place of a magic mongering with them, the cubes, spheres, cylinder, and also the top, soap-bubble, doll, dances, marches, circus, and scores of other free plays and games; and in place of two or three fish, insects, animals, plants,

Reprinted from G. Stanley Hall, "The Ideal School as Based on Child Study," *The Forum* (Sept. 1901-Feb. 1902), pp. 26-29.

several score must be provided, and a museum and *catalogue raisonné* of toys must be at hand. Eating bread, milk, fruit, with some simple table manners, and using paper napkins, sometimes do wonders for these human larvae. Feeding brightens the mind and saves the disposition; a full stomach opens the mouth, and good courses of lessons could be derived from the viands themselves.

The kindergarten should fill more of the day, and should strive to kill time. In the Berlin Institute children sleep at noon in a darkened room, with music, crackers, or even bottles, and thus resist man's enemy, fatigue, and restore paradise for themselves. Part of the cult here should be idleness and the intermediate state of reverie. We should have a good excuse to break into these, and at this age children should be carefully shielded from all suspicion of any symbolic sense. Thus in play and in play only, life is made to seem real. Imitation should have a far larger scope. Children should hear far more English and better, and in the later years the ear should be trained for French or German. Color should never be taught as such. The children of the rich, generally prematurely individualized or over-individualized, especially when they are only children, must be disciplined and subordinated; while the children of the poor, usually under-individualized, should be indulged. We should lose no syllable of the precious positive philosophy of Froebel, the deepest of all modern educational thinkers; but we must profoundly reconstruct every practical expression that he attempted of his ideas, and must strive to induce at least a few college-trained men and women to turn their attention to the kindergarten, thus making the training schools feel, what they have hitherto known so little of, the real spirit and influence of modern science. Teachers should study every child, not necessarily by any of the current technical methods. They should learn far more than they can teach, and in place of the shallow mannikin child of books they should see, know, and love only the real thing. After this metempsychosis, the kindergarten should be, and should become, an integral part of every school system.

II. The age of about seven or eight is a transition period of the greatest interest for science. Then most children have less chewing surface by three or four teeth; there is a year or more of increased danger to the heart; the breath is shorter and fatigue easier; lassitude, nervousness, visual disorders, and cough are somewhat more imminent; and the blood is more often impoverished. The brain has practically finished for life its growth in weight and size; and all work and strain must be reduced. Some important corner in its time of development, not yet fully understood, is turned.

III. At eight or nine there begins a new period, which, for nearly four years, to the dawn of puberty, constitutes a unique stage of life, marked off by many important differences from the period which precedes and that which follows it. During these years there is a decreased rate of growth, so that the body relatively rests; but there is a striking increase of vitality, activity, and power to resist disease. Fatigue, too, is now best resisted, and it is amazing to see how much can be endured. The average child now plays more games and has more daily activity, in proportion to size and weight, than at any other stage. It would seem, as I have proposed elsewhere with ground for the theory, as though these four years represented, on the recapitulation theory, a long period in some remote age, well above the simian, but mainly before the historic, period, when our early forebears were well adjusted to their environment. Before a higher and much more modern story was added to human nature the young in warm climates, where most human traits were evolved, became independent of their parents, and broke away to subsist for themselves at an early age. In this age, which we will call the juvenile, the individual boy to-day is a precious key for the reconstruction of a stage in the history of the race otherwise very obscure.

However this may be, child nature suggests very plainly that this period should be mainly devoted to drill, habituation, and mechanism. The age of reason is only dawning, and is not yet much in order; but discipline should be the watchword here. Writing, and even reading, for instance, should be neglected in our system before eight, and previous school work should focus on stories, the study of nature, and education by play and other activities. Now writing and reading should be first taught with stress. Their nascent period is now beginning. If we teach them before, we are apt to make the average child a bad writer for life by precocious over-emphasis on the finer muscles. Modern studies show that the zigzag of the eye back and forth along the printed line is as dangerous as is the too early wigwag of the pen. At best the strain laid upon these tiny muscles is dangerous. Too early drill in read-writing is also enormously wasteful, because intensive effort gives facility now in an amazingly short time. Now first the smaller muscles in the average child, so important for mind and will training, can bear hard work and much strain. Accuracy, which when out of its season is fraught with so many dangers for mind and body, is now in order.

Verbal memory is now at its very best, and should be trained far more than it is. We are now educating the automatic bases of both mind and morals, and habits are never so easily formed or made stable. Manual training and games should be extremely diverse, manifold, and thorough. It is the time to break in the human colt, which is by nature in some sense the wildest of all wild animals. If the piano or any other musical instrument is to be learned, this is the time for drill, especially on scales and exercises. An instrumentalist's technique is rarely good if its foundations are not laid in this age. Names, even technical ones, come now. Drawing, too, should now come into prominence, beginning in its large and perfectly free form before writing, and only near the end of the period becoming severely methodic and accurate. Art training should not result in intimidation, but first everything should be drawn—battles, fires, shipwrecks, and railroad accidents, with plenty of human figures and action, and no angles, straight lines, or regular curves, which have come very late in the history of the race. This would make drawing, as it should be, a real expression of the child's soul, and the child would copy what he, and not what the adult, sees.

The mother tongue will be the vehicle of nearly all the work of this period; but it will be on the short circuit from ear to mouth, which existed for unknown eons before writing or reading, and not chiefly on the long circuit and biologically very recent brain-path from eye to hand. Teachers praise written work in home and at school—compositions, essays, class work; but all these appeal to new and undeveloped powers of nerve and muscle. It is because we try to establish good English upon these foundations, so precarious at this stage, that we have so much and so just complaint of bad English. We ruin both handwriting and idiomatic speech by precocity. The child should live in a world of sonorous speech. He should hear and talk for hours each day; and then he would lay foundations for terse and correct English, and would keep read-writing, as it should forever be, subordinate to hearing and speaking. He would write as he speaks, and we should escape the abomination of bookish talk. At this stage written work should be required far less than at present.

Further, to secure these ends, we must first lay less stress upon correct spelling—which is, after all, of far less importance than we think—and also upon correct, adult Addisonian syntax. Good grammar is too much to expect yet. We must strive first for utterance and expression, which may be homely if only vigorous and adequate. Hence, much that we call slang has its place, and is really a revival of English in its most formative stage. The prim properties we idolize are not yet, but it is the hour of delight in cogency of expression. We do not yet know what slang to teach or how to teach it, but we ought to give the best of it an important place. The boy is not totally depraved because he loves the speech of Chimmie Fadden, of Mr. Ade, or of "The Charwoman," because such language is fresh from the mint where all words were made. Our end is the cultivation of expression, which must bring out clearly and strongly what is in the boy's soul. This expression must be of a kind at least no less effective for other boys than for us. A training that gives the power of writing or even talking upon any subject or upon none in particular is bad and vicious. Children have no right to write unless it is upon some subject that they know and upon which they feel strongly. Theme and composition should be strictly confined to the fields of interest, and then expression will find or make a vent for itself. Moreover, we should not teach language, as such, or apart from objects, acts, and concrete reality-truth. We must burn most of our language books.

A leading theorist, who provided the educational reformers with scientific and philosophic ammunition from his fertile and imaginative genius, was the multi-talented William James. Psychologist, philosopher, visionary, James was without doubt one of America's greatest intellectual products.

The Pragmatic philosophy that he helped to develop, with its voluntaristic appeal to the American mind, became the backbone of the new education. With some modifications and re-emphases, it became the Instrumentalism of John Dewey. The psychology of William James (functionalism) was, like Spencer's and Hall's, evolutionary. Though Spencer concluded that adjustment and adaptation to environment was the proper mental attitude and Hall became enamoured of the recapitulation theory as a major thesis of psychology, James (like Ward) stressed the positive, creative, active role of the mind in the evolutionary process. The world is not to be passively adapted to; it was to be actively transformed. Man's behavior rested not upon his adaptations but upon his reactions. In his famous *Talks to Teachers on Psychology,* James made this point in the clear and lucid prose that characterized his writing.

104. Talks to Teachers

William James

No reception without reaction, no impression without correlative expression,—this is the great maxim which the teacher ought never to forget.
An impression which simply flows in at the pupil's eyes or ears, and in no way modifies his active life, is an impression gone to waste. It is physiologically incomplete. It leaves no fruits behind it in the way of

Reprinted from William James, *Talks to Teachers on Psychology* (New York: Henry Holt & Co., 1899). pp. 33-37.

capacity acquired. Even as mere impression, it fails to produce its proper effect upon the memory; for, to remain fully among the acquisitions of this latter faculty, it must be wrought into the whole cycle of our operations. Its *motor consequences* are what clinch it. Some effect due to it in the way of an activity must return to the mind in the form of the *sensation of having acted*, and connect itself with the impression. The most durable impressions are those on account of which we speak or act, or else are inwardly convulsed.

The older pedagogic method of learning things by rote, and reciting them parrot-like in the schoolroom, rested on the truth that a thing merely read or heard, and never verbally reproduced, contracts the weakest possible adhesion in the mind. Verbal recitation or reproduction is thus a highly important kind of reactive behavior on our impressions; and it is to be feared that, in the reaction against the old parrot-recitations as the beginning and end of instruction, the extreme value of verbal recitation as an element of complete training may nowadays be too much forgotten.

When we turn to modern pedagogics, we see how enormously the field of reactive conduct has been extended by the introduction of all those methods of concrete object teaching which are the glory of our contemporary schools. Verbal reactions, useful as they are, are insufficient. The pupil's words may be right, but the conceptions corresponding to them are often direfully wrong. In a modern school, therefore, they form only a small part of what the pupil is required to do. He must keep notebooks, make drawings, plans, and maps, take measurements, enter the laboratory and perform experiments, consult authorities, and write essays. He must do in his fashion what is often laughed at by outsiders when it appears in prospectuses under the title of 'original work,' but what is really the only possible training for the doing of original work thereafter. The most colossal improvement which recent years have seen in secondary education lies in the introduction of the manual training schools; not because they will give us a people more handy and practical for domestic life and better skilled in trades, but because they will give us citizens with an entirely different intellectual fibre. Laboratory work and shop work engender a habit of observation, a knowledge of the difference between accuracy and vagueness, and an insight into nature's complexity and into the inadequacy of all abstract verbal accounts of real phenomena, which once wrought into the mind, remain there as lifelong possessions. They confer precision; because, if you are *doing* a thing, you must do it definitely right or definitely wrong. They give honesty; for, when you express yourself by making things, and not by using words, it becomes impossible to dissimulate your vagueness or ignorance by ambiguity. They beget a habit of self-reliance; they keep the interest and attention always cheerfully engaged, and reduce the teacher's disciplinary functions to a minimum.

Of the various systems of manual training, so far as woodwork is concerned, the Swedish Sloyd system, if I may have an opinion on such matters, seems to me by far the best, psychologically considered. Manual training methods, fortunately, are being slowly but surely introduced into all our large cities. But there is still an immense distance to traverse before they shall have gained the extension which they are destined ultimately to possess.

No impression without expression, then,—that is the first pedagogic fruit of our evolutionary conception of the mind as something instrumental to adaptive behavior. But a word may be said in continuation. The expression itself comes back to us, as I intimated a moment ago, in the form of a still farther impression,—the impression, namely, of what we have done. We thus receive sensible news of our behavior and its results. We hear the words we have spoken, feel our own blow as we give it, or read in the bystander's eyes the success or failure of our conduct. Now this return wave of impression pertains to the completeness of the whole experience, and a word about its importance in the schoolroom may not be out of place.

It would seem only natural to say that, since after acting we normally get some return impression of result, it must be well to let the pupil get such a return impression in every possible case. Nevertheless, in schools where examination marks and 'standing' and other returns of result are concealed, the pupil is frustrated of this natural termination of the cycle of his activities, and often suffers from the sense of incompleteness and uncertainty; and there are persons who defend this system as encouraging the pupil to work for the work's sake, and not for extraneous reward. Of course, here as elsewhere, concrete experience must prevail over psychological deduction. But, so far as our psychological deduction goes, it would suggest that the pupil's eagerness to know how well he does is in the line of his normal completeness of function, and should never be balked except for very definite reasons indeed.

Acquaint them, therefore, with their marks and standing and prospects, unless in the individual case you have some special practical reason for not so doing.

One of the key concepts introduced in Jamesian psychology was the "stream of consciousness," which was his way of expressing his belief that consciousness was an active business, engaged in the constant task of interpreting the data of experience. This placed on the individual the responsibility of constant and inescapable choice with regard to these data—to ignore, to emphasize, etc.

In the last analysis, James went on to say, education consists of the organizing of resources in the human being, "of powers of conduct which will fit him to his social and physical world." Education then, said James, could be briefly defined as "the organization of acquired habits of conduct and tendencies to behavior." The educated man, drawing upon his storehouse of examples and abstract conceptions, would be able to cope with novel and unique circumstances. The uneducated man could deal only with "the most habitual circumstances," his capacity for the novel, the different, was nil.

We have seen thus far a few examples of some of the major voices that called for the reform of the schools at the turn of the century and some of the theoretical support for educational change. There were, of course, other sources. Greatly increased non-Nordic immigration to America created the problem of "Americanization" of the immigrant and his children, and a failing apprenticeship system was unable to cope with the demands of an increasingly industrial society. All turned to the schools for an alleviation of social problems. From the agriculturalist who wished to revitalize American rural life and halt the mass exodus of rural youth to the urban industrial centers to the settlement worker who wished to restore a sense of community to the urban industrial neighborhoods, voices were raised for educational reform. As the emminent jurist, Roscoe Pound, has observed, our real and abiding faith is not in government but in education.

In essence, the school was being asked to expand its role, to take upon itself functions that other social institutions had demonstrated themselves incapable of handling adequately. The family and the community were not performing their traditional educational tasks, so the school was being asked to fill the void. This new interpretation of the proper relationship of the school to society was given eloquent statement by the then director of the University of Chicago Laboratory School, Dr. John Dewey, in 1899. Dewey was defending the radical curriculum of his school, particularly with regard to its manual training, against his critics. The following reading has been excerpted from his "The School and Society," originally given as three lectures to the parents and supporters of the Laboratory School and subsequently published as a pamphlet under the same title.

105. The School and Social Progress

John Dewey

We are apt to look at the school from an individualistic standpoint, as something between teacher and pupil, or between teacher and parent. That which interests us most is naturally the progress made by the individual child of our acquaintance, his normal physical development, his advance in ability to read, write, and figure, his growth in the knowledge of geography and history, improvement in manners, habits of promptness, order, and industry—it is from such standards as these that we judge the work of the school. And rightly so. Yet the range of the outlook needs to be enlarged. What the best and wisest parent wants for his own child, that must the community want for all of its children. Any other ideal for our schools is narrow and unlovely; acted upon, it destroys our democracy. All that society has accomplished for itself is put, through the agency of the school, at the disposal of its future members. All its better thoughts of itself it hopes to realize through the new possibilities thus opened to its future self. Here individualism and socialism are at one. Only by being true to the full growth of all the individuals who make it up, can society by any chance be true to itself. And in the self-direction thus given, nothing counts as much as the school, for, as Horace Mann said, "Where anything is growing, one former is worth a thousand re-formers."

Whenever we have in mind the discussion of a new movement in education, it is especially necessary to take the broader, or social, view, Otherwise, changes in the school institution and tradition will be looked at as the arbitrary inventions of particular teachers, at the worst transitory fads, and at the best merely improvements in certain details—and this is the plane upon which it is too customary to consider school changes. It is as rational to conceive of the locomotive or the telegraph as personal devices. The modification going on in the method and curriculum of education is as much a product of the changed social situation, and as much an effort to meet the needs of the new society that is forming, as are changes in modes of industry and commerce.

. . . . .

The change that comes first to mind, the one that overshadows and even controls all others, is the industrial one—the application of science resulting in the great inventions that have utilized the forces of nature

Reprinted from *John Dewey on Education: Selected Writings,* edited by Reginald D. Archambault, courtesy of Random House, Inc., pp. 294-310.

on a vast and inexpensive scale: the growth of a world-wide market as the object of production, of vast manufacturing centers to supply his market, of cheap and rapid means of communication and distribution between all its parts.

. . . . .

Back of the factory system lies the household and neighborhood system. Those of us who are here today need go back only one, two, or at most three generations, to find a time when the household was practically the center in which were carried on, or about which were clustered, all the typical forms of industrial occupation. The clothing worn was for the most part not only made in the house, but the members of the household were usually familiar with the shearing of the sheep, the carding and spinning of the wool, and the plying of the loom. Instead of pressing a button and flooding the house with electric light, the whole process of getting illumination was followed in its toilsome length from the killing of the animal and the trying of fat to the making of wicks and dipping of candles. The supply of flour, of lumber, of foods, of building materials, of household furniture, even of metal ware, of nails, hinges, hammers, etc., was in the immediate neighborhood, in shops which were constantly open to inspection and often centers of neighborhood congregation. The entire industrial process stood revealed, from the production on the farm of the raw materials till the finished article was actually put to use. Not only this, but practically every member of the household had his own share in the work. The children, as they gained in strength and capacity, were gradually initiated into the mysteries of the several processes. It was a matter of immediate and personal concern, even to the point of actual participation.

We cannot overlook the factors of discipline and of character-building involved in this: training in habits of order and of industry, and in the idea of responsibility, of obligation to do something, to produce something, in the world. There was always something which really needed to be done, and a real necessity that each member of the household should do his own part faithfully and in coöperation with others. Personalities which became effective in action were bred and tested in the medium of action. Again, we cannot overlook the importance for educational purposes of the close and intimate acquaintance got with nature at first hand, with real things and materials, with the actual processes of their manipulation, and the knowledge of their social necessities and uses. In all this there was continual training of observation, of ingenuity, constructive imagination, of logical thought, and of the sense of reality acquired through first-hand contact with actualities. The educative forces of the domestic spinning and weaving, of the sawmill, the gristmill, the cooper shop, and the blacksmith forge, were continuously operative.

.   .   .   .   .

At present, concentration of industry and division of labor have practically eliminated household and neighborhood occupations—at least for educational purposes. But it is useless to bemoan the departure of the good old days of children's modesty, reverence, and implicit obedience, if we expect merely by bemoaning and by exhortation to bring them back. It is radical conditions which have changed, and only an equally radical change in education suffices. We must recognize our compensations—the increase in toleration, in breadth of social judgment, the larger acquaintance with human nature, the sharpened alertness in reading signs of character and interpreting social situations, greater accuracy of adaptation to differing personalities, contact with greater commercial activities. These considerations mean much to the city-bred child of today. Yet there is a real problem: how shall we retain these advantages, and yet introduce into the school something representing the other side of life—occupations which exact personal responsibilities and which train the child in relation to the physical realities of life?

When we turn to the school, we find that one of the most striking tendencies at present is toward the introduction of so-called manual training, shopwork, and the household arts—sewing and cooking.

This has not been done "on purpose," with a full consciousness that the school must now supply that factor of training formerly taken care of in the home, but rather by instinct, by experimenting and finding that such work takes a vital hold of pupils and gives them something which was not to be got in any other way. Consciousness of its real import is still so weak that the work is often done in a half-hearted, confused, and unrelated way. The reasons assigned to justify it are painfully inadequate or sometimes even positively wrong.

If we were to cross-examine even those who are most favorably disposed to the introduction of this work into our school system, we should, I imagine, generally find the main reasons to be that such work engages the full spontaneous interest and attention of the children. It keeps them alert and active, instead of passive and receptive; it makes them more useful, more capable, and hence more inclined to be helpful at home; it prepares them to some extent for the practical duties of later life—the girls to be more efficient house managers, if not actually cooks and sempstresses; the boys (were our educational system only adequately rounded out into trade schools) for their future vocations. I do not underestimate the worth of these reasons. Of those indicated by the changed attitude of the children I shall indeed have something to say in the next chapter, when speaking directly of the relationship of the school to the child. But the point of view is, upon the whole, unnecessarily narrow. We must conceive of work in wood and metal, of weaving, sewing, and cooking, as methods of life, not as distinct studies.

We must conceive of them in their social significance, as types of the processes by which society keeps itself going, as agencies for bringing home to the child some of the primal necessities of community life, and as ways in which these needs have been met by the growing insight and ingenuity of man; in short, as instrumentalities through which the school itself shall be made a genuine form of active community life, instead of a place set apart in which to learn lessons.

. . . . .

The great thing to keep in mind, then, regarding the introduction into the school of various forms of active occupation, is that through them the entire spirit of the school is renewed. It has a chance to affiliate itself with life, to become the child's habitat, where he learns through directed living, instead of being only a place to learn lessons having an abstract and remote reference to some possible living to be done in the future. It gets a chance to be a miniature community, an embryonic society. This is the fundamental fact, and from this arise continuous and orderly sources of instruction. Under the industrial *régime* described, the child, after all, shared in the work, not for the sake of the sharing, but for the sake of the product. The educational results secured were real, yet incidental and dependent. But in the school the typical occupations followed are freed from all economic stress. The aim is not the economic value of the products, but the development of social power and insight. It is this liberation from narrow utilities, this openness to the possibilities of the human spirit, that makes these practical activities in the school allies of art and centers of science and history.

. . . . .

Our school methods, and to a very considerable extent our curriculum, are inherited from the period when learning and command of certain symbols, affording as they did the only access to learning, were all-important. The ideals of this period are still largely in control, even where the outward methods and studies have been changed. We sometimes hear the introduction of manual training, art, and science into the elementary, and even the secondary, schools deprecated on the ground that they tend toward the production of specialists—that they detract from our present scheme of generous, liberal culture. The point of this objection would be ludicrous if it were not often so effective as to make it tragic. It is our present education which is highly specialized, one-sided, and narrow. It is an education dominated almost entirely by the mediaeval conception of learning. It is something which appeals for the most part simply to the intellectual aspect of our natures, our desire to learn, to accumulate information, and to get control of the symbols of learning; not to our impulses and tendencies to make, to do, to create, to produce, whether in the form of utility or of art. The very fact that manual training, art, and science are objected to as technical, as tending toward mere specialism, is of itself as good testimony as could be offered to the specialized aim which controls current education. Unless education had been virtually identified with the exclusively intellectual pursuits, with learning as such, all these materials and methods would be welcome, would be greeted with the utmost hospitality.

While training for the profession of learning is regarded as the type of culture, as a liberal education, that of a mechanic, a musician, a lawyer, a doctor, a farmer, a merchant, or a railroad manager is regarded as purely technical and professional. The result is that which we see about us everywhere—the division into "cultured" people and "workers," the separation of theory and practice. Hardly 1 per cent of the entire school population ever attains to what we call higher education; only 5 per cent to the grade of our high school; while much more than half leave on or before the completion of the fifth year of the elementary grade. The simple facts of the case are that in the great majority of human beings the distinctively intellectual interest is not dominant. They have the so-called practical impulse and disposition. In many of those in whom by nature intellectual interest is strong, social conditions prevent its adequate relization. Consequently by far the larger number of pupils leave school as soon as they have acquired the rudiments of learning, as soon as they have enough of the symbols of reading, writing, and calculating to be of practical use to them in getting a living. While our educational leaders are talking of culture, the development of personality, etc., as the end and aim of education, the great majority of those who pass under the tuition of the school regard it only as a narrowly practical tool with which to get bread and butter enough to eke out a restricted life. If we were to conceive our educational end and aim in a less exclusive way, if we were to introduce into educational processes the activities which appeal to those whose dominant interest is to do and to make, we should find the hold of the school upon its members to be more vital, more prolonged, containing more of culture.

But why should I make this labored presentation? The obvious fact is that our social life has undergone a thorough and radical change. If our education is to have any meaning for life, it must pass through an equally complete transformation. This transformation is not something to appear suddenly, to be executed in a day by conscious purpose. It is already in progress. Those modifications of our school system which often appear (even to those most actively concerned with them, to say nothing of their spectators) to be mere changes of detail, mere improvement within the school mechanism, are in reality signs and evidences of evolution. The introduction of active occupations, of nature-study, of elementary science, of art, of history; the relegation of the merely symbolic and formal to a secondary position; the change in the moral school atmosphere, in the relation of pupils and teachers—of discipline; the introduction of more active, expressive, and self-directing factors—all these are not mere accidents, they are necessities of the larger social evolution. It remains but to organize all these factors, to appreciate them in their fulness of meaning, and to put the ideas and ideals involved into complete, uncompromising possession of our school system. To do this means to make each one of our schools an embryonic community life, active with types of occupations that reflect the life of the larger society and permeated throughout with the spirit of art, history, and science. When the school introduces and trains each child of society into membership within such a little community, saturating him with the spirit of service, and providing him with the instruments of effective self-direction, we shall have the deepest and best guaranty of a larger society which is worthy, lovely, and harmonious.

SECTION 3

Some Progressive Schools

Although Joseph Rice, in his series of dramatic articles for *The Forum* in 1893, found many shocking examples of corrupt and merely mundane educational practices, he also found some to illustrate his contention that there was a "progressive" spirit at work on the educational scene. One such example he offered was that of the Cook County Normal School in Illinois, which had been operating since about 1883 under the directorship of Colonel F. W. Parker. Under

Parker, the school had assembled a faculty that Rice claimed was "one of the most enthusiastic, earnest, progressive, and thoughtful corps of teachers that may be found anywhere." In the following selection, Rice described this school for his readers.

106. The Cook County Normal School

Joseph M. Rice

Of all the schools that I have seen I know of none that shows so clearly what is implied by an educational ideal as the Cook County Normal School, the school that for ten years has been in charge of Colonel Francis W. Parker, who, as is almost too well known to require mention, has done as much if not more than any other single person to spread the doctrine of the new education throughout our country. That the school does not accomplish all that it desires to do and that it still has a long road to travel before it reaches perfection, no one feels more keenly than Colonel Parker himself. As in other schools mistakes are made by the pupils in grammar and in spelling, some problems in arithmetic are inaccurately performed, some of the nature-paintings are daubs, some of the color-work is unharmonious, some of the wood-work made by the children could not command a high price in the market. Indeed, taken all in all, the results as measured on the scale of one hundred are no better and no poorer than those in other progressive American schools.

In one regard, however, namely, as a source of inspiration to those who desire to enter the profession, it is almost an ideal. This is true for two reasons: First, the school is almost unique in its suggestiveness, due to the attempt on the part of the teachers to conduct all the work on purely psychological principles, to the completeness of the school from the standpoint of the "all-side" development of the child, and to the manner in which are utilized the opportunities to bring the child into close contact with nature in the beautiful park of twenty acres in which the school is situated. Secondly, Colonel Parker possesses to a remarkable degree the power to inspire his students. Of many institutions it may be said that they are the sources of knowledge, but of few that they are the sources of wisdom. Colonel Parker does not aim to convert his students into storehouses of knowledge, into walking encyclopedias, but rather to impress them with the idea that when they leave the school they will have received but a glimpse of the infinite; and they do feel when they leave

Reprinted from Joseph M. Rice, "The Public Schools of Minneapolis and Others," *The Forum*, XV (Mar-Aug 1893), pp. 373-376.

him that the development of the human mind is indeed a difficult problem, and that in justice to their pupils they are in duty bound ever to seek such light as will guide them in solving the problem. Colonel Parker sends out into the world no full-grown trees, but only seedlings. In unfavorable soil the seedlings wither or are stunted in their growth; but when the soil in which they are planted is favorable to their growth, they develop into tall and beautiful trees.

The faculty of the Normal School is one of the most enthusiastic, earnest, progressive, and thoughtful corps of teachers that may be found anywhere, and they are continually growing. The reason why the results in the primary and grammar grades are not, under these favorable conditions, superior to those obtained in other progressive schools is that it is extremely difficult to find teachers equal to the task and to retain the competent ones after they have become imbued with the spirit of the school. The corps of teachers in the elementary department is, therefore, a very unstable one, and, it being consequently necessary continually to initiate new teachers into this difficult work, it is natural that imperfections should arise. That it is much more difficult for the grades than it is for the normal department to obtain thorough teachers and to retain them after they have had experience in the school is also natural, when the salaries paid to the grade teachers are only, say, one-third as large as those paid to the teachers of the normal department. The great difficulty under which the schools of Quincy, Massachusetts, have been laboring, since Colonel Parker made them famous, is that the Quincy teachers are so much in demand that the mere fact of having taught for a year or two at Quincy raises the teachers above the Quincy salaries. Last year as many as one-third of the whole number of teachers left the Quincy schools because higher salaries had been offered to them in other cities.

In the primary and the grammar grades of the school, the work is conducted on the same general lines as that of Minneapolis and La Porte. A great deal of attention is given to the unification of studies, Colonel Parker being a strong advocate of this educational principle; and in his talks to his students he is constantly impressing its value upon their minds. Throughout the school, the curriculum includes the sciences, literature, and the artistic lines of work such as designing, color-work, and drawing and painting from nature. There is also a complete course in manual training. Language, and to a certain extent arithmetic, are taught incidentally in connection with the other subjects rather than directly, and from the start the pupils are led to illustrate their compositions. In geography the work is made as objective as possible by means of the moulding-board, relief maps, pictures, and the magic-lantern, and from time to time the pupils are taken on geographical excursions. In history and in literature the work is in many respects excellent. The courses for the whole school are planned by the members of the normal school faculty who have special charge of the various subjects throughout the school. In the lowest primary grade, which for many years has been in charge of Miss Griswold, the work appeared to me to be very suggestive, and particularly in regard to busy-work. Several groups of children were doing busy-work at the same time, and in no two groups was it alike. In one group the pupils were painting a flower that they had just been studying, in another they were writing a story about an animal that had just been utilized in a lesson in reading as well as in number, in a third they were reading silently in their reading-books. In teaching children to read much attention is given to phonics. . . .

Probably the most famous of the early experimental schools was that started by the Deweys at the University of Chicago in 1896. This "laboratory school" was under the direct supervision of Dewey until 1904 (when he embarked for his epochal stay at Columbia). The school was to test empirically the theoretical educational principles evolved by John Dewey and stated in "The School and Society." The following readings are excerpts from the account of this school written by two of its teachers. The first illustrates the pedagogical practice as it affected a group of six-year-olds embarked upon the exciting study of "occupations serving the household."

107. Teaching Methods in the Laboratory School

K. C. Mayhew and A. C. Edwards

The general method of the classroom, for the most part, followed a certain daily order. At the beginning of the period, the children were given time for the exchange of the amenities of the day usual to a group of persons meeting after an absence. This general conversation was soon directed by the teacher to the business of the day. The results of previous work were reviewed in a group process, and plans for further develop-

From *The Dewey School, The Laboratory School of the University of Chicago, 1896-1903*, by Katherine Camp Mayhew and Anna Camp Edwards. Copyright, 1936, By D. Appleton-Century Company, Inc. Reprinted by permission of Appleton-Century-Crofts, Division of Meredith Publishing Company, pp. 80-85.

ment were discussed. Each child was encouraged to contribute, either out of his past experience or his imagination, ways and means of meeting the problem of needs that might arise under new circumstances. These suggestions were discussed by the group, and with the aid of the teacher, the plans for the work of the day were decided upon and delegated. At the close of the period, there was again a group meeting when the results, if successful, were summarized, and new plans for further work at the next period suggested.

The first project of the year started off with the building of a farm-house and barn out of large blocks varying in size up to six inches. In order to find the dimensions of their square houses, the children added the lengths of the blocks on one side and found the sum to be twelve inches or one foot. A plan for a chicken coop of manilla paper was then discussed and was finally marked off in two- and three-inch lengths, a rough approximation to keep in scale with the house. In the meantime, attention was centered on the farm itself, and the decision was made to raise corn and wheat and to have sheep and a dairy. The land was divided into fields and pastures, which were then fenced. For this they gathered twigs (to take the place of logs in making a rail fence), cut them into six-inch lengths, and built the fence three rails high. Around their pastures, however, they decided to have a stone fence, as they thought this was stronger. Work continued to some extent on the farm-house. Boards were cut to proper lengths, with spaces for the door and windows. A chicken coop was started. In planning the back part of this, when laying off spaces for the windows and doors, it suddenly struck the children that the door was wider than it was high. One of the children went to another table and measured the door already laid off for the front of the farm-house, and came back with the correct dimensions. This was an encouraging indication of a developing power of initiative and judgment. The square, the triangle, and the ruler were used freely. Although they had used the latter only a short time, they were very apt in its use. They knew the inch and half-inch, but hesitated on the quarter-inch. In general, it was found that they all took manual directions very well and showed great ability to plan and a high degree of independence in the execution of their plans, doing all the measuring and sawing themselves. As the project developed they suggested many of the things necessary in the making of a suitable house. The interest was well-sustained. In the kindergarten these children had been accustomed to making things that could be finished in one day, but they worked on this for almost two weeks without any loss of interest.

Early in the fall the group measured off and cleaned a space in the school yard five by ten feet for planting their winter wheat. A method of plowing was discussed and at one child's suggestion, a sharp stick was used and the field prepared in which the wheat was sown. In their sand-box farm their imaginary crop had come to fruition and, like the sheaf brought in from the farm, was ready for threshing. The various parts of the whole plant and their uses were discussed with the conclusion that the seed was of most value to people. A list was made of the wheat foods they had eaten—breakfast foods of coarsely ground wheat, and bread and cake from the finely ground flour. They played that they were farmers and discussed the best means of getting the seeds from the hulls, as they called the process of threshing. At first they picked it out by hand. This was too slow, so they suggested beating it with a stick and found that only the edge of the stick struck the ground. The problem was taken to the shop director, and with the help of some questioning, the children decided that if the farmer had two sticks joined together, more of the stick would hit the grain and thus the work would be done more quickly. The handle of the flail was made twice as long as the part that hits the grain. The next stop was to experiment with the wheat they had threshed and winnowed. Accordingly, it was pounded in a mortar and compared to some fine, white flour. They saw that the inside of the grain was soft and white like the fine flour, but that it was mixed with coarse, yellow particles. A child suggested putting this meal through a sieve to separate the coarse from the fine. This was done, but although the meal was a good deal finer, some of the yellow particles still remained. They then wanted to put it through a still finer sieve, but as there was none convenient, the process of bolting was explained to them, and the flour was sifted through some cheese cloth. This took out all the yellow particles and left the flour fine and white. They had in the end about three tablespoonsful of it, which was used in making a cake.

The experimental work with the food products of the farm and the effect of heat upon them as demonstrated in the cooking bulked large in the daily activities of these children. The interests in this phase of their occupational work was keen and assumed great importance in the development of the whole project and particularly in their use of numbers. When they talked about grains in the classroom, they cooked cereals in the kitchen. For this they needed to learn to measure, to know how many teaspoons equal one tablespoon, how many tablespoons equal one cup, and so on. They discovered that two halves make a cupful, just the same as three thirds, or four quarters, and they came to talk about $\frac{1}{2}$, $\frac{1}{3}$, or $\frac{1}{4}$ of a cupful, with ease and certainty. It was easy for them to see that $\frac{5}{3}$ of a cup of water is 1 and $\frac{2}{3}$ of a cup.

Much also of the number work was related to the construction work done on their farm or in connection with it. When their sand-table farm had to be divided into several fields for wheat, corn, oats, and also for the house and the barn, the children used a one-foot ruler as a unit of measurement and came to understand what was meant by "fourths and halves"—the divisions made, though not accurate, were near enough to allow them to mark off their farm. As they became more familiar with the ruler and learned the half-foot, and the quarter-foot and inch, finer work was naturally expected of them and obtained. Their use of this tool made it easy to distinguish those children who had had a kindergarten education from those who had just entered the group. When building the farm-house, four posts were needed for the corners and six or seven slats, all of the same height. In measuring the latter, the children frequently forgot to keep the left-hand edge of the ruler on the left-hand side of the slat, so the measurements had to be repeated two or three times before they were correct. What they did to one side of the house, they also did to the other and naturally worked more rapidly and more accurately as the work was repeated.

A new game of dominoes, invented by one of the teachers, did much to interest the children in the composition of numbers. Each domino had lines in place of dots. These when joined make numbers. A child is asked to take eight blocks. At first, he takes one block at a time, eight times. He builds his eight and is asked what he sees in it. He may see four and four or five and three. When all the compositions of eight are exhausted, he is asked how he can take eight blocks more rapidly than just one at a time. He may say: "Take six in one hand and two in the other," or "four in one hand and four in the other," and then proceeds to demonstrate this, by building an eight with a six and two, a four and four, and so on. This was done with all numbers up to twenty. When they came to the number ten, a child was asked to count the fingers on both hands and when he answered ten, was told that he had counted "once around his fingers," and a symbol for that was "1 (once) O round." The children agreed this might have been the development of our "10." Twenty was then twice (2) around and so on. In making eleven, twelve, and the "teens," they built their ten and began again to build another ten, but the blocks gave out (purposely). One of the blocks from each child's set was marked with a blue chalk line, and this marked block represented ten. So when they made eleven, twelve, etc., they made it with the ten block and one or two more. They were interested and understood quickly. The report comments "the children of these two groups seem to be mathematically inclined, and numbers are a pleasure to them."

An interest in reading also developed during these weeks, starting in a game which necessitated it. All the things they had found in their outdoor excursions were placed on a table. Sentences were written on the board, such as: "Find a cocoon," and the child who could read it was allowed to run and get the cocoon. After playing this game a few times, the same sentences were shown printed in large type, so that they would get the printed forms simultaneously with the script. They seemed very eager to read and decided themselves to make a weekly record of their work. This record was printed from time to time in large type and was reread with undiminished interest. One of the children brought David Starr Jordan's *The Story of Knight and Barbara* to school. Knight and Barbara were children of three and six, who retold and illustrated the stories that had been told to them. The children were so pleased with the book that they thought they would like to make one like it and at once set to work on the fable of the Hare and the Tortoise as the first story for their book. The story was told to them and they retold about one half of it at one sitting. This took some time as considerable discussion was necessary to make their story logical and clear. The story was written on the board and, when completed, was printed in large type on the charts, and later in small type for their books. The group seems to have shown the same sustained interest in reading and in finishing these books that they did in the making of their farm and, in general, exhibited a rather remarkable ability to concentrate on all phases of their work.

Progressive education, as Dewey saw it, was the response of the school to meet the changed circumstances and demands of an industrialized society that had uprooted so many of the educative aspects of the pre-industrial home and community.

William Wirt, in the booming industrial city of Gary, Indiana, was one of Dewey's followers who attempted this task—essentially that of restoring the community concept within an urban industrial complex. His "Gary Plan" made the school the nucleus of a community, the center of intellectual and artistic endeavors. Open twelve months of the year, the Gary schools under Wirt were set up as complete communities (in miniature) to serve as centers of social improvement. Although the alleged economies of the Gary schools were hotly contested, one observer at least was completely "sold" on the system. This was the influential journalist and critic, Randolph Bourne. Bourne's laudatory articles in *The New Republic* put the "Gary Plan" before its many readers, giving it a place second to none in the pre-war progressive scene. In the following selection from the April 24, 1915, issue of *The New Republic*, Bourne describes vocational training in the Gary schools.

108. Apprentices to the School

Randolph S. Bourne

Vocational training in the schools of Gary means that whatever work is necessary in the way of repairing, conserving, beautifying or enhancing the facilities, is done by the school itself. These large, lavishly equipped modern school-buildings require a force of mechanics to keep them in repair. Their shops are the industrial and manual shops for the school. The children work in them with skilled union workmen, who are employed not primarily as "manual training" teachers, but as assistants to the building superintendent. The mechanics teach by allowing the children to help them as apprentices. They earn their salaries by repair and construction work, while the children who desire it get an incomparable vocational training at practically no cost to the town. Where the ordinary trade-school must have large classes to make the enterprise pay, the Gary vocational work may be done with the smallest groups, for the shops are paying for themselves anyway.

Manual training takes on quite a new meaning as you move about, watching the boys in the carpenter-shop making desks or tables, or cabinets for the botany collections, or book-racks for the library, sending them on to the paint-shop when they have finished; boys in the sheet-metal shop hammering zinc for the roof; young electricians repairing bells; a couple of plumbers tinkering with pipes; little groups of serious and absorbedly interested boys in the foundry and forge and pattern-making shop, all cooperating like the parts of a well-ordered factory. There was obviously enough real work to keep busy for his hour a day every child who desired training in a trade. Where school and workshop are thus fused, the need for "continuation" and "cooperative" courses—where the boy alternates between shop or factory and school—disappears. The child has the advantages of both.

The ordinary school, and even the specialized vocational school, is rarely doing more in its industrial, manual, or domestic science work than playing a rather dreary game with toys. There could scarcely be a greater contrast between the real shops of the Gary schools and those ordinary

Reprinted by permission from Randolph S. Bourne. "Apprentices to the School," *The New Republic*, II, 25 (April 1915), pp. 302-303.

"shops" and kitchens with their dozens of little machines at which at a given time the entire class does its little stereotyped "stunt." In Gary the domestic science room is a real kitchen in which the daily luncheon is prepared and served at cost to the teachers and pupils who desire it. The cook is a real cook, and the girls come in as observers, helpers or workers, just as the boys go into the shops. The nearest approach to a luxury is the pottery shop, but this is itself perhaps the best symbol of that fusion of the artistic and the practical that is the Wirt genius. What are you to say when you walk into the art studio and find half a dozen girls and boys high on a scaffolding painting a frieze which they have themselves designed, while others are at work on stained-glass designs to go in varnished paper on the panels of the door?

There is a genial, joyous quality about all the work that gives every room a charm—the foundry with its deep shadows, the smooth gray pottery shop with its turning wheels and bright glazed jugs, the botany room with its mass of greenery. Even the history room at Emerson School had the atmosphere which comes from concentrated interest and the slow accretion of significant material. Emerson itself is a spacious and dignified building with innumerable little touches of taste that one usually associates only with the high schools of exceptionally wealthy and cultivated suburban communities. It is a delightful paradox that so beautiful a life should appear to be lived where every activity seems to be motivated by direct utilitarian application. I said that you have to plough your mind up to understand this kind of school. Certainly I have never seen a place which more nearly permitted to seem real that old ideal of the joy of work which we imagine must have existed back in guild days. It may be left to the imagination what children trained in such a school are likely to have to say to the industrial society in which we live.

The practical work of the school is only limited by local school needs, but the shoeless condition of some of the Froebel children inspired the starting of a shoe shop where old shoes were made over. Both Emerson and Froebel have a printery from which come all the blanks, reports, programs, etc., used in the school, as well as the bulletins and papers by which the various classes are tempted to preserve the good things they write. The commercial pupils have charge of all the accounting and bookkeeping as well as the supplies. The children who work in the shops are paid in checks, which are calculated on the basis of prevailing union wages for the working-time. This provides opportunities for a banking system, which is also in charge of the commercial class. In the Jefferson School the boiler-room is an integral part of the machine-shop.

The botany class was responsible for the beautiful and elaborate conservatory at the entrance of the Emerson School, and for the window hot-house in the botany room, where practical experiments are made. The botanists also have charge of the shrubs and trees on the grounds, and the vegetable gardens which they work communistically all through the summer. Their study of food and textile products ramified into the domestic science work, just as the zoology study was fused with physiology. This latter class had a playground zoo, with foxes and coyotes, raccoons and prairie-dogs, about whose habits and adventures they were preparing a brochure, which was already in press at the printery. When I stepped into the zoology laboratory itself. I found that I was in an even more animated zoo. Crows, chickens and pigeons in cages at the back of the room were lusty with vociferous greeting. The imperturbability of the children amidst this racket showed me how well aware they were that this was the way a zoology room ought to behave.

Such a school, where the child works almost unconsciously into a vocation which appeals to him as neither play nor drudgery, is far more "vocational" than even the specialized school. The child, beginning so young in shop or laboratory, and assimilating the work very gradually, is able to lay deep foundations of interest and skill. The Gary school is distinctly unspecialized. In a sense it gives a completely "liberal education." The child emerges a skilful amateur. The industrial and scientific work no more "train" him to take a definite place in the industrial world than the cultural work trains him to be a college professor. But he does leave school well equipped to cope with a dynamic, rapidly changing industrial society which demands above all things versatility, and which scraps methods and machines as ruthlessly as it does men. Only the man of rounded training and resourcefulness who can turn his hand quickly to a variety of occupations has much chance of success. Our public school, in spite of its fancied "liberal" curriculum, has really been turning out only very low-grade specialists. It has made no effort to produce the type of mind most needed today—the versatile machinist, the practical engineer, the mind that adapts and masters mechanism. This is probably the best intellectual type our society produces. This exactness, resourcefulness, inventiveness pragmatic judgment of a mechanism by its product, the sense of machinery as a means, not an end, are exactly the qualities that society demands in every profession or trade.

The Gary school is the first I have seen that promises to cultivate this kind of intelligence. It frankly accepts the machine not in the usual sense of the vocational schools, as an exacting master that the child is to learn docilely to obey, but as the basis of our modern life, by whose means we must make whatever progress we may will. The machine seems to be a thing to which society is irrevocably pledged. It is time the school recognized it. In Gary it is with the child from his earliest years. It is the motive of his scientific study. The physics teacher at the Emerson School told me that he thought the fascinating and irresponsible automobile had done more to educate the younger male generation than most of the public schools. Tinkering with an automobile was a whole scientific training.

I dropped into his physics class, and found a dozen twelve-year-old girls and their nine-year-old "helpers" studying the motor-cycle. With that fine disregard for boundaries which characterizes Gary education, the hour began with a spelling lesson of the names of the parts and processes of the machine. After the words were learned, the mechanism was explained to them as they pored over it, and their memory of vaporization, evaporation, etc., called into play. The motor-cycle was set going, the girls described its action, and the lesson was over, as perfect a piece of teaching as I have ever heard. The intense animation of that little group was all the more piquant for having as a background the astounded disapprobation of three grave school superintendents from the East.

To these physics classes the ventilating, heating and electric systems in the schools are all textbooks. The climate is studied. The shops provide many physics problems. There was a class of boys having explained to them the physical principles of various types of machines. The impetuous rush of those little boys as they were sent into the machine-shop to take apart a lawn-mower, a bicycle, and a cream-separator, and the look of elation on their faces, would alone make Gary unforgettable to me. It was evident that this was indeed a different kind of school.

Another public-school system moving along progressive educational lines was that of the little (pop. 5,600 in 1903) Wisconsin town of Menomonie. This system received considerable nationwide recognition, due to the journalistic talents of a follower in the Joseph Rice tradition who essentially duplicated his earlier expedition into the educational world. Adele Marie Shaw, during the period of 1903-1904, wrote a series of articles for *The World's Work* dealing with the schools of the country. The Menomonie system was one of the jewels of progressively oriented education unearthed by Shaw, and she lavished her praise upon it.

Initiated by the philanthropic activities of James Huff Stout, the Menomonie schools emphasized manual training, although a strong physical training system was also one of its features (it included boys and girls), as well as instruction in hygiene. The schools were community-oriented in the literal sense, utilized by adults as well as by children, and were excellent examples of the concept of the school as the nucleus of the community. Some of the activity that took place in the Menomonie schools may be seen in the following reading, which is a portion of the concluding Menomonie article of Adele Shaw which appeared in *The World's Work* under the title "The Ideal Schools of Menomonie."

109. The Ideal Schools of Menomonie

Adele Marie Shaw

These grammar-school lads that I saw were at work in a self-reliant, businesslike fashion upon a hickory step-ladder, a whitewood medicine-cabinet, a birch towel-roller, an oak piano-stool, red-birch inkstands, foot-stools, salt-boxes, collar and cuff boxes, plate-racks, picture-frames, and waste-baskets.

Care is taken to suit the instruction to the environment. I was attracted by a particularly smooth, strong sled. "We make sleds usually in the late fall," Mr. Bauersfeld explained. "Sleds and snow-shovels—and skees. When the band-saws break in a mill near by Mr. Stout gets them for us, and the sleds are shod with the best of steel." Everywhere I saw this inventive economy using old material in new ways. Some of the boxes were constructed from worn-out desk-tops.

"We make kites in the spring," Mr. Bauersfeld went on, "sometimes seventeen different kinds; and then we have a kite day and race airships on the kite-strings. They get a good deal of practice in mechanics out of the rigging of their airships," he twinkled.

Beyond the carpentry-room there was a little recitation-hall. A long work-counter allowed space for any practical demonstration the conductor of the classes wanted to use. From that and from a tool-room as complete and systematic as any library, with classified nails and classified saws, and from a fireproof vault where varnishes are stored which the pupils use in learning the arts of stains, fillers, shellac, and French polishing I emerged to see more *results*.

In this school Mr. Stout works out an occasional problem outside the curriculum. Once he asked a class of boys at the beginning of a year to

Reprinted from Adele Marie Shaw, "The Ideal Schools of Menomonie," *The World's Work*, VII (Nov. 1903-Apr. 1904), pp. 4541-4542.

"make something" quite independently. "Make anything you want to," he said. They wrestled faithfully, and the results were atrocious but interesting. Mr. Stout had found out what was in their minds. The objects were locked up and forgotten till the end of the year. Then they were produced, and great was the mirth of the class over their own work. They had learned since making these articles how to appreciate grace of outline as well as mechanical perfection. They could no longer conceive such crudities.

The material for this woodwork is bought in the rough, green lumber, and the instructors reduce it to any shape they wish. I looked at a mass of oak and birch and some slabs of red cherry that will some day be the superintendent's desk. It was carefully set up in the dry-kiln, the hot air circulating between the planks. Close at hand was the planing-mill, where blocks and boards are cut by the instructors into any shape desired. The economy and utility of this way of purchasing is evident even to a novice.

From the wood-working department I went into the iron-working rooms. I had spent much time in the immense forge-shop, where twenty-two "down-draft forges" were busy, and I had wandered in the din of anvils, and peered into hooded fires, and been startled by a trip-hammer controlled by a high-school boy of fifteen. I had gone somewhat breathless through a kind of royal machine-shop, where striplings were handling gigantic forces with a steady concentration that made the air alive. I had given to the extraordinary equipment of the mechanical drawing-room a more intelligent and less thrilled attention. I was ready for more lathes and draughting-boards. But I was not prepared for the foundry.

The pit and the crane, the bucket-ladle capable of producing a two-ton casting, the melting-room with its brass furnace, its "cupola" for iron, its floor of removable iron plates, its iron loading-stage beneath the floor, were vital with the sense of human mastery over material. In the faces of the boys bent over the machines this mastery had been plain—the tension of their work blended with the fine contentment of power rightly applied.

This was the work of the boys. The girls study "domestic science" in a department of six large sunny and well-arranged rooms.

DOMESTIC SCIENCE

The real interest in this work to a quick-witted girl is furnished in the pleasure of acquiring knowledge in the study of fabrics and textiles, manufactures and materials, in the working out of an original problem. A girl is given a group of foods to be reduced to their food elements by the study of scientific tables. If in the group (designed perhaps for a breakfast) the girl finds a food whose nourishing elements exist in an equal amount in a cheaper material, then the substitution is made and the cost reduced. To a group of girls is frequently given the preparation of one or two or three meals the cost of whose raw materials shall not exceed a definite amount. These meals are served to invited guests, chiefly fathers and mothers, and the entertainers take turns in acting as hosts and waiters.

One of these meals I saw in the process of serving. A high-school girl had been given a dollar, out of which she was to provide for twenty-five people. Here is the record:

Cream Tomato Soup
Croûtons

Veal Loaf   Potatoes

Bread and Butter
Milk

Tomatoes, 12 cents; veal, 40; potatoes, 14; bread, 15; milk, 15; butter, 10. Total, $1.06. Twenty-seven people served.

Deftness and a trim and accurate handling of materials, with the brain planning behind the work, are the objects for which the department labors under Miss Laura G. Day. Home experiments are recorded methodically, so that at the end of the year every child has card-catalogued her independent struggles. The children are known and their homes are known. Deception is practically impossible.

Progressive education of the pre-World-War-I years was oriented about the leitmotif of social reform through the schools. No better summation of this phase of progressive education may be found than was contained in the final section of *My Pedagogic Creed* by John Dewey.

110. Summation of a Creed

John Dewey

I Believe that

—education is the fundamental method of social progress and reform.

Reprinted from *John Dewey on Education: Selected Writings,* edited by Reginald D. Archambault, courtesy of Random House, Inc., pp. 437-439.

—all reforms which rest simply upon the enactment of law, or the threatening of certain penalties, or upon changes in mechanical or outward arrangements, are transitory and futile.

—education is a regulation of the process of coming to share in the social consciousness; and that the adjustment of individual activity on the basis of this social consciousness is the only sure method of social reconstruction.

—this conception has due regard for both the individualistic and socialistic ideals. It is duly individual because it recognizes the formation of a certain character as the only genuine basis of right living. It is socialistic because it recognizes that this right character is not to be formed by merely individual precept, example, or exhortation, but rather by the influence of a certain form of institutional or community life upon the individual, and that the social organism through the school, as its organ, may determine ethical results.

—in the ideal school we have the reconciliation of the individualistic and the institutional ideals.

—the community's duty to education is, therefore, its paramount moral duty. By law and punishment, by social agitation and discussion, society can regulate and form itself in a more or less haphazard and chance way. But through education society can formulate its own purposes, can organize its own means and resources, and thus shape itself with definiteness and economy in the direction in which it wishes to move.

—when society once recognizes the possibilities in this direction, and the obligations which these possibilities impose, it is impossible to conceive of the resources of time, attention, and money which will be put at the disposal of the educator.

—it is the business of every one interested in education to insist upon the school as the primary and most effective interest of social progress and reform in order that society may be awakened to realize what the school stands for, and aroused to the necessity of endowing the educator with sufficient equipment properly to perform his task.

—education thus conceived marks the most perfect and intimate union of science and art conceivable in human experience.

—the art of thus giving shape to human powers and adapting them to social service is the supreme art; one calling into its service the best of artists; that no insight, sympathy, tact, executive power, is too great for such service.

—with the growth of psychological service, giving added insight into individual structure and laws of growth; and with growth of social science, adding to our knowledge of the right organization of individuals, all scientific resources can be utilized for the purposes of education.

—when science and art thus join hands the most commanding motive for human action will be reached, the most genuine springs of human conduct aroused, and the best service that human nature is capable of guaranteed.

—the teacher is engaged, not simply in the training of individuals, but in the formation of the proper social life.

—every teacher should realize the dignity of his calling; that he is a social servant set apart for the maintenance of proper social order and the securing of the right social growth.

—in this way the teacher always is the prophet of the true God and the usherer in of the true kingdom of God.

World War I provided a turning point for educational thought and reform—a re-orientation of progressive educational practices and emphases. A professional organization, the Progressive Education Association, came into being in 1919, and educational reform acquired a centralized and organized voice. Passing into the hands of professional educators, the educational reform movement tended to be taken over by this group. Their professional jargon, which frequently managed to confuse prolixity with profundity, was but one instance in this professional isolation from the non-professional public. Progressivism in education was being cut off from its traditional ties with the lay public and becoming the intellectual plaything of the professional group.

A further influence, the attempt to make a science of education, set reform education apart from the interest and comprehension of the lay public. Based upon the emphasis toward scientism initiated by Edward L. Thorndike, this trend received a tremendous boost through the psychological testing for the U.S. Army during World War I. Extended usage of the famous "army alpha," a classification test, seemed to show the great potential for education in the measurement of intelligence.

This faith in the efficacy of psychological tests received a mixed response from educators. While some saw the classification of intelligence as a panacea for educational practice, others pointed out that as instruments of general classification the tests had merit, but to assume that they revealed a fixed and unalterable measure of *intelligence* was naive. Not only was a testing obsession naive, it was downright dangerous, stated some. John Dewey was one who saw the tendency to fit individuals into predetermined numerical niches of I.Q. scores as a perversion of democratic social progress. The controversy raged hot and heavy—and in a sense, although on a far more sophisticated level of psychometry, it still goes on.

Science was applied to the curriculum as well as to the psyche of the pupils. Studies of educational needs of society resulted in mountainous complications of statistical correlations, graphical analyses, and an imposing array of "scientific" trappings. No hazy metaphysical speculations for this segment of educational progressives, the cold clear light of empirical science would clear away the vague and terribly unscientific educational musings of an earlier decade. The curriculum constructors (or constricters, depending upon one's bias) went to work with a vengeance to make the art of education over into the science of pedagogy. What did people actually do as adults, what skills did they really acquire from their education? Answer these questions and you are on the way towards a curriculum scientifically articulated to real needs and requirements. What were the most efficient ways to transmit these skills to the students? A new methodology was born. Coldly efficient and economic, science became for some the savior of education.

On another progressive front, the post-war era of the 1920's ushered in an entirely different orientation. Far from both scientism and the earlier group-oriented social reformism, this facet of progressive educational thought saw as its mission the salvation of the creative individual from the threat of mass society. In the face of debilitating social pressures that were perceived as increasing encroachments upon the individual as a unique, creative entity, this group saw education as the means of salvation for individual expression. The school would enable the child to effectively free his own individual potential, to express himself as the unique human entity that he was, to counteract an increasingly constrictive conformist society.

These notions, enforced by the imported insights of Freud and his interpreters, gave birth to yet another phase of progressive education —the "child-centered" pedagogy of "creative self-expression." With a strong element of Rousseau confounded by psychoanalytical neologisms, this facet of progressive education quickly became the butt of cartoonists and wits. Indeed, to this day, it is quite probable that in the minds of many, this *was* progressive education. The earnest seekers of individual creative self-expression were satirized unmercifully in press and popular literature. Inevitably associated with the bearded bohemianism of Greenwich Village (indeed, the Village was a geographic locus of child-centered pedagogy), this group of progressive educators persevered in spite of ridicule and frequent abuse.

One of the most famous (or infamous) of the child-centered pedagogues was Caroline Pratt, whose "Play School" (later called the "City and Country School") was caricatured as the epitome of Greenwich Village expressionistic pedagogy. The following readings illustrate some of the activities of the Pratt school, as recorded by Caroline Pratt and Jesse Stanton in a 1926 book, *Before Books*. The first reading describes a group of thirteen children, aged three years, nine months to four years, six months, in the year 1920.

111. Before Books

Caroline Pratt and Jesse Stanton

FIRST WEEK

An illustration of the fact that the children connect the chimney and smoke was Murray's making smoke from the erasers just after Craig had brought him a chimney for his house. Craig, in placing a chimney on Mark's house, said, "This is for the little stove in the nursery." Murray's low house, which he said was a "country house," led to a discussion of the bungalow with rooms all on one floor. Cardboard was used as a roof for this house and after a time, Murray said, "This old roof is worn out," and taking it away, brought a fresh piece of cardboard and put it on. New articles of food that have appeared in grocery play are: prunes, macaroni, cinnamon, molasses, bread, butter, eggs, and fish. As Bianca brought Matthew too many groceries, we had a discussion as to what happens to

Reprinted by permission from Caroline Pratt and Jesse Stanton, *Before Books: Experimental Practices in the City and Country School* (New York: Adelphi Co., 1926), pp. 91-95.

food after being delivered. The processes of cooking it and eating it, and the disposal of refuse by putting it in the garbage can were gone over. The process of preparing clay for modelling purposes, by adding water, letting it stand, and then kneading it was discussed. Ice has been brought in from the yard and melted on the stove. When a child put ice in his pocket, we discussed the temperature of the body and the heating of clothing from the heat given off by the body. Medicine was administered to a sick animal that had been poisoned, and I told the children at the time of the danger of spoiled food. When we saw an ice wagon delivering ice on a trip later in the week, I emphasized again the necessity for keeping food at a low temperature. The use of the telephone in ordering food and the way of using the phone book were discussed. As a station for passengers has been built this week, we had a discussion of sleeping cars and the reason for dirt in trains described in the story of "The Journey."

SECOND WEEK

Murray, Matthew, Selma and I talked over freight on Monday, when Murray brought over a very long train for his track. I explained that freight trains were loaded with many different kinds of things—coal, food, furniture, machinery, etc. The children were interested in the new tin waste pipe for a nearby house, but this interest did not hold very long. They noticed the difference in color between the old and new pipe and Murray asked if they were going to paint the new pipe. The man said, "Yes." As the children did not ask "why," I did; and I showed them where the old pipe had rusted through. Christina asked one day, "Does flour make bread?" So we talked about the different foods it is used for. Murray said when they were playing foxes in the yard that the mother was going to lay an egg, so they could have some little foxes. I explained the mammalian method of reproduction. At lunch time on Wednesday, a story was told in which a pig was mentioned. He was branded at once as a smelly animal, so I told the children about the different ways of keeping pigs, and how this affected them. Skunks were mentioned as really smelly animals. The people in one of the children's stories went out and ate grass. This was challenged at once by, "People don't eat grass." I said, "No, but what grows in the field that they could eat?" Matthew said, "Blueberries," and someone else said, "Yes, but not if it was winter." When the block play has dealt with the transportation of milk, the empty cans have been returned to the country. On a trip last week, the children noticed empty milk bottles outside the houses. The only meat Murray seemed to be familiar with was chicken. He also said "pig," so I gave him the names of ham, bacon, and sausage;

and after he had slaughtered the cow—beef, roast beef, and beefsteak. A fire engine discussion again brought out the fact that Matthew, Christina, and Murray are clear on the point that water puts out the fires. I showed the children the ashes in our stove, in an attempt to clear up that difficulty. (See under IV Content of Play and Discussions, January, Third Week.) Paper and wood and matches were needed to start a fire, the children said. In this connection, it may be interesting to note that when Murray delivered meat at Bianca's house on Thursday, she was in the hall putting on her leggings; Christina wanted to put the meat on to cook at once, but Murray said no, they would have to wait for Bianca to get a match and light the fire. This shows how much more carefully the children are following through an idea. On Friday, we discussed the time of the appearance of the sun, moon, and stars in connection with Christina's drawing. All seemed clear on this. I am working with Bianca on the English names for parts of the body, using the dolls as illustrative material.

I had a discussion with the children playing butcher as to different methods of getting orders. Chops and chicken seemed to be the only meats known. Matthew knew that horses have to eat oats, and Bianca added, "If you don't eat you get dead." Christina made a garden by putting nails in a piece of wood and named the following flowers: sweet peas, dandelions, daisies, and poppies. New heels on Mark's shoes led to a discussion of the shoemaker and his business. We talked about the different parts of shoes —soles, heels, and tongues. At luncheon the next day, while talking about human tongues, a child said, "All shoes have tongues, too." Some one else added, "Except pumps," and another child, "And button shoes." Railroad tracks were covered with the sawdust collected from under the bench one morning, and the children told me it was "sand, to keep the engine from slipping." Mark's train, which carried food, led to a discussion of the dining car as well as the sleeping car. Both Christina and Matthew knew about this. Bianca ran a train which she called a "porter train." A lumber yard was talked about as a place where carpenters go when they want to get wood to build a house. The sand in the new sand pile was used as cement one day, so we talked about the uses of cement. Murray was playing with a piece of metal and he put his cup on it. As it swung back and forth it hit the metal and made a noise. Murray said, "That's a bell buoy." In answer to my question as to a bell buoy's use, he said, "It tells the ship not to go near the rocks." Hospital play showed a knowledge of the taking of rectal temperature, and the application of mustard plaster. We talked about the possibility of taking temperature by mouth, also. At lunch time on Friday, I was called away for a moment, and on my return, I found the children laughing heartily and saying, "Wouldn't it be funny if we drank our milk with our ears?" This was greeted with shrieks of laughter. Then another child would say, "Wouldn't it be funny if we drank our milk with our eyes?" "With our nose?"

Another well-known child-centered school was the "School of Organic Education" of Fairhope, Alabama. This was the product of Marietta Johnson. It was glowingly described by the Deweys in their *Schools of Tomorrow* (1915) and thus achieved a measure of fame in the world of progressive education. Founded in 1907, the school was pedagogically closer to Rousseau than to Dewey. Marietta Johnson went on to become an influential member of the Progressive Education Association in the post-World-War-I years. The following reading is her statement of the educational principles that governed and guided the School of Organic Education.

112. The School of Organic Education

Marietta Johnson

We believe the educational program should aim to meet the needs of the growing child. We believe that childhood is for itself and not a preparation for adult life. Therefore, the school program must answer the following questions:

What does the child of any particular age need to minister to the health of his body, to preserve the integrity of the intellect, and to keep him sincere and unselfconscious of spirit?

The answers to these questions will constitute the curriculum of the school, and as we grow in understanding of the nature and needs of childhood, the curriculum will change.

We believe that all children need music; therefore we give the younger children singing and dancing and singing games and all sorts of rhythmic work. As the children grow older, this work becomes folk dancing and folk singing, with reading of notes, singing harmonies, and learning to play an instrument at about ten or twelve years of age.

Time is given to dramatics throughout the school life.

Reprinted by permission from Marietta Johnson, "The Educational Principles of the School of Organic Education . . ." *Twenty-sixth NSSE Yearbook* (1927), Part I, pp. 349-351.

We believe that all children need creative handwork. This is the fundamental method of thinking. Therefore, all sorts of material are provided for self-expression. For the very young children, merely making things of clay and sand and using blocks may be sufficient. Later, this develops into real projects, using tools and art and craft materials. The creative handwork continues through all ages up to college. We believe it should continue through the college program. Handwork should grow out of, or be related to, work in history, literature, etc., as far as possible.

We believe that all childhood needs stories. The stories for the very young children would naturally take the form of folklore, and fables, and fairy tales; later on, the form of history, literature, and geography, after learning to read at about eight or nine years of age. This reading work would also result in composition and the study, perhaps, of grammar in the high-school period. The literature, history, and geography stories begun in the early years, would be replaced by the study of history, literature, and science as such in the high-school and college years.

The speech centers are developed very young. A child may learn a language other than his own at an early age, whereas he should not be obliged to read his own until he is eight or nine years of age. We would, therefore, give the children some experience in using a foreign language, such as Spanish or French.

All children need fundamental conceptions of number. The work of measuring, weighing, estimating, counting, begun in the early years, would naturally require the use of figures at about eight or ten, when the mechanics of number would be acquired with great delight. Later, the applied problems, and still later, the abstract problems, which are enjoyed during the high-school and college years.

In order to preserve unselfconsciousness in growth, no grades or marks should be given and no intellectual tasks set by the teacher. The children should be grouped according to chronological age. The teacher should provide suitable work for the group, with individual variation where necessary. The child should not do as he pleases; he does not know what is good for him. In order to preserve the unity of his intellectual and emotional life, intellectual work should accompany and follow sincere interest and desire, and the reward for all learning should be the inner satisfaction and the consciousness of power which comes through understanding.

All children should have free play, so every daily program should include much time in the open, much time in free, self-prompted occupations, and some time to dream. The fullest social association should be given.

We believe that education is life, growth; that the ends are immediate; that the end and the process are one. We believe that all children should have the fullest opportunity for self-expression, for joy, for delight, for intellectual stimulus through subject matter, but we do not believe that children should be made self-conscious or externalized by making subject matter an end. Our constant thought is not what do the children learn or do, but what are the "learning" and the "doing" doing to them.

We believe all children need Nature—not so much for facts as for experience and attitude. The Nature walks and talks of the little children would develop into serious Nature Study, gardening, and science of the older groups.

Every schoolroom must be a health center. In the measure that the school provides activities and exercises which tend to produce a sound, accomplished, beautiful body, an intelligent, sympathetic mind, a sweet, sincere spirit, it is educational. In the measure that it does not, it is not educational, however informational it may be.

We believe that society owes all children guidance, control, instruction, association, and inspiration—right conditions of growth— throughout the growing years until physical growth is completed. No child may know failure—all must succeed. Not "what do you know," but "what do you need," should be asked, and the *nature* of childhood indicates the answer.

As an example of more specific practices followed in the progressive school of the 1920's, the next selection throws some light upon the arrangement of studies. The school described is the Beaver Country Day School of Brookline, Massachusetts.

113. The Beaver Country Day School

Eugene R. Smith

Leaving this discussion of general principles, let us consider some of the more specific arrangements that result from them.

The social science central subject includes, as we have said, history, geography, civics, and current events. It might be said to be woven of two continuous threads of thought, one concerned with the pupils themselves, their surroundings, and their communities, from the smallest up to the United States and North America; the other taking up that which is more

Reprinted by permission from Eugene R. Smith, "The Principles of Curriculum-Making in The Beaver Country Day School," *Twenty-sixth NSSE Yearbook* (1927), Part I, pp. 323-325.

remote in time and place, and developing into a study of the world in general. In each one of the threads are involved the divisions already mentioned. The method for the study of those things immediate to the children, and particularly of those concerning their own country, is natural spiral as well as cumulative. The more important matters recur from year to year, each time with new and broader emphasis. The other thread is largely progressive, although of necessity repetition and enlargement must enter in from time to time. The thread concerned with the United States is thinner in the early stage, centering around holidays and other civic events, and coming often from likenesses and contrasts rather than from directly planned attack. Later on, it increases until it becomes the main thread, with the other as its adjunct.

In the three primary years, the children respond very strongly to primitive life, possibly because it is less complex and more easily understood by them than is present-day civilization, and so can be more easily used as material for imagination. Possibly also, because it to some extent parallels and interprets their own experiences in reaching out for the foundational things of life. This response is particularly strong in regard to the fundamental needs of food, clothing, and shelter. This second thread, therefore, takes the pupils into the lives of early uncivilized, or little civilized, peoples. Geography is accordingly little more than a condition of life until the third grade, where the more important land and water divisions and other geographical units become somewhat familiar.

The early civilizations, including those of Egypt, Palestine, and Greece, are used in the fourth year, with increasing consideration of geography in its relation to peoples and their problems. Much connection between this and the home-country thread comes out here through industrial and other comparisons. For example, the making of paper from papyrus may stimulate investigation of paper making to-day, clothing problems then and now may be compared, or the progress of the art of various countries may be traced.

In the fifth year, we found a very strong interest in the history of Europe, strongest perhaps in the period of chivalry. Consequently, Roman history is followed by mediaeval history and leads up to the European foundations for the study of United States history. The geography of Europe naturally accompanies its history, but since earlier Roman history gives an impetus for the study of Africa, that continent precedes Europe. The study of Africa, once started, naturally goes beyond what is needed for the Roman period and its general aspects are completed at this time.

The period of American exploration opens the sixth year, bringing in the continents of South and North America as a necessary accompaniment. The geography of the Oriental countries is studied almost as a separate subject, taken to complete the view of the world. Yet in many ways, it also connects with, and contrasts with, other parts of the social studies.

The first years of the junior high school probe rather deeply into present-day life, centering study about our own problems, but following our trade relations, our transportation, and our foreign affairs into all corners of the globe. It is expected that at the end of the eighth year the pupils shall have considerable knowledge and wide interests in regard to mankind, the conditions affecting his progress, and his problems, past and present.

The social sciences of the later years of the course are necessarily college preparatory histories, for which current outlines and textbooks are the foundation.

The mathematics is not hurried in the early primary years, coming in the first and second classes rather as a response to practical needs and game interests than as a superimposed task. Gradually, it takes a larger part in the curriculum, following the recommendations of various psychologists and committees and particularly the report of the National Committee. In this, as in all of the tool subjects, progress is regularly tested by standardized tests, which are used not only for diagnostic purposes, but also as a safeguard to the maintenance of curriculum standards and completeness.

The formal English is based on the usage necessary at each stage of progress: that usage is both oral and written, and comes partly from other subjects and partly from the inspiration of each pupil's reading in poetry and prose. Literature increases its proportion of the time as the pupils grow older. Oral English is required throughout the high school and much opportunity is given for presiding at meetings, writing and presenting plays, and other practical language applications.

The academic subjects for the last four years are to a large extent determined by college entrance requirements, although their content is sometimes modified or supplemented to suit individual or group needs. These requirements are, of course, considered as minimal essentials, rather than complete outlines. . . .

A well-known, but worth repeating, illustration of the progressive methodology is the unit of study related to boats. This unit, conceived for the third grade of the Lincoln Experimental School of Columbia University, was initiated by Miss Nell Curtis of the Lincoln staff. The following chart is the final unit of study as it evolved under two years of experiment by Miss Martha Groggel.

114. Study Unit on Boats

A UNIT OF STUDY RELATED TO

BOATS

THIRD GRADE

PROBLEMS-QUESTIONS

STIMULA-TION

In the spring of last year many of the boys of this group were interested in trains and other means of travel.

Many summer experiences with boats.

Wood in supply box cut in shapes suggestive of boats.

Bulletin prepared by the teacher.

Trip to see Half-Moon.

Trip to see boat models.

To construct boats that will look like a certain kind and with which children can play.

How do boats "go"?

Who first thought of making a sailboat?

How did people get the idea for different shapes for boats?

To know more about the people who traveled on the seas in early times.

To find out about the making of boats.

How many different kinds of boats do we have today and how is each kind used?

How did early people use their ships?

To find out about the different parts of a boat.

How do people know how much to put into a boat before it will sink?

Reprinted by permission from Otis W. Caldwell, "The Lincoln Experimental School" *Twenty-sixth NSSE yearbook*, Part 1, pp. 281-282.

SUBJECT MATTER CONTENT WHICH HELPED SOLVE THE PROBLEMS

INDUSTRIAL ARTS
Construction of boats: Making pattern, shaping hull, making sail, making keel, casting weight for keel, making rack for boat, and testing boat.
How boats developed from early times to the present day.
The difficulty involved in building a toy boat so it will balance in water.
Different kinds of sail boats.
The need for a keel on a boat.
Different methods of propelling a boat.
Modern inventions in connection with the propulsion of boats.
What makes boats float.
Different uses of boats today.

HISTORY
The Half-Moon directed interest to Hendrick Hudson and his ship.
Historic ships: Santa Maria, Mayflower.
Reference work, reading and discussions about:
Vikings: What color and kinds of clothing did they wear? What did they eat? What kind of houses did they have? What were their boats like? Did Vikings have stores? How did Viking writing look? Story of Lief Erickson. The gods of the Vikings. Their beliefs.
Phoenicians: Scenery, boats, people, trade, beliefs, clothing, cities, industries, etc.
Egyptians: Scenery, country, boats, beliefs, tools, writing, etc. Story of the building of Solomon's Temple.
Early Mediterranean peoples.

GEOGRAPHY
Pictures of boat from newspaper which interested children in world geography.
Geography related to countries studied.
Norway: Country, climate, people and occupations.
Phoenicia: Country, climate, people, trading routes, daily life of early people compared with that of today.
Egypt: Country, climate, trading, etc.
Map interest: Norway, showing ancient home of the Vikings. The Mediterranean countries, showing cities of Phoenicia and routes on which the King of Tyre sent materials for Solomon's Temple.
Plasticene map of Mediterranean Sea and surrounding countries on which children sailed card-board models of early boats.
Globe in frequent use to locate places mentioned.
Outline world map, locating countries.
Interest in determining distances (reading scales on map).
How far is it from Norway to Phoenicia?
How far is it from Norway to America?
Building Lower Manhattan on floor with blocks to exhibit boats.
Map was drawn on floor; buildings in New York City that helped most with sea travel.

ARITHMETIC
Measuring for boat patterns and measurements in boat making.
Figuring the number of board feet used by class in building boat racks.
Arithmetic problems in connection with science experiment of water displacement and floating objects.
What is a gram?
What is a cubit?
Dimensions of Solomon's Temple compared with dimensions of the Lincoln School.
Children saw a cubit measure at the Museum.

FINE ARTS
Sketching and painting pictures of Half-Moon.
Sketching and painting boat models.
Drawing blackboard frieze showing history of boats.
Ten easel pictures showing story of Lief Erickson.
Cut paper pictures of boats.
Painting Egyptian boats seen at Museum.
Painting Viking pictures showing clothing.
Painting modern boats.
Making clay tablet.

COMPOSITION—LITERATURE
Stories written about the trip to see Half-Moon.
Stories of other trips by individual children.
Original poems about boats and the sea.
Labels and invitations for boat exhibit.
Written and oral reports about boats. Vikings, Phoenicia and Egypt.
Stories for bulletin, room paper, council news, or absent class members, telling of class interest and study.

READING
Reference material pertaining to topics under discussion, found in school library or at home.
Children's reading material: Lief and Thorkle, Viking Stories, Early sea people, Boat Book prepared by other Third Grade, material prepared by student teachers.

SCIENCE
How can we tell if our boats will float and balance? Try out in delta table.
Three experiments: Why do some objects float and why do some sink?
How do people know how much to put into boat before it will sink?

DRAMATIZATION
Play-Story of Lief Erickson, spontaneously prepared by class.

MUSIC
Old Gaelic Lullaby. Volga Boat Song. Sail Bonnie Boat.

PROBABLE OUTCOMES

DESIRABLE HABITS AND SKILLS
Better skill in sketching.
Better skill in handling brush and paints.
A beginning of the development of how to sew.
Developing the habit of making a pattern before
    constructing an article.
Developing skill in shaping wood by means of
    plane and spokeshave.
Developing skill in using gouge and mallet.
Developing skill in reading distances on map.
Rapid growth in map drawing.
Developing habit of reading the newspaper.
Better skill in measuring.
Ability to gather information on a certain subject
    and reporting to class.
Increased ability in writing.

ATTITUDES AND APPRECIATIONS
Economic:
An appreciation of the use of weights and
    measures.
What it means to construct a real boat that will
    float and balance properly.
Appreciation of the change in the lives of the peo-
    ple caused by the discovery of iron and the use
    of sails.
Appreciation of paper as a writing material.
Appreciation of the modern inventions in con-
    nection with the propulsion of ships.
Social:
What the early people contributed to the world.
The number of people and industry it takes to
    supply materials for the construction of one
    building.
Comparison of the ideas of fairness of the early
    people with the present day.
Recreational:
Developing a joy in painting, sketching and draw-
    ing.
Growing interest in reading books about historical
    peoples, inventions or boats.
Playing with boats made.
Interest in the construction of a toy-boat.
Interest in the construction of a real boat.
The pleasure in making maps.
The pleasure of playing with maps.
Aesthetic:
Appreciation of the beauty in line and construc-
    tion of boats.
The adventure of the ship.

INFORMATION
Knowledge of the development of the boat from
    raft to steamship.
Who Hendrick Hudson was.
General idea of historic ships.
An interesting acquaintance with Vikings, Phoe-
    nicians, and Egyptians.
General geographical knowledge of the world.
What a cubit measure is.
Knowledge of how to draw maps.
Some idea of what makes objects float.
Some idea of how to make boats balance in water.
Some idea of how to construct a toy-boat.
How the early people made their clay tablets.
How to make a clay tablet.
The need for molds in casting metals.
Some idea of how iron is made into different
    shapes.

TOTAL

PERSONALITY

AS

MODIFIED

BY THE

FOREGOING

EXPERIENCES

NEW INTERESTS LEADING TOWARD FURTHER ACTIVITIES

Interest in world geography and travel.

Maps and actual distances between given places.

The time it takes to get to certain places.

Interest in silk through answering the questions:

What kind of clothing did the Vikings wear?

How is velvet made?

Interest in what clay is: How it is prepared for our use and how it was prepared by early people for making clay tablets.

Interest in the Egyptian and Phoenician alphabet and how our alphabet was developed from it.

The materials the Egyptians used for writing.

Interest in metals.

Interest in weight of different metals through casting of lead for keels.

How metals are shaped.

Interest in the construction of modern buildings through reading about Solomon's Temple and comparing it with the construction of the Lincoln School.

Interest in other phases of transportation.

Although the Lincoln School, the Beaver Country Day School, the School of Organic Education, etc. were private experimental schools, the progressive urge of the 1920's was present in the public-school systems as well. One of the best examples in this area took place in Winnetka, Illinois, under the leadership of Superintendent of Schools, Carleton Washburne.

The "Winnetka System" was one of an individualized curriculum with regard to what Washburne called "the common essentials" (science, three R's, social studies). The pupil proceeded through these tool subjects at his own pace, rather than at an arbitrarily set rate of progress. Completing a phase or "parcel" of work, the pupil would request a teacher evaluation and, if successful in the test, could move on to attack another "parcel" of academic work.

The individualized "Winnetka System" achieved excellent results with its pupils as measured by standardized tests. The following reading is from a 1929 article in *School and Society,* describing Winnetka schools. Its proud tone may be explained by the fact that the author was Carleton Washburne.

115. Winnetka

Carleton Washburne

Now it is reading time. Each child is reading his own book. The children have all been tested as to their reading ability. No child has a book which is too difficult for him.[1] No two children have the same book. Each child reads individually. The teacher goes about among them, letting them read one at a time to her. But they read aloud to her alone, not to the rest of the class. She gives each one drill where he needs it. Most of them need little or none. Charles has finished his book and is writing a composition on it—a book review which serves the double purpose of showing the teacher that he understands his book and of being an exercise in English composition. Another child is taking a brief oral test on a book she has finished, the teacher having a test card with which to make such

Reprinted by permission from Carleton Washburne, "Winnetka," *School and Society,* XXIX, 733 (January 12, 1929), pp. 43-44.

[1] Books are selected on the basis of reading tests, from the Winnetka Graded Book List, by Carleton Washburne and Mabel Vogel. Rand McNally and Company. 1928.

testing easy. A third is simply handing in a book slip stating that the book has been read. This child does not know whether or not she will be tested on the particular book. As a matter of fact, the teacher has seen her reading it, absorbed, and knows no test is necessary.

And now it is time for social science.

Instead of remaining in the fourth grade—which is just beginning this subject—let us step into a sixth-grade room and watch the eleven-year-olds at work.

In social science for the first time we find all the children working on the same general topic. Some, it is true, have nearly finished reading the story of the Vikings, others are nearer the beginning. This Viking study includes both the history and geography of these bold Norsemen, for one can not understand the Vikings without knowing something of the country in which they lived. Throughout the Winnetka schools history and geography are a single subject, not two separate subjects. People's lives must be lived somewhere. To participate in their lives with them involves geography as well as history.

As we look at the material, we find it written simply, dramatically, interestingly. We find that the picturization of the life of that different civilization is made so vivid that the child is experiencing it himself.

As he reads about the Vikings, the child draws maps or fills in maps, showing where they lived, showing the topography of their country and showing their journeys. As soon as any child completes a topic he comes to a practice test by which he can check up his own knowledge of the subject. Having satisfied himself through this practice test that he knows the essential facts, he asks the teacher for a real test, which is again complete and diagnostic, as in the case of other individualized subjects.

But social science—history and geography—is not only an individual subject. It is not merely an amassing of facts. Important as it is that children shall know certain basic facts, it is still more important that they shall have an experience in social living, that they shall have stimulus to creative work. It is in order to make it possible to use social science in this way that the children do not proceed strictly individually in this one subject. If a child completes a topic before his fellows, he may use his surplus time for arithmetic or language or spelling or reading or, if he wishes to do so, for additional work on this particular topic. The child who is unusually slow in mastering the topic may borrow some time from his more completely individualized subjects, so as not to hold the rest of the group back. The fact that all academic subjects, except social science, are completely individualized makes it possible, without violating the principle of individual mastery, to have all children on the same general topic in this one field. Let us watch this sixth-grade group.

They are studying the life of the Vikings. They are trying to imagine themselves living in those days of adventure. They have decided to have a "Viking Day," and to this end they have already begun to make their room over into a Viking feast hall. At one end there is a throne, on which the Viking Chief will sit. Two girls are making tapestries to hang beside the throne. Each boy is soon at work on his shield, making his own design. A group here is making a Viking boat. Another group has gone down to the lumber yard to borrow some lumber for a Viking feast table. A few girls are planning together what they can have for their Viking feast. They are reading in books about what the Vikings ate. The art supervisor drops in and gives the children suggestions and help in the designs of their tapestry or the shields, and answers the eager questions of some of the girls concerning the costumes they are making. Perhaps the children sing as they work, an old Norse folk-song which they have learned in their music period, because the music supervisor knows that the children are interested in the Vikings. They plan to sing this song at their feast.

One boy is telling some of his friends of a plan for making drinking horns. "My father works at the stockyards," he says. "He can bring us some steers' horns. We can paint them and use them to drink our mead."

In such an activity as this, ample opportunity is given for the widest range of ingenuity and initiative. Each child is encouraged to vary from his fellows, to express himself, to create. Yet all are utilizing their special interests or abilities for the welfare of the group enterprise.

The Viking feast hall is not for the purpose of teaching children about the Vikings. The amount of time they will spend on this one project is entirely disproportionate to the amount of valuable information they will get from it. It is the *outcome* of their reading concerning the Vikings— the *outcome* of their factual work, rather than a means to the mastery of facts. To teach facts exclusively through such projects would be to limit very seriously the things with which children become familiar. Much learning can be done more economically through the direct means of reading and study. Out of this reading and study, however, may grow ideas for action. These are given full play and are made the basis for creative expression and a training in group cooperation.

SECTION 4

The Social Frontier

The idea of the school as the instrument of social change and progress was clearly stated in the early theoretical days of progressivism. The social-reformist impulse, however, had fallen to a low ebb even in theoretical discussions in the decade of the 1920's. But in the 1930's the crisis in American society of the depression, economic collapse, and the threat of social and political upheaval brought an urgent re-emphasis on social reform to American education. One of the leaders of progressive education, George S. Counts, stated his views in 1932 of the new demands on education in a resounding challenge, *Dare the Schools Build a New Social Order?* Too long had the schools dealt only with the symptoms of social ills, he declared; now they had to act directly to cure the disease itself in reforming the very basic order of society.

116. Dare the School Build a New Social Order?

George S. Counts

Like all simple and unsophisticated peoples we Americans have a sublime faith in education. Faced with any difficult problem of life we set our minds at rest sooner or later by the appeal to the school. We are convinced that education is the one unfailing remedy for every ill to which man is subject, whether it be vice, crime, war, poverty, riches, injustice, racketeering, political corruption, race hatred, class conflict, or just plain original sin. We even speak glibly and often about the general reconstruction of society through the school. We cling to this faith in spite of the fact that the very period in which our troubles have multiplied so rapidly has witnessed an unprecedented expansion of organized education. This would seem to suggest that our schools, instead of directing the course of change, are themselves driven by the very forces that are transforming the rest of the social order.

The bare fact, however, that simple and unsophisticated peoples have unbounded faith in education does not mean that the faith is untenable. History shows that the intuitions of such folk may be nearer the truth than the weighty and carefully reasoned judgments of the learned and the wise. Under certain conditions education may be as beneficent and as powerful as we are wont to think. But if it is to be so, teachers must abandon much of their easy optimism, subject the concept of education to the most rigorous scrutiny, and be prepared to deal much more fundamentally, realistically, and positively with the American social situation than has been their habit in the past. Any individual or group that would aspire to lead society must be ready to pay the cost of leadership: to accept responsibility, to suffer calumny, to surrender security, to risk both reputation and fortune. If this price, or some important part of it, is not being paid, then the chances are that the claim to leadership is fraudulent. Society is never redeemed without effort, struggle, and sacrifice. Authentic leaders are never found breathing that rarefied atmosphere lying above the dust and smoke of battle. With regard to the past we always recognize the truth of this principle, but when we think of our own times we profess the belief that the ancient rôles have been reversed and that now prophets of a new age receive their rewards among the living.

That the existing school is leading the way to a better social order is a thesis which few informed persons would care to defend. Except as it is forced to fight for its own life during times of depression, its course is too serene and untroubled. Only in the rarest of instances does it wage war on behalf of principle or ideal. Almost everywhere it is in the grip of conservative forces and is serving the cause of perpetuating ideas and institutions suited to an age that is gone. But there is one movement above the educational horizon which would seem to show promise of genuine and creative leadership. I refer to the Progressive Education movement. Surely in this union of two of the great faiths of the American people, the faith in progress and the faith in education, we have reason to hope for light and guidance. Here is a movement which would seem to be completely devoted to the promotion of social welfare through education.

Even a casual examination of the program and philosophy of the Progressive schools, however, raises many doubts in the mind. To be sure, these schools have a number of large achievements to their credit. They have focused attention squarely upon the child; they have recognized the fundamental importance of the interest of the learner; they have defended the thesis that activity lies at the root of all true education; they have conceived learning in terms of life situations and growth of character; they have championed the rights of the child as a free personality. Most of this is excellent, but in my judgment it is not enough. It constitutes too narrow a conception of the meaning of education; it brings into the picture but one-half of the landscape.

If an educational movement, or any other movement, calls itself progressive, it must have orientation; it must possess direction. The word itself implies moving forward, and moving forward can have little meaning in the absence of clearly defined purposes. We cannot, like Stephen Leacock's horseman, dash off in all directions at once. Nor should we, like our presidential candidates, evade every disturbing issue and be all things to all men. Also we must beware lest we become so devoted to motion that we neglect the question of direction and be entirely satisfied with movement in circles. Here, I think, we find the fundamental weakness, not only of Progressive Education, but also of American education generally. Like a baby shaking a rattle, we seem to be utterly content with action provided it is sufficiently vigorous and noisy. In the last analysis a very large part of American educational thought, inquiry, and experimentation is much ado about nothing. And, if we are permitted to push the analogy of the rattle a bit further, our consecration to motion is encouraged and supported in order to keep us out of mischief. At least we know that so long as we thus busy ourselves we shall not incur the serious displeasure of our social elders.

The weakness of Progressive Education thus lies in the fact that it has elaborated no theory of social welfare, unless it be that of anarchy or extreme individualism. In this, of course, it is but reflecting the viewpoint of the members of the liberal-minded upper middle class who send their children to the Progressive schools—persons who are fairly well-off, who have abandoned the faiths of their fathers, who assume an agnostic attitude towards all important questions, who pride themselves on their open-mindedness and tolerance, who favor in a mild sort of way fairly liberal programs of social reconstruction, who are full of good will and humane sentiment, who have vague aspirations for world peace and human brotherhood, who can be counted upon to respond moderately to any appeal made in the name of charity, who are genuinely distressed at the sight of *unwonted* forms of cruelty, misery, and suffering, and who perhaps serve to soften somewhat the bitter clashes of those real forces that govern the world; but who, in spite of all their good qualities, have no deep and abiding loyalties, possess no convictions for which they would sacrifice over-much, would find it hard to live without their customary material comforts, are rather insensitive to the accepted forms of social injustice, are content to play the rôle of interested spectator in the drama of human history, refuse to see reality in its harsher and more disagreeable forms, rarely move outside the pleasant circles of the class to which they belong, and in the day of severe trial will follow the lead of the most powerful and respectable forces in society and at the same time find good reasons for so doing. These people have shown themselves entirely incapable of dealing with any of the great crises of our time— war, prosperity, or depression. At bottom they are romantic sentimentalists, but with a sharp eye on the main chance. That they can be trusted to write our educational theories and shape our educational programs is highly improbable.

Among the members of this class the number of children is small, the income relatively high, and the economic functions of the home greatly reduced. For these reasons an inordinate emphasis on the child and child interests is entirely welcome to them. They wish to guard their offspring from too strenuous endeavor and from coming into too intimate contact with the grimmer aspects of industrial society. They wish their sons and daughter to succeed according to the standards of their class and to be a credit to their parents. At heart feeling themselves members of a superior human strain, they do not want their children to mix too freely with the children of the poor or of the less fortunate races. Nor do they want them to accept radical social doctrines, espouse unpopular causes, or lose themselves in quest of any Holy Grail. According to their views education should deal with life, but with life at a distance or in a highly diluted form. They would generally maintain that life should be kept at arm's length, if it should not be handled with a poker.

If Progressive Education is to be genuinely progressive, it must emancipate itself from the influence of this class, face squarely and courageously every social issue, come to grips with life in all of its stark reality, establish an organic relation with the community, develop a realistic and comprehensive theory of welfare, fashion a compelling and challenging vision of human destiny, and become less frightened than it is today at the bogies of *imposition* and *indoctrination*. In a word, Progressive Education cannot place its trust in a child-centered school.

This brings us to the most crucial issue in education—the question of the nature and extent of the influence which the school should exercise over the development of the child. The advocates of extreme freedom have been so successful in championing what they call the rights of the child that even the most skillful practitioners of the art of converting others to their opinions disclaim all intention of molding the learner. And when the word indoctrination is coupled with education there is scarcely one among us possessing the hardihood to refuse to be horrified. This feeling is so widespread that even Mr. Lunacharsky, Commissar of Education in the Russian Republic until 1929, assured me on one occasion that the Soviet educational leaders do not believe in the indoctrination of children in the ideas and principles of communism. When I asked him whether their children become good communists while attending the schools, he replied that the great majority do. On seeking from him an explanation of this remarkable phenomenon he said that Soviet teachers merely tell their children the truth about human history. As a consequence, so he asserted, practically all of the more intelligent boys and girls adopt the philosophy of communism. I recall also that the Methodist sect in which I was reared always confined its teachings to the truth!

The issue is no doubt badly confused by historical causes. The champions of freedom are obviously the product of an age that has broken very fundamentally with the past and is equally uncertain about the future. In many cases they feel themselves victims of narrow orthodoxies which were imposed upon them during childhood and which have severely cramped their lives. At any suggestion that the child should be influenced by his elders they therefore envisage the establishment of a state church, the formulation of a body of sacred doctrine, and the teaching of this doctrine as fixed and final. If we are forced to choose between such an unenlightened form of pedagogical influence and a condition of complete freedom for the child, most of us would in all probability choose the latter as the lesser of two evils. But this is to create a wholly artificial situation: the choice should not be limited to these two extremes. Indeed today neither extreme is possible.

I believe firmly that a critical factor must play an important role in any adequate educational program, at least in any such program fashioned for the modern world. An education that does not strive to promote the fullest and most thorough understanding of the world is not worthy of the name. Also there must be no deliberate distortion or suppression of facts to support any theory or point of view. On the other hand, I am prepared to defend the thesis that all education contains a large element of imposition, that in the very nature of the case this is inevitable, that the existence and evolution of society depend upon it, that it is consequently[1] eminently desirable, and that the frank acceptance of this fact

[1] Some persons would no doubt regard this as a *non sequitur,* but the great majority of the members of the human race would, I think, accept the argument.

by the educator is a major professional obligation. I even contend that failure to do this involves the clothing of one's own deepest prejudices in the garb of universal truth and the introduction into the theory and practice of education of an element of obscurantism.

. . . . .

If we may now assume that the child will be imposed upon in some fashion by the various elements in his environment, the real question is not whether imposition will take place, but rather from what source it will come. If we were to answer this question in terms of the past, there could, I think, be but one answer: on all genuinely crucial matters the school follows the wishes of the groups or classes that actually rule society; on minor matters the school is sometimes allowed a certain measure of freedom. But the future may be unlike the past. Or perhaps I should say that teachers, if they could increase sufficiently their stock of courage, intelligence, and vision, might become a social force of some magnitude. About this eventuality I am not over sanguine, but a society lacking leadership as ours does, might even accept the guidance of teachers. Through powerful organizations they might at least reach the public conscience and come to exercise a larger measure of control over the schools than hitherto. They would then have to assume some responsibility for the more fundamental forms of imposition which, according to my argument, cannot be avoided.

That the teachers should deliberately reach for power and then make the most of their conquest is my firm conviction. To the extent that they are permitted to fashion the curriculum and the procedures of the school they will definitely and positively influence the social attitudes, ideals, and behavior of the coming generation. In doing this they should resort to no subterfuge or false modesty. They should say neither that they are merely teaching the truth nor that they are unwilling to wield power in their own right. The first position is false and the second is a confession of incompetence. It is my observation that the men and women who have affected the course of human events are those who have not hesitated to use the power that has come to them. Representing as they do, not the interests of the moment or of any special class, but rather the common and abiding interests of the people, teachers are under heavy social obligation to protect and further those interests. In this they occupy a relatively unique position in society. Also since the profession should embrace scientists and scholars of the highest rank, as well as teachers working at all levels of the educational system, it has at its disposal, as no other group, the knowledge and wisdom of the ages. It is scarcely thinkable that these men and women would ever act as selfishly or bungle as badly as have the so-called "practical" men of our generation—the politicians, the financiers, the industrialists. If all of these facts are taken into account, instead of shunning power, the profession should rather seek power and then strive to use that power fully and wisely and in the interests of the great masses of the people.

The point should be emphasized that teachers possess no magic secret to power. While their work should give them a certain moral advantage, they must expect to encounter the usual obstacles blocking the road to leadership. They should not be deceived by the pious humbug with which public men commonly flatter the members of the profession. To expect ruling groups or classes to give precedence to teachers on important matters, because of age or sex or sentiment, is to refuse to face realities. It was one of the proverbs of the agrarian order that a spring never rises higher than its source. So the power that teachers exercise in the schools can be no greater than the power they wield in society. Moreover, while organization is necessary, teachers should not think of their problem primarily in terms of organizing and presenting a united front to the world, the flesh, and the devil. In order to be effective they must throw off completely the slave psychology that has dominated the mind of the pedagogue more or less since the days of ancient Greece. They must be prepared to stand on their own feet and win for their ideas the support of the masses of the people. Education as a force for social regeneration must march hand in hand with the living and creative forces of the social order. In their own lives teachers must bridge the gap between school and society. and play some part in the fashioning of those great common purposes which should bind the two together.

This brings us to the question of the kind of imposition in which teachers should engage, if they had the power. Our obligations, I think, grow out of the social situation. We live in troublous times; we live in an age of profound change; we live in an age of revolution. Indeed it is highly doubtful whether man ever lived in a more eventful period than the present. In order to match our epoch we would probably have to go back to the fall of the ancient empires or even to that unrecorded age when men first abandoned the natural arts of hunting and fishing and trapping and began to experiment with agriculture and the settled life. Today we are witnessing the rise of a civilization quite without precedent in human history—a civilization founded on science, technology, and machinery, possessing the most extraordinary power, and rapidly making of the entire world a single great society. Because of forces already released, whether in the field of economics, politics, morals, religion, or art, the old molds are being broken. And the peoples of the earth are everywhere seething with strange ideas and passions. If life were peaceful and quiet and undisturbed by great issues, we might with some show of wisdom center our attention on the nature of the child. But with the world as it is, we cannot afford for a single instant to remove our eyes from the social scene or shift our attention from the peculiar needs of the age.

In this new world that is forming, there is one set of issues which is pecularily fundamental and which is certain to be the center of bitter and prolonged struggle. I refer to those issues which may be styled economic. President Butler has well stated the case: "For a generation and more past," he says, "the center of human interest has been moving from the point which it occupied for some four hundred years to a new point which it bids fair to occupy for a time equally long. The shift in the position of the center of gravity in human interest has been from politics to economics; from considerations that had to do with forms or government, with the establishment and protection of individual liberty, to considerations that have to do with the production, distribution, and consumption of wealth."

Consider the present condition of the nation. Who among us, if he had not been reared amid our institutions, could believe his eyes as he surveys the economic situation, or his ears as he listens to solemn disquisitions by our financial and political leaders on the cause and cure of the depression! Here is a society that manifests the most extraordinary contradictions: a mastery over the forces of nature, surpassing the wildest dreams of antiquity, is accompanied by extreme material insecurity; dire poverty walks hand in hand with the most extravagant living the world has ever known; an abundance of goods of all kinds is coupled with privation, misery, and even starvation; an excess of production is seriously offered as the underlying cause of severe physical suffering; breakfastless children march to school past bankrupt shops laden with rich foods gathered from the ends of the earth; strong men by the million walk the streets in a futile search for employment and with the exhaustion of hope enter the ranks of the damned; great captains of industry close factories without warning and dismiss the workmen by whose labors they have amassed huge fortunes through the years; automatic machinery increasingly displaces men and threatens society with a growing contingent of the permanently unemployed; racketeers and gangsters with the connivance of public officials fasten themselves on the channels of trade and exact toll at the end of the machine gun; economic parasitism, either within or without the law, is so prevalent that the tradition of honest labor is showing signs of decay; the wages paid to the workers are too meager to enable them to buy back the goods they produce; consumption is subordinated to production and a philosophy of deliberate waste is widely proclaimed as the highest economic wisdom; the science of psychology is employed to fan the flames of desire so that men may be

enslaved by their wants and bound to the wheel of production; a government board advices the cotton-growers to plow under every third row
of cotton in order to bolster up the market; both ethical and æsthetic
considerations are commonly over-ridden by "hard-headed business men"
bent on material gain; federal aid to the unemployed is opposed on
the ground that it would pauperize the masses when the favored members of society have always lived on a dole; even responsible leaders
resort to the practices of the witch doctor and vie with one another in
predicting the return of prosperity; an ideal of rugged individualism,
evolved in a simple pioneering and agrarian order at a time when free
land existed in abundance, is used to justify a system which exploits
pitilessly and without thought of the morrow the natural and human resources of the nation and of the world. One can only imagine what
Jeremiah would say if he could step out of the pages of the Old Testament and cast his eyes over this vast spectacle so full of tragedy and of
menace.

The point should be emphasized, however, that the present situation
is also freighted with hope and promise. The age is pregnant with possibilities. There lies within our grasp the most humane, the most beautiful,
the most majestic civilization ever fashioned by any people. This much at
least we know today. We shall probably know more tomorrow. At last
men have achieved such a mastery over the forces of nature that wage
slavery can follow chattel slavery and take its place among the relics of
the past. No longer are there grounds for the contention that the finer
fruits of human culture must be nurtured upon the toil and watered by
the tears of the masses. The limits to achievement set by nature have been
so extended that we are today bound merely by our ideals, by our power
of self-discipline, by our ability to devise social arrangements suited to
an industrial age. If we are to place any credence whatsoever in the word
of our engineers, the full utilization of modern technology at its present
level of development should enable us to produce several times as much
goods as were ever produced at the very peak of prosperity, and with the
working day, the working year, and the working life reduced by half. We
hold within our hands the power to usher in an age of plenty, to make
secure the lives of all, and to banish poverty forever from the land. The
only cause for doubt or pessimism lies in the question of our ability to
rise to the stature of the times in which we live.

Our generation has the good or the ill fortune to live in an age when
great decisions must be made. The American people, like most of the
other peoples of the earth, have come to the parting of the ways; they
can no longer trust entirely the inspiration which came to them when the
Republic was young; they must decide afresh what they are to do with

their talents. Favored above all other nations with the resources of nature and the material instrumentalities of civilization, they stand confused and irresolute before the future. They seem to lack the moral quality necessary to quicken, discipline, and give direction to their matchless energies. In a recent paper Professor Dewey has, in my judgment, correctly diagnosed our troubles: "the schools, like the nation," he says, "are in need of a central purpose which will create new enthusiasm and devotion, and which will unify and guide all intellectual plans."

This suggests, as we have already observed, that the educational problem is not wholly intellectual in nature. Our Progressive schools therefore cannot rest content with giving children an opportunity to study contemporary society in all of its aspects. This of course must be done, but I am convinced that they should go much farther. If the schools are to be really effective, they must become centers for the building, and not merely for the contemplation, of our civilization. This does not mean that we should endeavor to promote particular reforms through the educational system. We should, however, give to our children a vision of the possibilities which lie ahead and endeavor to enlist their loyalties and enthusiasms in the realization of the vision. Also our social institutions and practices, all of them, should be critically examined in the light of such a vision.

Less passionate than the Counts declaration, but equally concerned with the limited traditional role of the school in society, was the thinking and writing of Boyd H. Bode. A philosopher of education at Ohio State University, Bode's careful criticism of education and progressivism in the 1930's stressed the failure of the school to act toward changing and improving society. His essay, "The Confusion of Present-Day Education," of which selections follow, was an important contribution to *The Educational Frontier,* a yearbook of the John Dewey Society edited by William Heard Kilpatrick. This volume, with essays by John Dewey, John Childs, V. T. Thayer, H. Gordon Hullfish, and R. B. Raup as well as Kilpatrick and Bode, became the theoretical basis for the call to action on the social frontier of education.

117. From The Confusion of Present-Day Education

Boyd H. Bode

In brief, a survey of our economic development would seem to indicate that equality of opportunity does not mean what it meant a hundred years ago. In those earlier days the argument that free competition among individuals served to develop desirable qualities or traits had some plausability. But now great industrial and economic units have come upon the scene, and in them the individual tends to become submerged. Our "American way of life" has disappeared or, at any rate, is fast disappearing; and no appeals or sentimental attachment to the past can alter that fact. Genuine loyalty to the past does not mean opposition to change, but an active concern for the kind of change that will reconstruct what is valuable in our tradition so as to suit present conditions.

If equality of opportunity is to be preserved, the purposes or aims of our economic and industrial organizations must be widened so as to include other considerations besides that of pecuniary profit. If, for example, the idea of public interest could become sufficiently powerful to secure action with reference to the elimination of depressions, of economic insecurity, of unemployment, and of undesirable methods of selling and advertising, our whole national psychology would undergo a corresponding change. Since these matters are of direct concern to the average citizen, whether he happens to be an employee under the organizations immediately concerned or a member of the general public, they would be discussed in the newspapers, on the platform, and at the dinner-table; we should gradually acquire the habit of regarding our economic and industrial life from the standpoint of public interest. This wide participation would obviously be analogous to the participation by the Russian people in the Five-Year Plan; and a similar analogy would exist with respect to the relation between our schools and the rest of the social order. Translated into social terms, the escape from compartmentalization would mean an attempt to reconstruct the social pattern, which would then become a matter of common concern to the school and to the public outside the school.

The analogy can be pushed still another step. A democratic procedure, like Russian communism, involves a definite creed or point of view, and, like all creeds, it "loads the dice" in certain respects. It assumes at the out-

Reprinted by permission from Boyd Bode, "The Confusion in Present-Day Education," *The Educational Frontier* (New York: The Century Co., 1933), pp. 26-31.

set, for example, that coöperation, sharing, creative activity, are desirable qualities, and so it advocates the type of school organization with which progressive education has made us familiar. Second, it holds that all the values which enter into the process of reconstruction or reinterpretation must stand on their own merits with no special protection from the outside. In other words, it holds that the outcome of the reinterpretation must not be determined in advance so as to ensure special privileges for certain values as against the rest. This too is a definite creed, which could hardly expect to meet with universal acceptance.

This statement, however, of the presuppositions which determine democratic procedure in education also brings to light the distinctive feature that differentiates this procedure from the rest. This distinctive feature consists in the dictum that the individual must be permitted and encouraged to do his own thinking, to formulate his own social philosophy. It concedes in advance the possibility that some individuals will use the intellectual freedom which is accorded them to draw the conclusion that such freedom is reprehensible and a danger to society. Or, to state it differently, the reconstruction of values, without antecedent special privileges to any of them, may lead to the belief that certain values should be protected, that conclusions should be predetermined, that, in short, the democratic procedure is all wrong. Such an outcome might be considered regrettable from the standpoint of the school, but it could not be ruled out in advance without stultifying the whole idea of democratic procedure.

This implication of democratic procedure, it may be noted, has a direct bearing on the idea of "participation." In the Russian scheme, participation in the main means coöperation in the realization of a program that is laid out in advance. In our own schools the terms *participation* and *social* all too frequently limited in the same way. Pupils are encouraged to participate or to be social by exhibiting a spirit of helpfulness. There is, however, a different and in some ways far deeper meaning of these terms. If we take these terms to refer to the *search* for a program, i.e., if we take them to mean sensitiveness to values and an active concern for the reconciliation and conservation of conflicting values, the individual acquires a certain new distinctiveness. We are then forced to take special note of the fact that this reconstruction of values is something that the individual must do for himself. The reconstruction may be socially motivated to any degree, yet it remains a personal matter. Participation may easily degenerate into a form of herd action, in which the finest fruits of education are lost to sight.

At present the day may seem far distant when the school and the general public will be engaged extensively in matters of common concern. Meanwhile the school must do what it can to relate its activities to the larger concerns of the social order. The best hope for the school, in this connection, is to become more sensitive than it has been in the past to the need of reëxamining our national tradition. In stressing the interdependence of individuals in this modern world, something can be done, even in the lower grades, toward pointing out the need for widening our purposes in industrial and economic enterprises and for reconstructing our conception of the universe in which we live. With regard to this latter point, certain contrasts could be introduced to prepare for a better understanding of our tradition. Thus Franklin's proof that lightning is electricity and acts in strict conformity to natural laws gains a large measure of its significance from the fact that people previously held, and to some extent still hold, a widely different view on this subject. The same may be said regarding the evidence that diseases are "natural" phenomena. Or, again, the suggestion arising from the progressive remaking of our physical and social environment that intelligence should be entrusted with the task of recreating our standards of conduct and of values in accordance with changing conditions is a subject of violent disagreement. These illustrations serve to provide a clue to the determination of both subject-matter and method, and also to suggest how the continuity of the school with the social order, upon which our progressive schools have rightly placed so much emphasis, may be widened and directed. Eventually this growing insight should culminate in the comprehension of the basic conflicts that are to be found in every major domain of life—in religion, in economics, in government, and in the field of private and social conduct.

As was stated previously, the primary concern of a democratic educational procedure is to stimulate a reconstruction of our beliefs and habits in the light of their mutual relationships rather than to predetermine the nature of this reconstruction. The reconstruction will gravitate naturally and inevitably toward a philosophy of life or a social outlook, and it will take place with such assistance and encouragement as the schools can provide, but not according to any prescribed pattern. In a scheme of this kind we find clues for the selection of subject-matter and for methods of teaching. Can it also be claimed that such a scheme will provide a basis for social progress? It is obvious that a program of this kind, if really carried out, would not lead in every case to the same kind of social outlook. On the contrary, differences in attitude or points of view that exist among our population would tend to become more sharply accentuated and defined. But since a common program of some kind seems to be necessary, how can we hope that this kind of education would contribute to it?

The objection is plausible but has no finality. The differences in attitude or points of view to which reference was made above have always existed among our population. These differences, however, have not prevented the nation—except in the matter of economic-industrial development —from moving, on the whole, in the direction of a richer and more significant democracy. The evidence of this trend is to be found in the nature of the development exhibited by governmental functions. By and large, this development shows a growing concern for the welfare of the common man. Recognition of the rights of the common man is the basic article in our national faith, a faith that has hitherto proved more potent than our differences and disagreements. Is there any reason to suppose that this faith will be less dynamic if it becomes conscious of its larger implications and opportunities, if it gains a vision of a world in which its dream has become a reality?

It may be repeated that the kind of education which has been discussed here would doubtless carry people further apart in some respects, that it would emphasize certain differences in points of view. The point is that it would also do much toward cultivating common understandings and purposes. The time was when a liberal education meant the possession of a common body of knowledge and a common outlook on life. That time has gone by. About the only common element in present-day liberal education is that the same number of credits may be counted toward graduation. Liberal education has ceased to emphasize the possession of such a common tradition. To inherit the tradition of democracy, for example, is not like inheriting the classical tradition; it is more like inheriting a lawsuit. Yet this disturbing fact offers the opportunity of regaining, in a different form, the sense of solidarity among educated persons which is so largely lacking at the present time. All education, whether "liberal" or "technical," should help to create a sense that our traditions require reconstruction and thus provide community of understandings and interests, regardless of its content. In so doing it widens the area of common purposes by weakening the antagonisms that spring from complacent short-sightedness and from stupid loyalties to the past. Real education humanizes men. It does so, however, not by moulding them into unthinking acceptance of preëstablished patterns, but by stimulating them to a continuous reconstruction of their outlook on life.

It is in this need for reconstruction that we find the new educational frontier. At present educators are insensitive to this need, in direct proportion to their pretensions of scientific impeccability or to their sentimental absorption in the development of the individual child. A new emphasis is necessary if scientific method in education and the concept of individuality are to become meaningful. It is necessary if education is to make its proper contribution toward safeguarding the future. Without the clarity of vision that such education can bestow, there is imminent danger that class interests will brush aside the common good, or that in the storm and stress of conflict we shall lose our way and follow after strange gods. As our national faith gains a clearer understanding of itself, it will be deepened and strengthened and the genius of the American people will be set free to make its distinctive contribution to the welfare and happiness of mankind.

The social-reformist movement in education led to the launching of a journal, *The Social Frontier,* subtitled *A Journal of Educational Criticism and Reconstruction,* published monthly under the editorship of George S. Counts with Mordecai Grossman and Norman Woelfel as associate editors. The "Contents" of the first issue, October, 1934, is included below along with Counts' inaugural editorial. As a forum for the more "radical" social-reformist progressives, the journal held a wide and influential circulation throughout the thirties. By 1939 the journal was in financial trouble, however, and it was taken over by the Progressive Education Association; after several changes of editor and name, it ceased publication in 1943.

118. Contents of October 1934 Edition of The Social Frontier

119. Orientation

George S. Counts

American Society, along with world society, is passing through an age of profound transition. This fact has been proclaimed with ever greater emphasis and frequency by the march of ideas and events since the Civil War and particularly since the opening of the present century. It is proclaimed in the advance of science, technology, and invention, in the growing mastery of natural forces, in the changing forms of economy and government, in the increasing instability of the whole social structure, in the swelling armaments and the intensification of international rivalries, and in the wars, revolutions, and social calamities which seem to have become the order of the day throughout the world. Also it is proclaimed in the obsolescence of inherited conceptions of human relationships, in the decline of faith in traditional moral and religious doctrines, in the popularity of cults of cynicism and disillusionment, and in the appearance of revolutionary political theories, philosophies, and programs.

While the transition presents many facets, in its basic terms in the United States it is a movement from a simple agrarian and trading economy to a highly complex urban and industrial order with agriculture transformed into single-crop specialties. Since the days of Andrew Jackson the nation has evolved out of a loose aggregation of relatively self-contained rural households and neighborhoods into a vast society marked by minute differentiation of structure and function, close integration of parts, and common dependence on a far-flung productive and distributive mechanism whose operation requires an ever increasing measure of cooperation, general planning, and unified direction. In a word, for the American people the age of individualism in economy is closing and an age of collectivism is

Reprinted from George S. Counts, "Orientaton," *The Social Frontier,* I, 1 (October, 1934), pp. 3-4.

opening. Here is the central and dominating reality in the present epoch.

This fact means that the nation has entered a period freighted with unmeasured opportunities and responsibilites—a period when, in the words of Emerson, "the old and the new stand side by side, and admit of being compared; when the energies of all men are searched by fear and by hope; when the historic glories of the old can be compensated by the rich possibilities of the new era." In the years and decades immediately ahead the American people will be called upon to undertake arduous, hazardous, and crucial tasks of social reconstruction: they will be compelled to make some of the grand choices of history, to determine in which direction they are to move, to make decisions which will deeply affect the life of their country for generations and indeed for centuries—decisions concerning the incidence of economic and political power, the distribution of wealth and income, the relations of classes, races, and nationalities, and the ends for which men and women are to live. Moreover, owing to the revolutionary conquest of mechanical energy during the past one hundred years, the American people stand today on the threshold of unprecedented and unimagined potentialities of material and spiritual development. Also they stand in the imminent presence of economic collapse, political reaction, cultural regimentation, and war. They must choose among the diverse roads now opening before them. In particular they must choose whether the great tradition of democracy is to pass away with the individualistic economy to which it has been linked historically or is to undergo the transformation necessary for survival in an age of close economic interdependence.

In the making of these choices persons and institutions engaged in the performance of educational functions will inevitably play an important role. To the extent that they operate in the real world they will make their influence felt. Indeed, even if they should pursue a policy of evasion, in actual fact they would be throwing their influence on the side of outmoded anarchy and disorder. Whatever course they pursue they will either retard or hasten the adjustment to the new realities, they will either make easy or difficult the transfer of the democratic ideal from individual to social foundations. They will be called upon, not only to bring the heritage of knowledge, thought, and attitude abreast of general social advance, but also to make broad choices concerning alliances to be consummated, values to be preserved, interests to be defended, social goals to be striven for.

Already a few voices have been raised within the ranks of educational workers in acceptance of the challenge of social reconstruction. But as yet these voices are too timid to be effective, too tentative to be convincing, and too individual to speak a language of clear-cut purpose. They belong to persons who singly and in isolation have captured this or the other meaning of unfolding events. Before these persons, and perhaps countless others who have thus far remained inarticulate, can hope to become a positive creative force in American society and education, they must come into closer communication, clarify their thought and purposes, draw like-minded individuals into their ranks, and merge isolated and discordant voices into a mighty instrument of group consensus, harmonious, expression, and collective action. To contribute to the achievement of this object THE SOCIAL FRONTIER is being launched.

The journal makes no pretense to absolute objectivity and detachment, knowing such a goal to be impossible of achievement in that realm of practical affairs to which education belongs and in which positive decisions must be made. It represents a point of view, it has a frame of reference, it stands on a particular interpretation of American history. It accepts the analysis of the current epoch presented above and outlined in greater detail in *Conclusions and Recommendations, Report on the Social Studies** of the Commission of the American Historical Association.

THE SOCIAL FRONTIER assumes that the age of individualism in economy is closing and that an age marked by close integration of social life and by collective planning and control is opening. For weal or woe it accepts as irrevocable this deliverance of the historical process. It intends to go forward to meet the new age and to proceed as rationally as possible to the realization of all possibilities for the enrichment and refinement of human life. It will nurse no fantasies of returning to the simple household and neighborhood economy of the time of Thomas Jefferson; it will seek no escape from the responsibilities of today, either by longing for a past now gone beyond recovery or by imagining a future bearing the features of Utopia. It proposes to take seriously the affirmation of the Declaration of Independence that "all men are created equal" and are entitled to "life, liberty, and the pursuit of happiness." Also it proposes, in the light of this great humanist principle applied to the collective realities of industrial civilization, to pass every important educational event, institution, theory, and program under critical review. Finally, it will devote its pages positively to the development of the thought of all who are interested in making education discharge its full responsibility in the present age of social transition. Its editorial staff and board of directors hope that it will help fight the great educational battles—practical and theoretical—which are already looming above the horizon. And they trust that it will engage in the battles of the twentieth and not of the eighteenth century.

THE SOCIAL FRONTIER acknowledges allegiance to no narrow conception of education. While recognizing the school as society's central educational agency, it refuses to *limit* itself to a consideration of the work of this institu-

* Charles Scribner's Sons, New York, 1934, $1.50.

tion. On the contrary, it includes within its field of interest all of those formative influences and agencies which serve to induct the individual—whether old or young—into the life and culture of the group. It regards education as an aspect of a culture in process of evolution. It therefore has no desire to promote a restricted and technical professionalism. Rather does it address itself to the task of considering the broad role of education in advancing the welfare and interests of the great masses of the people who do the work of society—those who labor on farms and ships and in the mines, shops, and factories of the world.

The presidential election of 1932 brought to office Franklin D. Roosevelt with his promise of a "New Deal" for America, a promise made good in sweeping reform measures toward bringing an end to the depression crisis. One of the major areas of concern of the New Deal was the effect of the depression on the youth of America; in the first hundred days of the new administration, the Civilian Conservation Corps, was created; this was later followed by the National Youth Administration, both programs aimed at meeting this problem. Neither of these agencies was primarily concerned with education—the basic aim in fact seemed to be to hold young men and women off the labor market for as long as possible—yet both were educational enterprises of enormous proportions.

The agencies were set up to operate entirely independent of local schools and school administrations, first because F.D.R. wanted immediate action on a national scale in this area and second because the nation's schools were so little attuned to the urgent educational demands of the depression. The appeals of the social frontiersmen, it would appear, had been very little heeded by American schools; there was apparently no rebuilding of the social order underway, no progressive revolution in the schools.

The extent and purposes of the youth programs are outlined in the following selection from a government publication entitled *The National Youth Administration,* written by Palmer O. Johnson and Oswald L. Harvey, both educators and staff members of the NYA.

120. The Youth Problem

Palmer O. Johnson and Oswald L. Harvey

Only during recent years has the status of youth emerged in the United States as a major social problem. While the population was growing and spreading over the continent, there was plenty of room for young people in search of experience and a place in economic society. The vast majority of the people were engaged in comparatively simple rural enterprises, and educational needs were few and rudimentary. Not until the latter part of the past century were public educational facilities made available on an extensive scale. Occupational specialization and high-pressure production are of relatively recent development. The census of 1920 was the first to reveal an excess of urban over rural population.

The intensely rapid growth of population, the full impingement of industrial expansion and organization on economic and social life, and the final limitation of the frontier together have operated to force the American people into a recognition of population problems as a whole. As might be expected, various groups in the population have been faced with problems peculiar to themselves. Children were menaced with the oppressive conditions of child labor; poorly educated peasant immigrants suffered from industrial exploitation; and old people were faced with dismissal, abandonment, and economic insecurity. The problems of chief concern to youth, as one of these major groups, related primarily to education and employment. Job specialization demanded a more deliberate and specific form of vocational training; intelligent participation in civic affairs called for a more extensive and prolonged period of general education; and the complexity of social participation necessitated a period of conscious orientation and guidance which might serve to adjust the individual to the. conditions and demands of the group as a whole.

The recent major economic depression precipitated these problems of population adjustment. Defects in the social organization became glaringly evident and the need for concerted action became imperative. The Federal Government provided the essential lead and initiated the emergency program. By virtue of necessity relief was the primary motive. But relief alone, it soon became obvious, could not provide an adequate solution. So far

Reprinted from Palmer O. Johnson and Oswald L. Harvey, *The National Youth Administration,* Staff Study No. 13 (Washington: U. S. Government Printing Office, 1938), pp. 1-6; 88-90.

as possible the relief program had to be tempered with constructive planning which might help to resolve the fundamental problems of social and individual maladjustment and yield results of permanent social value. Plans of varying nature and effectiveness were introduced to meet the needs of the groups principally affected, and the National Youth Administration was set up as an integral part of the program.

Approximately one-sixth of the population of the United States falls within the age limits 16 to 24. With the declining birth rate this proportion may be expected to diminish correspondingly, until such time as population structure and size may have become fairly stable. In 1870 there were two persons over 25 to every youth between the ages of 15 and 25; by 1930 this ratio had risen to 3 to 1; and it is estimated that by 1960 it will be as high as 4 to 1. Thus youth would seem to become progressively less significant as a group for national consideration. Because youth constitute, however, the immediate group to assume active participation in political, social, and economic life, their preparation is vitally important to society as a whole. From this point of view they warrant the most concentrated attention.

Partly as an outcome of the population changes referred to above, youth fall heir to two especially significant social tendencies, one of which is to their advantage, the other not. As the proportion of young dependents in the population grows smaller and the proportion of wage-earning adults larger, it becomes possible to devote more and more attention to the needs of the youth group. Because of the need for an informed and educated citizenry, youth are being encouraged and will continue to be encouraged to attend school, and to progress so far as their abilities will permit; educational facilities are being extended and improved; and the total educational offering is becoming more diversified to provide for specific individual needs.

By contrast with the increased educational opportunities thus made available, however, vocational opportunities for youth may be expected to diminish. Technological improvements tend to increase the number of units of production per man, but they also give rise to constant shifting of occupations and corresponding periods of unemployment and readjustment for large groups of workers. They increase the amount of leisure time permitted to the individual, but they also demand a narrower and more specific type of skill and preparation on the part of the worker. Increasing competition for available jobs is an inevitable concomitant of technological improvement and a rapidly aging population. In the future job preference will probably be given to those with experience. This tendency is already evident. Job opportunities for youth may be expected in time to become more and more circumscribed. Youth may have to remain in school longer because of lack of economic opportunity and the preference for somewhat older and more experienced workers.

The significance of these coming events, however, has not yet been fully appreciated. Many youth have already left school, but only a few have been accommodated in industry. It is estimated that about two-thirds as many youth are out of school and seeking work as are in school or college.

Some of the unemployed youth would like to return to school or to continue with the studies which by necessity they may be forced to terminate. But either the school program has nothing more to offer that interests them, or the costs of further schooling are prohibitive. Although the facilities for free education have been provided, the costs of mainte-nance are such that many youth cannot afford to avail themselves of these facilities. It has been the common experience of social workers and school principals that children who drop out of school come most frequently from families in the lower income brackets; and it is the general impression that the representation of students in college is directly related to the income of their families. Various ways of providing for needy youth, such as low tuition fees, scholarships, and the cooperative plan of alternative periods of study and gainful employment, were in fairly common practice at the college level even before the depression; and the inadequacy of these provisions was recognized. That similar need existed and still exists among high school students was not fully appreciated until the depression made it obvious.

Thus, despite the educational opportunities already available, there are still many youth who, for want of a modicum of assistance, cannot utilize them. For this condition of affairs the schools are not wholly to blame. To the extent that their programs of study are insufficiently diversified and adapted to the individual needs of students, the fault is undoubtedly theirs. They are taking steps to remedy the defect, but progress, especially at the higher levels, is slow. Meeting the educational needs of youth who lack the necessary economic resources to attend school, however, is the function of the people themselves. It is not sufficient to establish com-pulsory attendance laws unless adequate school facilities are provided, or to offer free schooling for all unless added provisions, especially in terms of maintenance, are furnished to make attendance possible.

By raising the upper level of compulsory attendance to age 18, provid-ing the necessary resources for tuition and maintenance, and adapting the educational offering to the needs of youth, a large number of young persons now out of school and unemployed could be removed from the labor market and rehabilitated. Given guidance and appropriate training, the difficulties and stresses of their subsequent period of adjustment to employment conditions could be considerably reduced. Their problem is neither purely educational nor purely occupational, but a synthesis of both; it is essentially one of rehabilitation.

Unemployed youth out of school are caught between the upper and the lower millstones of necessity. On of the one hand, without training or experience they are of little or no value to an employer; current laws relating to accident liability and insurance influence employers to give preference, if any, to the older youth; and the demand for higher educational qualifications has grown more and more insistent. On the other hand, without resources to prolong their schooling, or without confidence in the programs offered by the schools, these unemployed youth cannot prosecute that period of further preparation conducive to adequate participation in gainful employment. As a result, unless they are given direct encouragement and considerable rehabilitation, they almost inevitably constitute a focus of social maladjustment. Upon them is the curse of not being wanted, with all its concomitants of apathy or resentment and of personality disintegration. The possibilities of their engaging in antisocial behavior under such circumstances are obvious.

The Federal Government intervened to help remedy the plight of unemployed youth by the establishment successively of the Civilian Conservation Corps and the National Youth Administration. Although relief was inevitably one of the purposes in their establishment, the stimulation of educational interests and the economic and social rehabilitation of youth were also regarded as major objectives of these agencies. Turning the talents of youth to constructive ends, they sought to employ them on projects of economic value as well as of educational significance. The record of achievement of these agencies is considerable.

. . . . .

EDUCATIONAL CONCEPTS AND POLICIES

As an emergency agency, flexible in its administration and with relatively large available funds, the National Youth Administration has been able to experiment in educational programs which, under ordinary circumstances, would have received little consideration by regular agencies of Government, and which even today are not fully recognized by the majority of educators.

Through the extension of educational opportunities to the underprivileged, the Youth Administration has uncovered a reservoir of competent youth desirous of continued education for whom almost no provision has been made in the past. It has demonstrated the possibility of providing educational opportunities at small cost which have proved of considerable advantage to the youth and to the institutions involved. And, by providing merely the essentials for the maintenance of youth, it has increased school and college enrollments by 300,000 to 400,000 without sacrificing quality to quantity.

Experimentation which grew out of the necessity for combining work with schooling has demonstrated possibilities of profound educational significance. Especially noteworthy in this connection are those work projects, sponsored by educational institutions, in which youth are maintained in residence at the institutions and undergo a course of training related to their employment on work of benefit to the institutions themselves. To the extent that the National Youth Administration has been successful in thus combining work and schooling, the more pointedly by contrast does it emphasize the inadequacies of the conventional current curriculum and guidance policies at both high school and college levels.

Although the nominal aim of the National Youth Administration has been to serve as a relief agency, it has actually fulfilled an educational function as well. Because relief was the primary objective, the educational policy of the Youth Administration has of necessity been of a temporizing and exigent nature. Had the educational function been considered as of primary rather than of secondary importance, it is not unlikely that the policies and programs here reported would have been considerably altered. To the conflicting practices inevitably resultant from this confusion concerning the relative importance of the functions of relief and education may in large measure be attributed many of the apparent discrepancies and inconsistencies in the present program.

URGENT PROBLEMS OF YOUTH

If there is today a "lost generation" of youth lacking work experience, lacking guidance, abandoned by the school, and disowned by industry, and if, as is often claimed, the new social and economic status of youth resultant from changes in the age composition of the population calls for national leadership in meeting the problems of youth, then it must be conceded that in large measure the National Youth Administration has contributed significantly toward the solution of these problems.

Without doubt the depression adversely affected the morale of youth. But by providing youth with an articulate agency for the expression of their needs and a focal point of direct action in meeting them, the National Youth

Administration has helped to restore their morale. The indictment that actual achievement has failed to measure up to the demand for service becomes, therefore, a criticism not of inadequacy in function so much as of limitations in application. Through each of its major programs the National Youth Administration has provided youth with facilities for continued education, work experience, practical guidance, and, so far as possible, placement in employment in private industry. There is much to indicate that the morale and health of youth participating in student aid and work projects employment have improved.

By experimenting with youth of unrevealed potentialities in unusual situations, the National Youth Administration has drawn attention to many inadequacies in the current provisions for vocational guidance. Many unemployed youth, poorly educated and untrained, are to all appearances fit for nothing but unskilled or semiskilled work; nevertheless, time and again, reports are received concerning the surprising extent of their achievements when given the right environment, an encouraging and skillful supervisor or foreman, and the chance to do constructive work.

Some of the misgivings of professional educators regarding the educational program of the Civilian Conservation Corps were expressed in an article by George A. Coe, then a faculty member of Union Theological Seminary and a frequent contributor to *The Social Frontier*.

121. What Kind of School Is a CCC Camp?

George A. Coe

Of all the numerous types of relief devised since the onset of the depression, the Citizens Conservation Corps is by all odds the best—the best for bodily health and vigor, and especially the best for mental health and balance. Moreover, the camps have provided something more than relief; they have had an educational fringe from the beginning, and now, under the inspiration of former Commissioner Zook and the leadership of Dean Marsh, education is becoming a definite aim and a planned activity. Each camp has an educational adviser who is under broad instructions to get

Reprinted from George A. Coe, "What Kind of School Is a CCC Camp?" *The Social Frontier*, I, 8 (May 1935), pp. 24-26.

acquainted with the needs and the aspirations of the young men, and then to employ on their behalf whatever means and agencies are available in the local situation. Each adviser starts, as it were, "from scratch." He is not encumbered by precedents nor by formal orders from supervisors, nor are any of the mechanics of "school" obligatory. If the resulting programs have a patchwork appearance, they have also the virtues of adaptation to the pupils informality, the experimental attitude, and all-'round plasticity. Such programs, or something to be developed out of them, will surely be a growing feature of the camps, however long or short their future may be. In fact, the main problem of their future is an educational one. Considered as relief, their efficiency is unquestionable; considered as schools, however, the kind and degree of their value remain to be determined.

The Need for Educational Appraisal

That an immediate educational appraisal of the CCC is needed should be evident. The Department of Superintendence implies as much when, without naming the Corps, it asks for an adequate program of work "and education" for our masses of unemployed youth. Already in various parts of the country research men are beginning to consider what outcomes should be expected from camp experience, and testing processes are being tentatively applied. Meantime, the popularity of the camps is so great that hasty proposals are being made with respect to their future. The Society of American Foresters, and Mr. Silcox, the head of our Forestry Service, have recommended that, in the interest of our forests, the camps be made a permanent feature of American life. On grounds broader than this there is a widespread belief that a year of camp life would be a wholesome experience for American youth generally, and that the present CCC camps furnish the right nucleus for such a development. The idea of learning through camping, already popularized by the Christian Associations, the Boy Scouts, and other agencies, is thus developing into a movement for a unique addition to our school system—unique on this continent, though not without partial precedents in Europe. Finally, from the head of our army comes the suggestion that military training be added to the present camp programs to the end of enlarging our reserve force. Each of these proposals for expansion carries within itself the danger of relegating education to the realm of wishful thinking, or at most to the status of a rather hit-or-miss by-product of a generous impulse. Any experienced teacher who inspects a CCC camp with the question in mind of its actual and possible effects upon growth in knowledge, attitudes, and habits will discover far more problems than solutions.

Any discerning eye, it is true, will delight in some features of CCC camp experience. To take part in making one's own habitation comfortable, sanitary, and neat; to build a playground and then use it oneself; to make the yard and the approaches to the camp attractive; to make flower-beds or rock gardens; to indulge such hobbies as photography, nature-study, and the building of radio receivers; to have regular hours; to adjust oneself to a co-operative group; to be in intimate contact with beauty in nature—all this means that important educational forces already are at work. It must be remembered, too, that each of these young men actually earns $30 a month by self-respecting toil, that $25 of this amount is paid directly by the government to his parents or to his dependents, and that the remainder may be spent as one will. For all this no educator can fail to be thankful. But can any educator forget that these young men are parts of a far larger human world; that this is the period in life in which, if ever, they will develop an active interest in and knowledge of this larger world; that their present experience of hardship and of uncertainty as to their future makes them peculiarly ready to inquire into the realities of life and of society, and that even so short a period as six months to a year just now may well be the decisive factor in determining their significance as adult citizens?

What, then, is a CCC camp considered as a school? In particular, do the camps contain the essential elements of a permanent educational plan? Can we, if we so desire, build a new unit of our school system upon what we already have here? The conditions for health and morale during a few months of economic distress are here, to be sure; but what about the other conditions and processes of education? Let us use our eyes.

PAUCITY OF EQUIPMENT AND INADEQUACY OF STAFF

The equipment of the camps is equipment for temporary relief, not for teaching and learning. The forest can be used for teaching forestry, of course, and such maintenance-operations as cooking and truck-driving, but these few occupations are of concern to only a small minority, and normal facilities for any other systematic teaching are not present even in skeleton form. The primary requirement of space for teaching and learning is not met. The educational adviser must use unadapted parts of mess halls and any available corner where men or materials can be assembled. So rudimentary a requirement as sufficient and proper illumination for evening study cannot be taken for granted. The basic physical fact is that a CCC camp is a temporary barracks for "feeding and sleeping" young men who must have immediate relief.

The endeavor to make these relief camps into educational camps has begun at the right point, namely, the installing at each camp of an educational adviser with almost *carte blanche* discretion as to program. But the adviser faces the stark fact that expenditure for his salary is not matched by financial provision for other imperative requirements—books, for example. He may have to wriggle to obtain gifts of books, or loans from public libraries—loans that are cautiously or reluctantly made because the administrative arm of the librarian is not long enough to reach to the camp. One can find camp "libraries" that contain nothing but one or two daily newspapers, piles of donated magazines, and less than half a dozen works of any kind upon the bookshelf. This, for the mental nourishment of two hundred young Americans! Materials and tools for laboratory and shop work are similarly scant. As for teachers, the adviser has to rely upon three unsteady sources: uncompensated speakers and leaders who may be enlisted in near-by communities; educated young men who happen to be found in the camp, and unemployed teachers who are receiving educational relief. Of these last only a few are provided, and the fluctuations in available public funds make even this resource a wavering one. Some of the most vital courses have here or there been dropped because relief funds are contracting.

Incidental Nature of Educational Program

The young men are required to spend seven or more hours daily at road-building, erosion-prevention, fire-prevention, and the like. There are available for systematic instruction and study only such energy and inclination as remain after a day's labor. That road-building itself has educational value need not be questioned, but to assume that effective cultural, civic, and vocational study requires only such left-over time and energy would be absurd.

The "enrolees" are not required to attend any classes, nor to do any studying, nor to meet any standards or take any tests. Naturally so, for the CCC is essentially a scheme of work-relief, and only incidentally and as an afterthought a scheme for schooling young men. If this situation has the advantage of putting the educational adviser upon his mettle because he must make courses attractive, it has the disadvantage—especially in view of the compulsory seven-hour work day—of representing education as a "take-it-or-leave-it" extra. Some camp commandants are willing to put pressure upon the young men, as by granting certain privileges only to those who attend educational classes, but such measures only accentuate the inherent maladaptation of the situation to the aims of education.

Military Administration and Educational Aims

The educational adviser is a subordinate official even in his own specialty —subordinate to a man who pursues a very different specialty. That the army officers who are in charge are not educators is not to their discredit, nor is it surprising that some of them flounder when they make decisions that affect teaching and learning. Indeed, there is something less than fairness in a system that subjects them to tests for which their training and experience have not prepared them. They are there as part of an emergency measure; they are required to do as best they can something that had to be done suddenly. The results are as good as we had any right to expect. It appears that in the by and large these military men, after some natural hesitation, are loyally supporting the new educational scheme. Some at least of the higher officers are strenuously for it. Yet the fact remains that military men are required to supervise a type of civilian service for which they have not been trained. If the camps are to become a permanent part of our school system, the present method of administering them will need to be changed, and undoubtedly it will be changed by making it either more specifically military in type or else more specifically civil. We shall have either camps managed by military men for military purposes (even though educational phraseology be employed), or else school camps managed by educators for purposes of civil education, general and vocational. Between the military and the civil we shall have to choose.

The question just raised leads on to a deeper one. We have not merely to determine who shall supervise a school, the meaning of "school" being agreed upon, but also to decide whether the old American meaning of the term shall be fundamentally transformed. Sleepily to assume that the present drive for militarizing the CCC means nothing more than adding a new frill to an old educational garment is to accept a cultural revolution without knowing that one is doing it. It is to surrender at this important point the definitely civil basis and control that hitherto have been taken for granted in our school system. This is not a merely theoretical or "academic" issue even for the present camps; if the camps are to become a permanent part of our school system, the issue is overwhelmingly practical and overwhelmingly important. What is to be the specific and basic difference between our camps and those of Hitler's Germany? There, too, a year in a work camp is looked upon as wholesome for youths; it is "educational" in the there-accepted sense of "education." But the all-controlling aim is that of Fascism The *Arbeitsdienst* is intended to fuse the youth of Germany into a particular kind of national unity, namely, the kind that unquestioningly and unanimously accepts political and economic orders from above just as a soldier accepts military orders. Hitler's scorn of democracy and of the whole idea of popular rule underlies his work-camp scheme. This is why it is military in tone and method. By the same sign, our own public education, to the extent that it becomes basically military, will promote the narrow virtues of the soldier, not the virtues of a citizen of a democracy going freely about his daily duties. It is not unfair to add that there are some Americans who hold essentially Fascist conceptions of government, and that many Americans are unawake to the almost world-wide growth of the plant that has flowered in Italy and Germany.

COMPREHENSIVE PLANNING VERSUS SCRATCHING THE SURFACE

The 360,000 young men now in these camps are only a minor fraction of those who have equal need of such help. Moreover, there are no camps for young women. What, then, do the proponents of a permanent system have in mind? Do they envisage camp education for only the present fraction of distressed young men, or for all distressed young men, or for all young men, or for all youth of both sexes? If the purpose is education, why not provide a year in the forest for all alike? But this, even if the age of eligibility were reduced from the present 18-25 to 18-22 or 17-21, would require a more than thirty-fold multiplication of present facilities! Moreover, these facilities would have to be transformed from lath and building-paper to permanent materials, and buildings and equipment for education would have to be added. Even if a less inclusive plan should be adopted, the erection of durable structures for housing, feeding, and education would be crushingly expensive; and, when all was done and ready, the camps, as educational units, would largely duplicate our high schools and junior colleges.

Beyond the question of financial cost there emerge also problems that concern educational validity. For example, is prolonged segregation from the society of women wholesome at this period in a young man's career? Is this the way to promote growth towards normal family life? Indeed, is it certain that a prolonged stay in the forest is altogether favorable for social growth in general? Can we assume that the values of a short vacation in the wilds will attach to a period several times as long, or that other social values than those of a vacation can readily be imported into such far places? The difficulty of carrying on vocational education at a distance from the varied industries of the country seems to be rather obvious. As for cultural and civic growth, the centres of population, large and small, appear as yet to be the most favorable environment. For it is in these centers that the issues that most involve culture, character, and citizenship become most visible;

it is here that the original material for study most abounds. That is, the present sites of our high schools and junior colleges are distinctly better than the forests for the educational purposes that permanent camps would have to pursue.

The short of the matter is that the CCC, though wisely conceived as a means of emergency relief, is only beginning to acquire social and educational perspectives. The camps will endure, supposedly, as long as the necessity for mass relief continues. Whether this period be long or short, the educational advisers who under present conditions can create only a few fragments of education, should be provided with the means and the personnel for something more systematic and organized. It is fortunate that Commissioner Studebaker has announced that he sees here a great educational opportunity. Yet we may as well realize that the CCC cannot offer, either economically or educationally, very much beyond palliatives for a fractured youth-experience. Only preposterously naïve thinking can take the camps as a guide to a permanent system.

The young men in the CCC were almost without exception school "dropouts," many of them, in fact, either functionally or totally illiterate. Even so, the enrollees could hardly be said to represent the lowest classes in American society of the thirties. The Negro, for example, was not generally included in the program, nor was any applicant with a police record accepted. Yet the educational function of the CCC was one not being performed by American education in its traditional role, and in this sense the CCC was of considerable importance. The following are comments made by enrollees, first on the educational program, then on the CCC generally.

122. Comments of CCC Enrollees

Of course a lot of boys could learn a lot more in here than they do if they wanted to. But I guess a lot of them can't learn any more and a lot of them don't want to learn any more.

. . . . .

If a guy wanted to learn something he really could learn in camp. The only thing was, I wasn't interested enough to take anything.

. . . . .

Reprinted by permission from Kenneth Holland and Frank E. Hill, *Youth in the CCC*, American Council on Education, Washngton, D. C., 1942, pp. 163; 237-240.

This mechanics class is O.K. We learned how to tear down a motor there. I like the things we study around camp better than the things I studied in school. You're allowed to do more as you please. You aren't tied down as you are in school. Then you can ask questions and talk up if you want to, and smoke.

. . . . .

Sure, I've learned something while I was in camp. I got my eighth grade diploma. I've learned a little typing, too. Of course I haven't learned it any too good, but I have learned something about typing. I plan to get more education now. I always felt that a person should have more education than grade school.

. . . . .

I don't see why they have it here. A lot of the boys don't need to go no further in school than they already have.

. . . . .

I couldn't read or write when I got to camp. The adviser got a woman to come out from town and teach me and some of the other fellows how. It was a big help.

. . . . .

It's all right for a boy who hasn't had a good education. All this stuff here is just sixth, seventh, and eighth grade work. Of course, there's some exceptions—like welding and the auto mechanics class I'm taking.

. . . . .

It bolstered my courage. I've got more ambition now.

. . . . .

Back home there were seven of us—five boys and two girls. In camp I got more room to sleep and it was quieter.

. . . . .

I was a bad egg before I went to camp. I was the black sheep of the family, I guess. Well, my folks treat me different now when I go home. I've been sending them money and helping them out.

. . . . .

It's better than home. At home I didn't get anything to eat.

. . . . .

I knew a boy right here in this camp that hadn't ever been nowhere and didn't know nothing when he came. When he left there was all the change in the world in that boy. He learned how to read and write and how to get along with people. It was a big improvement in him and the CCC done it.

. . . . .

Around home if you want to take a bath you have to go and get a bucket of water and go through all that stuff. Taking a shower in camp was a lot different. In camp it was a pleasure to take a bath.

. . . . .

Well, I think I have learned something from the work I have been doing in camp. I didn't know anything about laying tile or cutting rock before I came to camp. Working on the rocks, we get a little chance to do some masonry work when we build a fence with them. The work has given me more experience. Then you always know a little something about any job. You know what to do at the start and that's half the trick about getting a job. You are not so green as you would be otherwise.

. . . . .

I can't say that anything I learned in the CCC helped me to get that job. [A Negro ex-enrollee speaks of a job he obtained in a restaurant.] But in a way it might have. All those forty guys that were ahead of me were all just like I was before I went to the CCC. They never had a steady job before. Now I had been in the CCC for six months, so I had work experience. That gave me an edge on the other guys. No, they didn't *say* that is why they hired me, but that is how I figure it out.

. . . . .

I learned a lot from the work in the CCC and thought it very interesting. [From a leader-enrollee] We made slag roads. I had to supervise the fellows. We had to get logs from far away. We sent the trucks after them and loaded up each truck. The trucks would come in and dump their loads and then we'd lay a slag road out of 'em. I liked that sort of constructive work.

. . . . .

I didn't think the work we did was "made work." It was really important. We were building a national park. The boys were really improving the scenery. Yes, sir; the CCC really improved Wisconsin's scenery.

The idea of the "community school" was of a school entirely integrated into the life of a community which through the work of the school would act to improve and reform the whole society.

The community school in theory was put forward by the social frontiersmen, then worked out in experimental efforts in various communities throughout the United States. Paul R. Hanna's discussion of the idea with illustrations of the community school in practice entitled "The School: Looking Forward," was a part of the 1939 yearbook of the John Dewey Society, *Democracy and the Curriculum* edited by Harold Rugg.

123. The School and Community Development

Paul R. Hanna

We will now focus our discussion on [an additional] function of the School—that of *community development*. Modern research has demonstrated that changes in human affairs are partly the result of what *we* do. There was a time not so far distant when we relied upon supernatural powers to direct the daily course of events; and because these happenings were under the sole direction of some power outside ourselves we took a fatalistic attitude toward disease, famine, poverty, slums, and related phenomena that were detrimental to our welfare.

A new conception is developing in our modern world which looks at change as subject to control by human thought and will. We know that we have the natural resources, the man power and mechanical power to turn and direct our vast productive equipment of ingenious machines, and we have the engineering and managerial skill to organize the agricultural and industrial systems for continuous and capacity production. We know that the rational maintenance and improvement of this system need not be dependent upon chance and drift or the classical laws of economics, but upon our determination to use our resources—natural, human, and technical—to satisfy our human needs. Elimination of poverty, slums, illness, famine, and a host of similar "man-made" problems can be solved relatively soon if we use science and reason in organizing a set of social, economic, and political rules and regulations suited to the demands of our new technological age.

What agency in the community shall be given the responsibility for thus serving our common ends? What organization shall the democratic community establish to function as the laboratory in which community problems are studied and possible solutions proposed for the consideration and action of the citizens? In this volume the committee takes a position that the School as herein conceived serves the community in this capacity. It is the best housed, the best equipped, the best staffed, and most adequately financed of all the community agencies. Being responsible to the people at large, it is quickly responsive to needs as they arise in the community. In fact, the School serves as the "feelers" for the community and continually scouts

From Chapter XIV, "The School: Looking Forward," by Paul Hanna, from *Democracy and the Curriculum, The Life and Program of the American School* (Third Yearbook of the John Dewey Society): Copyright 1939 by D. Appleton-Century Company, Inc. Reprinted by permission of Appleton-Century-Crofts, Division of Meredith Publishing Company, pp. 392-396, 400-402.

out those problems which may yet be sufficiently widespread to cause general community concern. It is granted that there are numerous other agencies in the community, public and private, which also have programs of social service. The School does not replace all of these groups but rather serves as a coördinating factor. It differs from the general run of social service agencies to the degree that its program is all inclusive rather than particular. It serves to integrate all the separate efforts.

Thus, the School is thought of as the community's organ of social sensitivity and as a laboratory to which citizens bring common problems for solution. The purposes may be summed up as "community development."

URBAN COMMUNITY SURVEY AS INITIAL STEP

In *urban communities* the School functions typically as follows: The staff takes the initiative in discovering the state of affairs of the community in all types of human activity. On the staff are experts in sociological survey who are able to make as searching an analysis of the community as the Lynds made of Middletown.[1] The School gives opportunity to children, youth, and adults to participate in the fact-gathering phases of the survey. In the program of general education much of the classroom and laboratory work consists of working over the data collected in the survey. Children and youth find a vast amount of statistical work to be done, they meet problem-solving situations in designing tables and charts to record and report summaries of findings, they need a great deal of facility in oral and written expression as the data are studied and reported to the public, the work involves technics of study and general work habits—all these phases are essential to the educational program of the School as the survey progresses. Continuous analysis and reporting to the public by radio, press, public forums, exhibits of data, and dramatizations of findings, challenge the children, youth, and adults who are enrolled in the School.

Out of the survey findings comes a period of intensive community evaluation of the status of local affairs. Comparative studies with other communities show strengths and weaknesses.[2] The use of public forums, the pulpit, press, radio, clubs, and all other channels for democratic participation in policy-making results in a list of shortages in community welfare that should be attacked directly.

[1] Paul R. Hanna, *Youth Serves the Community* (New York, D. Appleton-Century Co., 1936). Describes projects done by schools in community survey.

Samuel Everett, editor, *The Community School* (New York, D. Appleton-Century Co., 1938). Also describes similar projects.

[2] The John Marshall High School of Minneapolis has made comparative community surveys for several years.

PROJECT OF COMMUNITY BEAUTIFICATION

For example, the survey may clearly disclose the lack of physical beauty and charm resulting from too little attention given to zoning laws, public parks and gardens, the landscaping of public buildings and private family dwellings, etc. The School focuses on the need and desirability of community action to improve the conditions. If sufficient community approval can be generated, the School then turns to designing plans of action.[3] Who formulates these plans of action? The children, youth, and adults attending the School actually create the plans and propose them to the public. If acceptable to the community, the student body of the School again plays the leading rôle. Principles of zoning are drawn up and presented to the civic authorities for consideration. Public parks, playgrounds, and recreation centers are planned in terms of the preferences of the community, availability of sites, climate, financial resources, etc. The School carries on a long-range program of discussion and education in order that the policies may be widely understood, and it is done largely through the students' activities. In the writing classes the students prepare bulletins and press releases. Students portray by posters, murals, models, and diagrams the reorganized and landscaped "city beautiful." Dramatizations created and produced by students show what the increased efficiency and beauty would mean to all the citizens of the community. Further, when public opinion has crystallized into a decision for action, the School students take the lead in starting the landscaping of private dwellings and public parks and highways. A nursery for experimental work with native and imported plants and shrubs demonstrates what is possible.[4] Sufficient quantities of new stock are produced here for use along highways and around public buildings. The public comes to the nursery for observation and instruction in gardening.

Much of the actual work of planting and some of the care of public gardens are done by the students. Again, caution is exercised that this does not develop into exploitation of child labor. This socially useful work occupies a small share of the student's time and energy from early adolescence through the period of general education, and participation may continue throughout active life if so desired by the individual.

The School over a period of a decade is able to point to convincing objective evidence that the community is far more beautiful, that life is

[3] In Santa Barbara, California, a community project of beautification a number of years ago is largely responsible for the fact that Santa Barbara has for several years won national recognition for being one of the most beautiful cities in America.

[4] Again in Santa Barbara the city schools have for years contributed to the improvement of plant life in public places as well as training gardeners and landscape workers.

lived more effectively because of the planned growth under new zoning ordinances and because of the care given to landscaping highways, public buildings, and residential areas, etc. Community consciousness will prohibit unsightly buildings, refuse heaps or unbeautified vacant lots. The city becomes known far and wide for its beauty.

Community Housing Project

Another shortage of our urban community discovered by the survey is likely to be in the housing facilities. The School organizes study groups in which the problems of housing are discussed.[5] The survey report shows a direct correlation between poor housing and high crime rate and high rate of disease. The effects of poor housing on other values in the neighborhood are obvious from the data.[6] A canvas of housing projects in other cities demonstrates how these social and economic ills are lessened when the community attacks the rehousing of its citizens.

The problem of housing is jointly studied by the School and all other agencies of the community interested in housing. Under the scholarly and expert supervision of the staff the students plan a long-term educational program designed to make the community conscious of the benefits to be had by housing projects. The sociological relations, the economic factors, and the health problems are clearly and forcefully presented to the public. As community opinion is built in favor of a housing program the School through its classes in regional planning, architecture, finance, etc., keeps the press, radio, and public forums supplied with concrete proposals for action. The students take the major responsibility for keeping the project moving forward toward community action. (As the project gets under way many adults enroll in the School work in order to understand better and contribute to the community housing plans.)

When construction work has actually begun, the project offers ample opportunity for the students to participate in the labor. Some students have apprenticeship experiences with the building trade and crafts; others participate in apprenticeship relations in the preparation and supervision of construction schedules. As the construction proceeds classes study materials and processes. In the laboratories they test insulations; they experiment with a variety of methods of lighting and heating; they test synthetic materials and compare them with natural construction materials. Classes follow

[5] Hanna, *op. cit.* Describes several projects on housing done by children and youth.
[6] With the boys of economically depressed areas of Cleveland Henry Harap reports interesting results of a study of housing.

the financing of the project. Others study the changes that the new houses may have on the life of families who will occupy them upon completion.

This problem offers opportunities for each student to assist families in properly furnishing the new homes and in reorganizing family attitudes and habits, thus increasing the possibility of their living happily in the new surroundings. Classes in home furnishings and interior decoration take possession of one of the new houses and completely furnish it in keeping with the income of the family which is to occupy it.[7]

. . . . .

These concrete descriptions of the manner in which the new School functions in *community development* complement the function of *individual development*. It must be noted that the two functions are not separate and certainly not antagonistic. Surely the welfare of each individual is enhanced by the beautification of the community, by rehousing, by higher standards of living resulting from improved agricultural practices, and from the conservation of soil and water. It is impossible to work realistically for the fuller development of the individual without directly attacking the improvement of the environment in which the child and youth are nurtured.

Further, as the individual participates in socially useful work of community development he is engaging in the most favorable experiences for his own personal development. In such coöperative and realistic enterprises he has the opportunity to formulate purposes, plan action to achieve the ends sought, carry out the plan, and judge the validity of his plan and method by the test of social approval. It is a demonstrated fact that for most people the most effective motivation is the approval of contemporaries for work done well for the social group. There is a joy in laboring for causes larger than one's own immediate ends that cannot be matched in any self-centered endeavor. The reaction of the group to the contribution made has the salutary effect of leading on to more of the same sharing.

There is no doubt that in our culture today advances in technology have outrun the corresponding advances in human relations, and as one of the results we find the educative experience of labor denied children and youth. Several million youth are today out of school and not employed. Psychology demonstrates that personality development is directly dependent on activity, on experience. For millions of our youth there is lacking these proper growth experiences. The vast reservoirs of energy dammed up in our youth need some outlet. The energy will be utilized for individually and socially destructive ends unless some modifications in our social arrangements are made toward channeling this energy in socially useful labor. Therefore as a prophylactic measure alone the School and its program of community development as herein described is a necessity; it organizes

---

[7] Public School No. 78 in the Bronx, New York City, has conducted a similar project in connection with the Hillside Housing Development.

the community life in the interests of the development of the individual through projects designed to develop the community.[8]

Again, the best theory of growth indicates that "study and learning" are carried on in solving the daily problems faced in living. To illustrate: Reading is best mastered as a tool in situations where the individual is eager to find the answer to some perplexing problem believing he will find pertinent information on the printed page. Here the focus is on "reading to learn" rather than "learning to read," and psychological research indicates that greater growth results from the former approach than from the latter. When the individual purposes to discover the fate of other cultures where soil erosion was unchecked, he is engaging in experience that will be rich in new understanding, in factual information, and in skills of reading and research. When the individual is constructing a model of the reorganized "city beautiful" he is "learning" many things—manipulative skills of handling tools and materials, art principles and technics, social relations of environment to human living, etc. When the individual is engaged in testing insulation materials for the rehousing development, he is not only "learning" the best insulation for the particular construction job, but at the same time he is learning the meaning of the scientific method, learning many science principles of reflection, conduction, and convection, learning many related economic facts and principles. In many ways he is "learning" as he carries on life in coöperative socially useful projects under the direction of the School.

The Eight-Year Study was an experimental project sponsored by the Progressive Education Association through its Commission on the Relation of School and College involving thirty secondary schools throughout the country. The study was a crowning effort of the thirties to explore new possibilities in curriculum and teaching in the secondary school. The findings of the study were published in a five-volume series entitled *Adventure in American Education,* the summary volume of which was *The Story of the Eight-Year Study* written by Wilford M. Aikin, who was chairman of the Commission. The following selections from Aikin's volume briefly outline the general findings of the study.

[8] The work projects of the CCC and NYA are more and more recognizing the principles as here stated. The newer projects contribute both to the development of the individual and of the community.

124. The Eight-Year Study

Wilford M. Aikin

What can be said now at the end of the Eight-Year Study? What has been learned through this experience? Have the hopes and expectations of those who inaugurated the project been fulfilled?

It should be recalled that the Commission had two major purposes:

1. To establish a relationship between school and college that would permit and encourage reconstruction in the secondary school.
2. To find, through exploration and experimentation, how the high school in the United States can serve youth more effectively.

Let us consider now the findings of the Study in the realm of school and college relations. The second part of this chapter presents conclusions based upon the experiences of the schools in their attempts to achieve the second major purpose: better service to American youth.

MANY ROADS LEAD TO COLLEGE SUCCESS

The proposal for co-operation, which was approved by colleges and universities generally in 1932, established an effective co-operating relationship between them and the Thirty Schools for the period of the Study. It permitted and encouraged the participating schools to go ahead with their plans for revision of their work. As stated early in this volume the Commission and the schools held that

success in the college of liberal arts does not depend upon the study of certain subjects for a certain period in high school;

there are many different kinds of experience by which students may prepare themselves for successful work in college;

relations more satisfactory to both school and college could be developed and established upon a permanent basis;

ways should be found by which school and college teachers can work together in mutual regard and understanding.

The study of the college experience of the graduates of the Thirty Schools was made to secure evidence which would confirm these beliefs or show

Reprinted by permission from *The Story of the Eight Year Study* by Wilfred M. Aikin. Copyright 1942, by McGraw-Hill, Inc., pp. 116-120, 122-125.

them to be unwarranted. The evidence is reported briefly in Chapter V and in detail in Volume IV of this Report. A careful examination of the findings can leave no one in doubt as to the conclusions that must be drawn:

> First, the graduates of the Thirty Schools were not handicapped in their college work.
>
> Second, departures from the prescribed pattern of subjects and units did not lessen the student's readiness for the responsibilities of college.
>
> Third, students from the participating schools which made most fundamental curriculum revision achieved in college distinctly higher standing than that of students of equal ability with whom they were compared.

These facts have profound implications for both school and college.

First, the assumption that preparation for the liberal arts college depends upon the study of certain prescribed subjects in the secondary school is no longer tenable. This assumption has been questioned for some time. Earlier studies threw some doubt upon it. The results of this Study disprove it. Success in college work depends upon something else. Real preparation for college is something much more important and vital than the accumulation of 15 prescribed units.

School and college relations based upon this untenable assumption are neither satisfactory nor sound. The relationship is an unhappy one. Colleges criticize the schools saying that students come to college unprepared for their work, that they are deficient in even the most rudimentary academic skills, that their habits of work are careless and superficial, and that they lack seriousness and clarity of purpose. Schools, on the other hand, charge that colleges regiment students, treat them too impersonally, counsel them inadequately, and fail to stimulate them intellectually. Teachers in secondary schools say that college professors are unwilling or unable to see the great problems of the high school, thinking of it only as a place of preparation for college and forgetting the school's obligation to the 80 per cent who stop their schooling at or before graduation from high school. Whether these criticisms are warranted or not, they reveal an unsatisfactory relationship. It does not seem that there can be much more happiness in either group until a sound basis of relationship is established.

The customary relations of school and college are unsound in that emphasis is placed upon outworn symbols—units, grades, rankings, and diplomas. To stand well with its patrons the high school must meet college requirements. If those requirements are not essentials, both school and college are forced into false positions. The college is placed in the position of saying that certain subjects, grades, and units are essential when it knows that they are not; and the school is placed in the false position of forcing students through work which may be of little value to them.

The conclusion must be drawn, therefore, that the assumption upon which school and college relations have been based in the past must be abandoned. It is evident that the liberal arts college has not examined its work thoroughly and realistically and based on that examination its prescription of what is essential in preparation. This Study has proved that some knowledges and skills heretofore generally assumed to be necessary are not needed. It has established, also, that necessary disciplines of mind and character may be achieved through many other subjects than those formerly assumed to be the only effective ones.

It does not follow that it is useless or impossible to describe what preparation is actually required for success in college. Indeed colleges need to know—teachers, pupils, and parents need to know—what knowledge, what skills, what habits, what attitudes constitute the foundation for satisfactory achievement in college. When these are determined, colleges should then require them for admission; schools could then be intelligent in their important task of preparation.

But this is more easily said than done. The college cannot state what preparation is essential unless it knows its own purposes. It must be said here that liberal arts college faculties seldom state clearly what they mean by liberal or general education. Perhaps they do not know. Individual professors often have clearly defined purposes. Sometimes departments such as English, history, economics have set up goals for their work. Rarely, however, have whole college faculties co-operatively thought their problem through and set forth their purposes and plans.

. . . . .

The Eight-Year Study has demonstrated beyond question that colleges can secure all the information they need for selection of candidates for admission without restricting the secondary school by prescribing the curriculum. For this purpose, evidence from such sources as the following would provide ample data:

1. Descriptions of students, indicating qualities of character, habits of work, personality, and social adjustment. Many of the record-forms prepared by the Commission's Committee on Records and Reports are helpful and suggestive in this connection.
2. The results of the use of instruments of evaluation
   a. Such standardized tests as are applicable to the school's work
   b. Other types of tests appropriate to the objectives of the school, such as those prepared by the Evaluation Staff of this Study
   c. Scholastic aptitude tests that measure characteristics essential

to college work and are independent of particular patterns of
school preparation

3. For colleges that require tests given by an outside agency, records
   of achievement in examinations that do not presuppose a particular
   pattern of content. An example is the Comprehensive English examination of the College Examination Board.

An admission plan such as this would not fix the content or organization
of the high school curriculum.

If such a plan were adopted generally by colleges, the secondary schools
of the United States could go about their business of serving all youth more
effectively. Uniformity would be neither necessary nor desirable in the work
of the school. One student would develop the essential skills, habits of
mind, and qualities of character through studies appropriate to his abilities,
interests, and needs; another student would develop the essentials of mind
and character through quite different studies. The secondary school
would then be encouraged to know each student well and to provide experiences most suitable to his development. This, in turn, would lead
to dynamic school curricula. The static, frozen pattern of subjects and
credits would disappear and secondary education would move ahead with
other dynamic forces toward the achievement of a greater democracy.

*The second major implication of the results of the Eight-Year Study is
that secondary schools can be trusted with a greater measure of freedom
than college requirements now permit.* The Thirty Schools, representing
secondary schools of various kinds in many sections, have not abused
their greater freedom. On the contrary, many college authorities wonder
that these schools did not use their freedom more extensively. It may be
thought that the participating schools were restrained from wild experimentation by the college members of the Directing Committee, but such
was not the case. In fact, they have constantly urged the schools to greater
adventure. However, custom is deeply embedded in secondary education. It
is not easy to break down traditional patterns of thinking and acting, nor
do teachers create new ones readily.

Perhaps the chief reason for confidence in the schools' use of freedom
is to be found in the genuine sense of responsibility which most teachers
feel. They are conscious of the far-reaching consequences of their work.
Because of this sense of duty they do not turn lightly from practices of
proved worth to engage in irresponsible experimentation. If some in the
colleges feared that the Thirty Schools would use their freedom recklessly,
they now know that their fears were without foundation.

Without exception the colleges involved state that this Study has been
very much worthwhile. Although there may be doubt concerning some of
the innovations in the schools, the colleges are unanimous in recognizing the

growth which the schools have achieved through participation in the enterprise. The Thirty Schools fervently hope that their new work can be continued and developed more fully. This can be done only if their present freedom is not taken away from them.

SECTION 5

Reconstructionism and Reaction

During the years of World War II, educational planning for the post-war world went forward with enthusiasm. The planners envisioned a world, a brave new one, in which schools would be expanded and enriched and which would play an increasingly important role in American society. For more than a century theorists in education had discussed the essential need of American democracy for a common school education offered to all American children. But in reality there had always been certain limitations and exclusions based on class or caste, on cultural, linguistic, or religious background of children. The vision of the planners of the 1940's, however, was of education literally for *all* American youth. The Educational Policies Commission of the National Education Association clarified and proclaimed the vision in a report published in 1944, *Education for All American Youth*. The ambitious optimism of the Commission's report is evident in the following selections.

125. What Youth Have in Common
Educational Policies Commission

The common qualities of youth are fully as important to education as their differences. For example:

Reprinted by permission from Educational Policies Commission, *Education for All American Youth* (Washington: National Education Association, 1944), pp. 16-19; 408-410.

All American youth are citizens now; all (or nearly all) will be qualified voters in the future; all require education for civic responsibility and competence.

All American youth (or nearly all) are members of family groups now and will become members of other family groups in the future; all require an understanding of family relationships.

All American youth are now living in the American culture and all (or nearly all) will continue to do so in the future; all require an understanding of the main elements in that culture.

All American youth need to maintain their mental and physical health now and in the future; all require instruction to develop habits of healthful living, understanding of conditions which foster health, and knowledge of ways of preventing disease, avoiding injuries, and using medical services.

All American youth will be expected to engage in useful work and will need to work to sustain themselves and others; all therefore require occupational guidance and training, and orientation to current economic conditions.

All American youth have the capacity to think rationally; all need to develop this capacity, and with it, an appreciation of the significance of truth as arrived at by the rational process.

All American youth must make decisions and take actions which involve choices of values; all therefore need insight into ethical values. Particularly do they need to grow in understanding the basic tenet of democracy—that the individual human being is of surpassing worth.

. . . . .

When we write confidently and inclusively about education for *all* American youth, we mean just that. We mean that all youth, with their human similarities and their equally human differences, shall have educational services and opportunities suited to their personal needs and sufficient for the successful operation of a free and democratic society.

These youth are created male or female, black or white, halt or hale. Birth and environment have tended to make some of them more alert or more shrewd or more bold than others. Environment and education have made them rich or poor, law-abiding or delinquent, employed or idle.

Their names are Dumbrowski, Oleson, Cabot, MacGregor, Veschinni, Adamatoulous, Okada, Chin, Valdez, Descartes, Kerchevsky, Schmidt, Smith, and Smythe.

They reside in farmhouses, cabins, trailers, packing boxes, skyscrapers, tenements, hotels, housing projects, houseboats, dormitories, mansions, prison cells, and just plain houses.

Among these youth are many of great potential talents. The American system of education has laid great stress on the development of these talents, wherever they may be found, for the benefit of the nation as well as of individuals. In the years to come, the nation will stand in even greater need of the leadership, the resourcefulness, and the creative abilities of its most capable citizens; and education must prize and cultivate their talents accordingly.

These youth—all of them—are to be the heirs and trustees for all that is good or bad in our civilization. What humanity will achieve a generation hence depends largely on them and on their education now.

Each of them is a human being, more precious than material goods or systems of philosophy. Not one of them is to be carelessly wasted. *All* of them are to be given equal opportunities to live and learn.

．　．　．　．　．

This Commission believes that, in the main, educators and lay citizens alike want the schools to extend their services so as to meet all the educational needs of all youth. Tradition, to be sure, and some vested interests impede change in education, as in every other institution. But, for the most part, these impediments do not arise from any active opposition to educational advancement. They will be largely swept away by a vigorous movement to shape education to the needs of all youth, when once that movement gains momentum.

Given the proposition that secondary education should serve *all* American youth, the chief difficulties are practical. We must plan education for youth in a greatly altered world, the character of which we cannot yet accurately foresee. And in this partially unpredictable world of the future, we must plan to carry education into areas largely unexplored. Facing these uncertainties, we are tempted to postpone planning, to counsel waiting until the outlines of the postwar world become more clear.

We must not wait, however. Events move too swiftly and on too vast a scale for us to be able to cope with them when they are almost upon us. Of some things we are already reasonably sure—the needs of youth, for instance. Others we can predict with some confidence, such as the distribution of employment among the major occupational fields. On a few matters we shall have to hazard conjectures, for example, the volume of private and public employment available for beginning workers.

Furthermore, a considerable body of tested educational experience is available. Much of it is still scattered, to be sure, in pioneering schools throughout the land. But these experiences could readily be brought together and placed at the disposal of everyone.

We will do well, then, to make our plans at once, using all that we know and all that can be reliably predicted; making conjectures now and then, when no better way appears; and revising our plans from time to time to accord with the changing course of events. Better by far to do this, tentative though it may be, than to keep on waiting for the certainty which never comes.

．　．　．　．　．

How Genuine Is Our Interest in Youth?

In the building of our country's future, the education of our youth comes first. The war has reminded us of many virtues and ideals that we had forgotten. One of them is the duty we owe to our children in the provision of their education, not education merely in terms of books, credits, diplomas, and degrees, but education also in terms of living and of preparation for future living.

Look about you. See what we now, in wartime, find it necessary and proper to do for our young men and women in the armed forces. Every one of them is taught some specific occupation, useful to him and to the nation. The health of all of them is zealously guarded by every resource of medical science. Their diet is ample and nutritious. There is useful work for each one of them. Opportunities for their recreation are provided everywhere. They are well-clad and cleanly-housed, well-fed and carefully educated. We compete among ourselves to see to it that they have books to read, music to hear, space to play. We stay at home that they may travel. We deny ourselves that they may have abundance. Their morale and their civic loyalty are our constant concerns. The uniform which proclaims them Americans is the complete and sufficient guarantee everywhere of just and considerate treatment for *all* American youth. This all costs time, effort, sacrifice, thought, and a great deal of money. But we would be properly ashamed to consider convenience when their welfare is at stake.

Shall these young people and their successors in the onward-moving generations be less precious to us when the firing ceases? Is our concern for their welfare, health, education, merely a selfish reflection of our desperate need for their youthful energies and lives on the field of battle? Are we going to forget youth as soon as we no longer need them to fight in the war which we allowed to happen? Where we now teach them how to work, shall we later tell them that their services are not wanted? Where we now assure them that the future of our nation lies in their keeping, shall we later tell young people, in effect, to keep out of civic affairs? Where we now provide college education for all persons qualified for leadership, shall we later return to college education as an economic privilege? Shall we, as soon as peace comes, declare an end to all hopeful cooperation for the welfare of our youth? Shall we then pinch the pennies for peace where we now deal out dollars for destruction?

The program here proposed will cost much more than the inadequate education of the past. There is no doubt of that. But consider this—if we make our economic system work even reasonably well after the war, we shall have a national income of around 110 billion 1940 dollars. Experts who have studied such matters tell us that, with such an income, we will spend:

25 billion dollars for foodstuffs, as compared with 16 billion in 1936
16 billion dollars for housing, as compared with 9 billion
13 billion dollars for household operations and equipment, as compared with 6.5 billion
8 billion dollars for automobiles, as compared with 4 billion
8 billion dollars for clothing, as compared with 4 billion
3 billion dollars for recreation, as compared with 1.6 billion.

Shall we, under such conditions, refuse to increase the 2.5 billion dollars which we have been spending for schools and colleges to educate children and youth of all ages? Shall we, with the highest per capita income of any nation in all history, use our increased wealth to feed, clothe, and house the adults in compartive luxury and neglect to spend any of our increase for the improvement of the education of our children and our youth?

Would you like your children to attend schools like those of Farmville and American City? They can, if you really want them to. Enough is known about how to operate such schools, there is plenty of timber and stone to build them, plenty of wealth to finance them. Your children, your community, your entire state and nation can have schools as good as, or better than, the schools described in this book as soon as you and enough other Americans demand them and do your own special but essential part in bringing them into existence.

The objective was proclaimed—education for all American youth —and was enthusiastically applauded by professional educators and laymen alike. The problems of implementing the ideal, however, were difficult ones that led within a few years to less and less agreement and very little applause. But in the immediate post-war years it appeared to many educators, particularly those of progressive thinking, that the major barrier which had prevented successful education of all youth through the secondary school was the curriculum of the school itself. Hence the curriculum must be reformed, it was thought, and focused on the life of the young and on their needs and interests. The leading group formed to attempt these sweeping curriculum revisions was the "Life Adjustment Movement," an account of the organization of which along with a statement of objectives follows. In actuality the "Movement" never got beyond the discussion stage, and even the talk was abandoned after 1950.

126. Development of the Life Adjustment Movement

J. Dan Hull

1. ORIGIN OF THE PROSSER RESOLUTION

In January 1944 the Division of Vocational Education of the Office of Education in the Federal Security Agency began the preparation of the bulletin *Vocational Education in the Years Ahead,* which was published in 1945. The manuscript was written by a working committee of ten members, but at regular intervals advice was sought from a consulting committee of forty leaders in vocational education.

On May 31 and June 1, 1945 a final conference of the consulting committee was held at the Wardman Park Hotel in Washington. At that meeting many problems were presented relating to the education for life needed by the large group of youth of secondary school age whose needs are not being appropriately met by preparation for college or through training for a specific vocation. The group assembled was able to offer but few solutions to the persistent problems which were presented.

At the closing session the Chairman asked Dr. Charles A. Prosser, Director of Dunwoody Institute, Minneapolis, to summarize the conference. As a part of his summarization, Dr. Prosser said:

> Throughout this conference, repeated references have been made to "neglected groups in vocational education." In closing, I am taking the liberty—in submitting the following Resolution—to point out the largest of these neglected groups of young people; and to propose that another conference like this one be held at an early date to consider what should be done for them.
>
> It is the belief of this conference that, with the aid of this report in

Reprinted by permission form *Education for Life Adjustment—Its Meaning and Implementation,* edited by Harl R. Douglass. Copyright, 1950, The Ronald Press Company, New York, pp. 3-4, 6-7, 9-10.

final form, the vocational school of a community will be able better to prepare 20 per cent of its youth of secondary school age for entrance upon desirable skilled occupations; and that the high school will continue to prepare 20 per cent of its students for entrance to college. We do not believe that the remaining 60 per cent of our youth of secondary school age will receive the life adjustment training they need and to which they are entitled as American citizens—unless and until the administrators of public education with the assistance of the vocational education leaders formulate a comparable program for this group.

We, therefore, request the U. S. Commissioner of Education and the Assistant Commissioner for Vocational Education to call at some early date a conference or a series of regional conferences between an equal number of representatives of general and of vocational education—to consider this problem and to take such initial steps as may be found advisable for its solution.

.   .   .   .   .

What Dr. Prosser meant by the 60 per cent is illustrated in a report presented by Assistant Commissioner John A. McCarthy of the State of New Jersey in the February, 1949, issue of *Tech Training* published by the American Technical Society of Chicago. A study was made to determine the need for a program of vocational education in Trenton, New Jersey. By checking with employers the payroll classifications of 25,445 workers in the industries of the area were determined as follows:

Engineers, others college trained	2.8%
Technicians less than college grade	3.6%
Clerical	7.6%
Skilled trades	18.5%
Laborers	19.5%
Semiskilled	48.0%

Visits to some of the industries gave insights into the jobs of the technicians, semiskilled workers, and laborers. Assistant Commissioner McCarthy summed up the findings as follows:

In general, those classified as semiskilled workers by employers are the repetitive workers in the mass production scheme. They do the same operations over and over again and gain increased ability through repetition. . . .

This is what the "60 percenters" do in Trenton, New Jersey. They may do other things in other communities, but in general what they do is so highly specialized that no adequate job preparatory program can be developed in the school to make them immediately employable on the specialized jobs. They can be trained more speedily and effectively in the actual job environment. Their training is short and intensive, extending from one hour to not more than two or three weeks.

All of this job specialization is not limited to industrial processes. Some of the "60 percenters" were doing highly specialized clerical operations—some on single-purpose machines which too are the result of mass production programs. These workers, mostly women, were operating key punch machines, card-sorting machines, invoice printing and duplicating machines, billing machines, photostat and other copying equipment all too highly specialized for in-school instruction. Much can be done to meet the needs of this group while they are in school, but their needs are not specific job preparation.[1]

The original Prosser Resolution sounded like an attempt to divide high school pupils into three separate and clearly defined groups. Fundamentally, however, it was an attempt by vocational educators to lead a pointed attack on problems common to all educators which cannot be solved by specific vocational training. The Resolution was given point by the fact that only 80 per cent of our youth enter the ninth grade and only 50 per cent remain to be graduated from high school. Obviously, such selectivity is not in harmony with our democratic philosophy.

Results of the National Conference.—Out of the National Conference at Chicago [May, 1947] came a three-phase action program aimed at

1. Creating a wide understanding of the problem and its implications.
2. Stimulating in states and selected communities programs or aspects of programs which will be suggestive to other states and schools.
3. Initiating, operating, and continuing the development of life adjustment educational services in every community.

There plans have been described in the bulletin, *Life Adjustment Education for Every Youth*. Students of secondary education will find in this bulletin no hypothesis or proposal which has not been suggested before. The ideas in it have often been advanced by professors of education and students of social problems. However, never before have they been so generally accepted after careful deliberation by those who have the actual responsibility for American secondary education. It is significant that here forward-looking educators propose to do something in an organized way about conditions which heretofore have received far too little attention.

To point up its efforts to translate theories into practice, the national conference at Chicago recommended the establishment of the Commission on Life Adjustment Education for Youth. The conference also recommended procedures for setting up the Commission.

. . . . .

[1] John A. McCarthy, "Industry Techniques to Solve Problems of 60 Percent Group," *Tech Training*, III, No. 3 (February, 1949), p. 8.

The Commission's Concept of Life Adjustment.—At a work conference which the Commission held in Washington, October 11-15, 1948, participants developed and accepted the following concept: "Life adjustment education is designed to equip all American youth to live democratically with satisfaction to themselves and profit to society as home members, workers, and citizens. It is concerned especially with a sizable proportion of youth of high school age (both in school and out) whose objectives are less well served by our schools than the objectives of preparation for either a skilled occupation or higher education."

Practically all the activities of most persons are related to their homes, their work, and their obligations as citizens. For this reason, the brief statement did not mention other areas of living. However, the Commission had previously named and described four additional important areas for all youth: ethical and moral living, self-realization, the use of leisure, health and safety, and consumer education.[4] As developed in regional and national conferences, life adjustment education means organizing and reorganizing schools to achieve useful living purposes. It means directing the activities of a school and adapting the content and methods of all courses so that each year all students are being prepared for important areas of living.

Basic to such education is a detailed and cumulative study of each pupil which will enable both teacher and pupil to plan appropriate learning activities. Basic also is a knowledge of society which will aid the pupil in making wise decisions in the light of his opportunities and limitations.

The Commission further described life adjustment education by saying:[5]

> It is concerned with ethical and moral living and with physical, mental and emotional health.
>
> It recognizes the importance of fundamental skills since citizens in a democracy must be able to compute, to read, to write, to listen, and to speak effectively. It emphasizes skills as tools for further achievements.
>
> It is concerned with the development of wholesome recreational interests of both an individual and social nature.
>
> It is concerned with the present problems of youth as well as with their preparation for future living.
>
> It is for all American youth and offers them learning experiences appropriate to their capacities.
>
> It recognizes the importance of personal satisfactions and achievement for each individual within the limits of his abilities.
>
> It respects the dignity of work and recognizes the educational values of responsible work experience in the life of the community.
>
> It provides both general and specialized education but, even in the

---

[4] *Life Adjustment Education for Every Youth* (Washington: Federal Security Agency, Office of Education), p. 61-90.

[5] *Ibid.*, pp. 4 and 5.

former, common goals are to be attained through differentiation both as to subject matter and experience.

It has many patterns. For a school, a class, or a pupil it is an individual matter. The same pattern should not be adopted in one community merely because it was effective in another. It must make sense in each community in terms of the goals which are set and the resources which are available.

It emphasizes deferred as well as immediate values. For each individual it keeps an open road and stimulates the maximum achievement of which he is capable.

It recognizes that many events of importance happened a long time ago but holds that the real significance of these events is in their bearing upon life of today.

It emphasizes active and creative achievements as well as adjustment to existing conditions; it places a high premium upon learning to make wise choices, since the very concept of American democracy demands the appropriate revising of aims and the means of attaining them.

It is education fashioned to achieve desired outcomes in terms of character and behavior. It is not education which follows convention for its own sake or holds any aspect of the school as an end in itself rather than a means to an end.

Above all, it recognizes the inherent dignity of the human personality.

In the post-war years the leaders of progressive education acted through the American Education Fellowship (the name was changed in 1944 from Progressive Education Association) to revitalize the movement toward bringing about a reconstruction of American society through the progressive school. At the forefront of these efforts was Theodore Brameld, a professor of education then at New York University, both in formulating the "reconstructionist" theory and in attempting to focus the influence of the AEF on the schools. The following report was written by Brameld for the AEF Policy Committee in 1947, and it reflects the spirit of the progressives of the time. These were the declining years of the movement, however, years of diminishing popular and professional support for its ideas; the organization of the AEF-PEA finally dissolved in 1955.

127. A New Policy for A.E.F.

Theodore Brameld

I

Since 1919 the American Education Fellowship (formerly called the Progressive Education Association) has served a distinctive role in the educational world. Its record of pioneering is long, its achievements influential. Few, if any, persons familiar with the last quarter-century of school history would deny this assertion, even though they may at times criticize some of the methods or outcomes for which the organization has been responsible. Nor would they deny that, directly or indirectly, its influence has extended far beyond the United States; throughout the world—China, India, South America, Australia, Europe—educators have studied and often adopted theories and practices developed by its own commission, published in its many pamphlets and volumes, and demonstrated by its members through projects, research, and school reorganization.

While it is impossible to summarize here in an adequate sense a list of its accomplishments, the AEF from its inception has stood first of all for a dynamic conception of education as vital experience in democratic learning and living. Therefore it has, on the other hand, opposed all forms of school autocracy—whether in the form of administrative organization which denies genuine participation to teachers, students, and parents; or in the form of classroom authoritarianism which places the child in a position of meekness and passivity, and which assumes that learning is chiefly an absorption of predetermined subject-matters. On the other hand, the organization has vigorously supported a great variety of efforts to make the school a living symbol of democracy in the way that superintendents and other officials share their own responsibilities and decisions with the entire personnel; in the way that students join in curriculum planning, rule-making, and school activities; in the way that the whole school radiates its influence through the community by utilizing resources, by influencing civic policy, by drawing adults into its program.

Many of these efforts, while they have by no means succeeded in transforming the entire traditional pattern, are bearing rich educational fruits. Not only have countless schools been modified. Other organizations of large membership have increasingly advocated and stimulated educational experimentation of kinds which were often initiated by the American Education

Reprinted from Theodore Brameld, "A New Policy for A.E.F.," *Progressive Education,* 25 (November, 1947), pp. 258-260, 262, 269.

Fellowship. This is not at all to assert, of course, that the AEF is solely responsible for recent progress toward a more workable conception of democratic education; what is asserted is that, in addition to its own very considerable responsibility, school leaders everywhere have of late been converging more and more toward the major objective which it first clearly formulated in America. The AEF welcomes this convergence wholeheartedly; it will not only continue to exert its own efforts in behalf of more democratic schools as it has defined them; it will seek to co-operate wtih all other educational groups dedicated to their establishment.

But the historic role of the AEF as a spearhead organization, is no longer fulfilled sufficiently by these types of effort. The degree of consensus about the criteria of sound public education in a democracy is now sufficiently large, at least in principle, so that many of the experiments which were earlier quite unique, even heretical, are no longer so regarded. Since accordingly we may predict that given enough time and financial support, American education will move forward along the lines earlier advocated, the question arises whether the AEF has completed its pioneering work—whether its membership and resources could not now better be utilized by dissemination among other organizations larger and richer. This is not only an honest question at the present juncture, it is crucial.

It is crucial, however, not merely or even chiefly because upon its answer depends the further existence of the AEF. Organizations of this sort, like others, can in no sense justify themselves merely because they have had an honorable career, or because many loyal members would feel sad if they dissolved. No, the answer is crucial because America and the world have entered a new period in their evolution—a period which creates unprecedented educational tasks because it generates unprecedented problems of great magnitude and danger. In an important sense, indeed, the responsibilities which education faces today and tomorrow are vastly more serious/ more compelling, than after the first World War. Whether the schools will assume their responsibility in time remains uncertain. That they have the obligation to do so, is, however, utterly certain. And it is precisely this obligation which provides the imperative for a reconstituted and rededicated organizational frontier.

The American Education Fellowship can and must once more therefore become this kind of organization. It can and must prove to teachers, parents, students, administrators, and to the public, that never in history has civilization itself been in greater jeopardy. At the same time, it can and must demonstrate that the opportunity is available to empower education, as never before, with vision and strength on behalf of a peaceful and humane world for the masses of mankind. Here is the vanguard task of the American Education Fellowship in the quarter-century we are now entering.

II

To examine and specify the main characteristics of this period should be one of the first lines of responsibility of the new AEF. That is, it should assist education on every level to understand how fraught with tension, friction, and overt conflict are both our domestic and international relations. Nothing short of the utmost realism and forthrightness will help citizens— young and old alike—to reorganize the depth, breadth, and obstinacy of contemporary problems. The habit of much education still to gloss over these problems because controversial or complex, still to ignore training in propaganda analysis and other techniques essential to their understanding, is proof enough that here alone the AEF could make a tremendous contribution.

The complexities of the social, political, and economic relations of this period should not, moreover, be an excuse for denying that they gravitate around two fundamental and related facts. The first is the fact of an unstable and precarious economy, with its accomplishment of insecurity, inflation, its cycles of boom-and-bust. The second is the fact of national rivalry and hostility with their potential of atomic war accompanied by the horrors of destruction and death on a scale never before imagined.

Yet despite their indisputability, neither of these factors receives a fraction of the attention that education, ostensibly devoted to freedom and truth, should be giving them. To consider the first a moment further, memories are not so short, of course, as to forget the economic events following World War I—the years of reckless prosperity and high living, of growing corporate power and disparities of wealth, followed by years of devastating depression, hunger and fear. During the 'thirties' some American educators became sufficiently concerned to voice their anger at this tragedy through the pages especially of one journal, *The Social Frontier,* and through the volumes especially of the Commission of the Social Studies (American Historical Association). They courageously analyzed the failures of a system which could cause such havoc, and they demanded thoroughgoing changes to eliminate those failures. Yet, as the depression waned and we became preoccupied with winning World War II, even their voices softened to a whisper. It was almost as though those theorists were right who have said that education is always chiefly a reflector of the social order—rather than a critic, leader, and re-creator of social order and culture. At the present moment, it is true that no section of American education is calling attention strongly and clearly to the fact that the prosperity of this decade is, in no essential way, different from that of the 'twenties'—that again we are living and spending recklessly, allowing big business free rein, permitting further concentrations of economic power, building a top-heavy profit structure which, if it rises unchecked, will again inevitably crash.

In only one great respect—though a most crucial one—the present decade differs from the 'twenties.' While America seems to have learned little from its recent economic experience, other parts of the world have learned much. All over the earth powerful movements of the common people are demanding that these absurd and destructive fluctuations of the industrial system should end—that public controls be exerted over economic processes of sufficient strength and rationality to guarantee stability, much greater equalization of wealth, and the securities of a rising standard of living which the proven potentialities of abundance make entirely feasible. America is out of step with the world. Yet her position is of such power and strategic importance that, if and when another and worse depression comes, she will shake and probably undermine many economic institutions elsewhere. Here, too, are facts which education ignores at its own peril and the world's.

The second fact—national rivalry and suspicion—receives, to be sure, a modicum of analysis in the schools. The roots of this terrifying reality, themselves largely economic, are seldom exposed, however, to the sunlight of honest scrutiny, and the solution of international order is too often treated both romantically and superficially. Once more the record of the past quarter century is helpful; in the 'twenties, thousands of schools studied the League of Nations and propagandized in behalf of peace. But they usually failed to show how any League was bound to fail sooner or later so long as national sovereignty remained intact, so long as bitter competition for foreign markets and natural resources was practiced by the same nations which hypocritically paid lip-service to internationalism. Thus when war came again, the disillusionment of millions of young men and women was in no small way the only clear effect of all efforts by the schools on behalf of peace.

And yet today it is important to inquire whether the only important "contribution" they are making is not, again, chiefly a repetition of the past. They may study and endorse the United Nations, to be sure; and that is helpful. But they seldom face the contradiction between high-minded objectives for all nations and the still dominant power of sovereignty of each nation. Students are taught that internationalism is desirable; they are also taught that the United States is supreme in its own right. They are taught that all countries must co-operate; they are also taught that we should keep the secret of atomic energy. They are taught that we should support the efforts of common peoples in other parts of the world to rise in power; they are also taught to be uncritical of a foreign policy which serves to thwart those efforts in countries like Greece, China, and Spain. They are taught the slogans of equality, freedom, and brotherhood; yet millions of them are taught (if in no other way than by failing to study alternatives) that the white race is superior to other races, that Christians are superior to Mohammedans or Jews.

The two great constructive purposes which should now govern the American Education Fellowship follow directly from this brief analysis. They are:

I. To channel the energies of education toward the reconstruction of the economic system—a system which should be geared with the increasing socializations and public controls now developing in England, Sweden, New Zealand, and other countries; a system in which national and international planning of production and distribution replaces the chaotic planlessness of traditional "free enterprise"; a system in which the interests, wants, and needs of the consumer dominate those of the producer; a system in which natural resources, such as coal and iron ore, are owned and controlled by the people; a system in which public corporations replace monopolistic enterprises and privately owned "public" utilities; a system in which federal authority is synchronized with decentralized regional and community administration; a system in which social security and a guaranteed annual wage sufficient to meet scientific standards of nourishment, shelter, clothing, health, recreation, and education, are universalized; a system in which the majority of the people is the sovereign determinant of every basic economy policy.

II. To channel the energies of education toward the establishment of genuine international authority in all crucial issues affecting peace and security; an order therefore in which all weapons of war (including atomic energy, first of all) and police forces are finally under that authority; an order in which international economic planning of trade, resources, labor distribution and standards, is practiced parallel with the best standards of individual nations; an order in which all nationalities, races, and religions receive equal rights in its democratic control; an order in which "world citizenship" thus assumes at least equal status with national citizenship.

IV

These two great guiding principles involve a multitude of specific educational tasks to which the American Education Fellowship should now devote itself. There precise delineation should involve every member and the closest cooperation with all groups and forces which share generally in its purposes. In this statement of policy, it is possible only to suggest what some of these tasks may be. We list them without elaboration or special concern for order of importance. [An outline of thirteen "tasks" follows.]

·　·　·　·　·

V

In making these important recommendations, the American Education Fellowship will continue, it should be reiterated, to support the kind of experimentation for which it is most famous. It will continue to emphasize "learning by doing," "community schools," "the integrated curriculum," "teacher-pupil planning" and other objectives of "progressive education" as these now become more widely accepted.

But such objectives are now subordinate even while indispensable to, the larger, more audacious and magnetic objectives impelled by a world in crisis. Faced by the alternatives of economic chaos and atomic war, on the one hand, of world-wide plenty and enforceable international order, on the other hand, this organization should become the clearest, most purposeful educational spokesman for the second of these alternatives. Thus, and only thus, can it become even more the great vanguard influence which it has been for nearly three decades—an influence which, as before, is certain to extend far beyond its own membership and even its own country.

To prove that education is not a mere mirror of dominant ideologies, *not* a device for bolstering outmoded economic systems and diseased nationalisms, but rather that education is a penetrating critic, dynamic leader, and imaginative re-creator which anticipates dangers *before* they crystallize into calamities, which helps simultaneously to reshape the culture of America and the world in accordance with the imperatives of our revolutionary age —this is the supreme obligation of the American Education Fellowship in our time. This is its new policy.

Progressive education had always been a center of controversy, from its early years the subject of vigorous attacks by critics mainly within the education profession. But by the 1950's a new sort of critic began to be heard and heard widely, the outraged layman vigorous in his criticism not only of progressivist methods in the school but of basic progressive theory regarding the function and responsibility of the school. The voices of these new critics were perhaps the outward and visible signs of basic changes in American society that brought the quick collapse of the "Life Adjustment Movement," the dissolution of the AEF-PEA, and in general the passing of progressivism as a movement in education.

Arthur E. Bestor, Jr., a professor of history then at the University of

Illinois, was one of the more serious and responsible of the new critics of progressive education. His books, *Educational Wastelands* in 1953, and *The Restoration of Learning* in 1955, were important contributions to the debate of the era. The following article is one of a series that appeared in the *New Republic* in 1953.

128. Anti-Intellectualism in the Schools

Arthur E. Bestor, Jr.

From the point of view of finances and equipment, the American public-school system is something of which to be immensely proud. Enrollment has increased steadily, until today four out of every five American children between the ages of five and 17, inclusive, are in school. We talk so much about overcrowding that we are apt to forget the significant fact that the equipment and resources of the public schools have increased far more rapidly than enrollment. Compared with 1870, every child now enrolled spends twice as many days per year in the classroom. The proportion of teachers to pupils is greater, and the teachers are required to have spent far more time in training. After adjustments are made for the changed value of the dollar, we find that nine times as much money is spent per year on the education of *each* child, and 13 times as much is invested in the buildings and equipment that each one uses. Inequalities and inadequacies exist, of course, and these must be eliminated. But the fact remains that the American people have generously and faithfully supported their schools. They have a right to ask whether school administrators have served the American people with equal faithfulness. Is the qualitative educational achievement of our public schools commensurate with the money and effort that have been invested in them?

Since the answer I am about to give is in the negative, I shall be automatically branded an enemy of the public schools by those who have a vested interest in the educational status quo. To repel such a charge, allow me to offer at the outset a full and frank confession of faith. I am a firm believer in the principle of universal, public, democratic education. I believe that publicly financed education from the nursery school through the highest levels of graduate and professional instruction is essential to American democracy as we know and value it. I have no sympathy whatever with anyone who proposes to cut school appropriations in such a way as to limit educational opportunity or to impair the quality of instruction. I

Reprinted by permission from Arthur E. Bestor, Jr., "Anti-Intellectualism in the Schools," *New Republic* (January 19, 1953), pp. 11-13.

believe in doing away with every barrier that race, religion or economic status interposes to prevent any American from pursuing to the highest levels any form of study for which he has the intellectual capacity, the desire and the will. I believe, finally, in academic freedom. I conceive it to be the scholar's duty to resist every effort to stifle the free and responsible investigation and discussion of public issues. And I stand ready to oppose to the uttermost any group that seeks to limit or pervert the curricula of schools and colleges in order to impose upon them their own narrow and dogmatic preconceptions concerning matters that are properly the subject of free inquiry.

The great issue today is not whether the American school system ought to be democratic—of course it ought. The issue is whether the school system ought to be *educational*. And the further question arises, if the public-school system ceases to be educational, can it possibly avoid being anti-democratic as well?

Some of the slogans by which professional educators mask their anti-intellectual purposes sound plausibly democratic. "It is the job of the school," reads one of the most influential current statements of educational policy, "to meet the common and the specific individual needs of youth." This, of course, is nonsense. If it were true, then the school would be in the business of supplying food, clothing and shelter. Obviously the school exists to satisfy the needs of individuals and of society. But it is designed to meet, and is capable of meeting, certain needs only. The school is one, but only one, of the agencies of society that minister to young people's needs. The family, the church, the medical profession, the government, private business —all exist to satisfy the needs of men and women, young and old. Some may not do the job as we would wish. But that affords no excuse for the school to neglect its task also, in a vain attempt to remedy the deficiency. The idea that the school must undertake to meet every need that some other agency is failing to meet is a preposterous delusion that can wreck the educational system without contributing anything to the salvation of society.

The school has its own job to do, and the nation is threatened with disaster if the school fails to do that job superlatively well. Many vital needs of men cannot be satisfied except through the extensive and rigorous application of intellectual means. No agency but the school can provide the systematic, disciplined, intellectual training required. This is, and always has been, the primary, indispensable function of the school. The nation is betrayed if the school shirks this responsibility or subordinates it to any other aim, however worthy in itself. The school exists to provide intellectual training in every field of activity where systematic thinking is an important component of success. It exists to provide it for every citizen who has the capacity and the will to apply intellectual means to the solution of the problems that confront him. And it exists to encourage intellectual effort on the part of every citizen, whether or not he possesses intellectual background to begin with.

This is not to say that the school can be indifferent to the vocational needs of its students, to their physical development, or to the problem of moral conduct. It merely means that the school shares responsibility in these matters with other agencies of society, and that it must make its contribution within the context provided by its own characteristic activity. Schooling is better than apprenticeship as preparation for a job, only if it leads a man to grasp the theory behind the practice. Physical education makes sense only if it is linked with a knowledge of physiology, only if it teaches a man to participate in sports for the sake of his own physical fitness, and only if it resolutely resists the diversion of school resources into the subsidizing of gladiatorial contests between muscular mercenaries. Finally, morality permeates all activities of life, assuming special form in each. In the schoolroom it appears primarily as intellectual honesty and as that species of reflectiveness which converts a mere taboo into an ethical imperative. In all these great spheres of life, the particular contribution which the school can make is determined by, and related to, the fact that it is an agency of intellectual training.

An increasing number of public-school administrators and educational theorists today refuse to define the purposes of the school in terms of intellectual training or of the recognized disciplines of science and scholarship. In my own state a publicly supported Illinois Secondary School Curriculum Program has circulated a series of questionnaires purporting to ask citizens, teachers and pupils what they "think is the job of the secondary school." History, mathematics, science and foreign languages are nowhere mentioned, hence no one is permitted to suggest that training in these fields might be even a part of "the job of the secondary school." Instead the school is supposed to be concerned with a pot-pourri of 55 "problems of high-school youth," in which "the problem of acquiring the social skills of dancing, playing party games, doing parlor stunts, etc." is given just as much emphasis as "the problem of acquiring the ability to study and help solve economic, social and political problems." The educators never tell how the school is going to give its students the latter, much-to-be-desired ability. Time will obviously not be allowed for systematic training in the disciplines of history or political science or economics. These have already been merged into the social studies, and the latter are eventually to be swallowed up, so the Illinois Curriculum Program hopes, by a "common learnings course" in which "materials from science, literature, history, mathematics, industrial education, homemaking, business education, art, music and all other areas of the curriculum would be included."

An inkling of what the educators mean when they propose to bring the great issues of public life down to the level of what they call the "real-life problems of youth" is afforded by an elaborate report on *The Schools and National Security,* which the Illinois Curriculum Program has recently published. The first task of the social studies, according to the chapter devoted to them, is to "reduce the tensions and meet the *needs* of children and youth." There are some starry-eyed promises about developing "a constructively critical attitude toward foreign policy" among pupils who, of course, are not to be burdened with any useless knowledge of history or geography or foreign languages. And when the report gets down to specific classroom work, it solemnly suggests that the schools can serve the nation in its present hour of peril by asking its students to "make studies of how the last war affected the dating pattern in our culture."

This nonsense is described as "life-adjustment education," and it masquerades as a democratic program for the schools. In point of fact it takes its origin from one of the most blatantly anti-democratic resolutions ever formulated by a conference of American educators. The first Commission on Life Adjustment Education for Youth was appointed by the United States Commissioner as a result of the following statement adopted by a group of educators in 1945:

> It is the belief of this conference that, with the aid of this report in final form, the vocational school of a community will be able better to prepare 20 percent of the youth of secondary-school age for entrance upon desirable skilled occupations; and that the high school will continue to prepare another 20 percent for entrance to college. We do not believe that the remaining 60 percent of our youth of secondary-school age will receive the life-adjustment training they need and to which they are entitled as American citizens—unless and until the administrators of public education with the assistance of the vocational-education leaders formulate a similar program for this group.

Consider for a moment the extraordinary implications of this statement. Sixty percent—three-fifths—of the citizens of the United States, it asserts without qualification, are incapable of being benefited by intellectual training or even training for skilled and desirable occupations. If this is true, it is a fact of the most shattering significance, for it declares invalid most of the assumptions that have underlain American democracy. It enthrones once again the ancient doctrine that the majority of the people are destined from birth to be hewers of wood and drawers of water to a select few who, by right of superior fitness, are to occupy the privileged places in society.

Let me be perfectly clear. I am not criticizing the work of experimental psychologists and of those professional educators who combine sound scholarship with a knowledge of pedagogy. What they have done to improve the methods by which the recognized disciplines are to be effectively taught is a worthy and important work. They are modest enough to recognize that they have neither the authority nor the competence to tamper with the purposes and the organization of the curriculum.

What I am criticizing is the arrogance of those secondary-school educators who believe that they own the schools and can mold them as they please without regard to the rest of the scientific, intellectual and professional life of the nation. I am condemning the sweeping conclusions concerning the intellectual incapacity of the American people which are being pronounced by educational administrators who are not themselves psychologists, which are supported by little more than subjective impressions, and which frequently confuse a lack of background and interest with a lack of intellectual capacity. I am condemning the reckless remaking of the public-school curriculum on the basis of these completely unverified conclusions. And I am condemning the substitution of high-powered propaganda for scientific objectivity in the process of carrying out what the educators describe as experiments.

It is my considered judgment that every one of these basic requirements of scientific, ethical experimentation upon human beings has been violated in the launching of the current programs of curricular change.

By dallying with "life-adjustment education" the schools are doing more than merely discarding intellectual training. They are actively teaching the public a concept for intellectual effort. By its very nature the school cannot be neutral in the matter of intellectual values, any more than a church can be neutral on the question of virtue. It either fosters respect for thought or it fosters the opposite. And if it does not foster respect for thought it obviously cannot foster respect for freedom of thought. If the schools are indifferent to intellectual values, the only conclusion which the public can draw is that intellectual values are worth very little, and that the destruction of them—the suppression of freedom of thought, of speech, and of teaching—is the destruction of something expendable.

In the long run the only real safeguard of intellectual freedom is widespread public respect for intellectual values. Only the public schools can give to the people at large a genuine understanding of intellectual effort and a sense of its vital importance to free men and to a free nation. To build our defense of freedom firm and deep, we need to eradicate, before it is too late, the anti-intellectual tendencies that have crept into our public-educational system. We must restore to the schools the clear and disciplined intellectual purpose that will make them once again the bulwarks of thought, and hence of freedom of thought.

In this effort we can count upon the support of an unknown number— but I suspect, an overwhelming majority—of the classroom teachers of the nation, who are distressed at the programs being imposed upon them.

We can count upon the support of a very considerable number of professors of education and public-school administrators who dissent from the party-line laid down by the powerful educational associations, by the public-school bureaucracy, and by the more vocal members of university departments of education. But because of the existence of this party-line and this structure of power, we cannot count upon the organized educational profession as such to safeguard the intellectual purpose and the intellectual integrity of our secondary schools.

It is the duty of scholars, scientists and members of the learned professions generally, to speak with a clear and independent voice in these matters. Cooperation with professional educators must continue, of course, in the devising of sound programs for the public schools. But on matters of high educational policy the learned world must speak with a voice unmistakably its own, and must not allow its words to be smothered or twisted or censored by others. It must speak directly to the general public, who make the final decisions on educational policy. It must express, continuously and unitedly, its considered judgment on the intellectual soundness of the programs that are offered in the public schools. Scholars have not done this effectively in the past, and the views of the professional educators have prevailed largely by default. If scholars will create for themselves an organ through which they can speak with clarity and force, I am confident that they will be listened to with respect. I have proposed to the learned societies of the country the creation of a Permanent Scientific and Scholarly Commission on Secondary Education, completely independent of the existing educational associations and of pressure groups whose interest in the public schools is sometimes of a dubious character.

Through such a Commission, I believe, the learned world can provide responsible leadership to the millions of Americans who believe both in democracy and in sound education and who are anxious to rescue the schools from those who act as if democratic education were synonymous with intellectual mediocrity.

Hollis L. Caswell, Dean of Teachers College, Columbia University, in 1951 made a carefully considered appraisal of the educational debate in a lecture, the Twenty-fourth Steinmetz Memorial Lecture, selections of which follow.

129. The Great Reappraisal of Public Education

Hollis L. Caswell

CURRENT CRITICISM OF SCHOOLS

Considering the nation at large, public education is currently encountering criticism of unusual intensity and scope. Organized groups are carrying on systematic attacks on public schools. Individuals who are highly critical of the schools receive wide attention in the press. Some important publications have taken editorial positions in sharp opposition to practices widely accepted in public education. David Harum, that homespun American philosopher, observed that a few fleas are good for a dog because they keep him from brooding on what a good dog he is. From this point of view people working in public education feel that there is little chance for undue complacency on their part, for they are attacked, not only by a few fleas, but by a swarm of yellow jackets as well.

Considered separately, these attacks may seem to represent the usual sort of criticism that any public activity in a democratic society must undergo and, I may add, should undergo. But it is my conviction that if we look deeper, studying the long-range import and seeking the interrelationships of current criticisms, far more is involved. It is my belief that a reappraisal is in progress of some of the most basic aspects of our public school system. Action may well be taken in meeting the issues currently raised that would divert our schools from the course of development pursued during the past century. That course of development has resulted in a distinctive American educational system. Many of the most pointed criticisms are directed toward those qualities that make it unique.

It is of great importance that the larger issues involved be recognized and understood. I do not intend to suggest that the American people may not decide to change their schools. They may even decide to reject some of the distinctive developments of the past century. What seems important to me is that we avoid drifting into far-reaching changes without awareness of what is at stake. With this point in mind, I shall undertake to describe and evaluate some of the fundamental features of our public school system that are being subjected to reappraisal as a result of the current wave of criticism.

Reprinted by permission from Hollis L. Caswell, "The Great Reappraisal of Public Education," *Teachers College Record,* LIV (1952-3), pp. 12-16; 22.

ATTACK UPON STANDARDS

One of the most common lines of attack relates to standards of achievement. It is asserted or implied that schools do not enforce desirable standards. As evidence, cases are cited of pupils in high school who read at elementary grade levels, or whose skill in arithmetic is comparably low, or whose knowledge of American history or of similar subjects is highly deficient. Now this is a difficult criticism to appraise, for there are such cases. To many people this seems conclusive evidence that schools are not requiring pupils to keep up with their work. The critics urge that definite standards be set and that pupils be failed until they meet them. This is a logical-sounding conclusion and in many communities teachers are under pressure to drop the policy that has been adopted quite widely of failing pupils infrequently.

This line of criticism strikes at one of the most distinctive features of the American educational system, our concept of equality of educational opportunity. As is true of so many things that seem simple and obvious on the surface, it involves a very complex issue. I shall attempt to indicate briefly why this situation exists and what the implications are of the apparently obvious and sensible proposal of the critics. In order to do this I shall have to make a brief excursion into our educational history.

The groundwork for our present educational system was laid about 1830. A great educational awakening occurred at that time, and state after state established its system of education. Each state had its own history and distinctive features, yet the same basic concepts were widely accepted. Certain of these concepts provide the setting out of which arises the present-day problem of standards.

The idea expressed earlier by our national leaders—that widespread education was essential to the safety of the Republic—was reiterated. Thus it was decided that education aimed at civic welfare should be provided for all the children of all the people. Our people were acquainted with educational systems in Europe that provided some educational opportunities for all citizens but limited them sharply for the lower classes. The typical plan was a dual educational system, one for the leaders and one for the masses. The upper-class children attended preparatory and secondary schools. The children of the masses attended primary and elementary schools. A few children of exceptional talent in the elementary school were permitted to transfer to secondary schools. This was achieved by giving examinations to children about eleven years of age in the school for the masses and "creaming off" a small fraction. The large group of lower-class children completed their education in the elementary school. The gap between those who went to elementary school only and those who were permitted to attend secondary school was very great indeed.

Our people would have no part of a dual school system. They established instead a single system open to all, regardless of economic or social background. Elementary and secondary schools were articulated into a single, continuous plan, and the concept of the American educational ladder was developed.

This concept involves many more problems on the operational level than educators realized for a long time. At first glance it seems simple enough. Merely let each pupil climb as far up the ladder as his ability permits and then drop out of school. So long as the standards for each "grade" are clearly defined and enforced, this, it seems, should provide equal opportunity. But by the early part of the present century, factors had entered the situation that greatly complicated it.

The people of the various states had realized more and more clearly the critical dependence of a democracy on education of the rank and file of people. Influenced by this and other considerations, such as the desire to limit child labor, they enacted compulsory attendance laws which extended the length of time pupils must attend school. Thus, today the laws in forty states require attendance to age sixteen and in eight states to age seventeen or eighteen. The common expectation is completion of high school as the earliest normal termination of schooling.

Now it became evident early in this century that even though pupils stayed in school for several years, a very large number were not successful in climbing the ladder. In 1909 Leonard P. Ayres, who later became president of the Cleveland Trust Company, published a pioneering study called *Laggards in Our Schools*. He showed that in some cities as many as 30 per cent of all children in school were repeating grades, and for the country as a whole, between 15 and 20 per cent were repeaters. He found that there were pupils fifteen, sixteen, and seventeen years of age in the first, second, and third grades. He reported that not more than one-half of all children entering the elementary school went beyond the sixth grade. His study raised a serious question whether a ladder constructed with year-by-year steps was one that the large group of children with tremendous differences in ability could successfully climb.

There followed for the next quarter of a century intensive study of what it means to provide equal educational opportunity for all the children of all the people. Scientific studies revealed some highly important facts, many of which were contrary to popular beliefs. For example, many studies reported that when there is question about failing or promoting a child, the odds are overwhelming that his achievement will be greater the next year if he is promoted than if he is failed. It was also found that a pupil will achieve significantly more in a given number of years in a curriculum through which he can progress without non-promotion than in one in which he is required to repeat grades. Findings such as these raised this kind of question: Is it better for a pupil who has been in school seven years to be in the fourth grade achieving at the fourth-grade standard or to be in the seventh grade achieving at the fifth-grade standard?

But the implications were more far-reaching than those which have to do with the readily measurable aspects of education, such as skill in reading. It became evident that having adolescent boys and girls of high-school age in classes with children in the elementary school was good for neither group. There were factors other than skill in reading, writing, and arithmetic that were far more powerful in determining what made a good grouping for instruction. The fifteen-year-old boy who could read only at the sixth-grade level needed to learn many of the same things as another boy of the same maturity who could read well enough to be in the tenth grade. Despite his slow reading a better program could be provided for the first boy in a high school than in an elementary school.

The result of a whole series of studies and experiments was an extension of the concept of equality of educational opportunity. Equality, it was agreed, should not mean *identical* opportunities but quite the opposite; that is, each individual should be afforded the educational opportunity that is best adapted to his particular needs and abilities. The standard to be applied under this concept is whether the individual is achieving as well as he can. It becomes necessary, consequently, to judge the capabilities of each student in evaluating his work. Persons holding the earlier conception would be horrified at finding a pupil in the twelfth grade reading at the seventh-grade level. They would feel that such a pupil should be in the seventh grade. Under the present conception a person would want to know whether the student had the ability to read above the seventh-grade level. If he could have learned to read better the school was at fault, but if he was reading as well as his ability would permit, then the chances are overwhelming that he would not have read that well had he been required to repeat grades.

One qualification of the concept of standards I have presented needs always to be kept in mind. That is, that it applies only to general education. When it comes to professional preparation and other types of specialization the nature of the task to be done and of the subject matter required imposes certain essential standards. In brief, in educating a man to be a citizen it is a good investment to make him the best citizen possible in terms of the capacities he possesses, but if he is being educated to be a surgeon it is not enough that he do as well as his ability permits; he must be able to save a reasonable proportion of his patients. He has to be a citizen for better or for worse, but he does not have to be a surgeon.

One implication of the principle of equality of educational opportunity which is often overlooked seems very significant to me. The critics who demand that the old concept of grade standards be applied focus attention on the student with low achievement. As a consequence, teachers are constantly striving to improve the records of slow-learning students. Now if you will note the concept as I have stated it, the capacities of each student are to set the standard for judging the adequacy of his achievement. In applying this concept one of the greatest needs in our present school program is, I believe, better provision for the gifted student. Every day we overlook talent of the highest order, which is a national resource of inestimable value. I have seen children in elementary schools who, under the guidance of skillful teachers, have achieved truly remarkable things in the creative arts, in scientific study, and in other fields. Much could be done in our high schools to differentiate courses and provide for independent study and special groups without violating democratic principles. The critics, by focusing the attention of teachers on pupils with low achievement, hold back the development of a program that would challenge our gifted children and youth.

The development of a twelve-year program of education adapted to the needs and capacities of all children and youth is a tremendously difficult undertaking. Only America has attempted so ambitious an enterprise. It is my belief that our schools have made great progress toward this goal but that much remains to be done. The basic question raised by the critics of standards is whether we shall have fixed, general standards of achievement grade by grade to which all pupils must conform, or whether we shall have standards that are set for each pupil in relation to his capacities. The former leads down the road to a selective educational system; the latter continues development of a program based on the principles of equality of opportunity.

.   .   .   .

[Two discussions follow entitled "Attack upon Methods" and "Non-Sectarian Policy," which have been deleted.]

Basic Issues Involved

In conclusion, I return to the theme with which I opened: Many of the critics are not attacking just extreme and fringe aspects of the program of public education; they are striking at basic and distinctive characteristics. There are no more central and important features of the program of American schools than our concept of equality of educational opportunity, the way in which modern methods of teaching have been developed out of research on learning, and our solution of the relation of religion and education. Yet current criticisms involve all of these.

At no time since the days of Horace Mann and Henry Barnard, in my opinion, has there been such widespread consideration of basic educational issues. This period will involve fateful educational decisions which might well result in major changes in the course of our educational development. In my view it may appropriately be characterized as "The Great Reappraisal of Public Education."

The great debate, the "reappraisal," continued, but the problem of extending education to all American youth remained and in the fifties came to be seen as a major problem in American society. To many Americans the heart of the problem was the education of the Negro. Discriminated against in separate but unequal schools for generations, by legal or *de facto* segregation in South and North, the Negro at last became a focus of educational effort. The progressive educator's vision of a transformed school and society had always, of course, included all American youth, whatever their color. But in the post-war years, culminating in the 1954 United States Supreme Court decision *Brown vs. Board of Education,* the legal inequalities in the education of the Negro were struck down, and the foundation was laid for an attack on racial segregation in education in all its forms.

130. Brown v. Board of Education

347 U.S. 483 (1954)

Appeal from the U.S. District Court for the District of Kansas.

Appeal from the U.S. District Court for the Eastern District of South Carolina.

Appeal from the U.S. District Court for the Eastern District of Virginia.

Certiorari to the Supreme Court of Delaware.

MR. CHIEF JUSTICE WARREN delivered the opinion of a unanimous Court.

These cases come to us from the States of Kansas, South Carolina, Virginia, and Delaware. They are premised on different facts and different local conditions, but a common legal question justifies their consideration together in this consolidated opinion.

In each of the cases, minors of the Negro race, through their legal representatives, seek the aid of the courts in obtaining admission to the public schools of their community on a nonsegregated basis. In each instance, they had been denied admission to schools attended by white children under laws requiring or permitting segregation according to race. This segregation was alleged to deprive the plaintiffs of the equal protection of the laws under the Fourteenth Amendment. In each of the cases other than the Delaware case, a three-judge federal district court denied relief to the plaintiffs on the so-called "separate but equal" doctrine announced by this Court in *Plessy* v. *Ferguson,* 163 U.S. 537. Under that doctrine, equality of treatment is accorded when the races are provided substantially equal facilities, even though these facilities be sparate. . . .

The plaintiffs contend that segregated public schools are not "equal" and cannot be made "equal," and that hence they are deprived of the equal protection of the laws. Because of the obvious importance of the question presented, the Court took jurisdiction. Argument was heard in the 1952 Term, and reargument was heard this Term on certain questions propounded by the Court.

Reargument was largely devoted to the circumstances surrounding the adoption of the Fourteenth Amendment in 1868. It covered exhaustively consideration of the Amendment in Congress, ratification by the states, then existing practices in racial segregation, and the views of proponents and opponents of the Amendment. This discussion and our own investigation convince us that, although these sources cast some light, it is not enough to resolve the problem with which we are faced. At best, they are inconclusive. The most avid proponents of the post-War Amendments undoubtedly intended them to remove all legal distinctions among "all persons born or naturalized in the United States." Their opponents, just as certainly, were antagonistic to both the letter and the spirit of the Amendments and wished them to have the most limited effect. What others in Congress and the state legislatures had in mind cannot be determined with any degree of certainty.

An additional reason for the inconclusive nature of the Amendment's history, with respect to segregated schools, is the status of public education at that time. In the South, the movement toward free common schools, supported by general taxation, had not yet taken hold. Education of white children was largely in the hands of private groups. Education of Negroes was almost nonexistent, and practically all of the race were illiterate. In fact, any education of Negroes was forbidden by law in some states. Today, in contrast, many Negroes have achieved outstanding success in the arts and sciences as well as in the business and professional world. It is true that public school education at the time of the Amendment had advanced further in the North, but the effect of the Amendment on Northern States was generally ignored in the congressional debates. Even in the North, the conditions of public education did not approximate those existing today. The curriculum was usually rudimentary; ungraded schools were common in rural areas; the school term was but three months a year in many states; and compulsory school attendance was virtually unknown. As a consequence, it is not surprising that there should be so little in the history of the Fourteenth Amendment relating to its intended effect on public education.

In the first cases in this Court construing the Fourteenth Amendment, decided shortly after its adoption, the Court interpreted it as proscribing all state-imposed discriminations against the Negro race. The doctrine of "separate but equal" did not make its appearance in this Court until 1896 in the case of *Plessy* v. *Ferguson,* . . . involving not education but transportation. American courts have since labored with the doctrine for over half a century. In this Court, there have been six cases involving the "separate but equal" doctrine in the field of public education. In *Cumming* v. *County Board of Education,* 175 U.S. 528, and *Gong Lum* v. *Rice,* 275 U.S. 78, the validity of the doctrine itself was not challenged. In more recent cases, all on the graduate school level, inequality was found in that specific benefits enjoyed by white students were denied to Negro students of the same educational qualifications. *Missouri ex rel. Gaines* v. *Canada,* 305 U.S. 337; *Sipuel* v. *Oklahoma,* 332 U.S. 631; *Sweatt* v. *Painter,* 339 U.S. 629; *McLaurin* v. *Oklahoma State Regents,* 339 U.S. 637. In none of these cases was it necessary to reexamine the doctrine to grant relief to the Negro plaintiff. And in *Sweatt* v. *Painter,* . . . the Court expressly reserved decision on the question whether *Plessy* v. *Ferguson* should be held inapplicable to public education.

In the instant cases, that question is directly presented. Here, unlike *Sweatt* v. *Painter,* there are findings below that the Negro and white schools involved have been equalized, or are being equalized, with repect to buildings, curricula, qualifications and salaries of teachers, and other "tangible" factors. Our decision, therefore, cannot turn on merely a comparison of these tangible factors in the Negro and white schools involved in each of the cases. We must look instead to the effect of segregation itself on public education.

In approaching this problem, we cannot turn the clock back to 1868 when the Amendment was adopted, or even to 1896 when *Plessy* v.

Ferguson was written. We must consider public education in the light of its full development and its present place in American life throughout the Nation. Only in this way can it be determined if segregation in public schools deprives these plaintiffs of the equal protection of the laws.

Today, education is perhaps the most important function of state and local governments. Compulsory school attendance laws and the great expenditures for education both demonstrate our recognition of the importance of education to our democratic society. It is required in the performance of our most basic public responsibilities, even service in the armed forces. It is the very foundation of good citizenship. Today it is a principal instrument in awakening the child to cultural values, in preparing him for later professional training, and in helping him to adjust normally to his environment. In these days, it is doubtful that any child may reasonably be expected to succeed in life if he is denied the opportunity of an education. Such an opportunity, where the state has undertaken to provide it, is a right which must be made available to all on equal terms.

We come then to the question presented: Does segregation of children in public schools solely on the basis of race, even though the physical facilities and other "tangible" factors may be equal, deprive the children of the minority group of equal educational opportunities? We believe that it does.

In *Sweatt* v. *Painter,* in finding that a segregated law school for Negroes could not provide them equal educational opportunities, this Court relied in large part on "those qualities which are incapable of objective measurement but which make for greatness in a law school." In *McLaurin* v. *Oklahoma State Regents,* the Court, in requiring that a Negro admitted to a white graduate school be treated like all other students, again resorted to intangible considerations: "his ability to study, to engage in discussions and exchange views with other students, and, in general, to learn his profession." Such considerations apply with added force to children in grade and high schools. To separate them from others of similar age and qualifications solely because of their race generates a feeling of inferiority as to their status in the community that may affect their hearts and minds in a way unlikely ever to be undone. The effect of this separation on their educational opportunities was well stated by a finding in the Kansas case by a court which nevertheless felt compelled to rule against the Negro plaintiffs:

> Segregation of white and colored children in public schools has a detrimental effect upon the colored children. The impact is greater when it has the sanction of the law; for the policy of separating the races is usually interpreted as denoting the inferiority of the negro group. A

sense of inferiority affects the motivation of a child to learn. Segregation with the sanction of law, therefore, has a tendency to [retard] the educational and mental development of negro children and to deprive them of some of the benefits they would receive in a racial[ly] integrated school system.

Whatever may have been the extent of psychological knowledge at the time of *Plessy* v. *Ferguson,* this finding is amply supported by modern authority.[11] Any language in *Plessy* v. *Ferguson* contrary to this finding is rejected.

We conclude that in the field of public education the doctrine of "separate but equal" has no place. Separate educational facilities are inherently unequal. Therefore, we hold that the plaintiffs and others similarly situated for whom the actions have been brought are, by reason of the segregation complained of, deprived of the equal protection of the laws guaranteed by the Fourteenth Amendment. This disposition makes unnecessary any discussion whether such segregation also violates the Due Process Clause of the Fourteenth Amendment.

Because these are class actions, because of the wide applicability of this decision, and because of the great variety of local conditions, the formulation of decrees in these cases presents problems of considerable complexity. On reargument, the consideration of appropriate relief was necessarily subordinated to the primary question—the constitutionality of segregation in public education. We have now announced that such segregation is a denial of the equal protection of the laws. In order that we may have the full assistance of the parties in formulating decrees, the cases will be restored to the docket, and the parties are requested to present further argument. . . . The Attorney General of the United States is again invited to participate. The Attorneys General of the states requiring or permitting segregation in public education will also be permitted to appear as *amici curiae* upon request to do so. . . .

It is so ordered.

[11] K. B. Clark, *Effect of Prejudice and Discrimination on Personality Development* (Midcentury White House Conference on Children and Youth, 1950); Witmer and Kotinsky, *Personality in the Making* (1952), Chap. 6; Deutscher and Chein, "The Psychological Effects of Enforced Segregation: A Survey of Social Science Opinion," 26 *J. Psychol.* 259 (1948); Chein, "What Are the Psychological Effects of Segregation under Conditions of Equal Facilities?" 3 *Int. J. Opinion and Attitude Res.* 229 (1949); Brameld, *Educational Costs,* in *Discrimination and National Welfare* (MacIver, ed., 1949), 44-48; Frazier, *The Negro in the United States* (1949), 674-681. And see generally Myrdal, *An American Dilemma* (1944).

The reappraisal of American education that had begun in the years just after World War II took a new direction in the late 1950's. Concern for improved education for the Negro and the "disadvantaged" child continued, but the new stress during these years was on education for the national interest, exemplified in the work of James B. Conant in his "reports" on American education. In general, a result of the competition arising of the "cold war," perhaps the consequence specifically of the Soviet *Sputnik I* of 1957, Conant emphasized the early identification and cultivation of talent in the schools geared to relatively specific technical needs of American society. The Conant recommendations combined much of the earlier criticisms of American schools by Bestor and others, some of the specific techniques and facilities of the progressive educators, as well as the social concerns of the times, all brought to focus educationally in the interest of the nation. As president emeritus of Harvard University and former ambassador to West Germany, Conant, in his studies of American schools, was received with intense interest on the part of educators and with wide publicity in the popular press. In the decade of the sixties he came to have enormous influence on education. The first of the Conant "reports," *The American High School Today,* prepared under the auspices of the Carnegie Corporation (as were the subsequent studies), was published in 1959. The introductory section of the study, which follows, suggests the general framework of the thinking underlying the recommendations for American schools.

131. The Characteristics of American Education

James B. Conant

The school board members and the school administrators to whom this report is directed are familiar with the basic assumptions underlying the present pattern of American education. They realize that the task of the American high school is a task which arises out of the historical developments of our schools, colleges, and universities and, in particular, reflects certain basic changes in the structure of our society which have occurred during this century. Some readers of this report, however, who have had

Reprinted by permission from James B. Conant, *The American High School Today* (New York: McGraw-Hill, 1959), pp. 1-9.

little or no opportunity to study American public schools may not be aware of the processes by which our school and college arrangements have come to diverge so markedly from those in other free nations. Therefore, as an introduction to a study of one segment of the educational pattern—the tax-supported high school—a brief summary of the characteristics of American public education may be in order.

To a foreign observer several aspects of the American educational scene seem so strange as to be almost incomprehensible. First of all, our colleges and universities are baffling. There are so many institutions with so great a variety of requirements for admission and with so many different types of program that a foreign visitor has difficulty in identifying those portions of a university which are concerned with what he regards as the true university function. In European universities there is no equivalent of our undergraduate liberal arts college, no provision for general education. European universities are essentially a collection of faculties concerned with the education of future members of the learned professions. The general or liberal education of the doctor, lawyer, theologian, engineer, scientist, or professional scholar is provided by special secondary schools, admission to which is determined by a highly selective procedure at age ten or eleven. Not more than 20 per cent of an age group are selected from the elementary school and enrolled in the preuniversity schools. Therefore there is a waste of talent under the European system. No one has estimated how much potential talent goes undeveloped in Germany, France, Italy, and Switzerland because of the early selection of the preuniversity students—a selection often influenced by the class system of European lands. The other 80 to 85 per cent stop their formal education at age fourteen and go to work. Of course, the selection of those who are to be enrolled in the preuniversity school is on the basis of academic ability, but family tradition plays a big role and many boys and girls from the farm and working class never even think of trying to enter a preuniversity school.

In the European preuniversity schools an eight- or nine-year rigorous course in languages, mathematics, science, history, and literature prepares the student to pass a state examination for a certificate which admits him to a university. The failures during the long course are many, and a considerable number fall by the wayside, but those who succeed finish with a mastery of two foreign languages, a knowledge of mathematics through calculus and of physics and chemistry at the level of our sophomore college courses. Those who are not enrolled in the preuniversity schools, except for a small fraction who enter an intermediate school, complete their full-time education at age fourteen.

One often sees a comparison made between the proportion of the youth of college age who are studying in an American college or university and the proportion of German, or Swiss, or French youth who are attending a university. It is true that something like a thrid of our young people are "going to college," and only about a fifteenth or twentieth of the boys and girls in a European country are university students. But the vast majority of the Americans are *not* university students in the European sense of the term—that is, students preparing for a profession. Actually, the percentage of young men who are preparing to be doctors, lawyers, engineers, scientists, scholars, and teachers of academic subjects is about the same in this country as in Europe—a surprisingly small percentage, by the way —something like 6 per cent of an age group.

To understand American colleges and universities, one must be aware of their history. The existence of a few American four-year colleges during colonial days and the persistence of these institutions during the early years of the American republic have had a determining influence on higher education in this country. Of perhaps equal significance has been the movement to establish agricultural and mechanical arts colleges which started just about a century ago. The passage of the Morrill Act during the Civil War provided federal support for a new type of college in each state, the "land-grant colleges," as they were soon called. As these institutions developed, collegiate instruction in such practical fields as animal husbandry came to have the same academic standing as that of education for the professions. A proliferation of professional and semiprofessional areas of instruction, running from architecture to wild life conservation, started in the closing decades of the last century and has continued in this century until today a catalogue of many an institution (privately controlled or publicly supported) bears little resemblance to a corresponding pamphlet issued by a European university.

The widening of the fields of instruction in the nineteenth century was part of a drastic educational reform that was taking place on both sides of the Atlantic. The main objective of this reform was the recognition of the physical and biological sciences as reputable subjects to be studied in a university. On this continent, because of the special history of the American people, the movement took on many special characteristics. The definition of what was a "university subject" widened and widened as the decades passed.

As the fields of study of applied science and practical subjects broadened at the university level, instruction at the secondary level also changed. A hundred years ago one assumed a lawyer would have studied Greek and Latin; it was argued that a classical education was essential for him as a professional man. Fifty years later, it was hard to make a convincing case that the preprofessional education of an electrical engineer or an agriculturist should include instruction in reading Latin. And at no time in the educational history of this country has mastery of a modern foreign language come to be recognized as the hallmark of a well-educated man or woman.

The transformation of the European university tradition on this continent is a theme about which much has been written. But the impact of this mutation on the high school seems at times to have been overlooked. Having spent considerable time talking to university professors and schoolteachers in several European countries, I have been impressed by the basic differences in the total pattern of tax-supported education on the two sides of the Atlantic. And, having tried to explain American public education to German audiences, I am aware of some of the peculiarities of our system—peculiar from a European standpoint. Yet I have found that by pointing out certain differences between American and European history one can lead a German, for example, to a better understanding of our schools (and also of some of our political institutions, but that is another story).

When Thomas Jefferson wrote of equality, he was certainly thinking of political equality. It is clear that the contrast between a new society without hereditary titles and an old society with an aristocracy was what he had in mind. The absence of conqueror and conquered, of a feudal system in our history, when pointed out to a European, provides a clue to understanding something of our present situation. So too does a realization of the importance of the pioneer movement westward in the nineteenth influence on the development of European nations, but the American century. Frontiers—in the American sense of the term—have had no frontier has in fact shaped our institutions. To a large extent, it was responsible for widening the concept of equality. For the American of the nineteeth century equality became, above all, equality of opportunity—an equal start in a competitive struggle. This aspect of equality acted like a magnet on inhabitants of other lands and attracted those immigrants whose settling on this continent so enriched our culture and invigorated our stock. And this wave of immigration placed on our tax-supported schools many educational tasks of a special nature. This fact is recognized by European educators who have studied our educational history, and more than one of them has spoken to me of the success of our public schools in bringing together the children of so many diverse peoples.

Equality thus came to mean for many new Americans not only political equality but also equality of opportunity. It came to mean too, especially west of the Alleghenies, equality of status of all honest labor. The land-grant colleges were both a symbol of equality of status and a means to the realization of the idea. One academic manifestation of this doctrine is our unwillingness to state frankly that a bachelor's degree has long since lost any meaning as a mark of scholastic attainment or the completion of a course of formal academic training. Whether one has a degree in engineering, agriculture, home economics, commerce, physical education, or in the arts and sciences, he is entitled to be called a "college graduate."

It is important to remember that the contrast between American and European education at the college and university level is nothing new. Except in terms of numbers, the differences were almost as great at the beginning of the century as they are now. Although only 4 per cent of the American youth were then attending a college or university compared to over 35 per cent today, the situation was as surprising to a European then as now. He then saw, as he still sees, a multitude of colleges and universities having no uniform standards for admission or for graduation, even in professional fields, and offering a wide range of practical subjects in which a student could major.

In the half-century that has elapsed, there have been no drastic changes in the basic pattern of education in either Europe or the United States. But in two respects the American pattern has diverged even more from that to be found in other countries; certain unique characteristics have been emphasized, so to speak. The percentage of youth attending a college or university has jumped from 4 to 35, and, at the same time, the percentage enrolled in grades eleven to twelve of the high school has about doubled. In 1910, only 35 per cent of the seventeen-year-olds were in school; today, the corresponding figure is over 70 per cent. These changes could easily have been predicted in 1900 by a student of American education. He would already have seen how enormous was the power of the twin ideals of equality of opportunity and equality of status; it was evident that the American people had come to believe that more education provided the means by which these ideas were to be realized. But two other factors also played a role. First, there was the urge for institutional expansion—the drive for larger faculties and student bodies in the colleges and universities; fifty years ago expansion was more than welcomed. Second, there was a radical change in the picture regarding the employment of youth. When this century began, approximately half of the boys and girls fifteen years of age were *not* attending school; many were at work. Thirty years later the percentage of this group attending school had reached 85. This alteration was not a consequence of state laws raising the school-leaving age; the laws were rather a consequence of profound economic and social changes. To explore adequately the background of this shift in the American scene would require many pages; suffice it to remind the reader that in the second decade of this century the campaign against child labor was being pushed vigorously at the state and national levels. Today, as a result of laws affecting employment, as well as the attitude of management and labor, it is difficult for boys even at the age of seventeen to obtain many types of jobs. In European countries three quarters or more of the youth go to work at fourteen or fifteen years of age.

As a consequence of the changes in universities and colleges in the nineteenth century and the alternation of the employment situation since World War I, the American public high school has become an institution which has no counterpart in any other country. With few exceptions, for the most part in large eastern cities, the public high school is expected to provide education for *all* the youth living in a town, city, or district. Such a high school has become known as a "comprehensive" high school in contrast to the "specialized" high schools which provide vocational education or which admit on a selective basis and offer only an academic curriculum. The local factors which have determined, and still determine, some of the features of a comprehensive high school are discussed later in this report, as are the pros and cons of the selective academic high school and the specialized vocational school.

Thousands of comprehensive high schools of considerable size exist throughout the United States. Though generalization about American public education is highly dangerous (and I shall avoid it as far as possible in this report), I believe it accurate to state that a high school accommodating all the youth of a community is typical of American public education. I think it safe to say that the comprehensive high school is characteristic of our society and further that it has come into being because of our economic history and our devotion to the ideals of equality of opportunity and equality of status.

It is hardly necessary to say that a European finds the educational tasks facing the teachers and administrators of a comprehensive high school almost beyond his comprehension. (But this is the case also with some Americans whose children have not attended such a school.) Almost as incomprehensible as the American college and the American high school is the characteristic arrangement in the United States for managing our tax-supported schools. When one tells a foreign visitor that we have tens of thousands of local school boards with vast powers over the elementary schools and the high schools, he is apt to say, "This is not a system but a chaos." To which I always reply, "But it works; most of us like it; and it appears to be as permanent a feature of our society as most of our political institutions." And then, in the hope of giving him some glimpse of the reasons why such an arrangement has developed and why, in spite of its obvious drawbacks, it has so many friends, one falls back again on history.

The doctrine of local responsibility and community independence can be related to our pioneer history without difficulty. Parish and county autonomy in the South, the seventeenth-century independence of New

England church congregations, and suspicion of centralized government are among the factors that shaped the present political structure of our school systems in many states. Yet there is no uniform arrangement. To describe with any accuracy the methods of choosing school board members and the powers of the boards in the forty-eight states, one would have to have a truly encyclopedic memory for details. Since, however, the school boards, almost without exception, do have a great degree of freedom in managing the local school, I have addressed this report in the first instance to school board members. And since in many communities the school boards are elected, I venture to hope the report may be of interest to citizens committees concerned with public education. I have directed my attention mainly to the comprehensive high school. I hope the preceding paragraphs may, in part, answer the questions of any reader who, like some of my friends two years ago, wonders why I have chosen to study high schools and what I mean by the "comprehensive" high school. I trust I have provided at least a clue to my belief in the significance of a unique American educational institution and the importance of supporting and improving thousands of examples of this institution throughout the United States.

REFERENCES

Childs, John L. *American Pragmatism and Education.* New York: Henry Holt & Co., 1956.

Clapp, Elsie Ripley. *The Use of Resources in Education.* New York: Harper, 1952.

Counts, George S. *Dare the Schools Build a New Social Order?* New York: The John Day Co., 1932.

Cremin, Lawrence A. *The Transformation of the School.* New York: Alfred A. Knopf, 1961.

DeGarmo, Charles. *Herbart and the Herbartians.* New York: Scribner's, 1896.

DeGarmo, Charles. *The Essentials of Method.* Boston: D. C. Heath & Co., 1892.

Dewey, John, and Dewey, Evelyn. *Schools of Tomorrow.* New York: E. P. Dutton, 1915.

Dworkin, Martin S. (ed.). *Dewey on Education.* New York: Teachers College,

Columbia University, 1959.

Hofstadter, Richard. *Anti-Intellectualism in American Life*. New York: Alfred A. Knopf, 1963.

Hofstadter, Richard. *Social Darwinism in American Thought*. Boston: Beacon Press, 1955.

Hofstadter, Richard. *The Age of Reform*. New York: Alfred A. Knopf, 1956.

Johnson, Marietta. *Youth in a World of Men*. New York: The John Day Co., 1929.

Joncich, G. M. (ed.). *Psychology and the Science of Education: E. L. Thorndike*. New York: Teachers College, Columbia University, 1962.

Kandel, I. L. *American Education in the Twentieth Century*. Cambridge, Mass.: Harvard University Press, 1957.

Kilpatrick, William H., *et al. The Educational Frontier*. New York: Appleton-Century, 1933.

Knight, Edgar W. *Fifty Years of American Education*. New York: The Ronald Press, 1952.

Lange, A. F., and DeGarmo, Charles. *Outlines of Pedagogical Doctrine*. New York: Macmillan Co., 1901.

Leidecker, Kurt F. *Yankee Teacher: The Life of William Torrey Harris*. New York: Philosophical Library, 1946.

Mayhew, Katherine C., and Edwards, Anna C. *The Dewey School*. New York: D. Appleton-Century, 1936.

Meyer, A. E. *The Development of Education in the Twentieth Century*. New York: Prentice-Hall, 1939.

Monroe, Will S. *History of the Pestalozzian Movement in thte United States*. Syracuse: C. W. Bardeen, 1907.

Naumburg, Margaret. *The Child and the World*. New York: Harcourt, Brace, 1928.

Parker, F. W. *Talks on Pedagogics*. New York: E. L. Kellogg & Co., 1894.

Parker, F. W. *Talks on Teaching*. New York: E. L. Kellogg & Co., 1883.

Pratt, Caroline. *I Learn from Children*. New York: Simon and Schuster, 1948.

Pratt, Caroline (ed.). *Experimental Practice in the City and Country School*. New York: E. P. Dutton, 1924.

Reisner, E. H. *Nationalism and Education Since 1789*. New York: Macmillan Co., 1922.

Robinson, James H. *The Mind in the Making*. New York: Harper, 1950.

Rugg, Harold. *Foundations for American Education*. Yonkers-on-Hudson, New York: World Book Co., 1947.

Rugg, Harold, and Shumaker, Ann. *The Child Centered School*. Yonker-on-Hudson, World Book Co., 1928.

Schaub, Edward L. *William Torrey Harris, 1835-1935*. Chicago: Open Court, 1936.

Spencer, Herbert. *Education: Intellectual, Moral and Physical*. New York: D. Appleton & Co., 1860.

Strickland, Charles E., and Burgess, Charles (eds.). *Health, Growth, and Heredity: G. Stanley Hall on Natural Education*. New York: Teachers College, Columbia University, 1965.

White, Morton G. *Social Thought in America*. Boston: Beacon Press, 1957.

Wiener, Philip P. *Evolution and the Founders of Pragmatism*. Cambridge, Mass.: Harvard University Press, 1949.

Epilogue

You historians. . . .
Forgetting reason, your pages run into thousands—the cost
Of paper alone must ruin you! To this you're forced by the vast
Profusion of acts and by the laws of your craft. But what yield,
What harvest is got from it, what fruit from clearing your field?
Who'll give to any historian as high a rate of pay
As he will give the man who announces the news each day?
——Juvenal, *Satires*

WHILE we promise to exercise proper academic restraint, and refrain from comment upon the relative pay scales of historians and news commentators, the issue raised so bluntly by this satiric poet is quite germane to a book such as this one. What fruit, indeed, may be harvested from these readings on American educational history? Does such a collection merely illustrate the compulsion of the historian to gather things together, trusting that somewhere in a lengthy potpourri of historical items the reader may detect some relevance to his own present? If this be the case, one might well enter a plea of guilty to the poet's charge of the unreasoning accumulation of thousands of pages as the historians' sole *raison d'etre*. Obviously, we feel that the charge is not a minor one, nor one to be ignored. By turning our attention to the present scene in education, we hope to present some evidence that the charge is unwarranted, that the past we have presented does bear relevance to the present, and that the educational present may be more readily comprehended through a knowledge of the educational past.

The most striking characteristic of contemporary American education is its brute size. Like Topsy, the educational involvement during the past decade has just "growed and growed." The extent of this growth may be noted by referring to the chart compiled by the *New*

Translation of the quotation from Juvenal's *Satires* by Hubert Creekmore, from the Mentor edition, published by New American Library.

THE NATION'S SCHOOL SYSTEM – A DECADE OF GROWTH

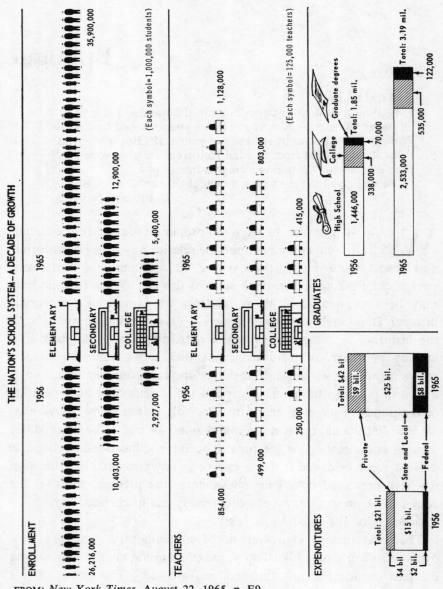

ENROLLMENT

1956   1965

ELEMENTARY

26,216,000   35,900,000

SECONDARY

10,403,000   12,900,000

COLLEGE

2,927,000   5,400,000

(Each symbol=1,000,000 students)

TEACHERS

1956   1965

ELEMENTARY

854,000   1,128,000

SECONDARY

499,000   803,000

COLLEGE

250,000   415,000

(Each symbol=125,000 teachers)

GRADUATES

High School   College   Graduate degrees

1956
Total: 1.85 mil.
1,446,000
338,000
70,000

1965
Total: 3.19 mil.
2,533,000
535,000
122,000

EXPENDITURES

1956
Total: $21 bil.
Private — $4 bil
State and Local — $15 bil.
Federal — $2 bil.

1965
Total: $42 bil
Private — $9 bil.
State and Local — $25 bil.
Federal — $8 bil.

FROM: *New York Times,* August 22, 1965, p. E9.

York Times from recent figures provided by the United States Office of Education.

This educational Leviathan is at present being subjected to a variety of opinions concerning its improvement, proper direction, and emphasis. This in itself is hardly anything new in education, as we have seen in some of our readings. Education emerges, as a rule, healthier and more viable from such disagreement. Indeed, the amazing flexibility of American education to adapt to new demands has, since Puritan days, been one of its major strengths. Let us hope that a day never comes when we all agree about just what education should be, when we have all committed ourselves irrevocably to a single educational dogma. The danger in such a situation is succinctly pointed up by a Nietzschean aphorism to the effect that:

> When the mind is made up, the ear is deaf to even the best arguments. This is the sign of a strong character. In other words, an occasional will to stupidity.

Hopefully, this "strength of character" will be absent from American education, thereby providing for the healthy dialogue of reasoned disagreement.

What are the main channels of such disagreement today in education? What is the relationship of these positions to the past?

As has been suggested, the contemporary scene offers several divergent views of the educational structure. Stipulating in advance the ramifications and nuances undoubtedly present within each, we see contemporary educational thought falling generally within four broad catagories.

I

The first category in educational thought today may be appropriately labeled the "retrenchment" group. The pedigree of this group is impressive. They trace their ancestry to the arguments of Socrates with the Sophists, to Cicero's thoughts on the education of a Roman orator, to the Renaissance humanists Vittorino da Feltre and Vergerio. Their thesis is a simple one, and it echoed from ancient Greece and Rome as clearly as it does from some modern American educators.

They call for a retrenchment of education, a reinstatement of the timeless humanistic values and emphases in education. Rather than molding education to fit the transitory needs and demands of a fleeting present, these people feel that there is a timeless core of wisdom, which has been transmitted to the present by the recorded experiences of the greatest thinkers, and that *this* should constitute at any given time the intellectual nucleus of education.

This position, as might be imagined, leads toward a bookish sort of education, and many "retrenchers" today are advocates of a "Great Books Curriculum," either partially or wholly.

The rise of the private school masters and the early academies in the United States was precipitated, as we have seen, by a confrontation of such an education with the pragmatic demands of a commercial civilization. The confrontation of modern retrenchers with modern "demand-need" educators (such as those that advocate that 96 per cent of the curriculum should be devoted to science and math, for example) is a parallel case in a scientifically oriented civilization.

The modern humanist retrenchers have fought on many fronts, disagreeing on one hand with Progressives, whom they perceived as committing education to the cultivation of gregarious little extroverts able to work and play well with others, and on the other hand with educational mechanics, who reduce all variables (including human) to neat statistical formulations.

Whatever the age or place, the educational retrencher is vigilant and on guard, ever ready to challenge those who threaten the integrity of education as the fullest transmission of the cultural and intellectual heritage. Defender of the humanist faith, he reveres the past glories of the race, which frequently causes him to be chastized as conservative or reactionary. In spite of ridicule and invective, however, the "retrencher" remains a potent force in education.

II

The second influential group may be labeled the "educational engineers." This contingent manifests great faith in the instrumental use of education to alleviate a multitude of social ills, ranging from unemployment and poverty to racial discrimination. Although many educators share this belief in the almost miraculous efficacy of education, the engineers are rather unique in that they tend to see this as the primary function of education.

Reducing educational problems as much as possible to a mechanistic level of manipulation, the engineers are greatly taken with statistical compilations, graphical analysis, and varieties of instructional machines. The human factor in education at times seems to get lost amid the manipulations of numbers and "things" that this group sees as its main task. Problems of quality often appear to be overshadowed by the theses of quantity and efficiency. From educational history, we can see that this position, at least in terms of its educational application, is closely related to that taken by advocates of the "monitorial" schools of Lancaster and Bell. The more recent engineers, of course, approach their task backed by lavish resources undreamed of by the monitorial masters, for example, W. W. Charters and others who, in the 1920's, attempted to develop a "science" of curriculum making through the job analysis approach. Perhaps an interesting example of this educational orientation currently may be seen in the centers established by the Office of Economic Opportunity, where education has been enlisted as an instrument in the fight against unemployment and poverty.

III

The romantic tradition in education remains a dimming but yet persistent voice in the contemporary scene. In this country, it reached its apogee, as we have seen, during the child-centered years of progressive education. Drawing from the European traditions initiated by Rousseau and developed by some of the transcendentalist educators in the nineteenth century, American educators like Marietta Johnson and Margaret Naumberg carried forward the romantic tradition in education into the twentieth century. Buttressed by frequently superficial interpretations of Freud's view of the role of the irrational, the romantic movement produced in the 1920's some remarkable schools and teachers in the child-centered wing of the progressive movement. Current romantic educators, though strong in the Rousseauean tradition, seem to lean more heavily upon the Freudian or neo-Freudian doctrines than on any of the earlier romantic doctrines. Considering the characteristics of this group, we would designate it "romantic-psychoanalytic" in current educational thought.

The ideal of this group is the world famous "Summerhill" of A. S. Neill, which has its imitators in this country as well as on the continent. The effort of the Summerhillians and of the group generally is to bring the insights of Freud and of current psychoanalytic theory into educational focus, all firmly based on certain romantic philosophic premises. From this orientation have come the illuminating criticisms of American education by Paul Goodman and others, as well as important insights by a member of professional educators pertaining to teaching methods, curriculum, and the role of the school in relation to the individual.

This modern, empirically demanding world has perhaps less sympathy for the romantics than earlier generations. Their pedagogical lexicon of "creativity" and "individual freedom" falls upon ears more conditioned to the language of space flights and cybernetics. But tradition in education is tenacious, and this tradition is ardently defended by the romantic-psychoanalytic group in education today. It would seem fair to say that probably more neophyte teachers are stimulated and encouraged by the noble words of Rousseau and the fascinating experiment of Summerhill than by any of the humanistic rhetoric of the retrenchers or the computerlike efficiency of the engineers. The belief in Man's essential nobility of character, in spite of this seemingly determined efforts to prove the contrary, remains if not triumphant at least a recurring theme.

IV

The fourth group to be considered is the educational "innovationists." Numerically large, the innovationists are thoroughly committed in general terms to American education as it exists, but they operate on an educational adaptation of one of the primary axioms of engineering—if the machine fails to work, kick it. The innovationists are convinced that the machine is basically sound, that it needs no major overhaul; but, as the label implies, they wish to remove, replace, or repair certain constituent parts. This position affords the tempting opportunity for any educator, or anyone else for that matter, to pursue whatever project he may have in mind, with the assurance that by changing, eliminating, or increasing a specific component, the educational system will operate smoothly.

The innovationists may be further classified into two distinct subgroups. The first subgroup is comprised of professional educators, members of state departments of education, of schools of education and teachers colleges, and many administrators and teachers in American schools. They have been labeled "educationists," or, in the aggregate, the "educational establishment," by some members of the second subgroup. The second subdivision is, of course, the "new" educator group, whose adherents are found mainly in the arts and science colleges, although some are present in schools of education as well. With close connections to the great philanthropic foundations, their members wield enormous influence, and they can be found in the most important administrative posts in American education today. Perhaps we could designate this second subgroup the "new establishment" since there is every indication of the will to gain power in education, to establish the necessary organization and to control and direct educational affairs.

The innovations proposed by either the educationists or by the new establishment are infinitely varied, differing from one group to the other and from one individual to another, and both subgroups frequently overlap and imitate each other's innovations. The educationists, for example, have initiated such projects as team teaching, foreign language laboratories, driver training, and Higher Horizon programs; and the new establishment has promoted "new math," the multicolored biology curriculum, and a uniform national testing system for the schools. Whatever the philosophy of the individual innovationists, they are all in essential agreement that American education urgently needs innovations, that any basic examination of education—theoretically, historically, or philosophically—causes only unnecessary delay, and that the innovation proposed this week will solve the major problem in education today. The innovationists want action. Understandably, they are not very interested in reflecting or planning in any broad educational contex, in raising the question of how a particular innovation may relate to education generally, or even in asking if yesterday's innovation actually solved the problem that seemed so important then. Untrammeled by theory and all the complexities involved in broad educational planning, the innovationists are concerned only with practice, with smoothing the educational way.

However valuable some of the specific innovations of this group may be, their doings can too often degenerate into educational fashion making by a few leaders or fashion pursuing by their many followers, either educationists or new educators. The innovationist orientation, with its emphasis on the present and on action, is as ancient as the process of education itself and the group is worth its own designation because of its enormous influence on education in America today.

A Concluding Postscript

It is hoped that the preceding outline of the four groups will explain partially the nature of contemporary educational thought. The categories are very general, of course, because the groups overlap each other and are continually changing. The history of American education is a history of a growing organism—flexible and retaining the plasticity necessary for change. And change it must if it is adequately to serve its masters, the people of America. Furthermore, there should be a sense of history, a willingness to reflect on the educational past, as an important element in determining the future.

We have tried to show some of the changes in education in America and some of the social and intellectual environments that surrounded these changes. American education is great because it has always retained its organic flexibility and adaptability, because our society has supported and tolerated such divergent opinions as represented by the four groups above. As such, the history of American education is a unique legacy, one worthy of sacrifice and attendant frustrations to ensure its preservation.

CONTEMPORARY REFERENCES

CURRENT EDUCATIONAL IDEAS

Belth, Marc. *Education as a Discipline*. Boston: Allyn and Bacon, 1965.
Brameld, Theodore. *Education for the Emerging Age: Newer Ends and Stronger Means*. New York: Harper, 1965.
Bruner, Jerome S. *The Process of Education*. Cambridge, Mass.: Harvard University Press, 1960.
Bruner, Jerome S. *Toward a Theory of Instruction*. Cambridge, Mass.: Harvard University Press, 1966.
Conant, James B. *The Education of American Teachers*. New York: McGraw-Hill, 1963.
Gardner, John W. *Excellence: Can We Be Equal and Excellent Too?* New York: Harper, 1961.
Goodman, Paul. *Compulsory Mis-Education and the Community of Scholars*. New York: Vintage, 1966.
Greene, Maxine. *The Public School and the Private Vision*. New York: Random House, 1965.
Lieberman, Myron. *Education as a Profession*. Englewood Cliffs, N.J.: Prentice-Hall, 1956.
Neill, A. S. *Summerhill: A Radical Approach to Child Rearing*. New York: Hart Publishing Co., 1961.
Skinner, B. F. *Walden II*. New York: Macmillan Co., 1948.

(The above books are available in paper editions.)

CIVIL RIGHTS

General Works:
Aptheker, H. (ed.). *A Documentary History of the Negro People in the U.S. . . .* New York: Citadel Press, 1962.
Board of Education, City of New York. *The Negro in American History*. Reprinted by the University of the State of New York, State Education Dept., Bureau of Secondary Curriculum Development, Albany, N.Y., 1965.
Bontemps, Arna W. *One Hundred Years of Negro Slavery*. New York: Dodd, Mead & Co., 1961.
Becker, John. *The Negro in American Culture*. N.Y.: Knopf, 1956.
Clift, Virgil A., Anderson, Archibald W., and Hullfish, Gordon (eds.). *Negro Education in America*. Harper, 1962.
De Huszar, George B. *Equality in America: the issue of minority rights*. New York: H. W. Wilson Co., 1949.

Rose, Arnold. *The Negro in America* (condensed version of Gunnar Myrdahl's *An American Dilemma*) Boston: Beacon Press, 1956.
1619-1790
Beer, George L. *The Old Colonial System,* 1660-1751. 2 vols. New York: Peter Smith, 1953.
Handlin, Oscar. *Race and Nationality in American Life.* Boston: Atlantic-Little, Brown, 1957.
Phillips, U.B. *American Negro Slavery.* New York: Peter Smith, 1918.
1790-1861
Bancroft, F. A. *Slave-trading in the Old South.* New York: Ungar, 1959.
Baines, Gilbert H. *The Antislavery Impulse: 1830-1844.* New York: Appleton-Century, 1933.
Filler, Louis. *The Crusade Against Slavery: 1830-1860.* New York: Harper, 1960.
Litwack, Leon F. *North of Slavery: The Negro in the Free States, 1790-1860.* Chicago: University of Chicago Press, 1961.
Nye, Russell B. *Fettered Freedom: civil liberties and the slavery controversy, 1830-1860.* East Lansing, Michigan: Michigan State University Press, 1963.
1861-1877
Carter, Hodding. *The Angry Scar.* New York: Doubleday & Co., 1959.
DuBois, W. E. B. *Black Reconstruction in America.* New York: Harcourt, Brace, 1935.
Franklin, John H. *The Emancipation Proclamation.* New York: Doubleday & Co., 1963.
Woodward, C. Vann. *Reunion and Reaction.* New York: Doubleday & Co., 1956.
1877-1901
Cash, Wibur J. *The Mind of the South.* New York: Alfred A. Knopf, 1960.
Harris, Robert. *The Quest for Equality.* Baton Rouge: Louisiana State University Press, 1960.
Woodward, C. Vann. *Origins of the New South, 1877-1913.* Baton Rouge: Louisiana State University Press, 1951.
Woodward, C. Vann. *The Strange Career of Jim Crow.* New York: Oxford University Press, 1955.
1901-1933
Frazier, Edward F. *Black Metropolis.* New York: Free Press, 1957.
Harlan, Louis R. *Separate and Unequal; Public School Campaigns and Racism in the Southern Seaboard States, 1901-1915.* Chapel Hill: University of North Carolina Press, 1958.
Locke, Alain. *The New Negro: An Interpretation.* New York: Boni, 1925.
1933-1945
Drake, St. Clair, and Clayton, Horace R. *Black Metropolis.* New York: Harcourt, 1945.
Ovington, Mary W. *The Walls Came Tumbling Down.* New York: Harcourt, 1947.
Simkins, Francis Butler. *The South Old and New.* New York: Alfred A. Knopf, 1947.
1945-1965
Ashmore, Harry S. *The Negro and the Schools.* Chapel Hill: University of North Carolina Press, 1954.
Brickman, William W., and Lehrer, Stanley (eds.). *The Countdown on Segre-*

gated Education. New York: Society for the Advancement of Education, 1960.

Brink, William, and Harris, Lewis. *The Negro Revolution in America*. New York: Simon and Schuster, 1964.

Glazer, Nathan, and Moynihan, Daniel. *Beyond the Melting Pot*. Cambridge, Mass.: Harvard University Press, 1963.

Humphrey, Hubert H. *Integration vs. Segregation: the crisis in our schools . . .* New York: Crowell, 1964.

Konvitz, Milton R., and Lesker, Theodore. *A Century of Civil Rights*. New York: Columbia University Press, 1961.

Lewis, Anthony, and The *New York Times*. *Portrait of a Decade: The Second American Revolution*. New York: Random House, 1965.

Mooney, Chase C. *Civil Rights and Liberties*. New York: Holt, Rinehart & Winston, 1964.

Roche, John P. *The Quest for the Dream*. New York: Macmillan Co., 1963.

Silver, James W. *Mississippi: the closed society*. Harcourt, Brace and World, 1964.

Savage, Henry. *Seeds of Time: The Background of Southern Thinking*. New York: Holt Rinehart & Winston, 1964.

RELIGION AND THE SCHOOLS

American Association of School Administrators. *Religion in the Public Schools*. Washington, D. C.: American Association of School Administrators, 1964.

American Council on Education. *The Relation of Religion to Public Education*. Washington, D. C.: American Council on Education, 1947.

American Council on Education. *The Function of the Public Schools in Dealing With Religion*. Washington, D. C.: American Council on Education, 1953.

Blanshard, Paul. *Religion and the Schools*. Boston: Beacon Press, 1963.

Boles, Donald E. *The Bible, Religion, and the Public Schools*. Ames, Iowa: Iowa State University Press, 1961.

Brickman, William W., and Lehrer, Stanley. (eds.). *Religion, Government and Education*. New York: Society for the Advancement of Education, 1961.

Brown, Nicholas (ed.). *The Study of Religion in the Public Schools*. Washington, D. C.: American Council on Education, 1958.

Butts, R. Freeman. *The American Tradition in Religion and Education*. Boston: Beacon Press, 1950.

Duker, Sam. *The Public Schools and Religion: The Legal Context*. New York: Harper & Row, 1966.

Dunn, William K. *What Happened to Religious Education: The Decline of Religious Teaching in the Public Elementary School 1776-1861*. Baltimore: Johns Hopkins Press, 1958.

Fraenkel, Osmond K. *The Supreme Court and Civil Liberties*. Dobbs Ferry, New York: Oceana Publications, 1963.

Kilpatrick, William H. et al. "Religion and Education: A Symposium," *Progressive Education*, No. 33 (Sept. 1956) pp 129-155.

McCluskey, Neil G. *Catholic Viewpoint on Education*. Garden City, New York: Hanover House, 1959.

McGrath, John J. (ed.). *Church and State in American Law*. Milwaukee: Bruce Publishing Co., 1962.

O'Neill, James M. *Religion and Education Under the Constitution*. New York: Harper, 1949.

Politella, Joseph. *Religion in Education, An Annotated Bibliography*. Oneonta, N.Y.: American Association for College Teachers of Education, 1956.

Thayer, V. T. *Religion in Public Education*. New York: Viking Press, 1947.

Thayer, V. T. *The Attack upon the American Secular School*. Boston: Beacon Press, 1951.

URBAN PROBLEMS

Board of Education, City of New York. *Higher Horizons Program, First Annual Progress Report* New York: Board of Education of the City of New York, 1960.

Chandler, B. J., Stiles, Lindley J., and Kituse, John I. (eds.). *Education in Urban Society*. New York: Dodd, Mead & Co., 1962.

Conant, James B. *Slums and Suburbs*. New York: McGraw-Hill, 1961.

Fortune Magazine. *The Exploding Metropolis*. New York: Doubleday & Co., 1958.

Green, Constance. *The Rise of Urban American*. New York: Harper & Row, 1965.

Kimball, Solon T., and McClellan, James E. *Education and the New America*. New York: Random House, 1962.

Lerner, Max. *America as a Civilization*. New York: Simon and Schuster, 1957.

McKelvey, Blake. *The Urbanization of America*. New Brunswick, N.J.: Rutgers University Press, 1963.

Meyerson, Martin, Tarrett, Barbara, and Ylvisaher, Paul (eds.). *Metropolis in Ferment*. Philadelphia: American Academy of Political and Social Science, 1957.

Mowrey, George E. *The Urban Nation, 1920-1960*. New York: Hill & Wang, 1965.

Schlesinger, Arthur M. *The Rise of the City, 1878-1898*. New York: Macmillan Co., 1933.

Schnore, Leo F. *The Urban Scene; Human Ecology and Demography*. New York: Free Press, 1965.

Stein, Maurice R. *The Eclipse of Community*. . . . Princeton, N. J.: Princeton University Press, 1960.

Weaver, Robert C. *The Urban Complex*. . . . Garden City, New York: Doubleday & Co., 1964.

Weaver, Robert C. *The Negro Ghetto*. New York: Harcourt, Brace and World, 1948.

Willbern, York. *The Withering Away of the City*. University, Alabama: University of Alabama Press, 1964.

Goodman, Paul. *Growing Up Absurd*. New York: Random House, 1956.

Goodman, Paul. *The Empire City*. New York: Bobbs-Merrill Co., 1942.

Goodman, Paul, and Goodman, Percival. *Communitas*. New York: Random House, 1947.

Index